❧ *THE*
ROMANCE
OF MERLIN
An Anthology

ARTHURIAN STUDIES
FROM GARLAND

The New Arthurian Encyclopedia
edited by Norris J. Lacy et al.

The Arthurian Handbook
by Norris J. Lacy and Geoffrey Ashe

The Romance of Arthur
edited by James J. Wilhelm and Laila Zamuelis Gross

The Romance of Arthur II
edited by James J. Wilhelm

The Romance of Arthur III
edited by James J. Wilhelm

King Arthur Through the Ages
edited by Valerie Lagorio and Mildred Leake Day

The Arthurian Revival in Victorian Art
by Debra N. Mancoff

"Arthur the Greatest King": An Anthology of Modern Arthurian Poems
edited by Alan Lupack

Arthurian Drama: An Anthology
edited by Alan Lupack

The Arthurian Yearbook
edited by Keith Busby

Sir Gawain and the Green Knight: A Dual-Language Edition
edited and translated by William Vantuono

❧ THE
*R*OMANCE
OF *M*ERLIN

An Anthology

EDITED BY *Peter Goodrich*

*G*ARLAND *P*UBLISHING, *I*NC.

New York & London ❧ 1990

808.803

Rom

The Romance of Merlin / edited by
Peter Goodrich.
      p. cm. — (Garland reference library of the humanities ; vol. 867)
Includes index.
      ISBN 0-8240-7042-9
      1. Merlin (legendary character) — Romances.   2. Merlin (legendary
character) — Literary collections.   3. Arthurian romances.   I. Goodrich, Peter,
1950–   . II. Series.
PN6071.M46R66   1990
820.8'0351 — dc20   90-43703

Printed on acid-free, 250-year-life paper

MANUFACTURED IN THE UNITED STATES OF AMERICA

CONTENTS

III.   Merlin in Medieval Romance

IV. Merlin in the Renaissance

V.   Merlin in the Nineteenth Century

VI. Merlin in the Twentieth Century

PREFACE

T H E   E N O R M O U S   popularity of Arthurian legend and other things
medieval during the past decade has prompted the publication of many
romances and critical studies, and made available both out-of-print materials
and significant new insights into the world of chivalric fantasy. No other
wizard in western culture defines the occupation of magic as fully as Merlin,
who from nonwizardly historical origins has developed over the centuries
into the archetypal master of all arts and technologies. Given the immense
importance and appeal of Arthur's mage, a literary anthology devoted to him
appears both desirable and necessary. From the wealth of popular literature
in all European languages, this collection focuses on the Anglo-American
tradition, in which Merlin is most popular and influential. This focus does
not disregard other valuable traditions and treatment of Merlin—especially
in French and German literature (in fact, the French contribution to the
English Arthurian tradition is impossible to avoid, and is thus acknowledged
in this book)—but is a choice of the editor to bring the contents down to
manageable proportions. Even so, the selection from an enormous volume
of Anglo-American texts of widely varying popularity and quality was not
easy to make. It is the first collection of Merlin texts in over a century, since
San Marte's *Die Sagen von Merlin* (Halle: Weisenhaus, 1853), and to the
pioneering spirit of San Marte and the other nineteenth-century medievalists on whose work much of our modern understanding is founded, this
anthology is partially dedicated.

   It is dedicated also to the many colleagues, friends, and family members
whose interest in Merlin has stimulated and developed my own. I gratefully
acknowledge my teachers Alan Gaylord, Thomas Garbaty, and Eric Rabkin,
who over a nearly fifteen-year period skillfully molded my understanding of
medieval literature and fantasy and patiently critiqued my efforts to explore
these subjects in writing. Many other scholars have also encouraged my
efforts, and without them this book would not have appeared. I especially
want to thank John Bollard, Nancy Marie Brown, Zacharias Thundy, and

Aubrey Gaylon—whose sudden passing while this book was in proof I acknowledge with sadness. Jeanie Watson, Maureen Fries, and Mildred Day are chief among the many others whose attention has revitalized my work whenever it has flagged. Freya Reeves Lambides and Alan Lupack of *Avalon to Camelot* commissioned an article on Merlin's development and graciously allowed me to reprint it with several alterations as the introduction to this volume. I wish to thank, too, David Higham Associates, Ltd., for permission to reprint selections from T. H. White, and The Bodley Head, Ltd., for those from C. S. Lewis. My faculty colleagues and administrators at Northern Michigan University contributed generously to this anthology with a faculty development grant. The talented people who have typed reams of text and helped to produce the book also merit thanks, especially Mary Letts, my patient and judicious editor at Garland, Gary Kuris, and the Garland staff. Most important of all are Meg, Andrew, and Katrina, whose love and unfailing support enable everything I do. This book is meant for them— small but tangible reward for a debt I never wish to be without.

PETER GOODRICH
Marquette, Michigan
February 1990

SELECTED PRIMARY WORKS INCORPORATING MERLIN

Myrddin Poems (900)	Attributed to Myrddin
Prophetiae Merlini (1135)	Geoffrey of Monmouth
Historia Regum Britanniae (1136)	Geoffrey of Monmouth
Vita Merlini (1150)	Geoffrey of Monmouth
Merlin (1200)	Robert de Boron
Merlínússpá (c. 1200)	Gunnlaugr Leifsson
L'Estoire de Merlin (1215)	(French)
Suite du Merlin (1230)	(French)
Arthour and Merlin (1250)	(English)
Boek van Merline (1260)	Jacob van Maerlant
Les Prophécies de Merlin (1272)	(French)
Historia di Merlino (1379)	(Italian)
Prose Merlin (1450)	(English)
Merlin (1450)	Henry Lovelich
Le Morte Darthur (1485)	Sir Thomas Malory
El Baladro del Sabio Merlin (1498)	(Spanish)
The Faerie Queene (1590)	Edmund Spenser
The Speeches at Prince Henry's Barriers (1610)	Ben Jonson
The Birth of Merlin (1620)	William Rowley (attributed)
The Life of Merlin (1641)	Thomas Heywood
England's Prophetical Merline,	
Merlinus Anglicus Junior (1644)	William Lilly
King Arthur: or, The British Worthy (1691)	John Dryden
Merlin, or the Devil of Stonehenge (1734)	Lewis Theobald
Merlin der Zauberer (1777), *Merlins weissagende*	
Stimme aus seiner Gruft (1810)	Christoph Martin Wieland
Merlin der Wilde (1829)	Ludwig Uhland
Merlin (1832)	Karl Leberecht Immermann
Idylls of the King (1859–1886)	Alfred Tennyson
Merlin l'Enchanteur (1860)	Edgar Quinet
A Connecticut Yankee in King Arthur's Court (1889)	Mark Twain

The Quest of Merlin (1891)   Richard Hovey
L'Enchanteur pourrissant (1904)   Guillaume Apollinaire
Merlins Geburt (1913), *Zauberer Merlin* (1924)   Eduard Stucken
Merlin (1917)   Edward Arlington Robinson
Der Neue Christophorus (1917–1974)   Gerhart Hauptmann
Taliessin Through Logres (1938),
     The Region of the Summer Stars (1944)   Charles Williams
That Hideous Strength (1945)   C. S. Lewis
Thor, with Angels (1948)   Christopher Fry
Porius (1951)   John Cowper Powys
The Once and Future King (1958)   T. H. White
The Dark Is Rising (1965–1977)   Susan Cooper
The Crystal Cave (1970), *The Hollow Hills* (1973),
     The Last Enchantment (1979)   Mary Stewart
The Island of the Mighty (1973)   John Arden and
                                                                 Margaretta D'Arcy
Le Testament de Merlin (1975)   Theophile Briant
Arthur Rex (1978)   Thomas Berger
Lancelot (1978)   Walker Percy
Merlin's Mirror (1979)   Andre Norton
Merlin (1979)   Robert Nye
Merlin, oder das Wüste Land (1981)   Tankred Dorst with
                                                                 Ursula Ehler
L'Enchanteur (1984)   Rene Barjavel
Merlin's Booke (1986)   Jane Yolen
Merlin (1988)   Stephen R. Lawhead
The Coming of the King (1989)   Nikolai Tolstoy

INTRODUCTION

T H E   F I G U R E   of Merlin has fascinated generations weaned from nursery rhymes to the tales of King Arthur. The combination of chivalry and marvel that these tales evoke has stimulated imaginations from the moment Merlin was yoked to Arthurian legend in the twelfth century by Geoffrey of Monmouth.

Merlin is in the public domain. He has long since entered that nonverbal space of consciousness which is the spawning ground of new fictional creations in archetypal modes; to paraphrase the myth critic Joseph Campbell, he is "the wizard with a thousand faces."

The figure of Merlin first developed recognizable form in medieval Britain from a combination of pan-European folk motifs and local legends. He does not originate simply as the literary adaptation of some other culture's creation, like the legendary founder of Rome, Aeneas—or Aeneas' great-grandson Brutus, the eponymous founder of Britain itself—but as a unique product of British or Brythonic culture in the Dark Ages.

Alfred Jarman has shown that he is descended from the medieval wild man of the woods tradition through the stories (now fragmentary) of Lailoken in Strathclyde, who became the forest prophet Myrddin in Welsh poetry. This man was apparently a chief who went mad at the Battle of Arfderydd in 573 and fled to the Caledonian Forest in Scotland. His madness condemned him to suffer unprotected the ravages of nature and to lament his fallen state, but also compensated him with the powers of insight and prophecy. Like many a medieval recluse, he was consulted about future events. Geoffrey of Monmouth presented these traditions in the *Prophecies of Merlin* (c. 1135) and especially the *Life of Merlin* (c. 1150). He also added a new dimension, whether deliberately or through ignorance, in that medieval best-seller *The History of the Kings of Britain* (c. 1136). Here he conflated the stories of Merlin's prophetic powers with a tale taken from Nennius of a clairvoyant child named Ambrosius, whose mother conceived him from the visitation of an incubus. Geoffrey made Merlin the adviser of King Vortigern's conqueror and successor Aurelius, the erector of Stonehenge, and the abettor of Uther's lust for Ygerne, which produced Arthur. Ever since then Merlin has been linked inextricably to the Arthurian legend.

Medieval romance writers, particularly on the Continent, lost no time in expanding upon the magical powers and roles initiated by these sources. Wace introduced the sword in the stone and suggested that he had fashioned the Round Table; Robert de Boron seized upon Geoffrey's incubus by making him the product of a demonic plot to produce the Antichrist; and de Boron's continuators in the French Prose *Merlin* added the tale of his love affair and captivity by the fairy Viviane (or Nivienne, Nyneve, Nimiane, Nimue), as well as elaborating interminably his prophetic and shape-changing gifts, military and engineering stratagems, sage counseling, storm-raising powers, and other magical accomplishments.

Merlin's dubious origins, penchant for practical jokes, and infatuation with Viviane also led to his eventual debasement. In this he shares the fate of Arthur and Gawain through the gradual adaptation of his legend to less aristocratic forms of literature than the chronicle and romance. Malory also appears to have felt uncomfortable with a character so firmly rooted in pre-Christian marvels and magic, since he drastically diminishes Merlin's abilities and achievements as depicted in his French sources. The wizard plays a significant part only in the first of the tales in Vinaver's edition, where he educates Arthur, and is soon shuffled off to the rock in Cornwall where he is shut up by the damsel of the Lake. Thereafter he is displaced by the ubiquitous Christian hermits as an explicator of knightly adventures.

By the Renaissance Merlin remained known primarily for his prophetic powers and magical artifacts. Renaissance tradition in Ariosto and Spenser, deriving partially from such chronicles as Ranulf Higden's *Polychronicon* (c. 1360), portrays him as the commander of demons and the creator of marvelous weapons, mirrors, murals and bas-reliefs, tombs, and springs. As a prophet he is repeatedly invoked to foretell the illustrious lineage of heroes and the dooms of overweening monarchs. In the seventeenth century this tradition encouraged popular astrologers and futurists like William Lilly to invoke him as the source and authority for their prognostications, while more serious writers like Ben Jonson appealed to him as a symbol of poetic foresight and wisdom in the training of princes, and playful writers like Thomas Heywood combined both prophecy and politics with the machinery of magical illusion.

Since prophecy was still considered by many as a reliable source of knowledge, these capabilities also linked Merlin with developing natural science. In combination with his clairvoyant and magic-making powers his shape-changing propensities even led alchemists and mystics to associate him with Mercury, the patron divinity of alchemy and a symbol of the Philosopher's Stone which can transmute base metal to gold. At the same time he remained in popular culture the son of the devil, who had repudiated (or not, according to a few writers) his sire's evil designs upon humanity. As the sciences grew more experimentally sophisticated and rational, however, his popularity in literature dwindled.

The Romantic era revived interest in Merlin, though the Romantic poets themselves wrote little about him. The Victorian writers Alfred Tennyson, Matthew Arnold, and Algernon Swinburne made him a major figure once again, along with Arthur and the knights of the Round Table. They saw in him the sage whose wisdom and grasp of eternity make possible Arthur's attempt to revive the Golden Age, undercut by his human desire and the feminine rhythms of nature. Writers following them also focused on the wizard's enchantment with Vivian, and increasingly, as two World Wars darkened their view of history, on Merlin's savage origins and madness.

The increasing rate of change in science and society also encouraged Merlin's adoption in two apparently contradictory ways: as an icon of fantasy, the prototypal magician; and as the forerunner of technological innovation, the scientist and inventor. Somewhere in between, a range of more or less fanciful romances seeking a plausible Dark Age Arthur also develop a plausible Merlin, as in Mary Stewart's Merlin trilogy. In fact, the mage now appears in a plethora of roles that evolve all of his former guises in literature and art, and he is more popular than ever before.

From this thumbnail history it is easy to see that, like Merlin's shapeshifting art in medieval romances, his masks are endlessly varied. His roles and abilities have been drawn from biblical and nonbiblical, historical and literary sources, thus developing a supra-archetypal figure who may appear in forms from devil to angel, Antichrist to Redeemer, wise old man to lustful dotard, shaman to scientist, wild man to sage. His literary appeal is rooted in contradictions and polarities, and the tensions generated by them propel the archetypal plots of fantasy. He has survived as an influential imaginative figure particularly by sustaining the eternal rivalries between Light and Dark, Law and Chaos, God and Mortal, Angel and Demon, Male and Female, Human and Beast, Mind and Matter, Wisdom and Love. All of these tensions are somehow internalized by the figure of Merlin—even while he is conventionally presented as a champion of the Light—and this ambiguity is the fundamental reason for his eternal mystery and popularity.

No other mage in English fiction demonstrates Merlin's capacity for development and transfiguration. His essence is not his debatable historicity but his aura of wizardry, his knowledge and abilities of magical realms vaster even than the realms of Arthur. Because magic is directed toward this-worldly achievement as distinct from the other-worldly focus of religion, Merlin usually acts as Arthur's wizardly double in the quest for a chivalric paradise on earth. Their "magic" is different, of course—for Arthur it is predominantly active and usually resides in external accouterments like Excalibur and its scabbard, or in the close-knit society of the Round Table, while for Merlin it is predominantly contemplative and implicit in his traditional nature as a semidivine being with supernatural abilities.

Merlin's legend is also represented in nearly every European language, and no other wizard in any language has achieved quite the same status or balance between opposites. The sword-bridge that the wizard suspends between potency and impotency, or religious and secular world views, seems to be the reason. The figure of Merlin, even while interpreted through the lens of Christian writers, has always resisted full incorporation into its belief system as a Christian prophet. Yet his concerns are as much religious as secular; he mediates between Christian and non-Christian beliefs, relating them both to the circumstances and aspirations addressed in Arthurian legend.

The figure of Merlin also heals the schism between eternal and practical types of magic. He is master of both—or as much a master as someone half-human can be. Edward Peters locates the separation historically in the twelfth-century cultural renaissance; it can be no coincidence that this is also the time when the figure of Merlin burst into Europe-wide popularity.

When we regard Merlin as a magician equipped with both divine and demonic qualities, we may interpret his wizardly attainments as hyperbolic attempts at human redemption and self-realization—as incarnating ways of overcoming the dichotomy between eternal and practical magic. The mechanics of magic, which are typically represented by the manipulation of hidden properties through various techniques of spell-casting and spirit control, are in Merlin signs of comprehension. His popularity rests less on the individual forms he takes in fiction than on an underlying homeopathy which makes him the archetype of all wizards—as we would wish them to be.

Merlin has always been an image of psychic maturing and atavistic release, of disengagement from the processes of nature balanced by a renewed and deeper involvement in them. This is true of him even at his most parodistic: just as the Wizard of Oz may be revealed as curator of humbug technology and pompous special effects, yet he remains capable of recognizing what is most characteristic of us. Oz rewards the Lion, Scarecrow, and Tin Man by giving them tokens of the courage, intelligence, and heart they desire because he cannot bestow the things themselves. By so doing he introduces them to what they really are, and prepares them to rule the Emerald City.

As such a figure he fulfills our desires—especially those directed toward mastery of our natural and social environments. His chief means for doing this are knowledge and its tool, language, which shapes the phenomenal world to his will. This ability to order phenomena grows out of the lesser ability to foretell it, and to make this possible a fascinating development in the wizard's character occurs. Merlin's oracular inspiration and prophetic gift originate in the wild-man figure as a product of neurosis. Since the condition of the wild man is "separation from wonted or due status" both socially and mentally, it is manifested schizophrenically (O'Riain, p. 184). But this figure is thereby initiated into the "collective unconscious" or universal memory of man; in literature the insight he gains evolves into the achievement of reintegrated personality, who thus becomes the servant of the divine will and the master of events rather than remaining at their mercy. This movement from neurosis to integration characterizes not just the wild-man figure, but the whole literary development of Merlin as he becomes the master wizard of English fiction. Yet the tension between neurosis and integration is retained by the convention of his half-human status and prophetic function. His doom signals an oscillating rather than linear movement, because neurosis is implicitly human, while integration is implicitly divine.

As dealers in illusion and reality, intermediaries between secular and sacred ontologies, all wizards share in this equivocal movement—though unlike Merlin they are absorbed ultimately into either heaven or hell. It is the foundation of their power and appeal.

Merlin's imaginative potential is consequently broader than that of gods on the one hand or humans on the other because it includes both divinity and humanity. Either aspect of him may be stressed in any given work, but all other wizard figures ultimately seem to be only one or the other. Their function is above all to resolve the tension within the psyche rather than—like ecumenical Merlin—to hold it fruitfully open.

The endless narrative possibilities opened up by his ambiguous nature are produced by these tensions between eternal verities and our human experiences. These tensions were also behind the open-ended interlace possibilities of medieval romance. Eugene Vinaver observes, "There is no limit to what a cycle might eventually receive within its orbit just as there is no limit to what the pictorial or sculptural ornament might absorb in its conquest of space: everything we see or read about is part of a wider canvas, of a work still unwritten of a design still unfulfilled" (pp. 80–81).

Thus the wizard is a culture hero who represents most of all "the power of the imagination to sustain its believers." In his equivocal goodness he also represents our desire for faith in the ultimate power of the supernatural to alter things for the better.

Merlin has always been the personified faculty of creative fantasy. His many literary functions and guises master time by changing or remaining determinedly anachronistic. Since his conscious disposition is generally benevolent, and since the fundamental tension implicit in his character and deeds appears to be between potency and impotency as expressed on the subhuman, human, and suprahuman levels, he is essentially portrayed as the good but ultimately fallible wizard who employs all his skills in the effort to reconstitute the Golden Age. Thus he is as infinitely adaptable as King Arthur, in tandem with whom he signifies cultural wholeness like the monomyth hero whose magical aspects they both incarnate. In turn his figure has become a conscious or subliminal source in Western society for uncounted adaptations of wizardly and Arthurian conventions.

Merlin has become tacit in our very conceptions of the wizard in any art or science. He has popular analogues in the legends of Virgil and Francis Bacon, in the characters of Prospero, Gandalf, Doctor Who, Mr. Spock, and Obi-wan Kenobi, in historical figures as dissimilar as the Elizabethan magus John Dee, Otto von Bismarck, Thomas Edison, and Albert Einstein, and in all media. In these myriad guises as well as under his own name Merlin is more alive today than ever. His story and Arthur's has for centuries been more than the national myth of Britain; it may eventually prove to be *the* myth of Western culture.

A Note on the Contents

I have chosen the texts in this anthology with three principles in mind. First, they represent the various ways in which the figure of Merlin has been developed throughout the ages; taken together, they constitute as complete a portrait of Merlin in English-speaking tradition (including the most seminal French influences) as is possible in one book. Second, they do not duplicate the material in other Garland anthologies, but supplement and extend it with regard to Merlin. Third, each work is significant, and enjoyable in its own right.

This volume adopts the chronological order in which the first versions of the individual texts were composed. Several of the texts date from a period later than their original composition, however. The Lailoken stories survive in fragments and in the twelfth-century *Life of St. Kentigern*, for example, but are considered nevertheless to contain elements of a tradition that predated the Myrddin poems of the ninth century and later. Even the Myrddin poems are available only in relatively late texts, and were circulated orally for several centuries before being set down in the versions that survive. "Merline," too, is a late version of the thirteenth-century *Of Arthour and of Merlin*, and is included here because it is in a more accessible form of English and demonstrates how the influence of the earlier poem survives Malory.

No selection from a literature so vast and varied as that surrounding Merlin can be perfect, of course, and many readers will miss texts that have been excluded. The contributions of other languages than English and French remain to be explored. However, the contributors to this volume all share the hope that it will contribute to better understanding of Merlin's protean appeal, and to greater enjoyment of his many guises.

Works Cited

Campbell, Joseph. *The Hero with a Thousand Faces*, 2nd ed. Bollingen Series 17. Princeton: Princeton University Press, 1968.

Gerald of Wales. *The Journey through Wales and The Description of Wales*. Lewis Thorpe, trans. Harmondsworth: Penguin, 1978.

Jarman, A.O.H. *The Legend of Merlin*. Cardiff: University of Wales Press, 1970.

O'Riain, Padraig. "A Study of the Irish Legend of the Wild Man," *Eigse* 14 (Summer 1972).

Peters, Edward. *The Magician, the Witch, and the Law*. Philadelphia: University of Pennsylvania Press, 1978.

Vinaver, Eugene. *The Rise of Romance*. Oxford: Oxford University Press, 1971.

For Further Reading

Gollnick, James, ed. *Comparative Studies in Merlin from the Vedas to C.G. Jung.* Lewiston, N.Y.: Edwin Mellen, 1990.

Goodrich, Norma Lorre. *Merlin.* New York: Franklin Watts, 1988.

Harding, Carol E. *Merlin and Legendary Romance.* New York: Garland, 1988.

Lacy, Norris J., et al., eds. *The Arthurian Encyclopedia.* New York: Garland, 1986.

Lacy, Norris J., and Geoffrey Ashe. *The Arthurian Handbook.* New York: Garland, 1988.

Lupack, Alan. *"Arthur, the Greatest King": An Anthology of Arthurian Poetry.* New York: Garland, 1988.

MacDonald, Aileen. *The Figure of Merlin in Thirteenth-Century French Romance.* Lewiston, N.Y.: Edwin Mellen, 1990.

Markale, Jean. *Merlin l'enchanteur, ou l'eternelle quête magique.* Paris: Retz, 1981.

Merriman, James Douglas. *The Flower of Kings: A Study of the Arthurian Legend in England Between 1485 and 1835.* Lawrence: University of Kansas Press, 1973.

Reiss, Edmund, Louise Horner Reiss, and Beverly Taylor. *Arthurian Legend and Literature: An Annotated Bibliography.* Vol. 1, The Middle Ages. New York: Garland, 1984.

Stewart, R.J., ed. *The Book of Merlin: Insights from the Merlin Conference.* Poole, Dorset: Blandford, 1987.

———. *Merlin and Woman: The Book of the Second Merlin Conference.* London: Blandford, 1988.

Taylor, Beverly, and Elisabeth Brewer. *The Return of King Arthur: British and American Literature since 1900.* London: Brewer, 1983.

Thompson, Raymond H. *The Return from Avalon: A Study of Arthurian Legend in Modern Fiction.* Westport, Conn.: Greenwood, 1985.

Tolstoy, Nikolai. *The Quest for Merlin.* Boston: Little, Brown, 1985.

Watson, Jeanie, and Maureen Fries, eds. *The Figure of Merlin in the Nineteenth and Twentieth Centuries.* Lewiston, N.Y.: Edwin Mellen, 1989.

Wilhelm, James J., and Laila Zamuelis Gross, eds. *The Romance of Arthur.* New York: Garland, 1984.

Wilhelm, James J., ed. *The Romance of Arthur II.* New York: Garland, 1986.

———. *The Romance of Arthur III.* New York: Garland, 1988.

Zumthor, Paul. *Merlin le Prophète.* Lausanne: Payot, 1943.

I.

MERLIN IN
THE DARK AGES

chapter 1

LAILOKEN

Aubrey Galyon and Zacharias P. Thundy

M A D N E S S O R frenzy is a frequent theme in medieval literature, and the wild man a recurring character. A character's madness usually takes one of three forms: battle frenzy, prophetic frenzy, or insanity occasioned by extreme sorrow or divine anger. These traditional sources of madness were deeply influenced by the Christian tradition of the ascetic or hermit life, in which a saint-to-be took up residence alone in the desert or wilderness so that his physical hardships would purify his soul and at least partially redress the preponderance of evil in the world. In this way the hermit or anchorite would atone for his own sinful nature and that of others. The earliest stories of Merlin originate from this context in Celtic lore.

Merlin takes his name from the Welsh poems translated in the next chapter, but he also has analogues in Irish and Scottish tradition. The many similarities among the Irish tale of mad Sweeney (Suibne in Gaelic), the Scottish lowland tradition of Lailoken, and the Welsh poems attributed to Myrddin demonstrate that their stories must have sprung from the same source or at least have influenced one another. This mutual influence is not surprising, since during the Dark Ages British tribes from Strathclyde settled in Wales, and frequent contacts existed between the kingdoms of southern Ireland and Wales and northern Ireland and Scotland. The stories existed in oral form long before they were recorded, but internal evidence suggests that Lailoken was the forerunner for Myrddin, and that Sweeney stems from both. What remains of the Lailoken stories is translated here.

The basic tale is of a warrior who goes mad in battle and rushes off to the forests for a life of bare subsistence among the beasts. For Sweeney the madness fulfills the curse of a saint; for both Sweeney and Lailoken it comes from a horrifying vision in the sky; for Merlin it originates in grief for slain relatives. In all three traditions the wild man is responsible for the battle and punished for his transgression, just as the Babylonian King Nebuchadnezzar is condemned in the Old Testament to seven years of madness for the sin of pride. Sweeney is associated with the Battle of Magh Rath in A.D. 637; Lailoken and Myrddin with the Battle of Arfderydd in 573. Condemned to live among the wild animals of the Caledonian Forest that covered northern Wales and southern Scotland, Lailoken/Myrddin had infrequent contacts with his former family and friends, but developed the abilities of second sight and prophecy often associated with wild men. Like Sweeney, who is finally pardoned by a saint, Lailoken meets and eventually obtains absolution from Kentigern, the patron saint of Glasgow.

Other popular motifs were associated with this story; some of them, like the Christian ascetic lifestyle itself, from eastern tradition. The most important of these are the incomprehensible prophecies with which Lailoken disturbs Kentigern and his priests, the significant laugh and exposure of King Meldred's unfaithful wife, and the triple death suffered as her revenge. All of these features reappear in later Merlin stories, most notably Geoffrey of Monmouth's *Vita Merlini* and the French romances of Robert de Boron and his continuators.

The many similarities among the Celtic wild-man stories were recognized by their composers or scribes: the beginning of "Lailoken and Kentigern" and end of "Lailoken and Meldred" refer to him as Merlin; Merlin's sister Gwendydd calls him "llallogan" (usually translated "twin-brother") in the Welsh "Apple Trees" stanzas; and Sweeney meets another madman in Scotland named "Ealladhan," who prophesies his own death and falls over a cliff. Such references suggest that the figure popularized as Merlin did indeed originate as a wild man afflicted with exile and prophetic insight in the Caledonian Forest of Strathclyde.

Bibliographic note: The references to Lailoken, like those to Sweeney, might not have survived at all without connection to a saint's legend. Interestingly, Kentigern, who died in 612 according to the *Annales Cambriae*, has a birth story much like Merlin's—he is born to a king's daughter who was mysteriously impregnated. Her lover was not an incubus demon, however, but a human suitor who lies with her disguised as a woman.

The primary source for this saint's legend is the twelfth-century *Life of St. Kentigern*, by Joceline of Furness, preserved in Cotton Vitellius C. VIII from the fifteenth century. Joceline's last chapter mentions Lailoken as a "homo fatuus," fool or simpleton, who disturbs Kentigern's devotions. An abridgment of Joceline's *Life* was ascribed to St. Asaph, and although both are later than Geoffrey of Monmouth's writings, it is possible that Geoffrey learned about Kentigern and Lailoken from contacts with the monks of St. Asaph's monastery, where he was appointed bishop in 1152. Walter Bower's *Scotichronicon* (1447) includes an abridgment of "Kentigern and Lailoken," and the fullest text, translated here, is from Cotton Titus A. XIX. in the British Library. The Titus manuscript continues with the story of Lailoken's association with King Meldred of Dunmeller (now Drumelzier) and the threefold death. For this translation we have used the edition of H. L. D. Ward, "Lailoken (or Merlin Silvester)," *Romania* 22 (1896): 504–526. Another translation and discussion of the Lailoken fragments is in Basil Clarke's *Life of Merlin* (Cardiff: University of Wales Press, 1973).

Kentigern and Lailoken

One day, when Blessed Kentigern was deep in prayer in a solitary part of the forest during the time he was leading the life of a hermit, a madman, naked, hairy, and wretched, ran toward him a in a fit of frenzy. His name was Lailoken; some say he was Merlin, the famous seer among the Britons, but this is not an established fact.

When Blessed Kentigern saw him, as legend has it, he approached the wild man with these words, "Whatever sort of God's creature you may be, I adjure you in the name of the Father, the Son, and the Holy Ghost to speak to to me. Are you from God? Do you believe in God? Who are you? Why are you wandering in this solitary wilderness with the beasts of the forest as your companions?" Stopping in his tracks, the wild man said, "I am a Christian, although I am not worthy of such a great name. I endure great torment in the wilderness for my sins. I am fated to live among the creatures of the wild since I am unworthy to perform my penance among men. It was I who caused the death of all those slain in that battle on the plain between Lidel and Carwannock; it is a battle well remembered by the people of this country. In the midst of that fray, the very sky began to gape open above my head, and I heard what seemed to be a great cracking sound, a voice in the sky saying to me, 'Lailoken, Lailoken, since you alone are guilty of the blood of all of your slain comrades, you alone shall suffer for their sins. You shall be handed over to the minions of Satan, and until the day of your death your companions shall be the beasts of the forest.' And, as I turned my eyes to the source of the voice, I saw a brilliance so dazzling that no man could bear it. I also saw numerous battle formations of an army in the sky, much like the streaks of lightning. In their hands the warriors held burning lances and shining javelins which they brandished at me with bloodthirsty fury. Then, as I turned away, a wicked spirit seized me and consigned me to live among the wild beasts of the forest, as you are my witness."

Having said these things, he leaped away into a secluded part of the woods known only to beasts and birds. Feeling great compassion for the wretch, Blessed Kentigern fell to his face upon the ground, praying, "Lord Jesus, this man is the most miserable of men. He lives in filth and solitude among the beasts as a beast, naked and an exile, having only green grass to eat as food. Bristles and hairs are a natural covering only for wild beasts, and grass of the earth, roots, and leaves only their fitting diet. This man is our brother. Though he has our frail form, our flesh, and our blood, he is lacking in everything that mankind needs except for the common air we all breathe. Does he have to live in the face of hunger and cold and in total deprivation with the beasts of the forest?"

Then the devout Bishop Kentigern, usually so restrained, was moved by the love of God and wept, his cheeks flowing with tears of compassion. Continuing to practice penance in the solitude of the forest, he besought the Lord in earnest prayer to help that wild man, that possessed one, unclean wretch, so that the present trials and tribulations that wracked his body might lead to the future salvation of his soul.

Later, as the legend has it, the aforementioned madman, coming quite often from his solitary haunts, used to sit perched on a cliff above the rushing waters of Mellodonor, in view of the city of Glasgow, near the northern wing of the local church. There, by pouring forth dreadful shrieks and lamentations, he would disturb Blessed Kentigern and his monks, who spent their time practicing the art of divine contemplation. Sitting there, the wild man predicted many things to come as if he were a prophet. Since he never repeated his predictions, which were quite obscure and barely intelligible, no one cared to believe him. His audience considered his words mere folly and recommended the Scriptures to him.

On the day this wild man was destined to depart from the afflictions of this world, he came to the rock spoken about earlier, as was his custom, wailing and shouting as the Blessed Kentigern was celebrating the morning mass. He importuned the saint in a loud voice to help him become worthy to receive the Body and Blood of Christ before he departed from this world. When the Blessed Kentigern was no longer able to bear the man's irreverent outcries, he sent one of his priests to bid the madman to be silent. The fortunate wretch answered him in kind and mild words, saying, "My lord, please go, I beg you, to the Blessed Kentigern and appeal to his kindness that he may deign to provide me with the divine Eucharist and Last Rites, since today I will depart from this life, a happy man, with the saint's help."

When the holy bishop heard this report from the mouth of his priest, he smiled piously and spoke to the bystanders who were pleading earnestly in behalf of the possessed man, "Isn't he that miserable creature who often tried to lead all of us, as well as a few others, astray with his words? Isn't he the one who has been living for many years among the beasts of the forest, a possessed man without the benefit of Christian fellowship? Since that seems to be the case, I do not believe it right to dispense to him the sacraments." The saint did, however, give orders to one of his priests, "Go and ask the man again about the sort of death he will die; also, find out whether he is really supposed to die today."

The priest went, and repeated to the madman what he was bidden to say by the holy bishop. The wild man replied that he would die this very day, felled by stones and clubs.

Then the priest returned to the bishop and told him what he had heard from the mouth of the wild man. The bishop asked the priest to go back to the wild man and tell him that he found it hard to believe that this was how he was going die and that he should speak truthfully and exactly as to the time and manner of his death. Then the bishop addressed those around him and said, "If perchance that wretch is speaking the truth without mincing words, then this day could very well be the last day of his life. Mind you, never before has he repeated the same thing in exactly the same words. Remember, he always used to reiterate the same speech, but always in different words so that his meaning has to be conjectured as different from what he said before."

Questioned a second time by the priest, the madman said, "Today my body will be pierced by a sharp wooden spear, and that is how I shall die." Returning to the bishop, the priest reported what he had heard from the demented man.

Calling his priests about him, the bishop said, "Just now you have heard it for yourselves. The man is still not consistent in his speech. So, I am afraid, I must deny him his request." Then the priests said, "Father, we beg you in the Lord's name not to be angry with us if we may offer your reverence our help in behalf of him. Let him be examined a third time, and maybe we will find out that he is trustworthy in some speech of his."

In accordance with their wishes, the bishop sent the priest a third time to inquire of that fortunate wretch how he would meet his end. The madman answered, "This very day, swallowed up by the waves, I shall end my life." The priest was highly indignant at this response and said, "Brother, you are acting foolishly and impiously; you are, indeed, a cheat and a liar. Even so, you request to be fortified with spiritual food from the hand of a holy and truthful man. So great a sacrament can be given only to the truthful and the righteous."

Then the demented wretch, suddenly transformed into a happy man with his senses restored by the Lord, immediately burst into more tears and said, "Lord Jesus, how long must I, the most miserable of men, endure such a hard fate? How long must I be afflicted with so many torments? Why do even your own faithful ones reject me though you yourself sent me here to them? Behold, they do not believe my words even though I haven't spoken to them anything except what you inspired me to say." Then turning to the priest, he said, "I urgently beg that the bishop himself, into whose care the Lord has assigned me this day, come to me and bring to me in his own hand the holy Eucharist that I have requested as a provision for my last journey, and then let him hear what God has ordained me to reveal to him."

Moved by the pleas of his clergy, the bishop came, bearing with him the blessed sacrament of bread and wine. As the saint neared him, that blessed wretch came down from the rock, prostrated himself at the feet of the saint and spoke as follows: "Welcome holy father, chosen soldier of the Most High. I am that same defenseless wretch who once appeared before you in the wilderness, a man handed over to the servants of Satan and fated to be a solitary wanderer until now. When you ordered me by the power of the true and and eternal God and in the name of the Trinity, I disclosed to you the cause of my sufferings. Moved by pity for my suffering and by my shrieks, you shed tears; then, seeing all the anguish and torment that I was enduring in my body on earth, you prayed God to turn these afflictions into everlasting happiness in the life to come. Thus, you gave a new meaning to the words of the Apostle, who said that the sufferings of this age can in no way compare to the future glory to be revealed in God's elect. The Lord, who listened to your prayers, has shown me mercy by restoring my senses and saved me from the power of Satan by delivering me, as befits a Christian believer of the Catholic faith, to God the omnipotent Father. Furthermore, after instructing me in many signs and symbols, He has sent me to you, especially in the sight of the other elect, so that you may believe my words and that this day you may send me to Him after I have received His most sacred Body and Blood."

When the holy bishop Kentigern heard that this was the very man who not long ago had encountered him in the wilderness—he also learned many other matters not recounted in this little book—his doubts vanished. Then, overcome by the devotion of the wretched man who wept and earnestly sought the grace of God, the saint shed tears profusely and spoke softly, "Behold, this is the Body and Blood of our Lord Jesus Christ, the one who is the true and everlasting salvation of all the living who believe in Him and the eternal glory of those who receive Him worthily. Whoever receives this sacrament worthily will have eternal life and will not die. He who receives it unworthily will die and not enjoy eternal life. Therefore, if you think that you are worthy of so great a gift, here it is placed on the altar of Christ. Approach it, then, in the fear of the Lord since you wish to receive Christ in all humility. I dare not give it to you nor forbid you from partaking of it since Christ Himself has deigned to make you worthy to receive it."

Then the happy wretch, having at once bathed himself with water, made his profession of faith in the One Triune God, approached the altar with humility, and partook of the sacrament of everlasting protection with great faith and sincere devotion. After giving himself the sacrament, he raised his hands to heaven and said, "I give you thanks, Lord Jesus, for I have now received that most holy Sacrament which I had been longing for." Then, turning to Blessed Kentigern, he said, "Your lordship, indeed, today my temporal life has reached its end. As you have already heard it from me, the most eminent of the British kings, the saintliest of the bishops, and the most noble of the lords will follow me within this year."

The bishop then responded, "Brother, do you yet persist in your madness? Are you not still being irreverent? But go in peace. May the Lord be with you."

Having received the priestly blessing, Lailoken bounded away like a wild goat slipping the hunter's noose and happily sought refuge in the underbrush. But since things predestined by the Lord cannot be ignored as though they will not come to pass, it happened that on that day Lailoken was stoned and beaten to death by some shepherds of King Meldred. At the very moment of death he fell down a precipitous bank of the River Tweed near the fortification at Dunmeller and fell onto a stake that was sticking up in a fish pond, thus impaling himself through the middle of his body with his head sticking down into the pond. In this way he gave up his spirit to the Lord just as he had foretold.

When Blessed Kentigern and his priests discovered that these things had happened to that deranged man just as he had foretold, they believed. They feared as well that the rest that he had predicted would also undoubtedly come to pass. They all began to quake with fear as tears poured down their cheeks and began to praise the name of the Lord, who always works wonders in His saints and is blessed forever in the world without end. Amen.

(Translated by Aubrey Galyon and Zacharias P. Thundy)

Meldred and Lailoken

According to another tradition, King Meldred, wishing to hear some new marvels from Lailoken, once captured him and ordered him bound with leather straps and held in the town of Dunmeller. Lailoken refused food and drink for the next three days and spoke not a word to the many who came to hear him. On the third day, as the king was sitting on an elevated throne in the high hall, his wife entered the room clad in a robe, wearing a crown of leaves on her head like a queen.

When the king saw her enter, he beckoned her to approach him and plucked off the leaves one after another from her hair. Seeing all this, the demented Lailoken burst into fits of uncontrollable laughter. The king, perceiving that Lailoken was in a cheerful frame of mind, took him aside and spoke to him in a sweet, flattering tone, "My good friend, Lailoken, tell me, I beg you, What are you laughing about? You have pierced my ears with the sharp peals of your laughter. If you answer my question, I will let you go free anywhere you wish."

At once Lailoken replied, "You had me arrested and ordered me bound with leather thongs for the sole purpose of hearing from me a new oracle. Very well. Now I will propose to you a new riddle about the latest developments. From poison comes sweetness and from sweet honey comes bitterness. But neither can remain both at the same time. This is my riddle. Tell me the solution if you can, and then you may let me go free." The king answered, "This is a very difficult puzzle, and I don't have the faintest clue for solving it. Since that is the case, tell me clearly another riddle on the same terms."

Then Lailoken proposed a second riddle similar to the first one and said, "Wickedness did good and eschewed evil; piety did evil and eschewed good. But neither can remain both at the same time." The king said, "Please don't speak to me in riddles. In plain language tell us the reason for your laughter and the solutions of your riddles. Then you shall be free from your prison." Lailoken answered, "If I speak in plain language, my words will cause you pain and me mortal grief."

The king replied, "Even if what you say is going to happen, I want to hear it from your mouth." Accordingly, Lailoken addressed the king, "Since you too are endowed with wisdom and are a good judge of character, give me your judgment of the following case and then I will obey your orders." The king said, "Tell me the case so that you may have my judgment."

Lailoken said, "A certain person confers the highest honor on his enemy and then the worst punishment on his friend. What do these two people really deserve?" The king answered, "The first one punishment and the second one reward." Lailoken said, "You have judged the case right. In like manner, your wife richly deserved the crown and you the most painful death. But it shall not be so provided; both of you remain the way you are."

The king became impatient, "Whatever you do is surrounded by mystery. Explain to us these riddles and whatever else that can be justly resolved. I'll grant you whatever you ask me." Lailoken said, "There is something I very much desire; you can easily grant me that besides my freedom. I want you to bury me in the eastern part of the city in the churchyard, where the faithful are interred, not far from the green chapel where the brook Pausayl flows into the River Tweed, which, indeed, will take place in a few days after my triple death. When the divided rivers meet at my grave, the architect of the united British nation will conquer the adulteress." By these words he indicated that the British would soon be disunited and defeated and that later their division would be healed. [*The "pactor britanicae gentis" is no doubt Cadwaladyr, whose miraculous return, as the uniter of the Cymry from Cumbria to Armorica, was often prophesied in the Merlinesque poems. It has also been reported that when King James VI of Scotland was crowned king of England, the River Tweed overflowed its banks and joined with Pausayl at Merlin's grave.*]

Lailoken revealed truthfully these and other future events that the king, the queen, and the court desired to learn after they had granted him his funeral request and had promised under oath that they would let him go safe and sound wherever he wished to go.

The prophet, now free from his leather bonds and ready to depart, rose up and said as follows, "What is more bitter than womanly poison that was infected from the beginning with the serpent's venom? What is sweeter than the just judgment that provides protection to the meek and humble from the poison of the wicked? Indeed, this very day this woman, your wife, conferred the highest honor on your archenemy, but you, on your part, tore your faithful friend into pieces. But neither is really so since you thought you were doing right when you did these things. The woman was absolutely unaware of the honor she was conferring on the enemy.

"The second puzzle is similar to the first one. Wickedness did good since the evil woman honored her own betrayer. Likewise, good did evil when the just man killed his faithful friend. But neither is really so since both did what they did out of sheer ignorance. A little while ago, when the queen committed adultery in the king's orchard, the leaves of the trees descended on her head to betray her and to reveal her adultery to the king. And it was this crime, wrapped in her robe and placed on her head, that the queen brought to the hall and flaunted in front of the court. When the king saw the leaves on her head, at once he beckoned her to his side and went about picking them off her head one by one. It was an honor that the woman conferred on the enemy who was about to reveal the crime. The king did his friend harm; however, he ordered him protected in order to prevent another crime."

After uttering this speech, Lailoken sought the impenetrable confines of solitude in the forest with no one in pursuit and all the people in awe.

The adulteress, feigning outrage, began to beguile the king with sweet speech and abundant tears. "My honorable lord and king, please don't believe the words of this madman. He said what he said in order that you might believe in him because with his riddles he had sought nothing else but release from the prison and freedom of movement. My lord, I am ready and willing to prove my innocence by means of proper trial. You, too, have heard like the rest of us what that most detestable traitor had said about his death: that he would die three times, which is no doubt impossible. Once dead, you are dead for good, and death cannot be repeated. So both his claims are plain lies. Besides, if he were a genuine prophet and seer, he would never have permitted himself to be captured or bound with thongs from which later he would beg to be freed. Therefore, if you now desist from pursuing him, you will be doing all of us an insult and your own kingdom a disservice. So that the honor of the realm may be preserved, since your majesty loves justice, you should not let such a horrendous crime go unpunished."

The king answered, "O most foolish woman, if I decide to comply with your request you will be proven to be the most abominable adulteress. In fact, Lailoken is a veritable prophet, for he said that, if I were to do publicly what you have now proposed to me, you will suffer great grief and I shall endure mortal anguish and our infamy will be proclaimed everywhere. But, if we leave things the way they are, the pain will remain hidden from the public's eye."

The woman, bursting into crocodile tears and saying in many words that the king did not wish to do what was good for him, went about secretly plotting Lailoken's death. After a few years, on the day that Lailoken received the last rites, he happened to pass at sundown through the meadow beside the Castle of Dunmeller [*now Drumelzier in Peebleshire*]. There he was confronted by some shepherds, who attacked him at the instigation of the nefarious queen. As Lailoken had predicted and as it has been written above, tradition has it that he met his death there. It is also said that the king buried Lailoken's lifeless body in the grave at the site that he himself had picked out when he was alive. Further, that town is about thirty miles from the city of Glasgow. Lailoken rests in a grave in the town's cemetery.

> Pierced by a spear, crushed by a stone,
> And drowned in the stream's waters,
> Merlin died a triple death.

(Translated by Zacharias P. Thundy)

chapter 2

MYRDDIN IN EARLY WELSH TRADITION

John K. Bollard

M Y R D D I N   I S   the Welsh name for a traditional figure who became known in the Latin works of Geoffrey of Monmouth as Merlinus and in other languages as Merlin. The difference in form between *Myrddin* (*Myrdin, Myrtin, Mirdyn, Mertin,* and *Merdin* are a few early Welsh spellings) and *Merlin* is no greater than similar variation in other names taken from Welsh into Latin and French Arthurian literature, as in Gwalchmai/Walwanus/Gauvain/ Gawain and Peredur/Perceval. The form *Merlinus* may have been chosen by Geoffrey to avoid connection with Old French *merde* 'excrement.'

Such things can rarely be determined with certainty, but the Welsh name Myrddin is not originally a personal name; it is perhaps derived by false etymology from the Brythonic place-name **Moridunon* 'Sea-fortress.' (The asterisk denotes an unattested, reconstructed form.) As the form of the place-name changed through time to **Mer-ddín* or **Myr-ddín* its significance was forgotten, and at some point *caer* 'fortress or stronghold' was prefixed to it, giving *Caerfyrddin* (in English, Carmarthen; *m* regularly becomes *f* [=*v*] in such Welsh compounds). The element *Myrddin* was subsequently understood as a personal name, by analogy with the structure of other eponymous place-names, such as *Caergybi* 'Cybi's fortress' and *Caer-gai* 'Cai's fortress.'

How early Myrddin came to be understood as a personal name is difficult to say, but there are a number of early traditions centering on a figure named Myrddin. However, although these traditions were articulated in Wales, they are not located in Wales. They refer primarily to events in the Celtic kingdoms of "the Old North," in what is now northern England and southern Scotland. As these kingdoms fell before the expansion of Anglo-Saxon domination, many of the names, figures, legends, and even a few very early poems (the earliest in a European vernacular), were relocated in Wales as the survivors of these kingdoms and their descendants themselves migrated to friendlier territory. One of these early Welsh poems, called *The Gododdin* and composed shortly after the year 600, celebrates the memory of the warriors of Gododdin, a British kingdom around Edinburgh, who died in an attack against the English at Catraeth (modern Catterick in Yorkshire). A passage in the later of the two surviving versions of *The Gododdin* states that "Morien defended the praise-poetry of Myrddin." This reading was probably interpolated into the poem at an uncertain later date, perhaps in an attempt to make sense of an obscure archaic passage. It does, however, indicate an early belief in the existence of a poet Myrddin connected with the traditions of the Old North.

In the *Book of Taliesin*, a fourteenth-century manuscript, a poem called *Armes Prydein Fawr* ("The Great Prophecy of Britain") also attests to this belief. This 200-line poem, which calls for an anti-Saxon alliance of the Welsh, Irish, Scandinavian Dubliners, Cornish, and the British of the North, was probably composed not much earlier than the year 930 and almost certainly before King Athelstan's English victory over the northern British, Irish, and Danes in the Battle of Brunanburh in 937. Two stanzas of this poem begin with *Dygogan awen*, "Poetic inspiration prophesies," and another begins *Dysgogan derwydon*, "Wise men prophesy." Yet another begins *Dysgogan Myrdin*, "Myrddin prophesies." Though no other reference to Myrddin or to events elsewhere connected with his name is included in this poem, this formula (unless it is a later interpolation) does indicate that by the tenth century Myrddin had become an archetypal prophet-poet whose name could be invoked to give authority to a prophetic expression of hope for eventual freedom from increasing English domination.

A good example of the place given to Myrddin as prophet at a somewhat later period can be found in the only medieval Welsh secular biography, the *Historia Gruffud vab Kenan*. This account of the life of Gruffudd ap Cynan (c. 1050–1137), ruler of the northern Welsh kingdom of Gwynedd, was originally written in the later twelfth century in Latin, but survives only in a Middle Welsh translation. After giving Gruffudd's genealogy on both sides of his family and justifying his rule through his descent, as a son of Adam, from God, the author goes on to say,

> Therefore, King Gruffudd being praiseworthy by worldly and spiritual descent, let us go on now to a prophecy of Myrddin, poet of the Britons, about him. Myrddin prophesies to us thus:
>
> A fierce eager one is prophesied,
> intending an attack from over the sea;
> Despoiler is his name; he despoils much.
>
> That is in Latin: "Saltus ferinus praesagitur uenturus de mari insidiaturus cuius nomen corruptor, quia multos corrumpet."
>
> O most beloved brothers of the Welsh, King Gruffudd ought to be remembered, he whom his worldly descent and the prophecy of Myrddin praise thus. And since that is completed, let us hurry on to his particular deeds, according as they have been left to us through old accounts. And may Christ be authority and support for us for that, and not Diana or Apollo.

The Welsh stanza given in this text was written sometime before 1100. Its applicability to Gruffudd ap Cynan is occasioned partly by the fact that Gruffudd was born and raised in Ireland, whence he could attack "from over the sea."

Most of what we know about the legend of Myrddin and its origins in early Welsh tradition is gleaned from a small number of poems in which Myrddin figures to a greater or lesser degree. These are mostly prophetic poems and the legendary elements are rarely a primary feature. Four of these poems are found in a manuscript of about 1250 known as the *Black Book of Carmarthen*, produced, according to tradition, in Carmarthen at the Augustinian Priory of St. John the Evangelist. It may, indeed, be the eventual connection of legends of a prophet from the Old North with the personal/place name Myrddin that accounts for the inclusion of these poems in this manuscript.

Bibliographic note: Most of the translations below, tentative and halting as they are, have been greatly improved by the gracious commentary of R. Geraint Gruffydd, Director of the Centre for Advanced Welsh and Celtic Studies, Aberystwyth. Perhaps it is needless to say that they would not have been even attempted without having at hand the fruits of A. O. H. Jarman's many years of invaluable textual and critical work on the Myrddin legend and its development. Among the most important, listing his editions first, are: *Llyfr Du Caerfyrddin* (Cardiff: University of Wales Press, 1982) (an edition in Welsh of the complete text of the *Black Book of Carmarthen*, including "The Conversation of Myrddin and Taliesin," "The Birch Tree Stanzas," "The Apple Tree Stanzas," and "The Little Pig Stanzas"); "Peiryan Vaban," *Bulletin of the Board of Celtic Studies* 14 (1951–1952): 104–108; (text of "Commanding Youth"); *Ymddiddan Myrddin a Thaliesin* (Cardiff: University of Wales Press, 1957, 2nd ed. 1967) (an edition and full discussion in Welsh of "The Conversation of Myrddin and Taliesin"); "Early Stages in the Development of the Myrddin Legend," ed. Rachel Bromwich and R. Brinley Jones, *Astudiaethau ar yr Hengerdd: Studies in Old Welsh Poetry* (Cardiff: University of Wales Press, 1978), pp. 326–349; *The Legend of Myrddin* (Cardiff: University of Wales Press, 1960); "The Welsh Myrddin Poems." in *Arthurian Literature in the Middle Ages*, ed. Roger Sherman Loomis (Oxford: Clarendon, 1959), pp. 20–30; Other texts and studies making this chapter possible include Rachel Bromwich, ed., *Trioedd Ynys Prydein: The Welsh Triads* (Cardiff: University of Wales Press, 1961, 2nd ed. 1978) (contains the texts of "The Three Skilled Bards" and "The Names of the Island of Britain," as well as important commentary on Myrddin and others); D. Simon Evans, ed., *Historia Gruffud vab Kenan* (Cardiff: University of Wales Press, 1977); J. Gwenogvryn Evans, ed., *The Poetry in the Red Book of Hergest* (Llanbedrog, 1911) (this diplomatic text of the *Red Book* poetry contains "The Prophecy of Myrddin and Gwenddydd, His Sister" and "The Separation-Song of Myrddin in the Grave"); M.E. Griffiths, *Early Vaticination in Welsh with English Parallels* (Cardiff: University of Wales Press, 1937) (an important study of the prophetic tradition in Wales); E. G. B. P[hillimore], ed., "A Fragment from Hengwrt MS. No. 202," *Y Cymmrodor* 7 (1886): 89–154 (this manuscript fragment, including "The Separation-Song of Myrddin," was recognized as part of the *White Book of Rhydderch* and rebound in its proper place in 1940); Ifor Williams, ed., "Y Cyfoesi a'r Afallennau yn Peniarth 3," *Bulletin of the Board of Celtic Studies* 4 (1924): 112–129 (contains a long fragment of "The Prophecy of Myrddin and Gwenddydd," and important texts of "The Apple Tree Stanzas," and "The Little Pig Stanzas").

Note on the pronunciation of Welsh names: Pronounce *a* as in f*a*ther, *ai*, *au*, and *ei* as in *ai*sle, *aw* as in n*ow*, *c* as in *c*at, *ch* as in Scottish lo*ch*, *dd* as in *th*en, *e* as in b*e*d, *f* as in o*f*, *ff* as in o*ff*, *g* as in *g*o, *i* as in b*i*d, *th* as in *th*ink, *u* as in b*u*sy or b*ea*d, *w* as in *w*ith or as the vowel in t*oo*th, *y* as in m*y*th or c*i*ty in a single or final syllable and as *a*live or gl*o*ve in other syllables. Pronounce *ll* with the tongue in the same position as for *l* by gently blowing air, without voice, past the side of the tongue (the *l* of English c*l*ean is very similar). The stressed syllable is almost always the next-to-last.

The Conversation of Myrddin and Taliesin

The first poem in the *Black Book* is "The Conversation of Myrddin and Taliesin." Taliesin was a late-sixth-century poet, twelve of whose poems have survived and around whom grew up a tradition of his omniscience and prophetic powers. He became a legendary figure and many later poems of prophecy and wisdom are attributed to him, especially in the *Book of Taliesin*. It may also be true that, like Taliesin, Myrddin was an actual early British poet; scholars are still debating that point. In any case, there is a tradition that Myrddin took part in the Battle of Arfderydd, which occurred, according to the tenth-century *Annales Cambriae* (Annals of Wales), in the year 573 (though 575 may be more accurate). Arfderydd has been plausibly identified as Arthuret, north of Carlisle in Cumberland. Not far from Arthuret is Carwinley, earlier *Karwindelhou*, from *Caer Wenddolau 'The Fortress of Gwenddolau,' which preserves the name of Gwenddolau ap Ceidio, the local ruler who apparently was defeated in the battle. As a result of events that are reflected in the poems below, Myrddin went mad at the Battle of Arfderydd and hid from his enemies in Celyddon Wood in southern Scotland. Here the theme of the prophetic wild man of the wood comes into play, a theme also known in early Celtic tradition in the stories of Lailoken and in the Irish story of *Suibhne Geilt* (recently translated by Seamus Heaney as *Sweeney Astray*).

"The Conversation of Myrddin and Taliesin" is a puzzling poem, not least because it deals only in part with the Battle of Arfderydd. Nor is much of the poem prophetic. Lines 1–22 describe an attack made by a certain Maelgwn, probably the famous Maelgwn Gwynedd, ruler of the north Welsh kingdom of Gwynedd, who is berated by Gildas in *The Ruin of Britain* and who died in 547. Other figures in this part of the poem are either unknown or appear only as vague shadows in early genealogical traditions. Such, for instance, are Elgan and Dywel, both of whom are connected with the southwestern Welsh kingdom of Dyfed. The first part of the poem, then, seems to commemorate a foray by Maelgwn Gwynedd into Dyfed, a tradition also reflected in Maelgwn's appearance in the Latin *Life of Saint Brynach*, in a manuscript of about 1200.

But at line 23 the meter, rhyme scheme, verb tense, and subject matter all change. It has been suggested that fragments of two different poems have been accidentally joined by turning over two leaves of the scribe's original. However, lines 1–22 all end in *-an*, and though the metrical scheme is a little different, the main rhyme of 23–38 is also *-an*. Furthermore, except where they are bracketed, the names of Taliesin and Myrddin are found in the manuscript identifying the speakers of each stanza, so a gap or jump in the scribe's original is unlikely. What, then, *is* the relationship between the two parts of the poem? This is hard to say, and much depends on the translation of the difficult line 23. Henry Lewis suggested that the line might be rendered "From the Battle of Arfderydd comes the cause," proposing that the battle of the first part of the poem was part of the lifelong preparations made by warriors for the later encounter discussed in the second part. But there are both linguistic and narrative objections to this reading, not the least being that none of the characters in lines 1–22 (except for Myrddin as speaker, of course) appears in the traditions about Arfderydd.

We do not know the cause of the Battle of Arfderydd, but there is a triad in a fifteenth-century manuscript preserving the names of the "Three Futile Battles of the Isle of Britain" in which we read, "The second was the Battle of Arfderydd, which was brought about because of the lark's nest." Might the parenthetical question posed in line 23 as it is translated below be a similar, more indirect reference to the tradition of the futility of this battle and its carnage? If so, then we can perhaps read the whole poem as a commentary by an unknown eleventh-century poet in the dual persona of the two archetypal prophetic poets on both the heroic qualities and the ultimate loss of the heroes of old. We might, furthermore, suggest that the first person in *to me came terror* (18) accords well with the tradition of the mad Myrddin in the later battle.

On metrical and linguistic grounds this poem cannot be much later than 1100. An approximate earliest date is provided in line 12 by the word *tarian* 'targe, a small, round shield,' borrowed from Old English *targe, targan*. The English borrowed it from Old Norse *targa* in the late tenth century. Thus "The Conversation of Myrddin and Taliesin" was most likely composed between 1000 and 1100. The absence of any reference to the Normans strongly suggests that the poem is pre-Norman.

It has been suggested (though not proven) that Geoffrey of Monmouth knew or knew of this poem and that it served as the impetus for the quite different conversation between Merlinus (Myrddin) and Telgesinus (Taliesin) in his *Vita Merlini* (c. 1148–1150).

The Conversation of Myrddin and Taliesin

[Myrddin:]
So wretched am I, so wretched,
because of what happened to Cedfyw and Cadfan.
There was bright, noisy battle;
there was a stained, resounding shield.

[Taliesin:]
There was Maelgwn whom I saw fighting.   5
His warband before a great host are not silent.

Myrddin:
Against two men in two groups they muster.
Against Errith and Gwrrith on pale white [steeds],
slender bays they bring, without doubt.
Soon will be seen the host with Elgan.   10
Alas for his death! On a great journey they came.

Taliesin:
Rhys One-tooth (but a span was his targe),
towards you there came swift death.
Cyndur killed; beyond measure they mourn.
Lords killed, generous [men] while they lived;   15
Three men of note, great their fame with Elgan.

Myrddin:
Over and over, more and more they came;
again and again to me came terror for Elgan.
They killed Dywel in his last battle,
the son of Erbin, and his folk.   20

Taliesin:
Maelgwn's host, bravely they came,
Resplendent warriors of battle on a bloody field.

The battle of Arfderydd (whence comes the cause?),
all during life they prepare for it.

Myrddin:
A multitude of bloodflowing spears on a bloody field;   25
a multitude of mighty warriors will prove mortal;
a multitude when injured; a multitude when forced to flee;
a multitude their retreat in their battle.

Taliesin:
Seven sons of Eliffer, seven men when tested;
seven spears they do not avoid at their seven stations.   30

Myrddin:
> Seven burning fires; seven opposing armies;
> one of the seven—Cynfelyn, always in the van.

Taliesin:
> Seven stabbing spears, seven rivers full
> of chieftains' blood they fill.

Myrddin:
> Seven score generous nobles went mad;   35
> in Celyddon Wood they ended.
> Since it is I, Myrddin, in the style of Taliesin,
> my prophecy will be just.

The Birch Tree, The Apple Tree, and The Little Pig

A marginal note on page 46 of the *Black Book* in the hand of Jaspar Griffith, an antiquarian and manuscript collector who died in 1614, reads:

> Myrddin son of Morfryn composed that which is written in the
> eight pages following, as Llywelyn ap Cynfric Ddu [a poet who
> died c. 1500] testifies in this manner:

> > Myrddin the wild, with a repulsive and mad sickness,
> > son of Morfryn, of doubtful ancient status [?],
> > sang a very similar, exceedingly frivolous poem
> > long ago in the wood from his enclosure
> > to his nasty, strange little pig
> > and his birch tree, like a fool.

In these eight pages the earliest surviving stratum of the Welsh Myrddin legend is preserved. Though Myrddin is not named in the first one, there is sufficient consistency in content and external references to allow us to assume that "The Birch Tree Stanzas" were conceived of as coming from the same prophetic source as the two poems that follow it in the manuscript. There is some inconclusive evidence, in the sharing of lines, images, structure, and references and in the consistent power of the poetic persona in these three poems, that suggests that they may indeed be sprung from a single mind. With minor variation, the order of stanzas in other manuscript versions is the same, though each version has some stanzas that the others do not. It may be, as A. O. H. Jarman suggests, that there is an original core of early stanzas dealing solely or primarily with Myrddin to which later and varied prophetic materials have been added. However, given the relative consistency of stanza order, it is also possible that one or more twelfth- or thirteenth-century poets composed these poems in much the form we have them, using traditional Myrddin material to give justification to both real hopes and *ex post facto* prophecies. Poets in the following centuries frequently imitated the prophetic style established in these three poems, though rarely including the legendary element.

"The Birch Tree Stanzas" are a good example of medieval Welsh prophetic poetry, using both general and specific references to evoke a sense of loss, a lament for the changes that have brought the Welsh under oppression. There is little hope of relief in this short poem. It may be significant that the place-names in these few stanzas range through north Wales, mid Wales, and south Wales, for though Wales was rarely unified politically, there was long a powerful sense of the cultural unity of the people. The more powerful Welsh rulers from the tenth to the thirteenth century struggled to turn this ideal into political unity, but never with lasting success. The redeemer Cadwaladr of the last line will turn up in most of the poems in this chapter. He is traditionally the last ruler of an independent Britain. According to *Annales Cambriae*, he died of a plague in 682. His name was subsequently invoked by Welsh poets as one of a series of heroes (including Arthur) prophesied to return to restore independence to the rightful inhabitants of the island. Often coupled with Cadwaladr's is the name of a certain Cynan, also prophesied to return.

"The Apple Tree Stanzas" contain some of the clearest references to the early tradition of the Myrddin story. Stanzas 5, 6, and 7 deal solely with this legendary material and contain no prophetic elements; stanza 4 has prophetic elements only in the last two lines. Early Celtic poetry is generally not narrative in form, and we must piece together, if we can, an underlying narrative from the allusions in these stanzas and some supporting materials. The name of Myrddin does not appear in the early versions of the Triads of the Island of Britain, though there are several triads that refer to various aspects of the Battle of Arfderydd. Thus traditions of this battle between Gwenddolau and Rhydderch Hael, the late-sixth-century ruler of the British kingdom of Strathclyde, are preserved independently of the Myrddin legend, which itself seems to be an offshoot of the Arfderydd lore that was transmitted to Wales from the north. In "The Apple Tree Stanzas" we find Myrddin in Celyddon Wood, driven there in his despair at having slain Gwenddydd's son at Arfderydd. Gwenddydd is named as Myrddin's *chwaer* 'sister' in one of the other poems below, but she may originally have been Myrddin's mistress. Myrddin was thus driven mad at having slain his nephew, or possibly his son—both important relationships in early Celtic society. Hiding (for fifty years, we are told) from Rhydderch and his men, Myrddin in his wild state has acquired the powers of prophecy and poetry, and he addresses the apple tree that protects him from being seen by his enemies. The whole poem is a combination of his lament at his own situation and of prophecy for Wales. Similarly, in "The Little Pig Stanzas," he addresses his prophecies to his sole companion in the wild. The form of this

poem may have been suggested by line 31 of "The Apple Tree Stanzas."
Oia/Oian/Hoian is a Middle Welsh interjection ranging in meaning from
something like "Oh" to "Alas."

A few after-the-fact prophecies can be identified fairly certainly as
references to known historical events in the Welsh struggles against the
Normans and English. "The Apple Tree Stanzas," lines 4–5, refer to the
Battle of Machafwy Vale on Wednesday, August 12, 1198, in which Geoffrey
fitz Peter defeated the forces of Gwenwynwyn, the Welsh ruler of Powys in
northeast Wales. Lines 8–9 of "The Little Pig Stanzas" (and possibly "The
Apple Tree Stanzas," 18) may refer to Llywelyn ab Iorwerth (1173–1240),
the ruler of Gwynedd who united much of Wales. (It is also tempting to see
in *taguistil* [= *tangwystl*] 'peace' in line 60 of "The Little Pig Stanzas" a veiled
reference to, if not the actual name of, Tangwystl, Llywelyn's mistress and
the mother of his eldest son, Gruffydd.) The five leaders from Normandy in
"The Little Pig Stanzas," number 4, are William the Conqueror, William II,
Henry I, Stephen, and Henry II. In 1171 Henry II went to Ireland, returning
in 1172 through St. David's (Tyddewi in Welsh, after Dewi Sant, "Saint
David"), where he heard mass. Stanza 7 seems to recount events of 1211. In
May 1211 King John fortified Degannwy in north Wales, but he then
retreated. In July he burned Bangor and took prisoner Rhopert, Bishop of St.
Deinioel's. The bishop, ransomed for 200 hawks, died soon after. Other
references undoubtedly recount actual events, but we cannot identify them
with any certainty.

In the translations below words or phrases not in the original are given in
square brackets [ ]. Later additions to the manuscript text are enclosed in
curved brackets { }. For instance, lines 17–18 of "The Apple Tree Stanzas"
were added later by a different scribe imitating the original hand. Perhaps
more significantly, the first of "The Little Pig Stanzas" seems to have been
added later (by the original scribe) in an empty space at the bottom of the
page before that on which stanza 2 originally began the poem.

Y Bedwenni: The Birch Tree Stanzas

1

Blessed its world, the birch in the Wye Valley
whose branches fall one by one, two by two,
and which will be when there is the battle in Ardudwy,
and bellowing of cattle around Mochnwy Ford,
and spears and battle-shout in Degannwy,   5
and Edwin in Môn when he rules,
and the green, light youths fighting
and giving them reddened garments.

2

Blessed its world, the birch in Pumlumon
which will see when there will be ferocity of stags,   10
and which will see the French in coats of mail,
and around Cefn yr Aelwyd, food for wild beasts,
and monks frequently [fighting] as knights.

3

Blessed its world, the birch in the uplands of Dinwythwy
which will know when there will be the battle in Ardudwy,   15
spears attacking around Edryfwy,
and a bridge on the Taf and another on the Tawy,
and another frail one on the banks of the Wye.
And the carpenter who will make them will be named Garwy.
The royal one of Môn will rule them.   20
Women under the Gentiles [=*Danes*], men in torment
are happier than I who await it;
at the time of Cadwaladr he shall sing a song.

Yr Afallennau: The Apple Tree Stanzas

1

Sweet apple tree, sweet its branches,
bearing precious fruit, famed as mine.
And I will prophesy before the owner of Machrau:
in Machafwy Vale on a Wednesday of blood,
rejoicing to Lloegr, exceeding red blades.   5
Oia, little pig! Thursday will come,
rejoicing to the Welsh, exceeding great battles,
swift swords defending Cyminod,
slaughter of Saxons on ashen spears
and playing ball with their heads.   10
And I will prophesy the truth without a lie:
A youth shall arise in the region of the South.

2

Sweet apple tree, great green tree,
its branches bearing fruit—it and its fine trunk.
And I will prophesy tumultuous battle,   15
Pengwern drinking-horns, mead their reward.
{And around Cyminod hewing down Angles,
hateful host, by the ruler of Eryri.}

3

Sweet apple tree and yellow tree
that grows beyond the ploughland, without ploughland around it.   20
And I will prophesy battle in Pictland,
defending their borders with the men of Dublin.
Seven ships they will come across the broad water,
and seven hundred, across the sea to conquer.
Of those that come, they will not go from us,   25
except for seven half-empty after their sorrow.

4

Sweet apple tree that grows beyond Rhun;
I have contended at its base in order to please a maiden,
with my shield on my shoulder and my sword on my thigh,
and in Celyddon Wood I have slept by myself.   30
Oia, little pig! Why should you think of sleep?
Listen to the birds whose desire is heard.
Kings across the sea will come on a Monday.
Blessed the world of the Welsh as a result of the attack.

5

Sweet apple tree that grows in a clearing,   35
its virtue hides it from Rhydderch's lords,
a crowd around its base, a host around it.
It would be a treasure to them, brave ranks [of warriors].
Now Gwenddydd loves me not and she welcomes me not.
I am hateful to Gwasawg, Rhydderch's supporter.   40
I have destroyed her son and her daughter.
Death has taken everyone; why does it not greet me?
And after Gwenddolau, no lords revere me,
no amusement gladdens me, no lover visits me.
And in the battle of Arfderydd my torque was of gold,   45
though I may not be a treasure today to [a maiden with] a swan's form.

6

Sweet apple tree, tender blossoms,
that grows secretly in the forests.
Tales I heard at the beginning of day
that Gwasawg, supporter of wealth, has been angered   50
twice and thrice and four times in one day.
Alas, Jesus! that my death came not
before there came by my hand the death of Gwenddydd's son.

7

Sweet apple tree that grows on a river bank,
passing by it a steward will not succeed in getting its splendid fruit.   55
While I was calm in mind I used to be at its base
with a fair, playful maiden, a slender and queenly one.

Two score and ten years in constraints of outlawry
I have been wandering with wildness and wild ones.
After irreproachable goods and pleasing minstrels,   60
now there visit only want with wildness and wild ones.
Now I sleep not; I tremble for my leader,
my lord Gwenddolau, and my neighboring kinsmen.
After suffering sickness and sadness around Celyddon Wood,
may I become a blessed servant to the Lord of Hosts.   65

8

Sweet apple tree, tender blossoms,
that grows in the uneven land of the trees.
The wild-wanderer prophesies a tale that will come:
Spears will be thrown by [those with] the countenance of bravery;
before renowned leaders, there will be a lord   70
with a horse of destructive leap, a heathen man.
Before a resplendent youth on daring journeys,
Saxons uprooted, poets flourishing.

9

Sweet apple tree and red-blossomed tree
that grows in hiding in Celyddon Wood.   75
Although it be sought, that will be vain because of its special virtue,
until Cadwaladr comes to his meeting of warriors
on the banks of the Tywi and the river Teifi,
and a fearful host of palefaces [=*the Saxons*] comes,
and the wild ones, the long-haired ones, are subdued.   80

10

Sweet apple tree and red-blossomed tree
that grows in hiding in Celyddon Wood.
Although it be sought, that will be vain because of its special virtue,
until Cadwaladr comes to his meeting at Rheon Ford,
Cynan before him attacking the Saxons.   85
The Welsh will prevail; splendid will be their leader.
Everyone will gain their rights; glad the honor of the Britons.
Horns of joy will be sounded, a melody of peace and fair weather.

Yr Oianau: The Little Pig Stanzas

1

{Oian, little pig and happy piglet!
Do not dig your lair on the mountain tops.
Dig in a secret place in the forest,
before the hounds of Rhydderch the Generous, defender of the faith.

And I will prophesy and it will prove true:　　　　　5
As far as Aber Taradir before the oppressors of Britain,
with all the Welsh in battle array,
Llywelyn his name, of the line of Gwynedd,
is the man who will overcome.}

2

Oian, little pig! There was need to flee　　　　　10
before the houndsmen of the courts if it were ventured,
lest pursuit come upon us and we [be] sighted,
and if we escape, we will not complain of our fatigue.
And I will prophesy before the ninth wave,
before the sole greybeard ravaging Dyfed.　　　　　15
Monasteries will arise, not for the unfaithful,
in the region of highland and wild animals.
Until Cynan comes to it to watch over it,
there will never be a return to its home.

3

Oian, little pig! Not easy do I sleep,　　　　　20
because of the tumult of sadness that is upon me.
Two score and ten years I bore the pain;
it is a sorry appearance that I have.
May I get from Jesus the support
of the kings of the heavens, highest lineage.　　　　　25
Not fortunately born is one of the children of Adam
who will not believe in God on the Last Day.
{I saw Gwenddolau as a splendid lord
gathering spoils on every border.
Under the red earth now he is silent,　　　　　30
chief of rulers of the North, greatest in generosity.}

4

Oian, little pig! There was need to pray
for fear of five leaders from Normandy;
and the fifth went across the salt sea
to conquer Ireland of pleasing homesteads.　　　　　35
He made war and uproar
and red arms and woe there.
And they without doubt shall come from there
and shall pay homage to the grave of Dewi.
And I will prophesy that there will be uproar　　　　　40
from the fighting of father and son, the land will know it,
and an incursion upon the ravaged homesteads of the men of England,
but may there never be deliverance to Normandy.

5

Oian, little pig! Be not sleepy.
There will come to us sad news: 45
Puny, perjuring leaders,
petty, hard stewards concerning a penny.
When there shall come across the sea ignoble men,
war-horses under them, two-faced,
two points on their unavoidable spears—   50
ploughing without reaping in a troubled world,
better a grave than life for all the needy.
Horns on the four-cornered women.
And when some lively sons are corpses,
there will be a morning of strife before Caersallog.   55

6

Oian, little pig and wretched piglet!
A pale wild wanderer tells me strange news,
and I prophesy a summer of conflict:
Amongst kinsmen, treachery from Gwynedd,
when peace will long be driven from the land of Gwynedd.   60
Seven hundred ships of pagans will come with the north wind,
and they will gather in Aber Deu Gleddyf.

7

Oian, little pig and blessed piglet!
A pale wild wanderer told me news that terrifies me:
When England encamps in Hiraethlyn   65
and makes Degannwy a steadfast fortress,
from the clash of England and Llywelyn,
there will be a youth in pursuit and a retreat from homes
when [Saint] Deinioel, son of Dunawd Deinwyn, is angered.
The Frank [=*Norman*] will be in flight; he will not ask the way! 70
In Aber Dulas a support will be destroyed;
slaughter around them, surrounding them.

8

Oian, little pig! Hoian! Hoiau!
If there were needy ones, God would make changes.
The pig which is alive will be mine;   75
let him seek that one which is dead.

9

Oian, little pig! It is bright day.
Hear the voice of the water birds, sad voices.
Years and long days will be ours,
and unjust lords, fruits withering,   80

and bishops will support thieves, vile churches,
and monks will deserve a load of sins.

10

Oian, little pig, sharp its nails,
A coarse companion when you go to rest.
Little knows Rhydderch Hael tonight at his feast   85
what I endured last night of sleeplessness:
snow up to my knees; overgrowth like a pack of hounds;
icicles in my beard; my course exhausted.
A Tuesday will come, a day of fury
between the warriors of Powys and the folk of Gwynedd,   90
and Hirell will arise from his long rest
to contend with his enemies for the boundaries of Gwynedd.
And if there be no share of mercy for me from my lord,
woe to me that it once was mine, sad my ending.

11

Oian, little pig! It will be no secret   95
when a battle-host sets out from Caerfyrddin,
two whelps leading them skillfully,
of the line of Rhys, giver of battle-momentum to an army;
when the Saxons are cut down in the battle of Cymerau,
blessed [will be] the world of the Welsh, a hardy folk.   100

12

Oian, little pig and white sow!
Do not sleep a morning sleep nor dig in the brush,
lest Rhydderch Hael come with his crafty hounds.
Before you reach the wood, your sweat will run.

13

Oian, little pig and white piglet!   105
If you had seen what I saw of grim violence,
you would not sleep a morning sleep; you would not dig in a hill;
you would not rush to the wasteland from a desolate lake.
When Saxons sit in Serpent Hill
and attack Castle Gollwyn from afar,   110
there will be splendid clothes and a brilliant number.

14

Oian, little pig! Listen in the hour
when the men of Gwynedd give their great battle.
Blades in hand, horns will be sounded.
Mail-coats will be pierced by sharp spears.   115
When the Normans come on the broad sea,

there will be clashing then by armies
and Britain conquered by the descendents of Yswain
and the destruction from London would be released.
And I will prophesy two rulers   120
who will create peace from heaven to earth.
Cynan, Cadwaladr—all of Wales
will be their meeting place which will be praised,
and bringing the land under rule of law and punishing denial
and a [false] oath and theft will be destroyed,   125
and deliverance will there be for us after trouble.
None of generosity will be cut away.

15
Oian, little pig! Green mountain.
Thin is my mantle; to me it is not sufficient.
Grey is my beard. Gwenddydd visits me not.   130
When the men of Bernicia come to the disgrace of a host,
the Welsh will prevail. Fair will be their day!

16
Oian, little pig and lively piglet!
Do not dig your lair nor eat more and more,
nor desire a field, nor love entertaining.   135
And counsel I will give to Gwenabwy:
Let there not be youthful, loving, courtly entertaining.
And I will prophesy the battle of Machafwy.
There will be red biers on Didmwy Hill
from the contention of the swaggering saddle warriors.   140
There will be a morning of woe and the arrival of woe.
A bear from Deheubarth will arise;
his justice will spread beyond the land of Mynwy.
Blessed it will be—Gwenddydd will await it—
when it comes to pass that the Prince of Dyfed will rule.   145

17
Oian, little pig! There are thorn blossoms,
deep-green is the mountain ridge, the land is fair.
And I will prophesy the battle of Coed Llwyfain
and red biers before the rush of Owein.
When the stewards make their feeble complaints,   150
perjury and treachery of the youths of the country.
And when Cadwaladr comes to conquer Môn,
the Saxons will be eliminated from the lands of Britain.

18
Oian, little pig! A great wonder
there will be in Britain, but it will not interest me.   155

When the countrymen come from the regions of Môn
to claim the Britons, there will be an uproar.
A leader of [good] fortune, with spears of glory will arise,
with brave, total ferocity from the banks of the Teifi.
He will make an uproar around Dyfed;   160
he will have a wealth of stags there.

19

Oian, little pig! So wonderful
that there will never be a single moment in the world in like manner:
so far the sound of Saxons and the spoils of battle
from the nobles of the Britons, grief's descendants.   165
And I will prophesy before sadness,
Britons instead of Saxons will rule the Picts.
And then there will come to us a gift of joy
after being long in humility.

20

Oian, little pig! Listen to the stags   170
and the singing of birds near Caer Rheon.
I had wished to seek a mountain of people
to look for the stormy countenance of lovers.
And I will prophesy a battle on the Iddon,
and the battle of Machafwy, and the battle of Afon,   175
and the battle of Cors Mochno, and a battle in Môn,
and the battle of Cyminod, and the battle of Caerlleon,
and the battle of Aber Gwaith, and the battle of Ieithion.
And when Dyfed may be a border land for stags,
a youth will arise; fortunate for the Britons.   180

21

Hoian, little pig! A troubled world there will be;
so sad its coming, but it will come:
Bare maidens, women wanton.
Kinsfolk will not respect their kinship,
ready or unready [i.e. unconstant] towards each other.   185
Alien, destructive, faithless bishops.

22

Hoian, little pig [with] small spots!
Listen to the voice of the sea birds, great their vigor,
musicians out-of-doors without a share of rights.
Though they stand in the door, a jewel will not come.   190
A wild man from afar told me:
Kings of extraordinary alliance[s],
Irish and Britons and Romans,

will make war and confusion,
and on the day corresponding to Thursday will come to you   195
and will fight fiercely about the banks of the Tywi.

23
Hoian, little pig [with] small thick legs!
Listen to the voice of the sea birds, great their tumult,
musicians out-of-doors without a share of honor.
Odious guests and authority belonging to a servant,   200
without keeping face, without a share of honor.
When there will be two brothers, two Iddases for land,
long carnage will be the outcome of their justice.

24
Hoian, little pig! No purpose comes to me
from hearing the voice of the water birds—loud their tumult.   205
Thin is the hair of my head; my mantle is not cozy.
The vales are my barn, my corn is not great,
summer is my store and it does not benefit me.
Before separating from God, of incomparable nature,
and I will prophesy: Before the end of the world,   210
women without modesty, men without manliness.

25
Hoian, little pig and piglet of a sow in heat!
Thin is my mantle; it is not sufficient for me.
Because of the battle of Arfderydd, it would not interest me
though the sky would fall to the ground and the sea flood.   215
And I will prophesy: After Henry,
a king who is no king, there will come tribulation.
When there is a bridge on the Taf and another on the Tywi,
war will come to Dyfed to you.

The Prophecy of Myrddin and Gwenddydd, His Sister

A poem found in the late-fourteenth-century manuscript known as the
Red Book of Hergest and in an early-fourteenth-century fragmentary text may
also be classed with the early poems of the Myrddin tradition. It has been
plausibly argued that the core of this poem was composed before 1100. "The
Prophecy of Myrddin and Gwenddydd, His Sister" is a long series of short
stanzas in the form of a dialogue between Myrddin and Gwenddydd.
Gwenddydd asks Myrddin to prophesy future Welsh rulers, and up through

stanza 57 we have, essentially, a list of historical rulers of Gwynedd. After that comes a series of uncertain stanzas, one of which (61) may refer to Llywelyn (or Llewelyn) ab Iorwerth in the phrase *brenhin llew* 'a kingly lion, a lion of a king.' After some references to the sons of King Henry and other unnamed English oppressors comes a series of more vague prophecies of the return of Cadwaladr and others, as well as references that cannot be identified. One interesting show of formal learning occurs in stanza 66 with its reference to Dionysus Cato, a Roman writer of the third and fourth centuries whose collection of moral apothegms, *Disticha Catonis*, was a popular text throughout the Middle Ages. The poem ends with prophecies of a final flood, the deaths of Gwenddydd and Myrddin themselves, a lament for lost heroes of old, and an exchange in which Myrddin and Gwenddydd commend each other to God. The full effect of this long poem is one of despair and of loss of faith and trust in this world.

Perhaps the most archaic element in this poem, or even in the entire Myrddin tradition, is the repeated word *llallawc* (once *llallogan*). This word occurs independently elsewhere in early Welsh poetry apparently meaning "friend," or perhaps (as a form of address) "lord." The word, however, is cognate with the name Lailoken/Lailochen/Laloecen/Laloicen, to give it the Latin forms found in the *Life of St. Kentigern*. Basil Clarke, in his edition of Geoffrey's *Vita Merlini*, suggests that the "Myrddin-original" was a real person named or called Llallawg or Llallogan who lost his reason at the Battle of Arfderydd. Given this possibility, and the difficulty of otherwise translating it with any confidence, Llallogan and Llallawg are retained in the translation given here—on the understanding that it may be either a generic noun ("lord, friend, dear friend") or an original name that became an attributive when the name Myrddin was attached to the legend. There are also in this poem some detailed correspondences with "The Little Pig Stanzas," especially in stanzas 59 and 69 ("Little Pig" 23, 25). These cross-references suggest a close coherence to the prophetic Myrddin tradition in the early thirteenth century.

Like all of the poems in this chapter, but even more so, the translations of this and the following poem are very tentative and in places altogether intractable. Ellipses (. . .) are shown where the translator fears to tread.

The Prophecy of Myrddin and Gwenddydd, His Sister

1

I came to you to relate [lore];
the judgment of the North is mine.
The wisdom of each people has been declared to me.

2

For the battle of Arfderydd and Ridding,
Gwenddydd, and all that will come upon me,
provider of a feast, where will I go?

3

I ask my Llallogan Myrddin,
a wise man, a prophet,
since he avoids me,
what lord will there be for us according to him?

4

In a song of Cadafel will be trust.
It is Wales. There will be resurgence.
Bounteous is the banner of Rhydderch the Generous.

5

Since Rhydderch possesses glory
and all Wales under him,
after him, who will come?

6

Rhydderch the Generous, slayer of the foe,
a heavy blow his attacking them;
a day of delight at Tawy Ford.

7

Rhydderch the Generous, an enemy for a while [?],
a refuge of the bards of a famed region;
where will he go if he goes to the ford?

8

I will tell Gwenddydd,
since she greets me skillfully,
that there will be no Rhydderch the Generous the day after tomorrow.

9

I ask my famed Llallawg,
eminent in an army:
Who will be after Rhydderch?

10

Because of Gwenddolau's death in the bloodshed of Arfderydd
I have become wild:
Morgant the Great, son of Sadyrnin.

11

I ask my famed Llallawg,
renowned in song as far as [?] the sea:
Who will rule after Morgant?

12

Because of Gwenddolau's death in the bloodshed of Arfderydd
do you wonder why there troubles me
a leader of the people of the land of Urien.

13

Your hair is the color of winter frost;
may God redeem your need.
Who will rule after Urien?

14

The Lord brought sorrow upon me;
I am sick at the last.
Maelgwn the Tall over the land of Gwynedd.

15

Long-lived may you be, my brother, my dear one.
Wretched is my vigor which gives me a [sorry] countenance.
After Maelgwn who will rule?

16

Rhun his name, swift his blow;
in the van of an army he will battle;
woe to Britain because of the day.

17

Since you are a friend and a paragon of slaughter,
you will be called a leader.
Where will Gwynedd go after Rhun?

18

Rhun his name, noble in war,
and I will prophesy it will happen:
fair girl, the land [will be] in Beli's hand.

19

I ask my famed Llallawg,
eminent in conflict:
Who will rule after Beli?

20

Since my sense has gone with the wild ones of the mountain,
and myself sad:
After Beli, his son Iago.

21

Since your sense has gone with the wild ones of the mountain,
and yourself sad:
Who will rule after Iago?

22

And my response to my dear one:
His feasts are without spirit;
after Iago, his son Cadfan.

23

The songs they sang
of the coming of fame to the four corners [of the world]:
Who will rule after Cadfan?

24

The land of Cadwallon, of great bravery,
in the four-cornered world it will be heard,
the head of the Angles will tumble down,
and throughout the world it will be praised.

25

From seeing your cheek so bloody
overmuch comes to my mind:
Who will rule after Cadwallon?

26

A tall man keeping an encounter,
and Britain as a single spear-shaft:
Best son of a Welshman, Cadwaladr.

27

He responds to me gently,
his powers are feeble:
Who will rule after Cadwaladr?
Idwal.

28

I ask you gently,
famed best of men of the earth:
Who will rule after Idwal?

29
After Idwal, will rule,
in the manner of invincible Dyfnfyn,
the white-shielded Hywel ap Cadwal.

30
I ask my famed Llallawg,
eminent in war:
Who will rule after Hywel?

31
I will tell his noble fame,
Gwenddydd, before leaving you:
After Hywel, Rhodri.

32
Cynan in Môn [=*Anglesey*] will be;
may he not guard his rights.
And before the son of Rhodri is called,
there will be the son of a foundling.

33
I ask from the world's retreat;
tell me calmly:
Who will rule after Cynan?

34
Because of Gwenddolau's death in the bloodshed of Arfderydd
terror working:
Merfyn the Freckled from the land of Manaw.

35
I ask my famed noble brother,
the light of song, best of men:
Who will rule after Merfyn?

36
I say there will be no delay;
the prophetic history of Britain will be pondered:
After Merfyn, Rhodri the Great.

37
I ask my famed Llallawg,
eminent in the day of conflict:
Who will rule after the son of Rhodri the Great?

38

On Conwy shore, affliction on a Wednesday
his tongue will be honored,
Anarawd of excellent nature.

39

I ask my famed Llallawg,
eminent in the day of praise:
Who will rule after Anarawd?

40

Next is where time is nearer
the messengers of our seal,
the leadership in Hywel's hand.

41

Those outlandish people who did not urinate
will be no nearer to Paradise.
A secular order is no worse than a church order.

42

I ask my . . . brother
whom I saw in fine fame:
Who will rule after those outlandish people?

43

For a year and a half nobles will be the subject of conspiracy;
their lives will be shortened;
defamed each carefree one.

44

Since you are a friend and a paragon of slaughter,
God's mercy upon your soul.
Who will rule after the nobles?

45

A lonely one will arise from hiding
who will not overprotect his honor;
Cynan of the hounds [=*warriors*] will possess Wales.

46

I ask from the world's retreat;
tell me calmly:
Who will rule after Cynan?

47

Men from afar, from overseas,
shall take strong fortresses;
they will declare[?] a nobleman king.

48

I ask from the world's retreat;
since you know its meaning:
Who will rule after a nobleman?

49

I will prophesy Serwen the Fair,
a white-shielded, steady messenger,
brave, strong, prison-encircling.
He will visit the region of treacherous chieftains.
He will repel yonder before him as far as Scotland.

50

I ask my brother, the fair [one],
since it is I who asks it:
Who will rule after Serwen the Fair?

51

Two white-shielded Belis will come,
fostered by him, who will cause confusion.
Do not expect peace; it will not be for you.

52

I ask my famed Llallawg,
eminent in conflict:
Who will rule after the two white-shielded Belis?

53

A sole fierce one, the generous one of defense,
sage, a defense in battle,
will rule the van of the uproar.

54

I ask my famed Llallawg,
eminent before an army:
Who is the sole fierce one
whom you prophesy there?
What is his name? From where will he come?

55

Gruffudd is his name, powerful, noble—
usual is a wound on the cheek of warriors—
who will rule over the land of Britain.

56

I ask my famed Llallawg,
eminent in battles:
After Gruffudd, whose?

57

I say there will be no delay;
the prophetic history of Britain will be pondered:
After Gruffudd, Gwyn the Proud [=*Owain Gwynedd?*].

58

I ask my famed Llallawg,
eminent in war:
Who will rule after Gwyn the Proud?

59

Oia, fair Gwenddydd of high lineage,
a pale wild wanderer will prophesy hateful tales.
A lineage will be over a land
that will not sustain a feast nor rightful recompense.
There will be two brothers, two Iddases for land;
as a result of their justice a long-standing blood-feud will be marveled at.

60

I ask my famed Llallawg,
eminent in battles:
Who will rule after them?

61

I will prophesy: not a servant of boars—
a lion of a king with an uprooting hand,
beak-like tongs, with the grasp of a wolf.

62

I ask my ample brother,
whom I saw nourished on mead:
After that who will be chief?

63

Count the number of the stars;
similar [the number of] his retinue.
A youth of two halves is he.

64

I ask my lordless brother,
an army's key, a lord's profit:
Who will rule after two halves?

65

A mixture of Irish in an army
and Welsh, and skilled in battle:
the lord of eight chief fortresses will he be.

66

I ask my cheerful brother,
who has read the book of Cato:
Who will rule after him?

67

I will tell it, from Rheged,
since she asks me in honor:
the whelp of Henry the arrogant king;
never in his life will there be deliverance.

68

I ask the famed, noble brother,
eminent in Wales:
Who will rule after the son of Henry?

69

When there is a bridge on the Taf and another on the Dyfi,
complete confusion will come upon England.
And I will prophesy: after the son of Henry,
a king who is no king, there will be tribulation.

70

I ask my brother, the fair one,
since it is I who ask it:
Who will rule after the king who is no king?

71

A somewhat foolish king will come
and the men of England will deceive him;
there will be no prosperity of the country under him.

72

Fair Myrddin, famous for genius of poetry,
angry, warlike in the army:
What will there be in the time of the foolish?

73

When England is moaning
and Wales froward,
there will be the wandering army.

74
Fair Myrddin of gifted speech,
do not tell me a lie:
What will be after an army?

75
One of the six will arise
who had been long concealed;
upon England there will be great stress.

76
Fair Myrddin of a lineage of renowned genius,
the wind turns inside a house:
Who will rule after that?

77
Decreed is the coming of Owain,
who will conquer as far as London
and give the Welsh the object of their desire.

78
Fair Myrddin, chiefest of fame for genius,
since I believe your word:
Owain, how long will he last?

79
Gwenddydd, listen to a sad tale:
the wind will be turned to the valley
for five years and two, as before.

80
I ask my ample brother,
whom I saw nourished on mead:
After that who will be chief?

81
When Owein is in Manaw
and battle in Pictland near at hand:
He will be a man, and men with him.

82
I ask my ample brother,
whom I saw nourished on mead:
After that who will be chief?

83

A chieftain of good upbringing who will conquer the land,
a country's delight through joy.

84

I ask my ample brother,
whom I saw nourished on mead:
After that who will be chief?

85

An outcry will go through the valley;
Beli the Tall and his proud men.
Blessed the world of the Welsh and woe to the heathens [=*Danes*].

86

I ask my famed Llallawg,
eminent in battles:
After Beli, whose?

87

An outcry will go through the river-mouth;
Beli the Tall and his numerous men.
Blessed the world of the Welsh; woe to the Irish.

88

I ask my famed Llallawg,
eminent in war:
Why comes woe to the Irish?

89

I will prophesy to the Christian world[?]:
Gwynedd, after your tribulation,
you will conquer every people.

90

The hounds of Morfryn, so united[?] were they,
Myrddin [Merfyn?] the Freckled, a powerful throng.
What will come to us, the two vows[?].

91

When Cadwaladr disembarks
and a broad host with him for Wednesday's jesting
to defend the men of Gwynedd,
wrong will come to the men of Chester.

92

Do not part unworthily with me
from shame of the encounter.
Where will Cadwaladr disembark?

93

When Cadwaladr disembarks in Tywi Vale
the river-mouths will be full of oppression.
The Britons will scatter the oppressors.

94

I ask my ample brother,
whom I saw nourished on mead:
Who will rule after that?

95

When there will be a churl of three languages in Môn,
and his flagon-bellied son,
it will be heard that Gwynedd is wealthy.

96

Who will scatter the English to the sea's edge?
Who is the fair one in flight?
Or the Welsh—who will be their deliverance?

97

A dispersal of heroes and the tumult of Rhydderch,
and the hosts of Cadwaladr
on the river Tarddennin;
they will break the key of the men [of Caerlleon?].

98

Do not part unworthily with me
from shame of the encounter:
What death will take Cadwaladr?

99

A bronze spear from a ship's planks will pierce him,
and the hand of an unbaptized man;
Shame will come to Wales from the day.

100

Do not part unworthily with me
from shame of the encounter:
How long will Cadwaladr rule?

101

Three months, three years of rights[?]
and three hundred full years;
battles, encounters will rule.

102

Do not part unworthily with me
from shame of the encounter:
Who will rule after Cadwaladr?

103

To Gwenddydd I will speak;
age upon age I will prophesy:
After Cadwaladr, Cyndaf.

104

I ask my ample [brother. . .].

105

One hand on a sword, the other on a cross,
let everyone take care for his life.
With Cyndaf there is no peace-making.

106

I will prophesy [?] to the Christian world:
Gwynedd, after your tribulation
you will conquer every people.

107

. . . and the people of the children of Adam
who spring from their praise
will have deliverance as far as Judgment Day.

108

From the time the Welsh go without aid in battle,
without maintaining their honor,
. . . like the cauldron of impediment[?].

109

I ask my ample [brother. . .]
. . . then who will be leader?

110

Noble wealthy Gwenddydd,
first, fairest in Britain,
over the merrymaking of the wretched Welsh.

111
When a deluge comes from Him to whom highest obligation [is due],
from the sea as far as the land,
doomed maiden, the end of the world.

112
After a deluge from Him to whom highest obligation [is due],
who will be the restorer,
and will there be a church and the share of a mass-priest?

113
No share of either mass-priest or poet
will there be, nor visiting the altar
until heaven falls to the ground.

114
Llallawg, since you answer me,
Myrddin ap Morfryn, a man of skill,
a sad tale you tell me.

115
I will tell it to Gwenddydd
since earnestly you ask me:
a deluge there will be, doomed maiden.

116
I will ask my ample [brother. . .].

117
What I have told thus far
to Gwenddydd, defender of chieftains,
shall come to pass every whit.

118
Llallawg, since it will befall me,
for the sake of the soul of your brothers:
What leader will be there?

119
Fair Gwenddydd, foremost of courtesy,
I will tell it earnestly:
There will be no leader ever after.

120
Alas, dear one, for the sad separating;
after you have been in battle,
brave, unconquerable battle-leader,
you, too, will be covered under the earth.

121

The airy wind will disperse the air,
[for] wisdom a foolish deceit is believed,
Gwenddydd, fortune until Judgment Day is sure.

122

Because of your death, mead-fostered [one],
I am destitute;
there is sorrow for [the news of] your death when it is brought,
[You of] excellent praise, who utters the truth?

123

From a secluded place rise up and declare
books of inspiration without fear,
and a tale of a maiden and a dream in sleep.

124

Morgenau dead, powerful Morial dead,
Morien dead, the rampart of battle;
heaviest the sorrow for [the news of] your death, Myrddin.

125

The Lord has brought my end upon me.
Morgenau dead; Mordaf dead;
Morien dead; dead those I love.

126

My one brother, do not rebuke me;
I am sick because of the battle of Arfderydd.
I seek guidance.
I commend you to God.

127

And I commend you
to the Lord of all creatures,
Fair Gwenddydd, refuge of songs.

128

The songs have remained
since praise has come to the four corners [of the earth].
Alas, God! How transitory they are.

129

Gwenddydd, be not sorrowful.
the burden has been put to the earth,
rejecting everyone who loves.

130
Alive I will not reject you,
and until Judgment Day I will remember you;
your blow, the heaviest tribulation.

131
Lively is the steed, easy the path,
bare the darkness, joyless the road.
I go after those that have gone.

132
I commend my brother in faith
to the Lord who made him.
Take communion before death.

133
I will not take communion from cursed monks
with their pouches on their thighs;
God himself will communicate me.

134
I commend my brother in faith
into the fortress on high.
May God care, Myrddin.

135
I commend my sister in faith
into the fortress on high.
May God care, Gwenddydd.
Amen.

The Separation-Song of Myrddin in the Grave

This poem, found in the *White Book of Rhydderch* with the rubric "Gwasg[a]rdgerd Verdin" and the *Red Book of Hergest* as "Gwasgardgerd Vyrdin yn y bed," seems to be largely a commentary on the moral state of the world in the face of English domination, with a relatively less predominant political element than in the foregoing poems. Like much Welsh prophetic verse, though, this poem does end on a positive note, prophesying that the Welsh will overcome.

Gwasgar(d)gerd, from *gwasgar* 'dispersal, separation, perplexity' plus *cerdd* 'song, poem,' is a word of uncertain meaning, though it might possibly refer to the fact that the speaker is in his grave. To render it literally as "separation-song" is simply to sidestep the problem with a translation of little meaning, and we should recognize that it may have had a specific or technical sense now lost to us. The first stanza and the longer title in the *Red Book*, adding the words "in the grave," seem to testify to the independent existence of a Welsh tradition in which Myrddin prophesies from the grave. The names of Gwenddydd and the shadowy Gwasawg, both from the earlier Myrddin tradition, appear in the last stanza (if, indeed, the poem is complete as we have it).

The Separation-Song of Myrddin in the Grave

1
A man speaks in the grave
what will happen before seven years;
March dead, chief lord of the North.

2
I drank wine from fair glass
with grim lords of war;
Myrddin is my name, son of Morfryn.

3
I drank wine from a bowl
with illustrious lords of war;
Myrddin is my name, unremitting.

4
When a man comes resisting on a black charger
to strike the men of England of destructive course,
there will be bitter rage in contending for
the White Mount, a blessed mount that suffers need,
the long want of the people of Wales.

5
There will be no safe ground in the cells of Ardudwy
        on the border of Wales
against the excellent boar of a bold host.

6
When the red one of Normandy comes
to challenge the English, vast expense,
a tax on every prophecy shall. . .[?]
a castle in Aber Hodni.

7

When the strong freckled one comes
        as far as Pengarn Ford,
men shall reproach, a hoof shall wear out,
the ruler of Britain then will be chief of judgment.

8

When Henry comes to challenge Mur Castell,
        to the border of Eryri [=*Snowdonia*],
oppression will call out over the sea.

9

When the Weak White one comes to challenge London
        on not-handsome horses,
he will name Canterbury a kingdom.

10

Thin their [acorn-]mast; thick their corn;
when he comes suddenly,
a youthful king, trouble makes him tremble.

11

A boy there will be, great his dignity,
who will conquer a thousand strongholds;
a child of life, a youthful king.

12

Strong towards the weak of a country in misery;
Weak towards the strong, the conqueror,
a leader [springs up], worse it is for his coming.

13

A world there will be intent on great heat;
women will have a long-lived herd of cattle;
a host of boys will make their confession.

14

A world there will be intent on its warmth;
may a churl do it good;
a girl will be proud, a youth rebellious.

15

A world there will be in which the [love-]tryst will end;
the young will fail in the face of misery;
in May cuckoos will die of cold.

16

A world there will be intent on the [hunting] pack;
the wilderness will be built upon;
not a shirt will be obtained without great price.

17

A world there will be intent on oaths,
evil life, and fault in churches;
word will be broken and relics,
truth reviled, falsehood spread;
faith weak; contention every other day.

18

A world there will be intent on clothing,
a lord will be a contender, a steward will be a vagabond,
the poet empty-handed, the priest handsome,
men reviled, denial spread.

19

There will be a world without wind, without rain,
without too much to plough, without overuse;
enough land will be one acre for nine.

20

When the men come without manliness,
and instead of the woods, getting corn,
in every hall a feast will arise.

21

When the pomp of trees is a forearm in length,
    there will be spring
    after a vicious ruler.
A cattle-stake will be worse than a shed.

22

On Wednesday, a day of fulfillment,
when spears will be worn out on a head,
Two will hide in a stockade of battle.

23

In Aber Sor men will take counsel
    after battle is spent;
a fair leader, a chieftain on the rampart.

24

In Aber Afon the host of Môn will be

English after [periods of] fair weather;
a long grave for those of great bravery.

25

In Aber Dwfr the duke will not hold it;
there will be [those] who may wreak cruelty;
and after battle, bitterness.

26

Battle there will be on the River Byrri
    and the Britons will overcome.
The men of Gower will perform [deeds of] valor.

27

In Aber Idon will be brought about battle,
    and disorderly spears,
and red blood on the cheeks of Saxons.

28

Gwasawg, your cry to Gwenddydd
was told to me by wild men of the mountain
    in Aber Craf.

Commanding Youth

The poem now called *Peiryan Vaban* (Commanding Youth) occurs in a single early-fifteenth-century manuscript between versions of "The Little Pig Stanzas" and "The Separation-Song of Myrddin." The poem itself is difficult to date, and it is somewhat of an anomaly in the Myrddin corpus. In general, it is even more of a moral or gnomic poem than the other Myrddin poems are, though there is a prophetic element in it as well. The poem contains references to Myrddin, Gwenddydd, Gwenddolau, Rhydderch, and even Gwasawg. It adds little to our knowledge of that legend, but it does seem to portray Myrddin as more of a warrior than elsewhere. Also reflected in this poem are traditions about Aeddan ap Gafran, or Aedán mac Gabráin, the sixth-century ruler of the Irish kingdom of Dalriada in western Scotland. Aedán led an army against Æthelfrith, the Anglo-Saxon king of Bernicia, and was routed in the Battle of Degsastan in 603. There must have been strong connections between Aedán and the British, for among other things he named one of his sons Arthur, when that British hero's fame was still fresh.

Commanding Youth

Commanding youth, cease your complaining.
May God protect you from the Irish heathens,
and on the way to Irish Hill [=*Galloway?*], the Devil's Encounter;
and the Franks and the Irish will scarcely part.
Aeddan will come from crossing the broad sea,   5
and a host from the Isle of Man will rise up with him,
and the islands on the way to Irish Hill.
The Devil's Encounter, as swift as a spear.

Commanding youth, cease your groaning.
Aeddan will come from crossing the broad sea,   10
and there will be neither youth nor tumult nor thunder.
Many a sally, many a warrior, many an owner of arms are Aeddan's,
many a long-headed spear, many a long spear-shaft,
seizing land. May Gafran prosper.
Many a breastplate, many a helm on head, cattle as to his intent,   15
many a red sword, many a surly lad, a fortress of bloody conflict,
many a lively steed, many a light, broad, shining shield.
And he says to Gwenddydd, when the light of day comes, there
     shall be prophecy.
And he says to Gwasawg he does not respect . . . nor sanctuary
     nor church.

Commanding youth, cease your weeping.   20
From troubled air it is usual to hear rain.
Aeddan will come with a host across the region.
And Gwenddydd knows not what his hands will do,
brothers in battle like the ardent ones,
because they will not suffer oppression, neither here nor there.   25
Except one who had been left in his affliction,
alas, a rarity[?] is wisdom from him.
Myrddin son of Morfryn was a white hawk
when the fierce battle would be fought,
when there would be joyous death, when there would be a
     broken shoulder,   30
when there would be heart's blood before he would be put to flight.
Because of the memory of Gwenddolau and his companions[?],
woe to me for my death—how slowly it comes.

Commanding youth, take your counsel.
It is usual for generous fortunate ones to deserve more.   35
From the encounter of Rhydderch the Generous, the indispensable one,
and if not a fortunate one, there will be no deliverance.
And I have prophesied between deep water and shallow,

since early his violence, lying at their anchor [?].
There was a time once when I sat in a court;   40
my covering was red and purple.
And today neither my cheek nor my body is fair;
for a comely maiden [it is] easy to spare me.
I call upon Christ; my cry will be heard.
May the gates of heaven be open for me.   45

Commanding youth, dry[?] your tears.
Weeping is not pleasant; it is not best.
Myrddin will come, great the intent,
because of the death of my brothers and Gwenddolau,
Llewelyn, Gwgon, best of the generous ones;   50
Einion, Rhiwallon, lord of all battles.
From the encounter of Rhydderch and renowned Aeddan
so clearly it is heard from the north to the south.
And he says to Gwenddydd, when it is daylight,
the woods will be filled with men and arms.   55

Commanding youth, seek your sleep.
Usual are pleasurable songs to supplicate for sleep.
Usual will be generous ones to suppliants; usual is it for lovers to
            love one another.
Usual is innate hatred between a man and one of equal strength,
but not usual is it for one of the same origin to be without affection.   60
Usual is it for an angry knight to be prince of a host,
and ravens on bodies, and a spear black.
Not usually does the wicked respect either cheek or eye
or brain-pan, though he be attacked.
After a long rest and resurrection from the grave,   65
let him who may be in the end with Jesus. Amen.
            —[Myr]ddin sang it.

The Names of the Island of Britain

One prose text in the *White Book of Rhydderch* deserves notice, for it gives
striking prominence to the name of Myrddin in a context that is clearly
independent of Geoffrey's account of early British history and it is based on
traditions that are earlier than the twelfth century:

These Are the Names of the Island of Britain

1.   The first name that was upon this island before it was seized or settled: Myrddin's Cloister. And after it was seized and settled: The Honey Island. And after it was conquered by Prydain son of Aedd the Great the name "The Island of Britain" was given to it.
2.   It has three chief adjacent islands and twenty-seven adjacent islands that are subordinate to it. The three chief adjacent islands are Môn [=*Anglesey*], Man, and the Isle of Wight. And three chief estuaries and seven score subordinate to it. And thirty-four chief ports, and thirty-three chief fortresses, and thirty-four chief wonders.
3.   This is the length of this island: from Penrhyn Blathaon in Scotland as far as Penrhyn Penwaedd [=*Penwith*] in Cornwall—that is nine hundred miles. This is its breadth: from Crigyll in Môn as far as Sarre—that is five hundred miles.
4.   There ought to be held in it a Crown and three Coronets. And in London should the Crown be worn, and in Penrhyn Rhionydd in the North one of the Coronets, and in Aberffraw the second, and in Cornwall the third.
5.   And there are three archbishoprics in it: one in Mynyw [*St. David's*], and the second in Kent [*Canterbury*], and the third in York.

The word *clas*, translated here as "cloister," is somewhat obscure in this context. It has a range of meanings including "monastic community," "a community or band of fellow-countrymen," and "enclosure, close, castle."

The claim of St. David's to archepiscopal status so hotly debated in the twelfth century was based on traditions of the primacy of that see that go back as far as the tenth century. Thus even section five does not preclude a date earlier than the twelfth century for this tract of onomastic and geographic lore. Less archaic elements have been added to this text in a later manuscript, including the statement, "And no one has a right to this island except the kindred of the Welsh themselves, the remains of the Britons who came long ago from Troy."

The Myrddin Triad

Though the legend of the mad or wild prophet in the trees is ancient in Welsh tradition, and though there are a number of triads (mnemonic triple groupings of lore) preserving the memory of the Battle of Arfderydd, Myrddin himself does not appear in the early redactions of the Triads of the Island of Britain. The only triad that names him is a later one that clearly shows the influence of Geoffrey of Monmouth's works and subsequent narrative developments, both in the Arthurian setting and in the bifurcation of the Merlinus/Myrddin character:

Three Skilled Bards were in Arthur's Court:
  Myrddin son of Morfryn,
  Myrddin Emrys [=*Ambrosius*],
  and Taliesin.

II.

MERLIN IN
GEOFFREY OF MONMOUTH

chapter 3

HISTORY OF THE KINGS OF BRITAIN

Aubrey Galyon and Zacharias P. Thundy

G E O F F R E Y O F Monmouth (d. 1154), writing in Latin, completed his *History of the Kings of Britain* around 1136. This work is one of the earliest accounts of Arthur and Merlin. His Arthur is, of course, a British (Celtic) leader who battles and defeats the Anglo-Saxon invaders that would ultimately overcome the British and establish themselves as the dominant nation in England. Geoffrey's Merlin (Myrddin in Welsh) probably owes certain features to the Welsh traditions found in the writings of Nennius, a monk of Bangor, Wales. The "fatherless boy," for example, whose blood Vortigern's magicians say must be mixed with the mortar to prevent Vortigern's edifice from collapsing, is also found in Nennius. However, Geoffrey's account of the building of Stonehenge, in which Merlin transports to the Salisbury Plain stones that giants had brought to Ireland from Africa, is not found in any other known sources.

The *Prophecies of Merlin* stem from a Welsh tradition that Merlin/Myrddin foresaw the defeat of the Saxons and the return of Celtic rule in Britain. The *Prophecies* were composed as a separate book a few years before the *History* was written and then included in that work by Geoffrey. The *Prophecies* are suitably opaque and cryptic; the Boar of Cornwall, however, can be identified as Arthur, and some after-the-fact references to historical events in Geoffrey's time may be discerned.

In his dedication of the *History* to Robert, Earl of Gloucester, Geoffrey says that Walter, the Archdeacon of Oxford, gave him an old book in "the British tongue" to translate into Latin; hence his *History*. Most scholars today believe that the old British book is a fiction of Geoffrey's, since no one such book could have contained all that is in the *History*. However, it is probable that many stories and episodes found in Geoffrey's *History* already existed in oral traditions handed down from generation to generation among the British. Some, if not all, of these traditions were also written down before the time of Geoffrey, who must have had access to several of them when he wrote his *History*. The fact that we do not have all of Geoffrey's sources does not entitle us to claim that the old British book is no more than a fiction of Geoffrey's.

    Bibliographic note: The account of Merlin and Vortigern's collapsing tower is found in Book VI of Geoffrey. The *Prophecies of Merlin* are found in Book VII, the building of Stonehenge in Book VIII. This translation is based on Geoffrey of Monmouth, *Historia Regum Britanniae: A Variant Version*, ed. Jacob Hammer (Cambridge: The Mediaeval Academy of America, 1951). Hammer's edition differs in several ways from the vulgate copy contained in the Cambridge University Library Ms. 1706 edited by Acton Griscom. Although edited from relatively late copies, it may derive from an original that predated the Cambridge manuscript; a few scholars have even speculated that such an original could represent Geoffrey's "very old book" or source. Despite the occasional differences in wording, the variant and vulgate versions of Merlin's prophecies both divide into three sections: a prophetic rendering of events up to and including Geoffrey's time, fanciful political events in Geoffrey's future, and an apocalyptic closing.
    A large scholarly literature examines Geoffrey's work. Among the most valuable contributions are John J. Parry and Robert Caldwell's "Geoffrey of Monmouth" in *Arthurian Literature in the Middle Ages*, ed. Roger Sherman Loomis (Oxford: Clarendon, 1959), pp. 72–73; J. S. P. Tatlock's *The Legendary History of Britain* (Berkeley: University of California Press, 1950), and Geoffrey Ashe's "A Certain Very Ancient Book," *Speculum* 56 (1981): 301–323. Additional episodes from the history may be found in *The Romance of Arthur*, ed. James J. Wilhelm and Laila Zamuelis Gross (New York: Garland, 1984), pp. 57–86. Merlin's *Prophecies* remain very much alive in modern-day occult literature, as asserted by R. J. Stewart's *The Prophetic Vision of Merlin* (London: Routledge and Kegan Paul, 1986).

Vortigern's Tower

[*The British king Vortigern is betrayed by his Saxon allies Hengist and Horsa, whom he had invited into Britain as mercenaries to help him solidify his hold on the throne. He is temporarily deposed in favor of his son Vortimer, who has some brief success in driving back the invaders, but Hengist's daughter, whom Vortigan has made his queen, Rowena, poisons Vortimer and the old king retakes the throne. With their thirst for more land and their superior forces, the Saxons eventually force him deep into Wales.*]

    Finally Vortigern asked his wizards what he should do. They all said that he should erect a very strong tower that would be a defense against his wicked enemies, who were causing him sorrow by eroding his kingdom. Searching a number of places for a location suitable to erect such a tower, he at last came to Mount Snowdon. There he called together masons and other craftsmen and began to lay the foundations for the tower. They mortared stones for a foundation, but whatever they built during the day sank into the ground during the night so that they did not know why or where their work had disappeared. When Vortigern heard of this, he again consulted his wizards to discover the cause of it. They told him that he should find a boy without a father, and that once such a boy was found, he must kill him and sprinkle the mortar and stones with his blood. They assured him that this expedient would make the foundation stand. He immediately sent search parties throughout every province, especially South Wales, to find such a person.

When one party came to the city that is now called Carmarthen, they found boys and girls playing in front of the city gate. They stopped there to observe the children's games and to inform the people about what they were searching for. During the game a quarrel pitted two youths, one named Merlin and the other Dinabutius, against each other. Dinabutius said to Merlin, " You fool, why do you dare compare yourself to me? Your family in no way equals mine, for I am sprung from kings and you don't even know who your father is."

Hearing this speech, the search party sent by Vortigern looked in amazement at Merlin and asked the bystanders who he was and who his parents were. They said that no one knew who his father was; they added, however, that the mother who gave birth to him was the daughter of the King of South Wales and that she lived with the nuns of the Church of St. Peter in that very city.

The men hurried to the prefect of the city and ordered him in the name of King Vortigern to send Merlin and his mother to the king. The prefect complied with the king's command and sent Merlin and his mother to him. When they were ushered into the presence of the king, he separated the two and began carefully to ask the woman by whom she conceived the youth. She said to him, "As your soul lives, my king, and as my soul lives, no man whom I know fathered that child upon me. But I know that once when I, then a maiden, was in my bedchamber, someone in the form of a handsome youth appeared to me, or so it seemed, and holding me tightly in his arms he kissed me many times, then suddenly disappeared, and became invisible. Yet from time to time this invisible man spoke to me and visited me; at last he lay with me in human form and left me pregnant. May it be known to your discreet majesty that no other man has known me otherwise."

Wondering at the words of this woman, Vortigern had his wise man Maugantius called so that he might declare whether what the woman had said could happen. Maugantius was thus brought before the king and when he heard what the mother of Merlin had claimed, he said, "In the books of philosophers and in a number of histories we find that many men have been engendered in this manner. For, as Apuleius in discussing the god of Socrates asserts, evil and unclean spirits called incubus-demons live in the sphere between the moon and earth. They are part human and part angelic in nature, and whenever they wish they can assume human form and consort with women. Perhaps one of these ravished that woman and fathered this youth."

When Merlin heard these things, he approached the king and said, "Why did you bring us to your court?" The king said to him, "My wise men have advised me to find a boy without a father and to mix his blood with the foundation of my tower to make it stand firm. We must build this tower, but we have not been able to lay a firm foundation yet, for whatever we build during the day is swallowed up by the earth during the night." Then Merlin said, "Order your wise men to come before me and I will prove that they are all liars." When the wise men were assembled and seated before the king, Merlin said to them, "Not knowing what prevents the foundation of the tower from staying solid and sound, you recommend to the king that my blood be mixed with mortar as if that would make the foundation remain firm. But tell me, if indeed you are wise men, what lies hidden under the foundation? For there must be something under it that prevents the structure from standing."

Stunned speechless, the king's counselors dared not utter a word in reply. Then Merlin said to the king, "My lord, call your workmen and have them dig up this ground until they find the pool of water that causes the structure to collapse. "When that was done, a pool of water was found, just as Merlin had said. The king then believed whatever Merlin said at that time and after. Turning to the wise men, Merlin said, "Tell me, liars and fakes, what, if you know, lies under the water of this pool?" Still speechless, they said not a word. Merlin said to the king, "Have ditches dug to drain the pool, and at the bottom you will see two hollow stones with two sleeping dragons in them." The king, believing that Merlin had already spoken the truth about the pool, had the pool drained. He marveled at Merlin's knowledge in all these things; the bystanders also marveled at Merlin's wisdom and proclaimed that God was in him.

The Prophecies of Merlin

While Vortigern was seated on the bank of the drained pool, two dragons came from the aforementioned hollow rocks; one was white, the other red. Breathing fire from the mouth and nose, they engaged in cruel combat. The white dragon prevailed and the chased the red one to the farther end of the lake. But the red one was ashamed at being beaten, and attacked the white one and forced it to retreat. While the dragons were thus fighting, the king commanded Ambrosius Merlin—that indeed was his full name—to say what the fight of these two dragons portended. Merlin started to cry uncontrollably. Inspired by the Spirit of Prophecy, he said:

Alas for the red dragon! The day of his extermination is fast approaching.

His lair will be occupied by the white dragon, who is none other than the Saxons whom you have invited. The red dragon represents the British people, who will be crushed by the white one. Mountains will be made level with valleys, and rivers of the valley will be flooded with blood. Religion will be destroyed, and bare, ruined churches will dot the nation. Nevertheless, in the end the downtrodden people will triumph over the oppressors who came from abroad. The wild boar of Cornwall will come to their assistance and trample the necks of oppressors under his feet. All the British Isles will be brought under his dominion, and he will control the groves of Gaul as well. The House of Romulus will tremble at his rage, and he will have a dubious departure in the end. The mouths of multitudes will celebrate his praises, and his triumphs will whet the appetite of poets.

Six of his descendants will hold his scepter after him, but the Germanic dragon will follow on their footsteps. The sea-wolf who rules over the African regions will praise him.

Once more religion will be disestablished, and there will be a major shift among the sees of the Church's primates. The See of London will be taken away and given to Canterbury. The seventh shepherd of York will become an exile in Brittany. St. David's will be given the pallium [*vestment worn by a bishop or archbishop*] of Caerleon, and a preacher in Ireland shall be struck dumb by a child growing in the womb. A shower of blood will pelt the earth, and mortal hunger will beset mankind. When these things begin to happen, the red one will feel bad about them, but after all these things have taken place he will thrive again.

The doomsday of the white dragon will be fast approaching, and the buildings in his little gardens will be torn down. Seven scepter-bearers will be killed, and one of them will be canonized. The wombs of mothers will be cut open and their children will be born premature. The people will raise a great supplication to have their lands restored to them. The man who is responsible for this turn of events will wear the mantle of the Bronze Man and for ages will guard the gates of London upon a bronze steed.

Later the red dragon will revert to his old customs and work hurt upon himself. Then the revenge of the Thunderer will catch up with him as every field will cheat the farmer of his produce. Death will carry off the people and every nation will be destroyed. The remnant will leave the land of their birth in order to plow alien fields; the good king—he will be counted as the twelfth among the royal saints—will prepare a navy for this purpose. Misery and and desolation will stalk the land, and threshing floors will turn into fertile forests.

Again the the white dragon will rise up and court a daughter of Germania. Our garden patches will again be sowed with alien seeds, and the red dragon will languish at the far rim of the pool. Afterwards the Germanic dragon will be crowned king and the Bronze Prince will be toppled. His reign has a preordained end, and he will not be able to extend his term. For a hundred and fifty years he will have to put up with trouble and turmoil; then for three hundred years he will wield his power.

Then the North Wind will blow against him and snatch away the flowers the West Wind has produced. Temples will be stripped of gold, and the sharp edge of the sword will work havoc. The Germanic dragon will hardly be able to stay in his lairs; the revenge for his betrayals will catch up with him. In the end he will manage to prosper for a short while, but his losses in Normandy will be a great blow to him.

A nation dressed in wood and iron corselets will seek him out and wreak vengeance on him for his evil deeds. This people will rehabilitate the natives, and the foreigners will be openly massacred; thus the seeds of the white dragon will be wiped out of our little gardens, and the members of the dragon's generation will also be decimated; the survivors will be reduced to slavery, and they will turn against their own mothers and hit them with spades and ploughshares.

Two more dragons will follow. Though one of them will be felled by the spear of envy, the other will assume a different name. The lion of justice will come next, and at his roaring the towers of Gaul and the dragons of the islands will quake. In his days gold will be wrung out of lily and the nettle, and silver will issue forth from the hooves of lowing cattle. Fops with curled hair will be clothed in multicolored fleece, but their outer garment will betray the inner man. The feet of these barking creatures will be lopped off. The animals of the wilderness will have peace, but mankind will bewail its miserable lot. Trade will be reduced into half, and the remaining half will later come to nought. The rapacity of kites will cease and the teeth of wolves will be blunted. The lion's cubs will be transformed into sea fish, and the eagle will build its nest on the summit of Mount Aravius. North Wales will flow red with the blood of mothers, and the house of Cornwall will kill six brothers. The tears of night will bedew the island, and everyone will be seduced into all manner of things.

Unfortunate are you, Normandy! The brain of the lion will be spilt on your land, and he, limbs severed, will be cast out of his own native land. The survivors will aspire to curry favor with the powerful and mighty, but the newcomers will enjoy all the favors. Devotion to duty will dispossess the man who inherited goods from the impious until he is endowed with his own father's mantle. Armed with the teeth of the wild boar about him, he will ascend the summit of mountains wearing a helmet. Albany will grow angry and, summoning her allies, she will engage in shedding blood. Between her jaws will be placed a bit made in the Bay of Brittany.

The eagle of the broken treaty will strip it of its gold and then take pleasure in building her third nest. The roaring whelps of lions will be ever awake and leave the woodlands to hunt under the walls of cities. No little havoc will they wreak upon those who stand in their way, and they will cut out the tongues of bulls. They will oppress the necks of roaring ones and relive ancestral times. After that from the first to the fourth, from the fourth to the third, and from the third to the second the thumb will be rolled in oil.

The sixth will destroy the walls of Ireland and transform forests into a plain. He will unite the different parts into a whole and will be crowned with the head of the lion. His beginning will be marked with fickle goodwill, but his end will be with the saints above. He will restore the seats of the blessed throughout their native lands, and set shepherds in appropriate places. He will give the pallium to two cities and he will endow virgins with gifts. He will thus earn the favor of the Thunderer and he will be set among the blest. From him will spring a lynx with penetrating eyes which will await the ruin of his people. Because of him Normandy will let go both islands and be stripped of her former dignity. Then will citizens be returned to the island, and discord fomented by foreigners will arise. Also a hoary old man, sitting on a snow-white horse, will divert the river of Periron and with a white wand measure out the dimensions of a mill upon that place.

Cadwallader will summon Conan and will make an alliance with Albion [= *Scotland*]. The foreigners will be massacred there; then rivers will flood with blood; then the mountains of Brittany will erupt; finally the diadem of Brutus will be established over all of them. Wales will be filled with joy, and the oaks of Cornwall will grow green. Then will the island be named after Brutus and the names given by outsiders perish. From Conan will come a bellicose boar that will busy his sharp tusks in the forests of Gaul. He will make stumps of the larger oaks, but he will be responsible for the protection of the smaller ones. Arabs and Africans will tremble before him, for the violence of his attacks will stretch to remote parts of Spain.

The ram of the Castle of Venus will follow, having golden horns and a silver beard, and from his nostrils he will breathe a cloud so dark that the entire surface of the island will be darkened. There will be a peace in his time and crops will be increased through the fruitfulness of the land. Women will become serpent-like in the way they walk; all their steps will be filled with pride. The Castle of Venus will be rebuilt and the arrows of Cupid will not cease to wound. The fountain of Amne will turn to blood, and two kings will duel over the lioness of the Ford of the Walking Stick. All ground will be abundant in produce, and humanity will not desist from fornication. Three centuries will witness these doings until entombed kings will lie disinterred in the city of London. Famine will return anew, mortality will be renewed, and city dwellers will bewail their forsaken cities. Without warning the boar of commerce will arrive and recall dispersed flocks to fields from which they were expelled. His breast will be food for the destitute and his tongue will satisfy the thirsty. From his mouth will flow rivers that will be drink for the parched throats of mankind. Then over the Tower of London will spring up a tree with just three branches, and the width of its leaves will darken the face of the whole island. Then the North Wind will come as an enemy of this tree, and an overpowering blast will break off the third branch. The remaining two will occupy the place of the cast-off branch until the one will destroy the other by the abundance of its foliage. Then the remaining branch will itself occupy the place of the other two and sustain birds from foreign lands. And this branch will be held harmful to the birds of this land, for fear of its shadow will deprive them of liberty of flight.

Then the ass of iniquity will rise quickly against the goldsmiths, but only slowly against the rapacity of wolves. In those days the oaks will burn throughout the forests, and acorns will be borne on the branches of linden trees. The Severn Sea will flow through seven mouths, and the waters of Usk will boil for seven months. The fish of that river will die from the heat, and serpents will be born from the bodies of the fish. The baths of the city of Bath will grow cold and their healthful waters bring forth death. London will bemoan the death of twenty thousand, and the River Thames will be turned to blood. Professed monks will be forced to wed, and their cries will be heard as far as the Alps.

In the city of Winchester there will erupt three fountains whose waters will divide the island into three portions. Whoever drinks from one will enjoy a long life and will not be oppressed by unexpected illness; whoever drinks from the second will die of insatiable hunger, and pallor and fright will mark his face. Whoever drinks from the third will fall victim to sudden death, and no one will be able to bury his body. Those wishing to avoid such great jaws of death will try to hide them with various coverings. But whatever substance is piled upon them will take the form of some other substance. If earth is piled there, it will turn into stones, stones into wood, wood into ashes, ashes into water. A maiden will be sent forth from the city of Canute's Forest to perform cures by her medicinal skills. When she will have exercised all her skills, she will dry up the noxious fountains by her breath alone. Then, when she refreshes herself with healthful waters, she will carry the Forest of Caledon in her right hand and the ramparts of the walls of London in her left. Wherever she walks, her path will be sulphurous and burn with a double-edged flame. The smoke from that flame will arouse Flemings and provide food for those beneath the sea. She herself will weep copious tears of pity and fill the island with her frightful cry. She will be slain by a stag of ten branches, four of which will sport golden crowns. The other six will become horns of oxen whose abominable bellows will stir up the three isles of Britain.

The Forest of Dean will come to life and breaking into human speech will shout, "Arise, Wales, and with Cornwall at your side speak thus to Winchester: 'The earth will swallow you up; move the see of your bishop to where ships come to port and let other members follow the head. For the hour comes when your citizens will perish for their crimes of perjury. The whiteness of your wools has blinded you and the variety of their dyes. Alas for the forsworn people, for on account of them the great city will be ruined.'"

The shipmen will rejoice in the growth of riches, and they will make two cities into one. A hedgehog loaded with apples will rebuild the town, and birds, attracted by the aroma of these apples, will flock there from diverse forests. He will add there a vast palace and surround it with six hundred towers. London will envy it and increase her walls threefold. The River Thames will encircle her on three sides, and news of that labor will be heard beyond the Alps. The hedgehog will hide his apples in his new city and make subterranean passageways there. At that time stones will speak, and the sea over which one sails to Gaul will be constricted into a narrow channel. A man on one bank will be audible to men on the other bank, and the land-mass of the island will grow greater. The secrets of those who dwell beneath the sea will be made known, and Gaul will quake with fear. Then a heron will come from the Calaterium Forest and fly around the coasts of the island for two years. By her nocturnal cry she will summon birds together and cause every winged creature to congregate with her. They will devastate cultivated fields and devour harvests of every kind. Famine will beset the populace and dreadful death will follow the famine. When this great calamity has ceased, these detestable winged creatures will approach the Valley of Galabes and raise it up into a high mountain. Upon the mountaintop the heron will plant an oak and make her nest in its branches. In the nest she will lay three eggs from which will come forth a fox, a wolf, and a bear. The fox will devour her mother and wear the head of an ass. Assuming this unnatural form, she will terrorize her brothers and force them to take refuge in Normandy. But there they will arouse the tusked boar and, returning together in a boat, will join in assault against the fox. But when defeat seems inevitable, the fox will feign death and move the boar to pity. Soon he will approach her body and standing over it will breathe on her eyes and her face. But the fox, still full of ancient cunning, will bite his left foot and tear it completely away from his body. Then jumping upon him, she will tear away his right ear and his tail and hide them in the mountainside caves. Thus deceived, the boar will demand that the wolf and the bear restore to him his missing parts. They, taking up his cause, will promise to fashion two feet, two ears, and a tail, which they will change into porcine members. He will acquiesce and await the promised restorations. Meanwhile the fox will descend from the mountains, change herself into a wolf, and approach the boar as if she wanted to speak to him. She will thus cunningly devour him completely. Then she will transform herself into the boar and pretend as though she has lost some body parts and is awaiting her kin. But afterward when they come to her, she will slay them with her quick jaws, and then she will have herself crowned with the head of a lion.

In her time there shall be born a serpent whose intent will be to destroy mankind. He will encircle London with his length and eat those who come his way. The mountain ox will assume the head of a lion and will polish his teeth white in the workshop of the Severn. He will summon to himself the flocks of Scotland and Wales, and they will dry up Thames as they drink. The ass will call to the long-bearded goat and exchange shapes with him. The mountain ox will become angry at that, and, calling the wolf to him, will turn his horns against them. After indulging in his savagery, he will eat them up flesh and bones, but he himself will be consumed by fire at the the top of Urian. The glowing embers of his funeral pyre will be changed into swans who will swim on dry land as if they were in a river. They will eat the fish in fish and the men in men. When old age touches them, they will become underwater lynxes, and deep under the waves they will work their insidious ways. They will sink ships and collect a hoard of silver.

The Thames will flow again and, gathering together its tributaries, will overflow the banks of its bed. It will submerge nearby cities and overrun mountains that stand in its way. Overflowing with treachery and evil, it will approach the fountain Galabes. Consequently insurrections will arise, inciting the North Welsh to make war. The oaks of the forest will come together and join in battle with the rocks of the people of Gwent. The raven will fly there with the kite and feast on the corpses of the fallen.

The owl will make her nest atop the walls of Gloucester and in her nest an ass will be born. The serpent of Malvern will raise him and instruct him in many treacheries. When he has seized the crown, he will ascend to the throne and terrify the populace of the country with his savage braying. In his time the mountains of Pachaia will totter, and the provinces will be stripped of their forests, for a fire-breathing worm will suddenly appear and consume the trees with his fiery breath. Out of him will come seven lions deformed with the heads of goats. They will debauch women with the horrible odor from their nostrils, and they will turn wives into prostitutes. A father will not know his own son because they will live together licentiously after the manner of beasts. Next a giant of evil will appear who will terrify everyone with his piercing eyes. Then the dragon of Worcester will rise up against him and try to destroy him. In the ensuing combat the dragon will be defeated and will be overwhelmed by the conqueror's wickedness. Casting away his clothing, he will mount the dragon. But the dragon will throw him skyward and beat his naked body with his tail stretched out to its fullest length. Regaining his strength, the giant will stab the dragon in the throat with a sword. Then, entangled in his own tail, the dragon will die of poisoning.

After him will come the boar of Totnes, who will oppress the populace with dreadful tyranny. Gloucester will unleash a lion that in various battles will harass the raging boar. The lion will trample him underfoot and terrify him with his gaping jaws. Finally the lion will quarrel with the kingdom itself and lord it over the nobles. Suddenly in the heat of the quarrel a bull will appear and strike down the lion with his right hoof. He will chase him out of the realm by pursuing him. But the bull will shatter his own horns against the walls of Exeter. The fox of Kaerdubali will take vengeance on the lion and eat him up with her teeth. Then the serpent from Lincoln will twine about the fox and make his presence known to the many dragons with his frightful hissing. Thereupon the dragons will battle each other and will rip one another into pieces. The winged one will overwhelm the one lacking wings and drive his poisonous claws into the other's muzzle. Two more will join battle, but they too will be killed. A fifth one will take the place of the two slain ones and with several contrivances will break the two survivors into pieces. Holding a sword, he will climb the back of one and sever his head from his body. Throwing off his clothing, he will climb upon another and hold that one's tail in his right and left claws. Naked he will conquer, because when clothed he accomplishes little. He will torment the rest and, sitting on their backs, he will drive them in circles about the kingdom.

Then a roaring lion will appear and there will be terror at his monstrous ferocity. He will reduce three times five portions to one, and alone he will rule the entire populace. A giant will appear in the splendor of snowy color and beget a white population. A luxurious living will sap the energy of the leaders, and their subjects will be turned into brutes. Afterward a lion fattened on the blood of men will appear among them. In the wheat field he will appoint a sickle-bearer as harvester, but the lion will destroy him as soon as he starts making his own moves.

A charioteer from York will calm the people and, having expelled his lord, he will stand tall in the chariot he drives. He will threaten the East with drawn sword, and the tracks of his chariot wheels will overflow with blood. Then he will turn himself into a fish in water and mate with a snake that entices him with her hisses. From that union will be born three lightning-quick bulls that, having consumed their pasture land, will be changed into trees. One of these will brandish a whip of vipers, and he will turn his back on the firstborn brother, who will try to seize the whip, but it will be carried away by the third brother. They will avert their eyes from each other until the time they have thrown away the poisoned drinking glass.

A farmer from Albion will take their place and down his back a snake will dangle. He will occupy himself tilling the soil so that the fields may become white for harvest. But the serpent will work at spilling his venom to prevent the plants from coming to harvest. The populace will perish in a deadly massacre, and the walls of the cities will crumble. The city of Gloucester will be given as a remedy, and she will intervene with the foster daughter of the whip-bearer; she will apply the right medicine and in a short time the island will be made whole.

Then a scepter will be held by two, one after the other; the horned dragon will serve them both. The first will come clad in iron and ride a flying serpent. Naked he will sit on the back of the serpent and will grasp its tail with his right hand. The seas will be stirred up by his cry, and he will instill dread in the second one. The second will, as a result, make the lion his ally. A quarrel will spring up between the two and they will battle each other. Each will succumb to wounds inflicted by the other, but the ferocious lion alone will survive. Then a man will come with lute and drum and soothe the savage lion. As a result, the different nations of the realm will live in peace and appeal to the lion to restrain himself. In the realm given him he will first try to balance the scales of justice; then he will stretch out his hand to grab Scotland. Because of this turn of events the northern provinces will suffer grief, and they will unbolt the doors of the temples.

The wolf will lead troops as the standard-bearer, and he will encircle Cornwall with his tail. A soldier in a war-chariot will resist him and transform the people of Cornwall into a boar. The boar will devastate the provinces, but in the end he will hide his head in the depths of the Severn.

A man will make a commercial alliance with the lion in a vat of wine, and the glimmering gold will blind the eyes of the onlookers. Silver will shine bright in the course of the events and will dazzle the winepressers. Mortals will be drunk on the wine placed in front of them, and disregarding heaven they will fix their eyes on the earth. The stars will avert their faces from them, and change their accustomed course in the skies. The indignant stars will deny rains and crops will suffer drought. Roots and branches will change places, and the freakishness of the situation will appear as a miracle. The brilliance of the sun will pale beside the amber glow of Mercury, and it will strike terror into onlookers. Mercury, born in Arcadia, will change his shield, and the helmet of Mars will summon Venus. The helmet of Mars will cast a shadow, and angry at this, Mercury will run away from his assigned orbit. Orion will unsheathe his sword, and Phoebus of the sea will agitate the clouds. Jupiter will go beyond his fixed paths, and Venus will desert her established circuits. The spite of the planet Saturn will pour forth torrents of rain on men and strike them down as though he were reaping the harvest with a bent sickle.

The twelve houses of the stars will weep because their guests have overrun their courses. The Gemini will break from their usual embrace and summon Aquarius to the Fountain. The scales of Libra will hang askew until the time Aries will place his curved horns beneath them. The tail of Scorpio will produce flashes of lightning, and Cancer will quarrel with the Sun. Dropping her maidenly restraint, Virgo will climb the back of Sagittarius. The chariot of the Moon will give trouble to the Zodiac, and the Pleiades will break forth in tears. They will refuse to take orders from Janus the doorkeeper, and the door closed to Ariadne will be overwhelmed by the waves. In the blinking of an eye the sea will surge up, and the dust of ancient battles will rise anew. With an ill-omened blast the winds will begin to fight again, carrying the battle-din to the stars above.

The Building of Stonehenge

[*As Merlin has foretold, Aurelius and Uther Pendragon return from exile in Brittany to triumph over both the Saxons and King Vortigern. King Aurelius of the Britons decides to build on Mount Amesbury a memorial suitable for all those who have died in the battles against the Saxons.*]

Then summoning carpenters and stonemasons from all parts of the realm, Aurelius ordered them to use all their skills to erect a structure of original design that would forever be a memorial worthy of the fallen heroes. But they all felt that their skills were not up to such a task and declined to undertake the project. Then Tremorinus, Archbishop of Caerleon, approached the king and said, "If any man has the art to execute your plan, it is Merlin, the bard of Vortigern. No man in the realm is more skillful than he in either foretelling the future or in contriving artful devices. Order him to come so that he may build the memorial you wish to construct."

After he had inquired at length about Merlin, Aurelius sent messengers throughout the different regions of the realm to find him and bring him to the king. As they traveled through the provinces, they found Merlin in the territory of the Gewissi at the fountain Galabes, which he was accustomed to frequent. Telling him what they wanted, they brought him to the king, who received him with joy. Aurelius, desiring to hear marvels, commanded him to tell of the future. Merlin replied to him, "Mysteries of that kind ought not be revealed except under great necessity. If I were to speak something vainly or amusingly, the spirit that teaches me would fall silent and would leave me when need for him arose." When Merlin had refused all such requests, the king no longer desired to inquire about the future, but spoke to him about the project he had in mind. Merlin said to the king, "If you wish to embellish the burial grounds of those men with a monument that shall stand forever, send for the choir of the Giants that is on Mount Killare in Ireland. For there is a structure of stone that no man of this age could erect unless his genius equaled his art. Those are huge stones whose power is nowhere to be matched. If they are erected in a circle in this place exactly as they were once placed in their present location, then they will stand forever."

When Aurelius heard these words, he burst out in laughter, asking, "How could stones of such size be brought here from so distant a country, as if Britain itself were lacking in stones sufficient for this project?" Merlin replied, "Do not be moved to idle laughter, my lord; for I do not speak idly. Those are mystical stones having medicinal properties. In ages past giants transported them from the farthest reaches of Africa and erected them in Ireland, where they dwelt at the time. They did this so that they could build baths at the foot of those stones for those who were laid low with infirmities. They washed the stones, letting the water and herbs run into the baths below so that those who bathed were healed of any affliction. In addition, they mixed the water and herbs into poultices that healed all wounds. Not a single one of those stones lacks medical powers."

When the Britons heard these words, they decided to send for the stones and to do battle with the people of Ireland if they tried to keep them. They chose Uther Pendragon, the brother of the king, and fifteen thousand troops to carry out the mission. Merlin was also chosen so that whatever had to be done could be done with his lore and advice. As soon as ships could be readied, they launched them, and arrived in Ireland with fair winds.

At the time the King of Ireland was Gilloman, a young man famed for his remarkable valor. When he heard that the Britons had set foot in Ireland, he mustered a large army and set out to meet them. When he had learned the reason for their venture, he laughed and said to those assembled around him, "It is no wonder the indolent Saxons were able to devastate the island of Britain, because the Britons are dupes and dolts. Whoever heard of such folly? Are the stones of Ireland one whit better than those of Britain so that we are provoked to fight over them? Arm yourselves, men, and defend your country. While I draw breath, they shall never carry off even the slightest stone of the choir of the giants."

Uther, when he saw that the Irish were prepared to fight, attacked them without a moment's hesitation. Quickly the Britons prevailed and put Gilloman to flight, the Irish army being wounded or killed.

Having obtained victory, the Britons moved on to Mount Killare. Coming to the stone structure, they expressed both joy and wonderment. Merlin came to those loitering about the stone and said, "Boys, try your strength to move those stones down and see whether art yields to strength or strength yields to art." With singleminded devotion to his command, the men busied themselves with all sorts of contrivances in their attempt to dismantle the stones. Some worked with ropes, some with cables, and some with scaling ladders in an effort to accomplish the task; but they were in no way successful. When they all despaired of the job, Merlin laughed and began to asemble his own machinery. Finally, when he had put together all that was necessary, he lowered the stones more easily than one could believe.

When he had lowered the stones, Merlin ordered them carried aboard ship, and thus with rejoicing they set forth on the return voyage to Britain; favorable winds sped them to shore and they bore the stones to the burial ground of the fallen heroes. When Aurelius was apprised of this, he sent messengers through all parts of the realm and commanded them to call clergy and laity to gather on Mount Amesbury so that they might dedicate the proposed monument with joy and honor. Thus, in accord with his edict, there came bishops, abbots, and members of every order that owed him fealty.

When they were all assembled on the appointed day, Aurelius placed the diadem on his own head and celebrated the Feast of Pentecost in regal manner, devoting the following three days to continual celebration. Meanwhile he bestowed vacant benefices upon members of his household to reward them for their labor in his service. Two metropolitan sees, York and Caerleon, had no pastors at that time. Desiring to heed the universal opinion of his subjects, he granted York to Sampson, an illustrious man famed for his great devotion; he gave Caerleon to Dubricius, whom divine Providence had already chosen as suitable for that position. When Aurelius had taken care of those and other affairs concerning his kingdom, he ordered Merlin to place the stones brought from Ireland upright around the sepulcher. In keeping with the king's wish, Merlin erected the stones around the sepulcher in the exact order in which they were found on Mount Killare in Ireland. Thus Merlin proved brains superior to brawn.

chapter 4

VITA MERLINI

John Jay Parry

THE FULL text of the remarkable Latin poem *Vita Merlini* (The Life of Merlin) survives in only one manuscript, Cotton Vespasian E. iv. in the British Library. It names Geoffrey of Monmouth as its author, and was probably written between 1148 (when Robert de Chesney, the former Oxford colleague to whom it is dedicated, was elected Bishop of Lincoln) and 1151, when Geoffrey was elected Bishop of St. Asaph. If Geoffrey was hoping for preferment from de Chesney, his appointment to this small monastery in northern Wales must have seemed a niggardly reward for his literary endeavors. On the other hand, he had received nothing whatsoever for the enormously influential *History of the Kings of Britain*.

The *Life of Merlin* is a miscellany, remarkable because it mixes so many modes of literature current in the Middle Ages. It includes Celtic folklore, political prophecies, pseudo-scientific learning, catalogues of information, and set-pieces of medieval oratory. Technically, it is a comedy in better than average Latin hexameter verse; its avowed purpose is to entertain its educated and predominantly priestly audience with a display of curiosities. Like most comedies, its playfulness accommodates a mixed style: plain and matter of fact when it narrates Merlin's adventures; elevated when Merlin or another character launches into a lament for human mortality, a poetic description, or prophecy, or a learned disquisition. It also offers a happy ending, in which Merlin retires to his forest house to worship and glorify God. Its variety and general light-heartedness do not prevent it from seriously addressing the fickleness and frequent bitterness of human destinies. We are likely to appreciate the *Vita* most when we read it for its witty play of active and contemplative imagination, as a crazy quilt of styles and subjects rather than a tightly plotted narrative like the modern short story.

Geoffrey drew partly on his earlier works for the Arthurian material in the *Vita*, recapitulating events before and during Arthur's career. However, he forms most of his narrative from the Welsh traditions concerning Lailoken and Myrddin in order to portray Merlin's own development from an unholy to a holy lifestyle through divine grace. While he asserts that the Merlin who engineers Arthur's conception and the Merlin who wanders mad in the Caledonian Forest are the same person, the second Merlin remains a distinctly different creation from the first. He is accompanied by a different cast of characters, like his wife Guendoloena, the bard Taliesin, and King Rhydderch, who is made husband of Merlin's sister Ganieda (called Gwenddydd in the earlier Welsh poems). Furthermore, he is much older than the Merlin who prophesies to Vortigern. The Battle of Arfderydd, at which he goes mad, occured nearly a century later than the approximate date of Vortigern's rule. To bridge for these differences, the *Vita* gives Merlin a role in Arthur's reign.

Modern readers are apt to be less interested in the pseudo-scientific material and lists of natural curiosities. Geoffrey borrowed most of them from a popular medieval encyclopedia of predominantly classical learning, Isidore of Seville's *Etymologies* (c. 600). Setting aside their obvious pedantry, these digressions about the ordering of creation, flowers, fish, islands, fountains, birds, and the like still exude an appealingly fabulous air. They also have symbolic correspondences to events during Merlin's life: among them, the ordering of creation to the disordering of British political realms, the islands to Merlin's isolation and Arthur's conveyance to Avalon, and the woodpecker to prophecy.

The medieval thirst for marvels, like today's, was voracious. Common, aristocratic, and clerical audiences all loved to hear of them, and Geoffrey was most willing to oblige at least the latter two. Nevertheless, the *Vita Merlini* did not have nearly the impact in the Middle Ages of Geoffrey's earlier works, although many of its motifs, such as the significant laughs and the threefold death, appear fully developed in the French Merlin romances and their subsequent Middle English versions. It has become an important reference point only for modern adaptations such as Laurence Binyon's *The Madness of Merlin* (1947), Mary Stewart's Merlin novels (1970, 1973, 1979), and Robert Nye's *Merlin* (1979), which return to Geoffrey of Monmouth and especially his Welsh sources for material, and which portray Merlin in his madness. With its many references to classical learning, specialized knowledge, and obscure people, places, and events, the *Vita* invites detailed study and still presents many mysteries to scholars. Geoffrey's last work is more influential today than it has ever been.

Bibliographic note: John Jay Parry (1889–1954) was a medieval scholar whose various bibliographies (alone and with collaborators) of critical Arthurian literature are still standard references for the field. In addition to *The Vita Merlini* (*University of Illinois Studies in Language and Literature* 10.3 [August 1925]), he edited *The Poems and Amyntas of Thomas Randolph* (1917) and the Welsh *Brut y Brenhinedd* (1937), and wrote *Andreas Capellanus: The Art of Courtly Love* (1941). His translation of the *Life of Merlin* is not strictly literal, but has not been bettered; it is based upon the complete Cotton Vespasian manuscript, and was compared with manuscript fragments and other printed editions for difficult points. Parry also discusses analogous stories in "Celtic Tradition and the *Vita Merlini*," *Philological Quarterly* 4 (July 1925): 193–207. Because our understanding of the British Dark Ages has advanced considerably since 1925, some of Parry's conjectural notes have been superseded, and I have omitted notes in the interests of space. Readers who wish to pursue their study of the poem should consult Parry's introduction and Basil Clarke's thorough edition, *Life of Merlin* (Cardiff: University of Wales Press, 1973). Another important study is J.S.P. Tatlock, "Geoffrey of Monmouth's *Vita Merlini*," *Speculum* 18 (July 1943): 265–287. A thoughtful discussion of Merlin's progress from unholy to holy man of the woods is in Penelope Doob's *Nebuchadnezzar's Children: Conventions of Madness in Middle English Literature* (New Haven: Yale University Press, 1974). Finally, an occult interpretation of the *Vita* has recently appeared: R.J. Stewart's *The Mystic Life of Merlin* (London: Routledge and Kegan Paul, 1986).

The Vita Merlini

I am preparing to sing the madness of the prophetic bard, and a humorous poem on Merlin; pray correct the song, Robert, glory of bishops, by restraining my pen. For we know that Philosophy has poured over you its divine nectar, and has made you famous in all things, that you might serve as an example, a leader and a teacher in the world. Therefore may you favor my attempt, and see fit to look upon the poet with better auspices than did that other whom you have just succeeded, promoted to an honor that you deserve. For indeed your habits, and your approved life, and your birth, and your usefulness to the position, and the clergy and the people all were seeking it for you, and from this circumstance happy Lincoln is just now exalted to the stars. On this account I might wish you to be embraced in a fitting song, but I am not equal to the task, even though Orpheus, and Camerinus, and Macer, and Marius, and mighty-voiced Rabirius were all to sing with my mouth and all the Muses were to accompany me. But now, Sisters accustomed to sing with me, let us sing the work proposed, and strike the cithara.

Well then, after many years had passed under many kings, Merlin the Briton was held famous in the world. He was a king and a prophet; to the proud people of the South Welsh he gave laws, and to the chieftains he prophesied the future. Meanwhile it happened that a strife arose between several of the chiefs of the kingdom, and throughout the cities they wasted the innocent people with fierce war. Peredur, king of the North Welsh, made war on Gwenddoleu, who ruled the realm of Scotland; and already the day fixed for the battle was at hand and the leaders were ready in the field, and the troops were fighting, falling on both sides in a miserable slaughter. Merlin had come to the war with Peredur and so had Rhydderch, king of the Cumbrians, both savage men. They slew the opposing enemy with their hateful swords, and three brothers of the prince who had followed him through his wars, always fighting, cut down and broke the battle lines. Thence they rushed fiercely through the crowded ranks with such an attack that they soon fell killed.

At this sight, Merlin, you grieved and poured out sad complaints throughout the army, and cried out in these words, "Could injurious fate be so harmful as to take from me so many and such great companions, whom recently so many kings and so many remote kingdoms feared? O dubious lot of mankind! O death ever near, which has them always in its power, and strikes with its hidden goad and drives out the wretched life from the body! O glorious youths, who now will stand by my side in arms, and with me will repel the chieftains coming to harm me, and the hosts rushing upon me? Bold young men, your audacity has taken from you your pleasant years and pleasant youth! You who so recently were rushing in arms through the troops, cutting down on every side those who resisted you, now are beating the ground and are red with red blood!" So among the hosts he lamented with flowing tears, and mourned for the men, and the savage battle was unceasing. The lines rushed together, enemies were slain by enemies, blood flowed everywhere, and people died on both sides. But at length the Britons assembled their troops from all quarters, and all together rushing in arms they fell upon the Scots and wounded them and cut them down, nor did they rest until the hostile battalions turned their backs and fled through unfrequented ways.

Merlin called his companions out from the battle and bade them bury the brothers in a richly colored chapel; and he bewailed the men and did not cease to pour out laments, and he strewed dust on his hair and rent his garments, and prostrate on the ground rolled now hither and now thither. Peredur strove to console him and so did the nobles and the princes, but he would not be comforted nor put up with their beseeching words. He had now lamented for three whole days and had refused food, so great was the grief that consumed him. Then when he had filled the air with so many and so great complaints, new fury seized him and he departed secretly, and fled to the woods not wishing to be seen as he fled. He entered the wood and rejoiced to lie hidden under the ash trees; he marvelled at the wild beasts feeding on the grass of the glades; now he chased after them and again he flew past them; he lived on the roots of grasses and on the grass, on the fruit of the trees and on the mulberries of the thicket. He became a silvan man just as though devoted to the woods. For a whole summer after this, hidden like a wild animal, he remained buried in the woods, found by no one and forgetful of himself and of his kindred. But when the winter came and took away all the grass and the fruit of the trees, and he had nothing to live on, he poured out the following lament in a wretched voice.

"Christ, God of heaven, what shall I do? In what part of the world can I stay, since I see nothing here I can live on, neither grass on the ground nor acorns on the trees? Here once there stood nineteen apple trees bearing apples every year; now they are not standing. Who has taken them away from me? Whither have they gone all of a sudden? Now I see them—now I do not!

Thus the fates fight against me and for me, since they both permit and forbid me to see. Now I lack the apples and everything else. The trees stand without leaves, without fruit; I am afflicted by both circumstances since I cannot cover myself with the leaves or eat the fruit. Winter and the south wind with its falling rain have taken them all away. If by chance I find some navews deep in the ground, the hungry swine and the voracious boars rush up and snatch them from me as I dig them up from the turf. You, O wolf, dear companion, accustomed to roam with me through the secluded paths of the woods and meadows, now can scarcely get across the fields; hard hunger has weakened both you and me. You lived in these woods before I did and age has whitened your hairs first. You have nothing to put into your mouth and do not know how to get anything, at which I marvel, since the wood abounds in so many goats and other wild beasts that you might catch. Perhaps that detestable old age of yours has taken away your strength and prevented your following the chase. Now, as the only thing left you, you fill the air with howlings, and stretched out on the ground you extend your wasted limbs."

These words he was uttering among the shrubs and dense hazel thickets when the sound reached a certain passer-by who turned his steps to the place whence the sounds were rising in the air, and found the place and found the speaker. As soon as Merlin saw him he departed, and the traveller followed him, but was unable to overtake the man as he fled. Thereupon he resumed his journey and went about his business, moved by the lot of the fugitive. Now this traveller was met by a man from the court of Rhydderch, King of the Cumbrians, who was married to Ganieda and was happy in his beautiful wife. She was sister to Merlin and, grieving over the fate of her brother, she had sent her retainers to the woods and the distant fields to bring him back. One of these retainers came toward the traveller and the latter at once went up to him and they fell into conversation; the one who had been sent to find Merlin asked if the other had seen him in the woods or the glades. The latter admitted that he had seen such a man among the bushy glades of the Calidonian forest, but, when he wished to speak to him and sit down with him, the other had fled away swiftly among the oaks. These things he told, and the messenger departed and entered the forest; he searched the deepest valleys and passed over the high mountains; he sought everywhere for his man, going through the obscure places.

On the very summit of a certain mountain there was a fountain, surrounded on every side by hazel bushes and thick with shrubs. There Merlin had seated himself, and thence through all the woods he watched the wild animals running and playing. Thither the messenger climbed, and with silent step went on up the heights seeking the man. At last he saw the fountain and Merlin sitting on the grass behind it, and making his plaint in this manner, "O Thou who rulest all things, how does it happen that the seasons are not all the same, distinguished only by their four numbers? Now spring, according to its laws, provides flowers and leaves; summer gives crops, autumn ripe apples; icy winter follows and devours and wastes all the others, bringing rain and snow, and keeps them all away and harms with its tempests. And it does not permit the ground to produce variegated flowers, or the oak trees acorns, or the apple trees dark red apples. O that there were no winter or white frost! That it were spring or summer, and that the cuckoo would come back singing, and the nightingale who softens sad hearts with her devoted song, and the turtle dove keeping her chaste vows, and that in new foliage other birds should sing in harmonious measures, delighting me with their music, while a new earth should breathe forth odors from new flowers under the green grass; that the fountains would also flow on every side with their gentle murmurs, and near by, under the leaves, the dove would pour forth her soothing laments and incite to slumber."

The messenger heard the prophet and broke off his lament with cadences on the cither he had brought with him, that with it he might attract and soften the madman. Therefore making plaintive sounds with his fingers and striking the strings in order, he lay hidden behind him and sang in a low voice, "O the dire groanings of mournful Guendoloena! O the wretched tears of weeping Guendoloena! I grieve for wretched dying Guendoloena! There was not among the Welsh a woman more beautiful than she. She surpassed in fairness the goddesses, and the petals of the privet, and the blooming roses and the fragrant lilies of the fields. The glory of spring shone in her alone, and she had the splendor of the stars in her two eyes, and splendid hair shining with the gleam of gold. All this has perished; all beauty has departed from her, both color and figure and also the glory of her snowy flesh. Now, worn out with much weeping, she is not what she was, for she does not know where the prince has gone, or whether he is alive or dead; therefore the wretched woman languishes and is totally wasted away through her long grief. With similar laments Ganieda weeps with her, and without consolation grieves for her lost brother. One weeps for her brother and the other for her husband, and both devote themselves to weeping and spend their time in sadness. No food nourishes them, nor does any sleep refresh them wandering at night through the brushwood, so great is the grief that consumes them both. Not otherwise did Sidonian Dido grieve when the ships had weighed anchor and Aeneas was in haste to depart; so most wretched Phyllis groaned and wept when Demophoon did not come back at the appointed time; thus Briseis wept for the absent Achilles. Thus the sister and the wife grieve together, and burn continually and completely with inward agonies."

The messenger sang thus to his plaintive lyre, and with his music soothed the ears of the prophet that he might become more gentle and rejoice with the singer. Quickly the prophet arose and addressed the young man with pleasant words, and begged him to touch once more the strings with his fingers and to sing again his former song. The latter therefore set his fingers to the lyre and played over again the song that was asked for, and by his playing compelled the man, little by little, to put aside his madness, captivated by the sweetness of the lute.

So Merlin became mindful of himself, and he recalled what he used to be, and he wondered at his madness and he hated it. His former mind returned and his sense came back to him, and, moved by affection, he groaned at the names of his sister and of his wife, since his mind was now restored to him, and he asked to be led to the court of King Rhydderch. The other obeyed him, and straightway they left the woods and came, rejoicing together, to the city of the king. So the queen was delighted by regaining her brother and the wife became glad over the return of her husband. They vied with each other in kissing him and they twined their arms about his neck, so great was the affection that moved them. The king also received him with such honor as was fitting, and the chieftains who thronged the palace rejoiced in the city.

But when Merlin saw such great crowds of men present, he was not able to endure them; he went mad again, and filled anew with fury he wanted to go to the woods, and he tried to get away by stealth. Then Rhydderch ordered him to be restrained and a guard posted over him, and his madness to be softened with the cither; and he stood about him grieving, and with imploring words begged the man to be sensible and to stay with him, and not to long for the grove or to live like a wild beast, or to want to abide under the trees when he might hold a royal scepter and rule over a warlike people. After that he promised that he would give him many gifts, and he ordered people to bring him clothing and birds, dogs and swift horses, gold and shining gems, and cups that Wayland [the Smith] had engraved in the city of Segontium [*Carnarvon, Wales*]. Every one of these things Rhydderch offered to the prophet and urged him to stay with him and leave the woods.

The prophet rejected these gifts, saying, "Let the dukes who are troubled by their own poverty have these, they who are not satisfied with a moderate amount but desire a great deal. To these gifts I prefer the groves and broad oaks of Calidon, and the lofty mountains with green pastures at their feet. Those are the things that please me, not these of yours—take these away with you, King Rhydderch. My Calidonian forest rich in nuts, the forest that I prefer to everything else, shall have me."

Finally, since the king could not retain the sad man by any gifts, he ordered him to be bound with a strong chain lest, if free, he might seek the deserted groves. The prophet, when he felt the chains around him and he could not go as a free man to the Calidonian forests, straightway fell to grieving and remained sad and silent, and took all joy from his face so that he did not utter a word or smile.

Meanwhile the queen was going through the hall looking for the king, and he, as was proper, greeted her as she came and took her by the hand and bade her sit down, and, embracing her, pressed her lips in a kiss. In so doing he turned his face toward her and saw a leaf hanging in her hair; he reached out his fingers, took it and threw it on the ground, and jested joyfully with the woman he loved. The prophet turned his eyes in that direction and smiled, and made the men standing about look at him in wonder since he was not in the habit of smiling. The king too wondered and urged the madman to tell the cause of his sudden laugh, and he added to his words many gifts. The other was silent and put off explaining his laugh. But more and more Rhydderch continued to urge him with riches and with entreaties until at length the prophet, vexed at him, said in return for his gift, "A miser loves a gift and a greedy man labors to get one; these are easily corrupted by gifts and bend their minds in any direction they are bidden to. What they have is not enough for them, but for me the acorns of pleasant Calidon and the shining fountains flowing through fragrant meadows are sufficient. I am not attracted by gifts; let the miser take his, and unless liberty is given me and I go back to the green woodland valleys, I shall refuse to explain my laughter."

Therefore when Rhydderch found that he could not influence the prophet by any gift, and he could not find out the reason for the laughter, straightway he ordered the chains to be loosed and gave him permission to seek the deserted groves, that he might be willing to give the desired explanation. Then Merlin, rejoicing that he could go, said, "This is the reason I laughed, Rhydderch. You were by a single act both praiseworthy and blameworthy. When just now you removed the leaf that the queen had in her hair without knowing, it, you acted more faithfully toward her than she did toward you when she went under the bush where lover met her and lay with her; and while she was lying there supine with her hair spread out, by chance there caught in it the leaf that you, not knowing all this, removed."

Rhydderch suddenly became sad at this accusation and turned his face from her and cursed the day he had married her. But she, not at all moved, hid her shame behind a smiling face and said to her husband, "Why are you sad, my love? Why do you become so angry over this thing and blame me unjustly, and believe a madman who, lacking sound sense, mixes lies with the truth? The man who believes him becomes many times more a fool than he is. Now then, watch, and if I am not mistaken I will show you that he is crazy and has not spoken the truth."

There was in the hall a certain boy, one of many, and the ingenious woman catching sight of him straightway thought of a novel trick by which she might convict her brother of falsehood. So she ordered the boy to come in and asked her brother to predict by what death the lad should die. He answered, "Dearest sister, he shall die, when a man, by falling from a high rock."

Smiling at these words, she ordered the boy to go away and take off the clothes he was wearing and put on others and to cut off his long hair; she bade him come back to them thus that he might seem to them a different person. The boy obeyed her, for he came back to them with his clothes changed as he had been ordered to do. Soon the queen asked her brother again, "Tell your dear sister what the death of this boy will be like." Merlin answered, "This boy when he grows up shall, while out of his mind, meet with a violent death in a tree."

When he had finished she said to her husband, "Could this false prophet lead you so far astray as to make you believe that I had committed so great a crime? And if you will notice with how much sense he has spoken this about the boy, you will believe that the things he said about me were made up so that he might get away to the woods. Far be it from me to do such a thing! I shall keep my bed chaste, and chaste shall I always be while the breath of life is in me. I convicted him of falsehood when I asked him about the death of the boy. Now I shall do it again; pay attention and judge."

When she had said this she told the boy in an aside to go out and put on woman's clothing, and to come back thus. Soon the boy left and did as he was bid, for he came back in woman's clothes just as though he were a woman, and he stood in front of Merlin to whom the queen said banteringly, "Say brother, tell me about the death of this girl." "Girl or not she shall die in the river," said her brother to her, which made King Rhydderch laugh at his reasoning; since when asked about the death of a single boy Merlin had predicted three different kinds. Therefore Rhydderch thought he had spoken falsely about the queen, and did not believe him, but grieved, and hated the fact that he had trusted him and had condemned his beloved. The queen, seeing this, forgave him and kissed and caressed him and made him joyful.

Meanwhile Merlin planned to go to the woods, and he left his dwelling and ordered the gates to be opened; but his sister stood in his way and with rising tears begged him to remain with her for a while and to put aside his madness. The hard-hearted man would not desist from his project but kept trying to open the doors, and he strove to leave and raged and fought and by his clamor forced the servants to open. At length, since no one could hold him back when he wanted to go, the queen quickly ordered Guendoloena, who was absent, to come to make him desist. She came and on her knees begged him to remain; but he spurned her prayers and would not stay, nor would he, as he was accustomed to do, look upon her with a joyful face. She grieved and dissolved in tears and tore her hair, and scratched her cheeks with her nails and rolled on the ground as though dying. The queen seeing this said to him, "This Guendoloena who is dying thus for you, what shall she do? Shall she marry again or do you bid her remain a widow, or go with you wherever you are going? For she will go, and with you she will joyfully inhabit the groves and the green woodland meadows provided she has your love."

To this the prophet answered, "Sister, I do not want a cow that pours out water in a broad fountain like the urn of the Virgin in summer-time, nor shall I change my care as Orpheus once did when Eurydice gave her baskets to the boys to hold before she swam back across the Stygian sands. Freed from both of you I shall remain without the taint of love. Let her therefore be given a proper opportunity to marry and let him whom she shall choose have her. But let the man who marries her be careful that he never gets in my way or comes near me; let him keep away for fear lest if I happen to meet him he may feel my flashing sword. But when the day of the solemn wedding comes and the different viands are distributed to the guests, I shall be present in person, furnished with seemly gifts, and I shall profusely endow Guendoloena when she is given away." When he had finished he said farewell to each of them and went away, and with no one to hinder him he went back to the woods he longed for.

Guendoloena remained sadly in the door watching him and so did the queen, both moved by what had happened to their friend, and they marveled that a madman should be so familiar with secret things and should have known of the love affair of his sister. Nevertheless they thought that he lied about the death of the boy, since he told of three different deaths when he should have told of one. Therefore his speech seemed for long years to be an empty one until the time when the boy grew to manhood; then it was made apparent to all and convincing to many. For while he was hunting with his dogs he caught sight of a stag hiding in a grove of trees; he loosed the dogs who, as soon as they saw the stag, climbed through unfrequented ways and filled the air with their baying. He urged on his horse with his spurs and followed after, and urged on the huntsmen, directing them now with his horn and now with his voice, and he bade them go more quickly. There was a high mountain surrounded on all sides by rocks with a stream flowing through the plain at its foot; thither the animal fled until he came to the river, seeking a hiding place after the usual manner of its kind. The young man pressed on and passed straight over the mountain, hunting for the stag among the rocks lying about. Meanwhile it happened, while his impetuosity was leading him on, that his horse slipped from a high rock and the man fell over a precipice into the river, but so that one of his feet caught in a tree, and the rest of his body was submerged in the stream. Thus he fell, and was drowned, and hung from a tree, and by this threefold death made the prophet a true one.

The latter meanwhile had gone to the woods and was living like a wild beast, subsisting on frozen moss, in the snow, in the rain, in the cruel blasts of the wind. And this pleased him more than administering laws throughout his cities and ruling over fierce people. Meanwhile Guendoloena, since her husband was leading a life like this with his woodland flock through the passing years, was [to be] married in accordance with her husband's permission.

It was night and the horns of the bright moon were shining, and all the lights of the vault of heaven were gleaming; the air was clearer than usual, for cruel, frigid Boreas had driven away the clouds and had made the sky serene again and had dried up the mists with his arid breath. From the top of a lofty mountain the prophet was regarding the courses of the stars, speaking to himself out in the open air. "What does this ray of Mars mean? Does its fresh redness mean that one king is dead and that there shall be another? So I see it, for Constantine has died and his nephew Conan, through an evil fate and the murder of his uncle, has taken the crown and is king. And you, highest Venus, who slipping along within your ordered limits beneath the zodiac are accompanying the sun in his course, what about this double ray of yours that is cleaving the air? Does not its division indicate a severing of my love? Such a ray indeed shows that loves are divided. Perhaps Guendoloena has left me in my absence and now clings to another man and rejoices in his embraces. So I lose; so another enjoys her. So my rights are taken away from me while I dally. So it is surely, for a slothful lover is beaten by one who is not slothful or absent but is right on hand. But I am not jealous; let her marry now under favorable auspices and let her enjoy her new husband with my permission. And when tomorrow's sun shines I will go and take with me the gift I promised her when I left."

So he spoke and went about all the woods and groves and collected a herd of stags in a single line, and the deer and she-goats likewise, and he himself mounted a stag. And when day dawned he came quickly, driving the line before him to the place where Guendoloena was to be married. When he arrived he forced the stags to stand patiently outside the gates while he cried aloud, "Guendoloena! Guendoloena! Come! Your presents are looking for you!" Guendoloena therefore came quickly, smiling and marvelling that the man was riding on the stag and that it obeyed him, and that he could get together so large a number of animals and drive them before him just as a shepherd does the sheep that he is in the habit of driving to the pastures.

The bridegroom stood watching from a lofty window and marvelling at the rider on his seat, and he laughed. But when the prophet saw him and understood who he was, at once he wrenched the horns from the stag he was riding and shook them and threw them at the man and completely smashed his head in, and killed him and drove out his life into the air. With a quick blow of his heels he set the stag to flying and was on his way back to the woods. At these happenings the servants rushed out from all sides and quickly followed the prophet through the fields. But he ran ahead so fast that he would have reached the woods untouched if a river had not been in his way; but while his beast was hurriedly leaping over the torrent Merlin slipped from his back and fell into the rapid waves. The servants lined the shore and captured him as he swam, and bound him and took him home and gave him to his sister.

The prophet, captured in this way, became sad and wanted to go back to the woods, and he fought to break his bonds and refused to smile or to take food or drink, and by his sadness he made his sister sad. Rhydderch, therefore, seeing him drive all joy from him and refuse to taste of the banquets that had been prepared for him, took pity on him and ordered him to be led out into the city, through the market place among the people, in the hope that he might be cheered up by going and seeing the novelties that were being sold there.

After he had been taken out and was going away from the palace he saw before a door a servant of a poor appearance, the doorkeeper, asking with trembling lips of all the passers-by some money with which to get his clothes mended. The prophet thereupon stood still and laughed, wondering at the poor man. When he had gone on from here he saw a young man holding some new shoes and buying some pieces of leather to patch them with. Then he laughed again and refused to go further through the market-place to be stared at by the people he was watching. But he yearned for the woods, toward which he frequently looked back, and to which, although forbidden, he tried to direct his steps.

The servants returned home and told that he had laughed twice and also that he had tried to get away to the woods. Rhydderch, who wished to know what he had meant by his laughter, quickly gave orders for his bonds to be loosed and gave him permission to go back to his accustomed woods if only he would explain why he laughed. The prophet, now quite joyful, answered, "The doorkeeper was sitting outside the doors in well-worn clothing and kept asking those who went by to give him something to buy clothes with, just as though he had been a pauper, and all the time he was secretly a rich man and had under him hidden piles of coins. That is what I laughed at; turn up the ground under him and you will find coins preserved there for a long time. From there they led me further toward the market place, and I saw a man buying some shoes and also some patches so that after the shoes were worn out and had holes in them from use he might mend them and make them fit for service again. This too I laughed at since the poor man will not be able to use the shoes nor," he added, "the patches, since he is already drowned in the waves and is floating toward the shore; go and you will see."

Rhydderch, wishing to test the man's sayings, ordered his servants to go quickly along the bank of the river, so that if they should chance to find such a man drowned by the shore they might at once bring him word. They obeyed the king's orders, for going along the river they found a drowned man in a waste patch of sand, and returned home and reported the fact to him. But the king meanwhile, after sending away the doorkeeper, had dug and turned up the ground and found a treasure placed under it, and laughingly he worshipped the prophet.

After these things had happened the prophet was making haste to go to the woods he was accustomed to, hating the people in the city. The queen advised him to stay with her and to put off his desired trip to the woods until the cold of white winter, which was then at hand, should be over, and summer should return again with its tender fruits on which he could live while the weather grew warm from the sun. He refused, and desirous of departing and scorning the winter he said to her, "O dear sister, why do you labor to hold me back? Winter with his tempests cannot frighten me, nor icy Boreas when he rages with his cruel blasts and suddenly injures the flocks of sheep with hail; neither does Auster disturb me when its rain clouds shed their waters. Why should I not seek the deserted groves and the green woodlands? Content with a little I can endure the frost. There under the leaves of the trees among the odorous blossoms I shall take pleasure in lying through the summer; but lest I lack food in winter you might build me a house in the woods and have servants in it to wait on me and prepare me food when the ground refuses to produce grain or the trees fruit. Before the other buildings build me a remote one with seventy doors and as many windows through which I may watch fire-breathing Phoebus and Venus and the stars gliding from the heavens by night, all of whom shall show me what is going to happen to the people of the kingdom. And let the same number of scribes be at hand, trained to take my dictation, and let them be attentive to record my prophecy on their tablets. You too are to come often, dear sister, and then you can relieve my hunger with food and drink." After he had finished speaking he departed hastily for the woods.

His sister obeyed him and built the place he had asked for, and the other houses and whatever else he had bid her. But he, while the apples remained and Phoebus was ascending higher through the stars, rejoiced to remain beneath the leaves and to wander through the groves with their soothing breezes. Then winter came, harsh with icy winds, and despoiled the ground and the trees of all their fruit, and Merlin lacked food because the rains were at hand and he came, sad and hungry, to the aforesaid place. Thither the queen often repaired and rejoiced to bring her brother both food and drink. He, after he had refreshed himself with various kinds of edibles, would arise and express his approval of his sister. Then wandering about the house he would look at the stars while he prophesied things like these, which he knew were going to come to pass.

"O madness of the Britons whom a plenitude, always excessive, of riches exalts more than is seemly! They do not wish to enjoy peace but are stirred up by the Fury's goad. They engage in civil wars and battles between relatives, and permit the churches of the Lord to fall into ruin; the holy bishops they drive into remote lands. The nephews of the Boar of Cornwall cast everything into confusion, and setting snares for each other engage in a mutual slaughter with their wicked swords. They do not wish to wait to get possession of the kingdom lawfully, but seize the crown. The fourth from them shall be more cruel and more harsh still; him shall a wolf from the sea conquer in fight and shall drive defeated beyond the Severn through the kingdoms of the barbarians. This latter shall besiege Cirencester with a blockade and with sparrows, and shall overthrow its walls to their very bases. He shall seek the Gauls in his ship, but shall die beneath the weapon of a king. Rhydderch shall die, after whom discord shall hold the Scots and the Cumbrians for a long time until Cumbria shall be granted to his growing tusk. The Welsh shall attack the men of Gwent, and afterwards those of Cornwall, and no law shall restrain them. Wales shall rejoice in the shedding of blood; O people always hateful to God, why do you rejoice in bloodshed? Wales shall compel brothers to fight and to condemn their own relatives to a wicked death. The troops of the Scots shall often cross the Humber and, putting aside all sentiment, shall kill those who oppose them. Not with impunity, however, for the leader shall be killed; he shall have the name of a horse and because of that fact shall be fierce. His heir shall be expelled and shall depart from our territories. Scots, sheathe your swords which you bare too readily; your strength shall be unequal to that of our fierce people. The city of Dumbarton shall be destroyed and no king shall repair it for an age until the Scot shall be subdued in war. Carlisle, spoiled of its shepherd, shall lie vacant until the scepter of the Lion shall restore its pastoral staff. Segontium and its towers and mighty palaces shall lament in ruins until the Welsh return to their former domains. Porchester shall see its broken walls in its harbor until a rich man with the tooth of a wolf shall restore it. The city of Richborough shall lie spread out on the shore of its harbor and a man from Flanders shall reestablish it with his crested ship. The fifth from him shall rebuild the walls of St. David's and shall bring back to her the pall lost for many years. The City of the Legions shall fall into thy bosom, O Severn, and shall lose her citizens for a long time, and these the Bear in the Lamb shall restore to her when he shall come.

Saxon kings shall expel the citizens and shall hold cities, country, and houses for a long time. From among them thrice three dragons shall wear the crown. Two hundred monks shall perish in Leicester and the Saxon shall drive out her ruler and leave vacant her walls. He who first among the Angles shall wear the diadem of Brutus shall repair the city laid waste by slaughter. A fierce people shall forbid the sacrament of confirmation throughout the country, and in the house of God shall place images of the gods. Afterward Rome shall bring God back through the medium of a monk, and a holy priest shall sprinkle the buildings with holy water and shall restore them again and shall place shepherds in them. Thereafter many of them shall obey the commands of the divine law and shall enjoy heaven by right. An impious people full of poison shall violate that settlement and shall violently mix together right and wrong. They shall sell their sons and their kinsmen into the furthest countries beyond the sea and shall incur the wrath of the Thunderer. O wretched crime! that man whom the Founder of the world created with liberty, deeming him worthy of heaven, should be sold like an ox and be dragged away with a rope. You miserable man who turned traitor to your master when first you came to the throne, you shall yield to God. The Danes shall come upon [you] with their fleet, and after subduing the people shall reign for a short time and shall then be defeated and retire. Two shall rule over them whom the serpent, forgetful of his treaty, shall strike with the sting in his tail instead of with the garland of his scepter.

"Then the Normans, sailing over the water in their wooden ships, bearing their faces in front and in back, shall fiercely attack the Angles with their iron tunics and their sharp swords, and shall destroy them and possess the field. They shall subjugate many realms to themselves and shall rule foreign peoples for a time until the Fury, flying all about, shall scatter her poison over them. Then peace and faith and all virtue shall depart, and on all sides throughout the country the citizens shall engage in battles. Man shall betray man and no one shall be found a friend. The husband, despising his wife, shall draw near to harlots, and the wife despising her husband shall marry whom she desires. There shall be no honor kept for the church and the order shall perish. Then shall bishops bear arms, and armed camps shall be built. Men shall build towers and walls in holy ground, and they shall give to the soldiers what should belong to the needy. Carried away by riches they shall run along on the path of worldly things and shall take from God what the holy bishop shall forbid. Three shall wear the diadem, after whom shall be the favor of the newcomers. A fourth shall be in authority whom awkward piety shall injure until he shall be clothed in his father, so that girded with boar's teeth he shall cross the shadow of the helmeted man. Four shall be anointed, seeking in turn the highest things, and two shall succeed who shall so wear the diadem that they shall induce the Gauls to make war on them. The sixth shall overthrow the Irish and their walls, and pious and prudent shall renew the people and the cities. All these things I formerly predicted more at length to Vortigern in explaining to him the mystic war of the two dragons when we sat on the banks of the drained pool. But you, dear sister, go home to see the king dying and bid Taliesin come, as I wish to talk over many things with him; for he has recently come from the land of Brittany where he learned sweet philosophy of Gildas the Wise."

Ganieda returned home and found that Taliesin had returned and the prince was dead and the servants were sad. She fell down lamenting among her friends and tore her hair and cried, "Women, lament with me the death of Rhydderch and weep for a man such as our earth has not produced hitherto in our age so far as we know. He was a lover of peace, for he so ruled a fierce people that no violence was done to any one by any one else. He treated the holy priest with just moderation and permitted the highest and the lowest to be governed by law. He was generous, for he gave away much and kept scarcely anything. He was all things to all men, doing whatever was seemly; flower of knights, glory of kings, pillar of the kingdom. Woe is me! for what you were—now so unexpectedly you have become food for worms, and your body moulders in the urn. Is this the bed prepared for you after fine silks? Is it true that your white flesh and royal limbs will be covered by a cold stone, that you will be nothing but dust and bones? So it is, for the miserable lot of mankind goes on throughout the years so that they cannot be brought back to their former estate. Therefore there is no profit in the bravery of the transient world that flees and returns, deceives and injures the mighty. The bee anoints with its honey what it afterwards stings. So also those whom the glory of the world caresses as it departs it deceives and smites with its disagreeable sting. That which excels is of brief duration, what it has does not endure; like running water everything that is of service passes away. What is a rose if it blushes, a snowy lily if it blooms, a man or a horse or anything else if it is fair! These things should be referred to the Creator, not to the world. Happy therefore are those who remain firm in a pious heart and serve God and renounce the world. To them Christ who reigns without end, the Creator of all things, shall grant to enjoy perpetual honor. Therefore I leave you, ye nobles, ye lofty walls, household gods, sweet sons, and all the things of the world. In company with my brother I shall dwell in the woods and shall worship God with a joyful heart, clothed in a black mantle." So she spoke, giving her husband his due, and she inscribed on his tomb this verse, "Rhydderch the Generous, than whom there was no one more generous in the world, a great man rests in this small urn."

Meanwhile Taliesin had come to see Merlin the prophet, who had sent for him to find out what wind or rainstorm was coming up, for both together were drawing near and the clouds were thickening. He drew the following illustrations under the guidance of Minerva his associate.

"Out of nothing the Creator of the world produced four [elements] that they might be the prior cause as well as the material for creating all things when they were joined together in harmony; the heaven which He adorned with stars and which stands on high and embraces everything like the shell surrounding a nut; then he made the air, fit for forming sounds, through the medium of which day and night present the stars; the sea which girds the land in four circles, and with its mighty refluence so strikes the air as to generate the winds which are said to be four in number; as a foundation He placed the earth, standing by its own strength and not lightly moved, which is divided into five parts, whereof the middle one is not habitable because of the heat and the two furthest are shunned because of their cold. To the last two He gave a moderate temperature, and these are inhabited by men and birds and herds of wild beasts. He added clouds to the sky so that they might furnish sudden showers to make the fruits of the trees and of the ground grow with their gentle sprinkling. With the help of the sun these are filled like water skins from the rivers by a hidden law and then, rising through the upper air, they pour out the water they have taken up, driven by the force of the winds. From them come rainstorms, snow, and round hail when the cold damp wind breathes out its blasts which, penetrating the clouds, drive out the streams just as they make them. Each of the winds takes to itself a nature of its own from its proximity to the zone where it is born. Beyond the firmament in which He fixed the shining stars He placed the ethereal heaven and gave it as a habitation to troops of angels whom the worthy contemplation and marvellous sweetness of God refresh throughout the ages. This also He adorned with stars and the shining sun, laying down the law by which the star should run within fixed limits through the part of heaven entrusted to it. He afterwards placed beneath this the airy heavens, shining with the lunar body, which throughout their high places abound in troops of spirits who sympathize or rejoice with us as things go well or ill. They are accustomed to carry the prayers of men through the air and to beseech God to have mercy on them, and to bring back intimations of God's will, either in dreams or by voice or by other signs, through doing which they become wise. The space beyond the moon abounds in evil demons, who are skilled to cheat and deceive and tempt us; often they assume a body made of air and appear to us and many things often follow. They even hold intercourse with women and make them pregnant, generating in an unholy manner. So therefore He made the heavens to be inhabited by three orders of spirits that each one might look out for something and renew the world from the renewed seed of things.

"The sea too He distinguished by various forms that from itself it might produce the forms of things, generating throughout the ages. Indeed, part of it burns and part freezes and the third part, getting a moderate temperature from the other two, ministers to our needs. That part which burns surrounds a gulf and fierce people, and its divers streams, flowing back, separate this from the orb of earth, increasing fire from fire. Thither descend those who transgress the laws and reject God; whither their perverse will leads them they go, eager to destroy what is forbidden to them. There stands the stern-eyed judge holding his equal balance and giving to each one his merits and his deserts. The second part, which freezes, rolls about the foreshorn sands which it is the first to generate from the nearby vapor when it is mingled with the rays of Venus's star. This star, the Arabs say, makes shining gems when it passes through the Fishes while its waters look back at the flames. These gems by their virtues benefit the people who wear them, and make many well and keep them so. These too the Maker distinguished by their kinds (as He did all things), that we might discern from their forms and from their colors of what kinds they are and of what manifest virtues. The third form of the sea which circles our orb furnishes us many good things owing to its proximity. For it nourishes fishes and produces salt in abundance, and bears back and forth ships carrying our commerce, by the profits of which the poor man becomes suddenly rich. It makes fertile the neighboring soil and feeds the birds who, they say, are generated from it along with the fishes and, although unlike, are moved by the laws of nature. The sea is dominated by them more than by the fishes, and they fly lightly up from it through space and seek the lofty regions. But its moisture drives the fishes beneath the waves and keeps them there, and does not permit them to live when they get out into the dry light. These too the Maker distinguished according to their species and to the different ones gave each his nature, whence through the ages they were to become admirable and healthful to the sick.

"For men say that the barbel restrains the heat of passion but makes blind those who eat it often. The thymallus, which has its name from the flower thyme, smells so that it betrays the fish that often eats of it until all the fishes in the river smell like itself. They say that the muraenas, contrary to all laws, are all of the feminine sex, yet they copulate and reproduce and multiply their offspring from a different kind of seed. For often snakes come together along the shore where they are, and they make the sound of pleasing hissing and, calling out the muraenas, join with them according to custom. It is also remarkable that the remora, half a foot long, holds fast the ship to which it adheres at sea just as though it were fast aground, and does not permit the vessel to move until it lets go; because of this power it is to be feared. And that which they call the swordfish because it does injury with its sharp beak people often fear to approach with a ship when it is swimming, for if it is captured it at once makes a hole in the vessel, cuts it in pieces, and sinks it suddenly in a whirlpool. The serra makes itself feared by ships because of its crest; it fixes to them as it swims underneath, cuts them to pieces and throws the pieces into the waves, wherefore its crest is to be feared like a sword. And the water dragon, which men say has poison under its wings, is to be feared by those who capture it; whenever it strikes it does harm by pouring out its poison. The torpedo is said to have another kind of destruction, for if any one touches it when it is alive, straightway his arms and his feet grow torpid and so do his other members and they lose their functions just as though they were dead, so harmful is the emanation of its body.

"To those and the other fishes God gave the sea, and He added to it many realms among the waves, which men inhabit and which are renowned because of the fertility which the earth produces there from its fruitful soil. Of these Britain is said to be the foremost and best, producing in its fruitfulness every single thing. For it bears crops which throughout the year give the noble gifts of fragrance for the use of man, and it has woods and glades with honey dripping in them, and lofty mountains and broad green fields, fountains and rivers, fishes and cattle and wild beasts, fruit trees, gems, precious metals, and whatever creative nature is in the habit of furnishing. Besides all these it has fountains healthful because of their hot waters which nourish the sick and provide pleasing baths, which quickly send people away cured with their sickness driven out. So Bladud established them when he held the scepter of the kingdom, and he gave them the name of his consort Alaron. These are of value to many sick people because of the healing of their water, but most of all to women, as often the water has demonstrated. Near to this island lies Thanet, which abounds in many things but lacks the death-dealing serpent, and if any of its earth is drunk mixed with wine it takes away poison. Our ocean also divides the Orkneys from us. These are divided into thirty-three islands by the sundering flood; twenty lack cultivation and others are cultivated. Thule receives its name "furthest" from the sun, because of the solstice which the summer sun makes there, turning its rays and shining no further, and taking away the day, so that always throughout the long night the air is full of shadows, and making a bridge congealed by the benumbing cold, which prevents the passage of ships.

"The most outstanding island after our own is said to be Ireland with its happy fertility. It is larger and produces no bees, and no birds except rarely, and it does not permit snakes to breed in it. Whence it happens that if earth or a stone is carried away from there and added to any other place it drives away snakes and bees. The island of Gades lies next to Herculean Gades, and there grows there a tree from whose bark a gum drips out of which gems are made, breaking all laws. The Hesperides are said to contain a watchful dragon who, men say, guards the golden apples under the leaves. The Gorgades are inhabited by women with goats' bodies who are said to surpass hares in the swiftness of their running. Argyre and Chryse bear, it is said, gold and silver just as Corinth does common stones. Ceylon blooms pleasantly because of its fruitful soil, for it produces two crops in a single year; twice it is summer, twice spring, twice men gather grapes and other fruits, and it is also most pleasing because of its shining gems. Tiles produces flowers and fruits in an eternal spring, green throughout the seasons.

"The island of apples which men call 'The Fortunate Isle' gets its name from the fact because it produces all things of itself; the fields there have no need of the ploughs of the farmers and all cultivation is lacking except what nature provides. Of its own accord it produces grain and grapes, and apple trees grow in its woods from the close-clipped grass. The ground of its own accord produces everything instead of merely grass, and people live there a hundred years or more. There nine sisters rule by a pleasing set of laws those who come to them from our country. She who is first of them is more skilled in the healing art, and excels her sisters in the beauty of her person. Morgen is her name, and she has learned what useful properties all the herbs contain, so that she can cure sick bodies. She also knows an art by which to change her shape, and to cleave the air on new wings like Daedalus; when she wishes she is at Brest, Chartres, or Pavia, and when she wills she slips down from the air onto your shores. And men say that she has taught mathematics to her sisters Moronoe, Mazoe, Gliten, Glitonea, Gliton, Tyronoe, [and] Thitis— Thitis best known for her cither. Thither after the battle of Camlan we took the wounded Arthur, guided by Barinthus to whom the waters and the stars of heaven were well known. With him steering the ship we arrived there with the prince, and Morgen received us with fitting honor, and in her chamber she placed the king on a golden bed and with her own hand she uncovered his honorable wound and gazed at it for a long time. At length she said that health could be restored to him if he stayed with her for a long time and made use of her healing art. Rejoicing, therefore, we entrusted the king to her and returning spread our sails to the favoring winds."

Merlin said in answer, "Dear friend, since that time how much the kingdom has endured from the violated oath, so that what it once was it no longer is! For by an evil fate the nobles are roused up and turned against each other's vitals, and they upset everything so that the abundance of riches has fled from the country and all goodness has departed, and the desolated citizens leave their walls empty. Upon them shall come the Saxon people, fierce in war, who shall again cruelly overthrow us and our cities, and shall violate God's law and his temples. For He shall certainly permit this destruction to come upon us because of our crimes, that He may correct the foolish."

Merlin had scarcely finished when Taliesin exclaimed, "Then the people should send some one to tell the chief to come back in a swift ship if he has recovered his strength, that he may drive off the enemy with his accustomed vigor and reestablish the citizens in their former peace."

"No," said Merlin, "not thus shall this people depart when once they have fixed their claws on our shores. For at first they shall enslave our kingdom and our people and our cities, and shall dominate them with their forces for many years. Nevertheless three from among our people shall resist with much courage and shall kill many, and in the end shall overcome them. But they shall not continue thus, for it is the will of the highest Judge that the Britons shall through weakness lose their noble kingdom for a long time, until Conan shall come in his chariot from Brittany, and Cadwalader the venerated leader of the Welsh, who shall join together Scots and Cumbrians, Cornishmen and men of Brittany in a firm league, and shall return to their people their lost crown, expelling the enemy and renewing the times of Brutus, and shall deal with the cities in accordance with their consecrated laws. And the kings shall begin again to conquer remote peoples and to subjugate their own realms to themselves in mighty conflict."

"No one shall then be alive of those who are now living," said Taliesin, "nor do I think that any one has seen so many savage battles between fellow citizens as you have."

"That is so," said Merlin, "for I have lived a long time, seeing many of them, both of our own people among themselves and of the barbarians who disturb everything. And I remember the crime when Constans was betrayed and the small brothers Uther and Ambrosius fled across the water. At once wars began in the kingdom which now lacked a leader, for Vortigern of Gwent, the consul, was leading his troops against all the nations so that he might have the leadership of them, and was inflicting a wretched death upon the harmless peasants. At length with sudden violence he seized the crown after putting to death many of the nobles, and he subdued the whole kingdom to himself. But those who were allied to the brothers by blood relationship, offended at this, began to set fire to all the cities of the ill-fated prince and to perturb his kingdom with savage soldiery, and they would not permit him to possess it in peace. Disquieted therefore since he could not withstand the rebellious people, he prepared to invite to the war men from far away with whose aid he might be able to meet his enemies.

"Soon there came from divers parts of the world warlike bands whom he received with honor. The Saxon people, in fact, arriving in their curved keels had come to serve him with their helmeted soldiery. They were led by two courageous brothers, Horsus and Hengist, who afterwards with wicked treachery harmed the people and the cities. For after this, by serving the king with industry, they won him over to themselves, and seeing the people moved by a quarrel that touched them closely they were able to subjugate the king; then turning their ferocious arms upon the people they broke faith, and killed the princes by a premeditated fraud while they were sitting with them after calling them together to make peace and a treaty with them, and the prince they drove over the top of the snowy mountain. These are the things I had begun to prophesy to him would happen to the kingdom. Next, roaming abroad they set fire to the houses of the nation, and strove to make everything subject to themselves.

"But when Vortimer saw how great was the peril of his country, and saw his father expelled from the hall of Brutus, he took the crown, with the assent of the people, and attacked the savage tribes that were crushing them, and by many battles forced these to return to Thanet where the fleet was that had bought them. But in their flight fell the warrior Horsus and many others, slain by our men. The king followed them and taking his stand before Thanet besieged it by land and sea, but without success, for the enemy suddenly got possession of their fleet and with violence broke out and, led over the sea, they regained their own country in haste. Therefore, since he had conquered the enemy in victorious war, Vortimer became a ruler to be respected in the world, and he treated his kingdom with just restraint. But Hengist's sister, Rowena, seeing with indignation these successes and protected by deceit, mixed poison, becoming on her brother's account a malignant step-mother, and she gave it to Vortimer to drink, and killed him by the draught. At once she sent across the water to her brother to tell him to come back with so many and such great multitudes that he would be able to conquer the warlike natives. This therefore he did, for he came with such force against our army that he took booty from everybody until he was loaded with it, and he thoroughly destroyed by fire the houses throughout the country.

"While these things were happening Uther and Ambrosius were in Breton territory with King Biducus and they had already girded on their swords and were proved fit for war, and had associated with themselves troops from all directions so that they might seek their native land and put to flight the people who were busy wasting their patrimony. So they gave their boats to the wind and the sea, and landed for the protection of their subjects; they drove Vortigern through the regions of Wales and shut him up in his tower and burned both him and it. Then they turned their swords upon the Angles and many times when they met them they defeated them, and on the other hand they were often defeated by them. At length in a hand to hand conflict our men with great effort attacked the enemy and defeated them decisively, and killed Hengist, and by the will of Christ they triumphed.

"After these things had been done, the kingdom and its crown were with the approval of clergy and laity given to Ambrosius, and he ruled justly in all things, but after the space of four years had elapsed he was betrayed by his doctor and died from drinking poison. His younger brother Uther succeeded him and at first was unable to maintain his kingdom in peace, for the perfidious people, accustomed by now to return, came and laid waste everything with their usual phalanx. Uther fought them in savage battles and drove them conquered across the water with returning oars. Soon he put aside strife and reestablished peace and begat a son who afterwards was so eminent that he was second to none in uprightness. Arthur was his name and he held the kingdom for many years after the death of his father Uther, and this he did with great grief and labor, and with the slaughter of many men in many wars. For while the aforesaid chief lay ill, from Anglia came a faithless people who with the sword subdued all the country and the regions across the Humber. Arthur was a boy and on account of his youth he was not able to defeat such a force. Therefore after seeking the advice of clergy and laity he sent to Hoel, King of Brittany, and asked him to come to his aid with a swift fleet, for they were united by ties of blood and friendship so that each was bound to relieve the distresses of the other. Hoel therefore quickly collected for the war fierce men from every side and came to us with many thousands, and joining with Arthur he attacked the enemy often, and drove them back and made a terrible slaughter. With his help Arthur was secure and strong among all the troops when he attacked the enemy, whom at length he conquered and forced to return to their own country, and he quieted his own kingdom by the moderation of his laws.

"Soon after this struggle he changed the scene of the war, and subdued the Scots and Irish and all these warlike countries by means of the forces he had brought. He also subjugated the Norwegians far away across the broad seas, and the Danes whom he had visited with his hated fleet. He conquered the people of the Gauls after killing Frollo to whom the Roman power had given the care of that country; the Romans, too, who were seeking to make war on his country, he fought against and conquered, and killed the procurator Hiberius Lucius who was then a colleague of Legnis the general, and who by the command of the Senate had come to bring the territories of the Gauls under their power.

"Meanwhile the faithless and foolish custodian Modred had commenced to subdue our kingdom to himself, and was making unlawful love to the king's wife. For the king, desiring, as men say, to go across the water to attack the enemy, had entrusted the queen and the kingdom to him. But when the report of such a great evil came to his ears, he put aside his interest in the wars and, returning home, landed with many thousand men and fought with his nephew and drove him flying across the water. There the traitor, after collecting Saxons from all sides, began to battle with his lord, but he fell, betrayed by the unholy people confiding in whom he had undertaken such big things. How great was the slaughter of men and the grief of women whose sons fell in that battle! After it the king, mortally wounded, left his kingdom and, sailing across the water with you as you have related, came to the court of the maidens. Each of the two sons of Modred, desiring to conquer the kingdom for himself, began to wage war and each in turn slew those who were near of kin to him. Then Duke Constantine, nephew of the king, rose up fiercely against them and ravaged the people and the cities, and after having killed both of them by a cruel death ruled over the people and assumed the crown. But he did not continue in peace, since Conan his relative waged dire war on him and ravaged everything and killed the king and seized for himself those lands which he now governs weakly and without a plan."

While he was speaking thus the servants hurried in and announced to him that a new fountain had broken out at the foot of the mountains and was pouring out pure waters which were running though all the hollow valley and swirling through the fields as they slipped along. Both therefore quickly rose to see the new fountain, and having seen it Merlin sat down again on the grass and praised the spot and the flowing waters, and marvelled that they had come out of the ground in such a fashion. Soon afterward, becoming thirsty, he leaned down to the stream and drank freely and bathed his temples in its waves, so that the water passed through the passages of his bowels and stomach, settling the vapors within him, and at once he regained his reason and knew himself, and all his madness departed and the sense which had long remained torpid in him revived, and he remained what he had once been—sane and intact with his reason restored. Therefore, praising God, he turned his face toward the stars and uttered devout words of praise. "O King, through whom the machine of the starry heavens exists, through whom the sea and the land with its pleasing grass give forth and nourish their offspring and with their profuse fertility give frequent aid to mankind, through whom sense has returned and the error of my mind has vanished! I was carried away from myself and like a spirit I knew the acts of past peoples and predicted the future. Then since I knew the secrets of things and the flight of birds and the wandering motions of the stars and the gliding of the fishes, all this vexed me and denied a natural rest to my human mind by a severe law. Now I have come to myself and I seem to be moved with a vigor such as was wont to animate my limbs. Therefore, highest Father, I ought to be obedient to Thee, that I may show forth Thy most worthy praise from a worthy heart, always joyfully making joyful offerings. For twice Thy generous hand has benefitted me alone, in giving me the gift of this new fountain out of the green grass. For now I have the water which hitherto I lacked, and by drinking of it my brains have been made whole. But whence comes this virtue, O dear companion, that this new fountain breaks out thus, and makes me myself again who up to now was as though insane and beside myself?"

Taliesin answered, "The opulent Regulator of things divided the rivers according to their kinds, and added moreover to each a power of its own, that they might often prove of benefit to the sick. For there are fountains and rivers and lakes throughout the world which by their power cure many, and often do so. At Rome, for instance, flows swift Albula, with its health-giving steam which men say cures wounds with its sure healing. There is another fountain called Cicero's, which flows in Italy, which cures the eyes of all injuries. The Ethiopians also are said to have a pool which makes a face on which it is poured shine just as though from oil. Africa has a fountain commonly called Zama; a drink from it produces melodious voices by its sudden power. Lake Clitorius in Italy gives a distaste for wine; those who drink from the fountain of Chios are said to become dull. The land of Boeotia is said to have two fountains; the one makes the drinkers forgetful, the other makes them remember. The same country contains a lake so harmful with its dire plague that it generates madness and the heat of too much passion.

The fountain of Cyzicus drives away lust and the love of Venus. In the region of Campania there flow, it is said, rivers which when drunk of make the barren fruitful, and the same ones are said to take away madness from men. The land of the Ethiopians contains a fountain with a red stream; whoever drinks of this will come back demented. The fountain of Leinus never permits miscarriages. There are two fountains in Sicily, one of which makes girls sterile and the other makes them fruitful by its kindly law. There are two rivers in Thessaly of the greatest power; a sheep drinking of one turns black and is made white by the other, and any one drinking of both spends its life with a variegated fleece. There is a lake called Clitumnus in the Umbrian land which is said at times to produce large oxen, and in the Reatine Swamp the hooves of horses become hard as soon as they cross its sands. In the Asphalt Lake of Judaea bodies can never sink while life animates them, but on the other hand the land of India has a pool called Sida in which nothing floats but sinks at once to the bottom. And there is a Lake Aloe in which nothing sinks but all things float even if they are pieces of lead. The fountain of Marsida also compels stones to float. The River Styx flows from a rock and kills those who drink of it; the land of Arcadia bears testimony to this form of destruction. The fountain of Idumea, changing four times throughout the days, is said to vary its color by a strange rule; for it becomes muddy, then green, then the order changes and it turns red and then becomes clear with a beautiful stream. It is said to retain each one of these colors for three months as the years roll around. There is also a Lake Trogdytus whose waves flow out, three times in the day bitter, and three times sweet with a pleasant taste. From a fountain of Epirus torches are said to be lighted, and if extinguished to resume their light again. The fountain of the Garamantes is said to be so cold in the day time, and on the other hand so hot all night, that if forbids approach on account of its cold or its heat. There are also hot waters that threaten many because of the heat which they get when they flow through alum or sulphur which have a fiery power, pleasant for healing.

"God endowed the rivers with these powers and others so that they might be the means of quick healing for the sick, and so that they might make manifest with what power the Creator stands eminent among things while He works thus in them. I think that these waters are healthful in the highest degree and I think that they could afford a quick cure through the water that has thus broken out. They have up to now been flowing about through the dark hollows under the earth like many others that are said to trickle underground. Perhaps their breaking out is due to an obstacle getting in their way, or to the slipping of a stone or a mass of earth. I think that, in making their way back again, they have gradually penetrated the ground and have given us this fountain. You see many such flow along and return again underground and regain their caverns."

While they were doing these things a rumor ran all about that a new fountain had broken out in the woods of Calidon, and that drinking from it had cured a man who had for a long time been suffering from madness and had lived in these same woods after the manner of the wild beasts. Soon therefore the princes and the chieftains came to see it and to rejoice with the prophet who had been cured by the water. After they had informed him in detail of the status of his country and had asked him to resume his scepter, and to deal with his people with his accustomed moderation, he said, "Young men, my time of life, drawing on toward old age, and so possessing my limbs that with my weakened vigor I can scarce pass through the fields, does not ask this of me. I have already lived long enough, rejoicing in happy days while an abundance of great riches smiled profusely upon me. In that wood there stands an oak in its hoary strength which old age, that consumes everything, has so wasted away that it lacks sap and is decaying inwardly. I saw this when it first began to grow and I even saw the fall of the acorn from which it came, and a woodpecker standing over it and watching the branch. Here I have seen it grow of its own accord, watching it all, and fearing for it in these fields I marked the spot with my retentive mind. So you see I have lived a long time and now the weight of age holds me back and I refuse to reign again. When I remain under the green leaves the riches of Calidon delight me more than the gems that India produces, or the gold that Tagus is said to have on its shore, more than the crops of Sicily or the grapes of pleasant Methis, more than lofty turrets or cities girded with high walls or robes fragrant with Tyrian perfumes. Nothing pleases me enough to tear me away from my Calidon which in my opinion is always pleasant. Here shall I remain while I live, content with apples and grasses, and I shall purify my body with pious fastings that I may be worthy to partake of the life everlasting."

While he was speaking thus, the chiefs caught sight of long lines of cranes in the air, circling through space in a curved line in the shape of certain letters; they could be seen in marshalled squadron in the limpid air. Marvelling at these they asked Merlin to tell why it was that they were flying in such a manner.

Merlin presently said to them, "The Creator of the world gave to the birds as to many other things their proper nature, as I have learned by living in the woods for many days. It is therefore the nature of the cranes, as they go through the air, if many are present, that we often see them in their flight form a figure in one way or another. One, by calling, warns them to keep the formation as they fly, lest it break up and depart from the usual figure; when he becomes hoarse another takes his place. They post sentries at night and the watchman holds a pebble in his claws when he wishes to drive away sleep, and when they see any one they start up with a sudden clamor. The feathers of all of them grow black as they grow older. But the eagles, who get their name from the sharpness of their sight, are said to be of such keen vision, beyond all others, that they are able to gaze at the sun without flinching. They hang up their young in its rays wishing to know by his avoidance of them whether there exists among them one of inferior breeding. They remain on their wings over waters as high as the top of a mountain and they spy their prey in the lowest depths; straightway they descend rapidly through the void and seize the fish swimming as their inheritance demands. The vulture, thinking little of the commerce of the sexes, often conceives and bears (strange to say) without any seed of her spouse. Flying about on high in the manner of the eagle she scents with distended nostrils a dead body far across the water. This she has no horror of approaching in her flight, although she is slow, so that she may satiate herself with the prey she wishes for. This same bird also lives vigorous for a hundred years. The stork with its croaking voice is a messenger of spring; it is said to nourish its young so carefully that it takes out its own feathers and denudes its own breast. When winter comes men say it avoids the storms and approaches the shores of Asia, led by a crow. Its young feed it as it grows old because it fed them when it owed them this care. The swan, a bird most pleasing to sailors, excels all others in the sweetness of its music when it dies. Men say that in the country of the Hyperboreans it comes up close by being attracted by the sound of a zither played loudly along the shore. The ostrich deserts her eggs, which she places under the dust that they may be taken care of there when she herself neglects them. Thence the birds come into the world hatched by the sun instead of by their mother. The heron, when it fears the rain and the tempests, flies to the clouds to avoid such a peril; hence sailors say that it portends sudden rainstorms when they see it high up in the air. The phoenix by divine dispensation always lives as an unique bird, and in the land of the Arabs rises with a renewed body. When it grows old it goes to a place very warm from the heat of the sun and gets together a great heap of spices and builds itself a pyre, which it lights with rapid movements of its wings, and it settles down upon this and is completely consumed. The ashes of its body produce a bird, and in this way the phoenix is again renewed throughout the ages. The cinnamolgus when it wishes to build a nest brings cinnamon, and builds of that because of its undoubted strength. From this men are in the habit of driving it away with arrows, after which they remove the heap and sell it. The halcyon is a bird that frequents sea pools and builds its nest in time of winter; when it broods the seas are calm for seven days and the winds cease and the tempests, relaxed, hold off, furnishing placid quiet for the bird. The parrot is thought to utter human speech as its own call when no one is looking directly at it, and it mixes 'ave' and 'chaire' with jocose words. The pelican is a bird accustomed to kill its young and to lament for three days confused with grief. Then it tears its own body with its beak and, cutting the veins, lets out streams of blood with which it sprinkles the birds and brings them back to life. The Diomedae when they resound with tearful noise and make lament are said to portend the sudden death of kings or a great peril to the realm. And when they see anyone they know at once what he is, whether barbarian or Greek; for they approach a Greek with beatings of the wings and with caresses and they make a joyful noise, but they fly about the others on hostile wings and approach them with a horrible sound as though they were enemies. The Memnonides are said to go on a long flight every fifth year to the tomb of Memnon, and to lament the prince killed in the Trojan War. The shining Hercynia has a marvellous feather which gleams on a dark night like a lighted lamp, and shows the way if it is carried in front of a traveller. When the woodpecker makes a nest he pulls out of the tree nails and wedges that no one else can get out and the whole neighborhood resounds with his blows."

After he had finished speaking a certain madman came to them, either by accident or led there by fate; he filled the grove and the air with a terrific clamor and like a wild boar he foamed at the mouth and threatened to attack them. They quickly captured him and made him sit down by them that his remarks might move them to laughter and jokes. When the prophet looked at him more attentively he recollected who he was and groaned from the bottom of his heart, saying, "This is not the way he used to look when we were in the bloom of our youth, for at that time he was a fair, strong knight and one distinguished by his nobility and his royal race. Him and many others I had with me in the days of my wealth, and I was thought fortunate in having so many good companions, and I was. It happened one time while we were hunting in the lofty mountains of Arwystli that we came to an oak which rose in the air with its broad branches. A fountain flowed there, surrounded on all sides by green grass, whose waters were suitable for human consumption; we were all thirsty and we sat down by it and drank greedily of its pure waters. Then we saw some fragrant apples lying on the tender grass of the familiar bank of the fountain. The man who saw them first quickly gathered them up and gave them to me, laughing at the unexpected gift. I distributed to my companions the apples he had given to me, and I went without any because the pile was not big enough. The others to whom the apples had been given laughed and called me generous, and eagerly attacked and devoured them and complained because there were so few of them. Without any delay a miserable madness seized this man and all the others; they quickly lost their reason and like dogs bit and tore each other, and foamed at the mouth and rolled about on the ground in a demented state. Finally, they went away like wolves filling the vacant air with howlings. These apples I thought were intended for me and not for them, and later I found out that they were. At that time there was in that district a woman who had formerly been infatuated with me, and had satisfied her love for me during many years. After I had spurned her and had refused to cohabit with her she was suddenly seized with an evil desire to to me harm, and when with all her plotting she could not find any other means of approach, she placed the gifts smeared with poison by the fountain to which I was going to return, planning by this device to injure me if I should chance to find the apples on the grass and eat them. But my good fortune kept me from them, as I have just said. I pray you, make this man drink of the healthful waters of this new fountain so that, if by chance he get back his health, he may know himself and may, while his life lasts, labor with me in these glades in service to God." This, therefore, the leaders did, and the man who had come there raging drank the water, recovered, and cured at once recognized his friends.

Then Merlin said, "You must now go on in the service of God who restored you as you now see yourself, you who for so many years lived in the desert like a wild beast, going about without a sense of shame. Now that you have recovered your reason, do not shun the bushes or the green glades which you inhabited while you were mad, but stay with me that you may strive to make up in service to God for the days that the force of madness took from you. From now on all things shall be in common between you and me in this service so long as either lives."

At this Maeldinus (for that was the man's name) said, "Reverend father, I do not refuse to do this, for I shall joyfully stay in the woods with you, and shall worship God with my whole mind, while that spirit, for which I shall render thanks to your ministry, governs my trembling limbs."

"And I shall make a third with you, and shall despise the things of the world," said Taliesin. "I have spent enough time living in vain, and now is the time to restore me to myself under your leadership. But you, lords, go away and defend your cities; it is not fitting that you should disturb beyond measure our quiet with your talk. You have applauded my friend enough."

The chiefs went away, and the three remained with Ganieda, the prophet's sister, making a fourth, she who at length had assumed and was leading a seemly life after the death of the king who so recently had ruled so many people by the laws he administered. Now with her brother there was nothing more pleasant to her than the woods. She too was at times elevated by the spirit so that she often prophesied to her friends concerning the future of the kingdom. Thus on a certain day when she stood in her brother's hall and saw the windows of the house shining with the sun, she uttered these doubtful words from her doubtful breast.

"I see the city of Oxford filled with helmed men, and the holy men and the holy bishops bound in fetters by the advice of the Council, and men shall admire the shepherd's tower reared on high, and he shall be forced to open it to no purpose and to his own injury. I see Lincoln walled in by savage soldiery and two men shut up in it, one of whom escapes to return with a savage tribe and their chief to the walls to conquer the cruel soldiers after capturing their leader. O what a shame it is that the stars should capture the sun, under whom they sink down, compelled neither by force nor by war! I see two moons in the air near Winchester and two lions acting with too great ferocity, and one man looking at two and another at the same number, and preparing for battle and standing opposed. The others rise up and attack the fourth fiercely and savagely but not one of them prevails, for he stands firm and moves his shield and fights back with his weapons and as victor straightway defeats his triple enemy. Two of them he drives across the frozen regions of the north while he gives to the third the mercy that he asks, so that the stars flee through all portions of the fields. The Boar of Brittany, protected by aged oak, takes away the moon, brandishing swords behind her back. I see two stars engaging in combat with wild beasts beneath the hill of Urien where the people of Gwent and those of Deira met in the reign of the great Coel. O with what sweat the men drip and with what blood the ground while wounds are being given to the foreigners! One star collides with the other and falls into the shadow, hiding its light from the renewed light. Alas, what dire famine shall come, so that the north shall inflame her vitals and empty them of the strength of her people. It begins with the Welsh and goes through the chief parts of the kingdom, and forces the wretched people to cross the water. The calves accustomed to live on the milk of the Scottish cows that are dying from the pestilence shall flee. Normans depart and cease to bear weapons through our native realm with your cruel soldiery. There is nothing left with which to feed your greed, for you have consumed everything that creative nature has produced in her happy fertility. Christ, aid thy people! Restrain the lions and give to the country quiet peace and the cessation of wars."

She did not stop with this and her companions wondered at her, and her brother, who soon came to her, spoke approvingly with friendly words in this manner, "Sister, does the spirit wish you to foretell future things, since he has closed up my mouth and my book? Therefore this task is given to you; rejoice in it, and under my favor devoted to him speak everything."

I have brought this song to an end. Therefore, ye Britons, give a wreath to Geoffrey of Monmouth. He is indeed yours for once he sang of your battles and those of your chiefs, and he wrote a book called "The Deeds of the Britons" which are celebrated throughout the world.

III.

MERLIN IN
MEDIEVAL ROMANCE

chapter 5

ROBERT DE BORON AND HIS CONTINUATORS

Nancy Marie Brown

IN THE first years of the thirteenth century a French poet named Robert de Boron set out to rework the familiar tales of Merlin and King Arthur into a more Christian story of the Holy Grail. Robert planned, it seems, a three-part epic beginning with *Joseph of Arimathea*, about the early history of the Grail; continuing with *Merlin*, about the founding of the Round Table; and concluding with *Percival*, about the Quest for the Holy Grail. Robert's poems, for the most part, have been lost—only the *Joseph* and 504 lines of the *Merlin* remain—but he, or an anonymous successor, later wrote a prose *Merlin*, which exists in several versions, each with a lengthy continuation by another writer. One of these continuations is a prose *Percival* (called the Didot-*Percival*, from the name of the best-known manuscript), which seems to reflect Robert's original sequel. The others are the *Estoire de Merlin* (The Story of Merlin), in that vast, five-part, "orthodox" version of the Arthurian romance known as the Vulgate Cycle; the *Suite du Merlin* (The Continuation of the Merlin Story), which was also part of a longer cycle, now in fragments; and the incomplete *Livre d'Artus* (Book of Arthur), which elaborates on episodes from the *Estoire de Merlin* (this sequel is not represented in the translations here).

Although the outline of his *Merlin* comes from Geoffrey of Monmouth's *History of the Kings of Britain*, Robert de Boron had no qualms when it came to shuffling the elements of history, omitting and reordering events to bring out his Christian moral. His *Merlin*, more a lesson in how good men should live in an evil world than a history of Britain's kings, is a simple, three-part narrative, each section revolving around one of his three major characters: Merlin, King Uther Pendragon, and King Arthur.

Part 1 (to Chapter 30 in Alexandre Micha's edition and including the first episode translated here) reveals Merlin's character. The good wizard is more than the otherworldly prophet of Geoffrey's history. He is a prankster, a shapeshifter and player of practical jokes, with an errand from God to teach men that they are incapable of distinguishing good from evil or appearance from reality without divine guidance, and that, therefore, they must distrust their faulty human reason and submit to God's will. Robert's Merlin is born through a plot of the devils to avenge Christ's harrowing of Hell. They create a man who will deceive his fellows—Merlin, born of a virgin and an incubus—but the child is saved from becoming this intended Antichrist by his mother's virtue. Instead, we read, he is "elected by God to perform a service that none but he can perform, since no other being knows what he knows," that is, to orchestrate the Quest for the Holy Grail. Merlin retains a demon's magical powers—including an impish sense of humor and the ability to change his shape whenever he wishes into that of any man of any class or age, ugly or handsome—and a demon's knowledge of past and present thoughts and actions. But God grants him also knowledge of the future, which demons do not possess. Robert completes his sketch by establishing a connection between Merlin and Christ—wise men see a star that signals his birth; a king seeks to kill him; at a young age he stuns his elders with his knowledge.

The lengthy second part of Robert's book (Chapters 31 to 79) is the story of King Uther Pendragon. While Merlin's personality and powers were revealed, Uther matures in the book from a joyful youth to a grave and pious king, his character shaped by Merlin's lessons. In the first lesson, translated here, Merlin teaches Uther and his brother Pendragon (then the king) that appearances are deceiving. The second lesson Uther and his brother learn is to believe Merlin even when he seems to be talking nonsense; the third, taught to Uther after Pendragon's death (Uther takes the name Uther Pendragon to honor his brother), is to submit entirely to Merlin's will—which is God's will. When Merlin tells Uther to found the Round Table as a replica of the table of the Last Supper, he explains, "I will tell you what I know Our Lord wants you to know."

The relatively short third part of Robert's *Merlin* (Chapters 80 to 91) tells King Arthur's story from conception to coronation. Uther, in his role as Everyman, forgets in the face of passion all Merlin has taught him, with the result that he finds himself helplessly caught in a dangerous civil war. What he does not realize—and what the reader of Robert's book by now ought to realize—is that his very predicament is part of God's plan. Otherwise, Merlin, who knows all things, would have prevented the war, just as, earlier, he saved Uther from a Saxon assassin. Through Merlin's magic Uther's passion is sated and Arthur is conceived and spirited away to be raised in safety; through Merlin's counsel peace is concluded; with his aid Uther wins his last battle; and, finally, through Merlin's persuasion and his (or God's) magic Arthur pulls the sword from the stone and is anointed king.

The continuations of Robert de Boron's *Merlin* pick up the story here, soon after Arthur's coronation. The Didot-*Perceval*, whose author may have been Robert himself, immediately introduces Perceval and the Quest for the Holy Grail. Arthur and his court exist only as backdrop for the Quest; Merlin's attention—and the reader's—is focused on Perceval, who eventually finds the Grail and, for his piety, is permitted to remain with it. When Merlin brings word to court that the Quest is ended, the knights of the Round Table "said they had no desire to stay any longer with King Arthur, and would cross over the sea to seek adventures." To retain his following Arthur launches a campaign in France, then goes on to Rome, during which time his regent, Mordred (who is not Arthur's illegitimate son, in this version, but his nephew), usurps the throne. Arthur and his kingdom are destroyed while Merlin watches, his responsibility having ended when the Quest for the Holy Grail was achieved. After the Matter of Britain is over, in the passage here translated, Merlin returns to Perceval and the Grail and passes from the sight of the world.

The authors of the *Estoire de Merlin* and the *Suite du Merlin* were much more interested in Arthur and his court, and not at all taken with Robert's Christ-like Merlin. They made Merlin into Arthur's premier counselor, war strategist, emissary, and court magician, the announcer and arranger of the adventures of Britain. What they found most appealing in Robert's characterization of Merlin, what they preserved and expanded, was not the Christian rationale, but the devilish, puckish side of the wizard, his pranks and magic and shapeshifting, his general unpredictability. To this they added another demonic trait—lust—which eventually causes Merlin's downfall and, it can be argued, Arthur's, since it leaves the king bereft of his best counselor and only magician. In both the *Estoire de Merlin* and the *Suite du Merlin* the wizard falls in love with a maiden (Viviane or Niviane or Nimue) who learns magic from him and eventually turns that magic against him, sealing him in a magical tomb—in the *Estoire*, alive, to be her plaything; in the *Suite*, dead. Although both of these sequels tell the early history of Arthur's reign, ending with Merlin's disappearance and leading up to the coming of Lancelot and the Quest for the Holy Grail, each has a different emphasis. The *Estoire de Merlin* concentrates on Arthur's wars against the Saxons, against Lot and the rebel kings, in France, and against the Emperor of Rome. Arthur wins each war largely because of Merlin's magical aid. As in Robert de Boron's original the wizard is always on the side of right; he is the king's guide and teacher and, wherever he may be, knows when the king is in need and (except when he is under the power of Viviane) arrives in time to extricate him from the predicament. He can be a friendly, playful, comic wizard, as the two passages translated here show; his only weakness is a quick eye for beautiful young maidens. The *Suite du Merlin*, by contrast, concentrates on the adventures of individual knights of the Round Table. The Merlin of this story is a much darker, more ambiguous figure. Rather than constantly being the king's guide and friend, he sometimes, as in the passage translated, withholds information from Arthur, and so contributes to the destruction of the realm.

The translation attempts to be literal while being fair to the humor, fast pace, richness of characterization, and depth of theme of the originals. It attempts, too, to preserve the form of the romances, which were meant to be read aloud. In such a work each word cannot matter—listeners invariably will miss a few here and there. Sentences must be clear and simple and loosely structured, as are the sentences—the thoughts—of speech. If a work is to be read aloud, it must, like a piece of music, repeat its themes, its melodies, hold each note long enough that it lodges in the listener's mind. These idiosyncrasies of the medieval prose romance can perhaps explain how one scholar could remark, "The grotesqueness of Boron's version is mostly due to his stylistic clumsiness: his style throughout his work fails to complement the interest of his material." Style, to that scholar, is the manipulation of the individual word: lyricism, mellifluence, poetry. To a storyteller style is something else: pace, surprise, suspense, humor, clarity, juxtaposition—all elements in which Robert de Boron and his continuators excel.

Bibliographic note: The editions translated here are: for Robert de Boron's *Merlin* (the French prose *Merlin*), the edition by Alexandre Micha (Geneva: Droz, 1980); for the *Estoire de Merlin*, that of H. O. Sommer in Volume 2 of *The Vulgate Version of the Arthurian Romances* (Washington, D.C.: Carnegie Institute of Washington, 1908); for the *Suite du Merlin*, that found in *Merlin*, ed. Gaston Paris and Jacob Ulrich (Paris: Firmin, 1886; rpt. New York: Johnston, 1965); and for the *Perceval*, that found in *Le Roman du Graal: Manuscrit de Modene*, ed. Bernard Cerquiglini (Paris: Union Generale d'Editions, 1981).

Robert de Boron's Merlin

Vortigern's Tower

(ch. 21–31 in Micha)

[*Vortigern, who had usurped the throne of England and made a marriage alliance he soon regretted with the hated Saxons, determined to build an unassailable tower. He brought in the best masons, but each time the tower rose above three or four courses, it tumbled down. His soothsayers said that if the blood of a boy conceived without a father were mixed into the mortar, then the tower would stand. So King Vortigern sent men to find such a child.*]

The king's messengers departed two by two. They searched so far, through so many lands and countries, that eventually two of them met up with two others and they decided to go on together for a while. So the four rode on until one day they came to a large open yard, at the entrance to a village, where a great many children were playing a ball game.

Merlin, who knew all things, saw them coming and knew they were looking for him. He ran over to one of the richest boys in the village—who he knew would swear at him—raised his stick, and struck him on the leg. The boy began to cry and swore at Merlin and called him a fatherless bastard.

When the men searching for a child conceived without a father heard this, all four of them went over to the boy who was crying and asked, "Who hit you?"

He replied, "The son of a woman who hasn't any idea what begot him! The bastard never even had a father!"

When Merlin heard that, he came over, laughing, and said, "I am the one you are looking for, the one you have promised to kill to bring his blood to King Vortigern."

When they heard that, they were astonished. "Who told you this?"

Said Merlin, "I knew it as soon as you vowed it."

"Will you come with us, then, to the king?"

"I'd be afraid you would kill me," he said. But he knew very well they didn't have the heart to do that; he said it to test them. Then he said, "If you promise not to kill me, I'll go with you and explain why the tower you want my blood for will not stand."

And when they heard that, they were quite astounded. "You tell us marvelous things! It would be a great sin to kill you." And one of them said, "I would rather perjure myself than kill you."

Said Merlin, "Come to the nunnery where my mother lives. I cannot go without taking leave of her and of Master Blaise, the good priest with her."

"We will go wherever you want."

So Merlin led the messengers to the nunnery where his mother was living.

Merlin went in, telling the household to make the men welcome. When they had dismounted, he took them to Blaise, saying, "Here are the men I told you were coming to find and kill me." And to the king's messengers he said, "I will describe your errand to this good man. Then, I pray you, tell him whether or not what I say is true. And do not lie! For I want you to know that if you lie, I will know it."

And the messengers said, "We will not lie. You can be sure we won't lie to you about this."

And Merlin said to Blaise, "Now listen well as I tell you what these good men came to say to you." [*The king's messengers listened, astonished that Merlin knew so much about them, as Merlin recounted to Master Blaise—who was Merlin's mother's confessor and had been charged by Merlin to write the book of the Holy Grail—the whole history of King Vortigern's tower and described for him in great detail the messengers' quest, down to the number of clerks who requested his blood and the number of messengers sent to find him.*]

"Good Master Blaise, ask them if I am telling the truth."

And Blaise asked the king's messengers if this marvel Merlin had described was true. They replied, "Have you heard and understood the whole story? So God helps us and lets us return to our own country and not all die at swordpoint, he did not, as far as we know, say a single untrue word to you."

Master Blaise made the sign of the cross and said, "He will grow still wiser, if he lives. It would be a great shame if you killed him."

"Sir, we would rather be perjured and lose our lives and have the king confiscate our estates. But he himself, since he knows everything else, knows very well whether or not we have the desire to do that."

Said Blaise, "What you say is true. I will ask him about it and about that

other thing, concerning you, so that you will marvel at what he says." They
called Merlin over—he had walked away so they could talk together
privately. And his master said, "All this is as you said; they admit it is true.
But they told me to ask you another thing, Do you know whether or not they
have the desire to kill you?"

Merlin laughed and said, "I know very well, thanks to God and to them,
that they do not have any desire at all to do that."

And the king's messengers said, "That is the truth. Will you come with
us, then?"

"Yes, without fail, if you promise faithfully to take me before the king and
to not let any harm come to me before I have spoken with him."

And so they promised. [*Merlin then took leave of Blaise, sending him to
Northumberland to wait for him; there they would continue the Book of the Holy
Grail. He also said goodbye to his mother, who begged him to let Blaise remain with
her; he said he could not.*]

Merlin rode away with the king's messengers. As they rode on, they came
to a village that was having a fair, and they passed through the village and
came upon a peasant who had bought a pair of sturdy shoes and pieces of
leather to repair them with when they wore out, for he planned to go on a
pilgrimage. When Merlin saw the peasant, he laughed. The king's messengers
asked why he was laughing. He replied, "Because of that peasant you see
there. Ask him what he means to do with the leather he is carrying, and he
will tell you, 'Repair my shoes.' Then you will see why I'm laughing, for I
tell you, certainly, he will be dead before he reaches home."

When they heard that, they thought it a great marvel and said, "We can
test if this is true." So they went up to the peasant and asked what he planned
to do with the shoes and the leather he was carrying. He said he planned to
go on a pilgrimage and would need the leather to repair his shoes. When they
heard him saying the same thing Merlin had, they thought it a very great
marvel and they said to each other, "This man seems quite strong and
healthy. Let's two of us follow him, and the other two go back to the road and
wait there, for it would be very good to know the truth of this marvel." So two
of them went after the peasant. They had not gone more than a league when
they saw him fall down dead, his shoes in his arms. When they saw that, they
turned back and found their companions and told them what they had seen.
"Those clerks were great fools who told us to kill such a wise man," their
companions said when they had heard. The other two messengers said they
would rather be flogged than cause him to be killed. This they said in private
and they didn't know Merlin knew it. But when they returned to him, he
thanked them for what they had said.

They asked, "What have we said that you should thank us for?" And
Merlin repeated their words just as they had said them. When they heard
that, they were amazed. "We cannot do or say a thing that this child will not
know of." [*Another day, they passed a funeral with a priest leading the procession,
singing loudly, and a good man, weeping, following the coffin. Merlin stopped and
began to laugh. His escorts asked why. The man was weeping over another man's son,
he said, while the one whose son it was sang. To test the truth of that, Merlin sent the*

messengers to the child's mother to ask why her husband was crying when it was the priest's son who had died.] Two of them went over to the woman and asked what Merlin had told them to. The woman was terribly frightened when she heard their question and replied, "Good sirs, for God's mercy! I know it well nor will I hide it from you, for you know the truth. And you seem to be good men. It is just as you say. But for God's sake, do not say anything to my husband or he will kill me."

When they heard this marvel, they returned and told their two companions. Then they agreed, the four of them, that there was never in the world such a good soothsayer.

So they rode on until they came within a day's ride of Vortigern. Then the messengers said, "You yourself should tell us what to say to our lord the king, for two of us should go ahead to announce we have found you. Tell us what you want us to say about you. He will most likely blame us for not killing you."

When Merlin heard them talk this way, he knew they wanted what was best for him. He said, "Do just as I tell you and you will not be blamed."

And they said, "Command us, then."

And Merlin said, "Go to Vortigern and tell him you have found me and recount exactly what you have heard me say. Tell him I will show him why his tower cannot stand—if he agrees to kill those who wanted me killed. Tell him also that I will reveal why they wanted me killed. When you have said all this, you will be totally safe, as he will tell you."

The messengers set off and came to Vortigern that night. When Vortigern saw them he was very glad and asked, "Have you done my will?"

And they replied, "As best as we could." Then they took him aside and told him in private everything just as it had happened—how they had found Merlin and that, if he had not wanted them to, they would never have found him. "But he came voluntarily to you."

And the king said, "What Merlin are you talking about now? Weren't you to find the child conceived without a father? And bring me the blood out of his body?"

They replied, "Sire, this is Merlin you are speaking of. You should know he is the wisest man and the best soothsayer that ever came before God. Sire, everything you made us swear, everything just as you commanded it—all this Merlin told us. He said your clerks do not know why the tower falls, but he can show you and them both, if you wish. And he told us many other great marvels. He sent us to you to find out if you would talk with him. But if you wish, we will kill him where he is, for two of our companions are there guarding him."

When the king heard that, he said, "If you pledge your lives that this Merlin will show me why my tower falls, then you need not kill him."

And they replied, "We pledge that gladly."

Then said the king, "Go fetch him for I would very much like to speak with him."

The messengers returned, and the king himself rode after them. When Merlin saw the messengers, he laughed and said, "You have pledged your lives for me!"

Said they, "That is true. We would rather our own lives be risked than that we should have to kill you, and he made us promise to do one or the other."

Replied Merlin, "I will quickly release you from that pledge."

So they rode on until they met the king.

When Merlin approached Vortigern, he saluted him and said, "Vortigern, come speak privately with me."

He took the king aside, calling over the messengers who had escorted him. When they were in counsel, Merlin said, "Sire, you had me sought because your tower would not stand, and you commanded that I be killed because of the advice of your clerks, who said the tower would stand by my blood—but they lied. If they had said it would stand *through* my blood, then they would have been telling the truth. Now, if you promise to do to them what they wanted you to do to me, I will show you why the tower falls and teach you, if you want to know, how to make it stand."

Vortigern replied, "If you show me what you say you will, I'll do with them whatever you wish."

And Merlin said, "If I lie even in the smallest word, do not believe anything else I say. Have your clerks come, and I will ask them why the tower falls. You will hear that they do not know the reason."

The king led Merlin to the fallen tower, and the clerks were sent for and brought before it. When they had arrived, the king had Merlin brought over by one of the messengers who had escorted him. Merlin said to them, "Sir Clerks, why is it, do you think, that this tower falls?"

They replied, "We know nothing of its falling, but we have told the king how it can be made to stand."

And the king said, "You told me marvels. You had me command a search for a man conceived without a father, and I do not know how such a man could be found."

Then Merlin said to the clerks, "Sir Clerks, you take the king for a fool. When you had him send for the man born without a father, you did it not for his need, but for your own—you had predicted that through this fatherless child you would all meet your deaths. For this reason—because you were afraid this child would kill you—you told the king to kill him and to put his blood in the foundation of the tower so that it would stand and never fall again. And you thought that in this way you could outwit the one the signs said would cause your deaths."

When the king's clerks heard the child relating such a marvel—what they thought no one besides themselves knew—they were very afraid. They believed they had been condemned to death. And Merlin said to the king, "Sire, now you see these clerks did not want to kill me for the sake of your tower, but for fear of what they themselves had predicted—that I would cause their deaths. Ask them, for they are not so brave that they would dare lie to you in front of me."

Said the king, "Is he telling the truth?"

And the clerks replied, "Sire, so we might face God without our sins, it is true. But we do not know how he knows these marvels. We pray to you, as to Our Lord—let us live until we have seen if he knows the truth about the tower and if he can make it stand."

Merlin said, "You will not die until you have seen why the tower falls." They thanked him. [*Under the tower, Merlin revealed, was a pool, and in it were two rocks, under which lay two dragons, a red and a white. The pool was drained and the dragons uncovered, and when all the court came out to watch the fight, Merlin pardoned the soothsayers on the condition they never again would work magic. The white dragon defeated the red. This, Merlin explained, meant that Uther and Pendragon, the heirs of the rightful king, would drive Vortigern from his throne; indeed, in the ensuing battle, they burned Vortigern to death in his tower.*]

Merlin's Introduction to Uther and Pendragon

(ch. 31–38 in Micha)

[*After Vortigern's death, the English made Pendragon king. He laid siege to the Saxon invader, Hengist, but the siege lasted a year with no profit, and he despaired. Five of his counselors advised asking Merlin's help, telling him the story of Vortigern's tower.*]

When Pendragon heard that, he was amazed and asked, "Where might such a good wizard be found?"

They said, "We do not know where in the land he might be. But we do know he is aware when someone speaks of him, and we know he is in this country. If he wishes to, he will come here."

Said Pendragon, "If he is in this country, I will find him." So he sent messengers throughout the land to find Merlin.

Merlin knew the king was seeking him. As soon as he could, after he had spoken to Blaise, he went to a village where he knew he could find the king's messengers.

He went as a woodcutter, a great ax on his shoulder and great boots on his feet. He was dressed in a short coat that was all torn. He had long hair standing all on end and wore a great beard. He looked very much like a wild man. He went to the house where the king's messengers were, and when they saw him they were amazed and said to one another, "That one looks like an evil man."

Merlin went straight up to them and said, "You are not obeying very well the command of your master to seek the wizard Merlin."

When they heard that, they said to one another, "What devil told that to this churl? What is he interfering for?"

And Merlin replied, "If I had the errand you have, I would find him sooner than you."

At this they all gathered around him, asking if he knew Merlin or had ever seen him.

He said, "I have seen him and I know where he lives. He knows very well that you are seeking him. But you will never find him if he does not wish to be found. He asked me to tell you this: it is useless for you to try, for even if you did find him, he would not go with you. He also directed me to say that the men who told your lord the good wizard was in this country were telling the truth. Now, when you return, tell your master he will not take the castle he is besieging until Hengist is dead. And out of the five men in the camp who asked him to seek Merlin you will find but three alive when you return. To these three men and to your master say that if they come to this village and hunt in these forests, they will find Merlin. But if they themselves do not come, they will never find anyone who can find him."

The messengers listened carefully to what Merlin said. But when he finished, he turned around, and in the turning, he disappeared. Then they made the sign of the cross over themselves, saying, "We have spoken to a devil. What should we do about what he told us?" They discussed it and said, "We will go back and recount to the king, and to those who know about these kinds of marvels, what we have seen and heard. Then we will know if those two are dead."

So they retraced their steps to the king's camp. When the king saw them, he asked, "Have you found the man you were sent after?"

"Sire," they replied, "we will tell you what happened to us. Send for your counselors and those who told you about this wizard."

The king sent for them, and when they had all arrived, they drew aside to take counsel. Then the messengers told about the marvel that had occurred and repeated everything the churl had said, including that two of the five men would be dead before the messengers returned. And when they asked for news, they were told that those two men were indeed dead.

When the counselors who had suggested Merlin be found heard that, they marveled greatly at this man who was so hideous, so ugly, and so old. They wondered if it could be Merlin himself the messengers spoke of—but they did not know he could take on other forms than his own. Nevertheless, the counselors concluded that no one would say these things except Merlin. So they said to the king, "We believe it was Merlin himself who spoke with your messengers, for no one else could tell of the death of these men, nor dare speak of the death of Hengist. Ask what village they found this man in."

And the messengers replied, "We found him in Northumberland. He came to our hostel."

Then the king's counselors were convinced it was Merlin. They said the king himself should go after him. So the king said he would leave the siege to his brother Uther and go to Northumberland and hunt the forests he had been told to hunt.

So the king quickly arranged everything and went to Northumberland. He asked for news, but found no one who could tell him anything. So he said he would go hunt the forests.

The king rode through the forests looking for Merlin. Soon one of his men came upon a great number of beasts with a hideously ugly herdsman guarding them. He asked whose man he was.

The herdsman said, "I am from Northumberland, the servant of a nobleman."

"Do you have any news of Merlin?"

"I myself, no. But yesterday I saw a man who said the king was coming to look for Merlin today in these woods. Has he come? Do you know anything about it?"

The king's man replied, "It is true that the king is looking for him. Can you direct him?"

And he said, "I will tell the king such a thing, but I will not tell you."

"I will take you to the king."

Replied the herdsman, "Then I would badly guard my beasts. Besides, I have no need of the king. But if he were to come to me, I could tell him about the one he is looking for."

"I will bring the king to you."

Then he parted from the herdsman and searched for the king. When he had found him, he recounted what he had seen. The king said, "Take me to him."

So he led the king to the place where he had found the herdsman and said to him, "See here, I have brought the king to you. Now tell him what you said you would tell him."

"Sire," the herdsman said, "I know very well that you seek Merlin. But you will not find him until he wants to be found. Go to one of your good villages nearby, and he will come to you when he knows you are waiting for him."

Then the king said, "How do I know you are telling me the truth?"

"If you do not believe me, don't do as I say, for it is folly to believe bad advice."

When the king heard that, he asked, "Are you saying now that your advice is bad?"

"No, you said that. But you know very well that my advice on this matter is better than the advice you could give yourself."

Said the king, "I will believe you."

So the king went to the village closest to the forest. After he had been there a while, a nobleman, very well turned out, well dressed and well shod, came to the king's hostel and said, "Take me to the king."

They took him in. When he was before the king, he said, "Sire, Merlin sent me to you. He wants you to know that the man guarding the beasts spoke the truth when he instructed you to come here. Merlin will come to you when he wants to. You do not yet have need of him. When you do, he will come voluntarily to you."

Replied the king, "I have need of him every day. Never have I had such desire to see any man as I have to see him."

"In case you said that, Merlin sent by me the good news that Hengist is dead and that Uther your brother has killed him."

When the king heard that, he was amazed. "Could this be true what you are telling me?"

"He did not instruct me to say more. But you would be a fool if you doubted him before testing it. Send to find out if it is true, then you will believe."

The king said, "That is good advice."

He sent two messengers on the best horses he had, commanding them not to stop riding until they knew if it was true that Hengist was dead. They departed and rode as fast as they could. When they had ridden one night, they met messengers from Uther bringing word of Hengist's death. The messengers told each other the news and they all returned to the king.

The man who had brought Merlin's message to the king had already left. The messengers returning and those who were coming went before Pendragon and told him privately how Uther had killed Hengist. When the king heard that, he forbade them, on pain of death, to speak of it to anyone else. And so things remained and the king marveled greatly how Merlin had known of the death of Hengist.

So the king waited in the village to see if Merlin would come. He thought in his heart he would ask Merlin how Hengist had been killed, for hardly anyone yet knew he was dead.

And so the king waited. One day, when he was coming from chapel, a very handsome nobleman, well dressed and well turned out and seeming to be noble in every way, came before him. He greeted the king, saying, "Sire, who are you waiting for in this village?"

Replied the king, "I am waiting for Merlin to come talk with me."

"Sire," he said, "you are not wise enough to recognize him when he is speaking to you. Call those you have brought who ought to recognize Merlin. Ask them if I could be Merlin."

The king was amazed and had those called who ought to recognize Merlin and said, "Good sirs, we are waiting for Merlin. But there is not a one of you who, as far as I know, would recognize him. If you would, tell me."

"Sire," they replied, "if we see him we will recognize him easily."

The gentleman who had come before the king said, "Good sirs, can one truly know another who knows not himself?"

"We are not saying we know everything about him. Just that we would easily recognize his face if we saw it."

"One does not know a man who knows only his outward appearance, as I will show you." The nobleman called the king into a chamber by himself. "Sire," he said, "I would very much like to be your and your brother Uther's man. Know that I am Merlin, for whom you have been looking. But these men, who believe they know me, know nothing about me. I will show you. Go outside and send in the ones who say they know me. As soon as they see me, they will say that you've found me. Except when I wish it, they can never recognize me."

When the king heard this, he was very glad. "I will do whatever you wish," he said.

He left the room as quickly as he could and called those who believed they knew Merlin. By the time they came, Merlin had taken on the appearance in which they had seen him before. And when they saw him, they said to the king, "Sire, we tell you certainly that this is Merlin!"

When the king heard that, he laughed. "Make sure you know him well."

"We are certain this is Merlin."

And Merlin said, "Sire, they are telling the truth. Now, tell me your desire."

Said the king, "I beg of you, if it is possible, that you love me and let me become more acquainted with you, for these gentlemen have said you are very wise and give very good advice."

Merlin replied, "Sire, you could not ask of me any advice that I will not give you, if I can."

Said the king, "I would dearly like to ask you, if you please, to tell me if I have spoken with you since I came to this land looking for you."

"Sire," said Merlin, "I was the man you found guarding the beasts."

When the king and those with him heard that, they were astounded. And the king said to them, "You do not know this man very well, for he walked right past you and you did not recognize him."

"Sire," they said, "we cannot see how such a thing could have happened. But we believe he can say and do what no man who ever lived could say or do."

Then the king asked Merlin, "How did you know of the death of Hengist?"

"Sire, I knew that while you were away Hengist would try to murder your brother. I went to your brother and told him, and he, thanks to God and to himself, believed me. He prepared himself. And I will tell you of the strength and courage and bravery of Hengist: He went alone into your camp at night to your brother's pavilion to kill him. But your brother, as I have said, did not doubt me, but thankfully was watching that night all alone—for he had not told anyone else. He had armed himself, but no one knew, for he kept it secret. So he watched outside his pavilion the night that Hengist came, carrying knives to kill him. Your brother let him enter the pavilion and search it. When he found no one and went to leave, your brother stepped in front of him and fought with him: and he was quickly killed, for your brother was in armor and Hengist was not—he had come only to kill him quickly and flee back."

When the king heard this news, he asked, "In what guise were you when you spoke with my brother? For I marvel that he believed you."

"Sire, I took on the appearance of a wise old man and spoke with him privately. I said that this night, if he did not guard himself, he would be killed."

"Did you tell him who you were?"

Said Merlin, "He still does not know who spoke with him, and he will not know before you tell him. And this is the reason I brought you here, for you would not have been able to take the castle while Hengist lived."

Then said the king, "Dear sweet friend, will you come with me? I have great need of your counsel and your aid."

"Sire," Merlin replied, "I will come very soon, but soon thereafter your men will grow very angry that you believe me. But if you care for your honor and are wise, you will not cease to believe me because of them."

Replied the king, "You have told me so much and done so much, that if it is true you have saved my brother, I will never doubt or disbelieve you."

"Sire, go speak with your brother. Ask him who told him what I just told you. If he can tell you who, do not believe anything else I might say to you. But know this: when I want you to recognize me, I will come to your brother just as I did when I warned him."

Said the king, "For God's sake, tell me what day my brother will speak with you."

"You may know it gladly, but watch, as you love me, that you do not tell anyone else [except Uther]. For if I find you have lied, I will not believe you ever again. And it will be a greater loss to you than to me."

Said the king, "As soon as I have lied to you once, do not believe me again. But I will test you in many ways."

"I want you to test me in as many ways as you wish. But know that I will speak with your brother on the eleventh day from when you next speak to him."

In this way Merlin introduced himself to Pendragon. He took his leave then and returned to his Master Blaise and told him these things. And Blaise put them down in writing, and through him we know them today.

[*Pendragon returned to Uther, and they compared what they knew about Hengist's death. Pendragon told Uther he knew who had warned him and astonished his brother by saying he would speak with the man again in eleven days.*] And so the two brothers agreed to stay together all that day.

Merlin, who knew all these things, told Blaise how the two brothers had spoken together concerning him, and how the king was planning to test him.

Asked Blaise, "What do you plan to do about that?"

Said Merlin, "They are young and jolly men. I could not make them love me in any better way than by doing much of their will and by making them laugh and be joyful."

[*Merlin, having decided to dupe Pendragon again, appeared on the eleventh day in the guise of a valet of Uther's mistress. He spent the entire day with the brothers without being recognized.*] When it drew near to vespers, Pendragon marveled greatly that Merlin had not come, for he had promised to speak with Uther that day.

They waited until compline. When it had passed, while Uther took care of some business and he and the king were conversing, Merlin went away and took on the appearance he had had the day he spoke to Uther. He went to Uther's lodging and told one of the knights to go fetch him.

The knight did so, saying that a nobleman was asking after Uther at his lodging. Uther went to the king and told him. The king said Uther should come back and get him if it was the wise old man who had saved him from death. Uther said he would without fail.

Uther went to his lodging and found the nobleman there. He recognized him immediately and was delighted to see him and told him many things, saying, "Sire, you saved me from death, but I marvel that my lord the king told me everything that you said and everything that I did after you parted from me. And he told me you would come here today. He prayed and commanded me that if you spoke with me, he would know it. He said also, when I came here, that if you were here, I should go get him. But greatly I marvel that he knew what you said to me."

Merlin replied, "He would not have known it if someone had not told him. Go get him, and ask him in front of me who told him."

Uther turned away to find the king, commanding those who guarded the door to let no one enter.

But Merlin, as soon as Uther had left, took on the appearance of the valet who had carried the letters.

When they returned and found the boy, Uther was amazed. "Sire, I am seeing marvels. I left here the nobleman I told you about, now I find no one here but this valet! Wait—I will ask my men outside if they saw anyone leave, or if they saw this valet enter."

So Uther went outside, and the king began to laugh heartily.

Estoire de Merlin

Merlin Dupes King Arthur

(pp. 122–124 in Sommer)

[*With Merlin's tactical and magical aid, Arthur defeated Lot of Orkney and the other petty kings rebelling against his right to rule. The army then disbanded and Arthur, with King Ban and Bors of Brittany, traveled to Bedigran, the chief city of the realm, to wait for Merlin, who earlier had shown Arthur where treasure was buried nearby.*]

The day after the king arrived there was a great feast, and when they had eaten the three kings went down to a pavilion by the river to look over the fields and meadows. As they looked along the riverbank, they saw a tall churl, carrying a bow and blunt arrows, coming toward them. There were wild ducks swimming in a brook, as is their nature to do. The churl raised his bow and shot at one; the arrow broke its neck. Then he sent a larger arrow after the first and killed the drake. He picked the ducks up, slipped their necks through his belt, and continued on toward the pavilion. The three kings were leaning out, watching him, and when he was within bowshot, King Arthur called out to him. The man came over to the pavilion and the king asked if he would sell the birds he had shot. The man said yes, gladly. So the king asked, "And what will you have for them?"

The man didn't say a word. He was wearing sturdy leather shoes, a homespun coat, and a hooded surcoat belted with a strip of sheepskin. He was tall and strong, swarthy and hairy, and he looked quite crude and ugly. Then he said, "I do not care for a king who loves his treasure too much—it is bad to have a miserly king who dares not make a poor man rich when he could easily do so. I will give you the birds, although I am no richer than you see. But you do not have the heart to give me even a third of the treasure that you found buried, even though it was neither through your honor nor your might that you found it."

When King Arthur heard these words from the churl, he turned to the other two kings and said, "What devil told this churl I found buried treasure?"

King Ban called the churl over and demanded who had told him. The man did not answer except to tell King Arthur to take the birds so he could go. Said King Ban, "First tell us, on your soul, who told you the king had found buried treasure."

The churl replied, "He told me—the wild man called Merlin. And he also told me he was coming today to speak with the king."

While he was speaking, Sir Ulfin came out of an inner room and crossed to where the king was questioning the churl, saying, "Tell me now, why I should believe you have spoken with Merlin."

Said the churl, "If you want to believe me, you can believe me. And if you don't, then don't believe me. For I've received nothing from you, so we're even."

When Ulfin heard that, he began to laugh, because he knew at once that this was Merlin himself. And when the churl saw Ulfin, he said to him, "Take these birds in to the seneschal so he can serve them for dinner tonight to this king of yours, who doesn't even have the heart to make a poor man rich—one who, what is more, could well repay him. And you know that he has this very day spoken with one to whom it matters very little whether or not he has anything on earth, no matter how great it is."

Then Ulfin began to laugh very loudly and said to him, "Sir, if you please, I would very much like to speak with you."

The churl said he would gladly speak with him.

The king looked at Ulfin and asked why he was laughing so hard, and Ulfin answered that he would know shortly.

The churl went inside, dressed as he was, and said to Kay, "Here, Sir Seneschal, now have these birds plucked so your king can enjoy them, for I have given them to him."

"Sire," said Ulfin, "this is hardly the first gift he has given you."

As he said that, Bretel came up, and overhearing Ulfin's remark, he recognized Merlin instantly and began to laugh. The king asked, "Now, why are you laughing?" Bretel replied that he would gladly tell him if the churl wanted him to. The churl said he did.

Then Ulfin said to the king, "Sire, don't you know Merlin, your friend? Didn't he say he would speak with you today, just as this churl says?"

"Yes," said the king, "why do you ask?"

"Sire," said Ulfin, "I asked because it is true, I know, that one can't know someone well after seeing him only two or three times, but that you do not recognize this man at all surprises me greatly."

The king was so astonished at what Ulfin said that he didn't know what to say except to pray that he would tell him who this churl was, if he knew.

"Sire," said Ulfin, "do you not know Merlin?"

Said the king, "Certainly, I do."

"Then look carefully at this good man. If you still don't see, he could easily say he has misplaced his service with you. Because this is Merlin himself, who has served and loved and aided you so much, doing and saying whatever he could against those who wished you ill."

King Arthur made the sign of the cross. The other two kings were very surprised and asked, "Merlin, is it truly you? We have never seen you in such a disguise."

Merlin replied that that could well be.

"Dear lords," said Ulfin, "perhaps you won't be so astonished if he shows you again the appearance you saw first?" They said they wished he would do that. Said Ulfin, "Then go into this chamber," and they went in. And Ulfin said to them, "Dear lords, never be amazed at the affairs of Merlin, for he will show you plenty of disguises. Whenever he wants, he transforms himself, changing his looks by magic, as is quite clear." Guinebaus, who was there, agreed it was so. "And," said Ulfin, "he disguises himself because there are many men in this country who would like to see him dead."

Then they all returned to Merlin to see him in his usual guise, and when they entered the room, there was Merlin. They ran up to him and made a great deal of him, like men who loved him dearly. And they began to laugh about the shots they had seen him make and the words he had said to the king. Then King Arthur said to him, "Now I know you love me, for you gave me your birds for free, and I will eat them for love of you." And Merlin said he would have it so.

The Begetting of Ector des Mares

(pp. 402–406 in Sommer)

[*When the time came for kings Ban and Bors to leave Camelot, Merlin escorted them to Brittany; their first night out, they came upon a castle surrounded by marshland.*]

The castle was very beautiful, and so well situated and fortified it could withstand any assault. It was completely encircled by a pair of walls, deep and high, with many towers and battlements—in all, well defendable. Inside the bailey were five towers, round and straight and reaching to the heavens; four were not unusual, but the fifth was marvelous and tall—with a parapet all around and so high that a man could barely shoot an arrow to the top. Outside the bailey there was a double moat filled with water, and all around the circles of walls and moats were the marshes, two leagues wide and so full of water and mire that a man who set out to cross them would drown. There was a single causeway leading to the castle, and it was so narrow that two horses could not pass abreast. At the entrance to this causeway was a forest of beautiful pine trees, tall and branchy, and in this forest was a meadow, one fourth its size. In the center of the meadow was a beautiful pine tree; from one of its branches hung a horn of ivory, whiter than new snow, on a chain of silver. Whoever wanted lodging at the castle, or who wanted to joust for the right to pass over the causeway, was to sound the horn. [*Merlin said it was the Castle des Mares (Castle of the Marsh), and belonged to a knight of great renown, Agravadain the Black. He recommended they stay overnight there, and King Ban, who had heard of Agravadain, offered to sound the horn. He blew it so that the marshes resounded, but still did not think it could be heard at the castle, so he sounded it quickly twice more. Agravadain, angry at hearing his horn blown so aggressively, charged down the causeway on his warhorse and challenged the kings. Learning they were Arthur's subjects, he lost his anger and invited them into the castle.*] They hailed squires and valets to help them dismount, and the lord himself took the two kings by the hands, because they seemed to him noblemen and princes. He led them to a chamber at the base of the central tower to disarm. While they were disarming, three beautiful maidens entered—two were Agravadain's nieces and the third was his daughter—carrying three mantles of fine red cloth trimmed with black ermine, which they placed on the shoulders of their lord and the two kings. But King Ban, who was lusty and amorous, stared at the maidens with great interest and desire, for they were marvelously beautiful and gracious and young, the eldest not yet twenty-four. And Agravadain's daughter was the most beautiful of them all. Merlin looked at her with great desire, and thought in his heart that the man who slept with that maiden would burn with joy. And if it were not, he thought, for the great love I have for my Viviane, I would take her in my arms this very night. And if I cannot have her, I will make it so that King Ban can. So he laid a simple enchantment on them, and as soon as he had done so, King Ban and the daughter of Agravadain loved each other passionately.

After the two kings were robed in the mantles the two maidens had placed on their shoulders, Agravadain entertained them royally until it was time for dinner. Then he had splendid, large tables set in the middle of the palace, and he seated the two brother kings at the head table, one beside the other, next to him and his lady wife, who was beautiful and young, not yet thirty years old. And the knights sat at tables in the middle of the palace. The three lovely maidens waited on the two kings and Agravadain. And Merlin was there, but he had taken on the appearance of a young lad of fifteen. He was dressed in a particolored coat of red and white, belted with a baldric of silk that had two ribbons of silk with rings of gold here and there and from which hung a small alms-purse of beaten gold. He had curly, blond hair and large, green eyes. He knelt before King Ban. He received many looks from one side and the other, for no one recognized him except the two brother kings; those of their party believed he belonged to the household of the lord of the castle. And because of the great goodness and beauty they saw in him, the maidens looked at him with great interest now and again. But the daughter of Agravadain had eyes only for King Ban because of Merlin's enchantment, and she blushed often and was anxious for the tablecloths to be taken away, for she greatly desired to be in his arms naked, and she did not know where this desire had come from.

These thoughts and this anguish came to the maiden through Merlin's enchantment. And for his part King Ban was so affected that he could not stop laughing and playing at the table, and he didn't know what had come over him. He was very angry he was acting that way, for he had a beautiful young wife who did not deserve that he wrong her; and also, he thought it would be treason—they had given him such great honor there—he thought there was no greater dishonor he could do than to shame the daughter of his host in such a manner. He was so ill at ease that he did not know what to do. To be sure, he said in his heart, he would not ask anything of her.

But Merlin, who knew all their thoughts, said to himself that that could not be, for it would be a great shame if they did not come together. For the land of Britain would win great honor through·the child that would be born, because of the great prowess he would have. This Merlin said to himself.

And when the tablecloths were taken away, and they had washed their hands, they all went and leaned out the windows and looked down at the marshes, and the land all around was so marvelously beautiful that they forgot everything until it was time to go to bed. Then they entered a chamber next to the master chamber where the maidens had prepared two beds as if for princes and the two kings went to bed in great splendor. And when the two kings were in bed, the lord of the castle went to bed next to his wife, and the three maidens went to another chamber nearby.

When they were all in bed, Merlin began his enchantment so that everyone in the castle would sleep except for King Ban and the damsel, who were both so strongly smitten with each other that they could neither rest nor sleep. Then Merlin, who wanted to finish what he had begun, went to the chamber where the maiden lay and took her very gently by the hand and said, "Rise, beautiful one. We will go to the one you so desire." And she was so enchanted that she could not contradict his will, but rose right away from her bed, naked except for her chemise and her fur robe, and Merlin led her by the hand past the bed of her father and the beds of the other knights of the castle—but they were so sound asleep that he could have torn the castle down over their heads without waking them. Merlin and the maiden went on until they came to the chamber where the two kings lay and found King Ban and King Bors, who was sleeping as soundly as the others under Merlin's spell. So they went straight to King Ban, who was quite in anguish, and Merlin said, "Lord, see the good and beautiful maiden who will give birth to the good and handsome knight who will bring great renown to the realm of Logres."

When the king saw the maiden and heard Merlin's words, he stretched out his hands and received her joyfully, as one who has great desire. He could not contradict the enchantment that had been made. But if he had not been enchanted, he would never have dared it even for the realm of Logres, for he greatly feared Our Lord. So he rose up and took the maiden in his arms, and she took off her fur robe and her chemise and went to bed with him and they drew together as lovingly and as naturally as if they had been together for twenty years, for neither one was afraid or ashamed in front of the other. All this Merlin had ordained.

In this manner King Ban and the maiden lay together all night until daybreak. And then Merlin, who was well aware of the time, came and made the damsel rise. When she had dressed herself in her chemise and her robe, the king took a small ring from his finger, saying, "Beautiful one, keep this ring and my love." And the damsel took it and put it on her finger, then drew away from him and commended him to God. And Merlin took her back to her bed and put her to bed totally naked. And she went to sleep right away, like one who had conceived a son of whom Lancelot would have great joy and great honor, because of his great goodness.

When Merlin had put the damsel to bed in the bed he had taken her out of, he returned to his own bed. Then he undid his enchantment and everyone in the castle awoke. It was still early. The squires and the sergeants rose and armed themselves and saddled the horses and loaded the coffers and cases. And Merlin went to King Ban, who was still asleep, for the enchantment was over. And although he knew he had lain with the damsel, he could not remember how it had happened—but he was sure it had been through Merlin's doing. And Merlin went to him and told him it was time to leave.

When the two kings and all the others had risen and dressed, the lord of the castle and the three maidens came to the two kings and greeted them. They returned their greeting. And when King Ban saw the damsel who had made love with him all night he looked at her very carefully, but she bowed her head as if she were ashamed that she had been so intimate with him and now was abandoned. And never before and never after could she love another man more than him, it seemed, for never could a man approach her without her saying to herself that she was the wife of a crowned king and ought not abandon herself to a lesser man. And she would not take a husband.

King Ban took her by the hand and said very softly, "Damsel, I must go. But wherever I am, I am your knight and your friend. I pray you, think of your welfare and take care of yourself, for you are pregnant with a son who, it is known, will give you great joy and honor." Of this Merlin the wise had spoken, and through him King Ban knew much that was to come.

The damsel replied in a low voice, "Lord, if that is so, God, by his grace, will give me greater joy than I have from your leaving, for never have lovers so soon parted. But if you must go, I will be comforted as best I can by the one I carry. If I live to see him, he will be for me a mirror and a remembrance of you."

At those words the king placed his hands on her shoulders and, sighing, commended her to God. Then the damsel turned and went into the chamber she shared with the two maidens, and the two kings and Merlin commended the lady of the castle to God, and also the lord, and thanked them profusely for the courtesy they had shown them. Then they mounted and rode out of the castle and passed along the causeway one after the other. And Agravadain accompanied his guests as far as the pines, then turned back.

Suite du Merlin

The Begetting of Mordred

(pp. 147–162 in Paris-Ulrich)

So it is said that a month after Arthur's coronation, the wife of King Lot of Orkney—Arthur's sister—came to the king's great court at Carduel [= *Caerleon*] in Wales. But Arthur did not know she was his sister. The lady came splendidly to court, in a great company of ladies and damsels and with a great host of knights. She brought also her four sons by King Lot, all very handsome children and so young that the eldest was only ten years old; he was called Gawain. The second oldest was Gaheris; the third, Agravain; and the fourth, Gareth. And so the lady came to court with all her children, whom she dearly loved. And she was graced with such beauty that one could hardly find her equal. She was highly honored by the king, not only because she was a crowned queen, but because she was of King Uther Pendragon's lineage.

King Arthur delighted in the lady's company and grandly entertained her and her children. As soon as he had seen this woman so filled with beauty, he loved her passionately, and he made her stay at court for two full months. During that time he lay with her and engendered Mordred, through whom great evil would come to the land of Logres and to all the world.

Thus the brother knew the sister carnally, and she carried the one who would betray him to his death and cast the land into destruction and martyrdom. [*The queen returned to Orkney and Arthur dreamed that a dragon and a troop of griffins laid waste the kingdom; he killed the dragon, but was mortally wounded. The dream troubled him so much he could not go back to sleep, so he waked his men early to go hunting. They rousted a stag and set off in chase, but Arthur rode so hard that he outstripped the others until, out of sight and hearing of them, his mount fell down dead beneath him.*] When Arthur found himself on foot, he did not know what to do, for his men were far behind him. So he chased after the stag, going at such a speed that in less than an hour he was totally lost—but even so he kept after the stag, believing his men must follow shortly and he would surely meet them.

When he was weary and covered with sweat and could not go any farther, he sat down by a spring. But as soon as he sat down, he began thinking about what he had seen in his dream that night. While he sat thinking, he heard dogs baying; the noise was so loud there must have been thirty or forty of them, and they seemed to be coming toward him. He thought it must be the hunting pack, so he raised his head and looked in the direction the noise was coming from.

It was not long before he saw a huge beast, stranger than he had ever seen in his entire life. And it was strange both inside and out, for from its belly came the noise of thirty hounds baying.

The beast hurried over to the spring and drank a great draught. Watching it, the king crossed himself, saying, "I am seeing the greatest marvel that has ever been seen. Of a beast as strange as this, I have never heard tell. For if she is marvelous outside, she is just as marvelous inside—I can hear quite plainly that she has live brachets inside her belly baying. Nowhere in the kingdom of Logres has such a marvel been seen." This the king said to himself. As soon as the beast began to drink, the animals inside her, baying, fell silent. When she finished drinking and drew away from the spring, they started baying again just as before. And they made the same noise as twenty brachets after a wild beast. So the beast went away from the fountain in a great racket of baying. The king watched it out of sight, so astonished at the marvel he was seeing that he did not know if he was sleeping or awake. And it hurried off so that the king soon lost both sight and sound of it. And when it was out of sight, he returned to what he was thinking about before.

[*A knight came by on foot, distraught that he had lost his horse, for he had chased the Beast for a year—it would be killed by the best of his lineage, and he was hunting it to test himself. As they talked, a squire appeared, searching for the king. The king ordered the squire to dismount and said he intended to follow the Beast. "Ha! Sire! You would not do such villainy to me and my Beast," cried the knight. He leaped onto the horse and, exchanging threats with the king, rode away on his quest. The squire set off to bring the king another horse, and Arthur lapsed back into thought.*] While he was deep in thought, Merlin came by looking like a four-year-old child. He recognized the king as soon as he saw him, and greeted him—but he did not give any sign he knew it was the king. The king raised his head and said, "Child, God bless you! Who are you?"

Merlin replied, "I am a squire from a strange land. But I am very surprised to see a knight like you worrying so much, for it seems to me that no man who is worth anything would worry over something he could get good advice about."

The king stared at the child, amazed that he spoke so wisely. "Child, I do not believe any man under God could give me advice for what I am thinking about."

Said Merlin, "Surely you cannot think anything I do not know, nor do anything I do not know. Sire, you are amazed over nothing! For everything you see in your sleep will happen in the future—so it pleases the Creator of the world. If you saw your death in your sleep, you should not be surprised."

When the king heard Merlin talk that way, he was not amazed—he was astounded!

And Merlin said, "So that you will marvel even more, I will describe to you what you dreamed last night."

Said the king, "By my head, if you can do that, it will be the greatest marvel I have ever seen or heard of."

Said Merlin. "I will tell you. Then you will have even more to think about than you did before." So he described the dream just as the king had dreamed it.

And when the king heard that, he crossed himself for the marvel he had witnessed and replied, mistakenly, "You are not a man one should believe—but a demon. You could not know these secret things you have described to me through the wisdom of a man."

And Merlin replied, "Because I described secret things to you does not give you the right to say I am a demon. But I will prove to you that you are a devil and the enemy of Jesus Christ and the most traitorous knight in this land. For you are an anointed king! And into that honor and that dignity you were placed by the grace of Jesus Christ and no other. Arthur, you have committed such a grave sin! For you have lain carnally with your own sister, whom your father begot and your mother carried, and you have engendered on her a son who is as God knows well—for through him great evil will come to the earth."

To this replied the king, very shamed by these words, "Enemy of God, you could not be certain of what you accuse me unless you knew for sure that I had a sister. And you could not know this, nor anyone else, for I myself do not know it. And no one, it seems to me, could be more certain of such a thing than I myself. And I know nothing about it!"

"By my faith," said Merlin, "that is not true. I am more sure of this than you are, for you yourself say you know nothing about it. I know very well who your father and your mother and your sisters are. And although it has been a long time since I saw them, I know very well that they are alive and well."

This comforted the king greatly. Nevertheless, he did not at all believe the child was telling the truth, for he still believed it was a demon talking to him. But nevertheless he said, "If you were to identify my father and my mother and my sisters, so I could know for certain from what lineage I come, you could not ask for anything in my kingdom that I would not give you."

Said Merlin, "Do you swear to that as king? For know it well that if you lie to me, greater evil will come to you than you could believe."

Said the king, "I swear to you. Faithfully."

"Then I will tell you. You will be certain quite soon. I say you are a nobleman of so high a lineage as to be the son of a king and a queen. And your father was a nobleman and a good knight."

"What!" said the king, "am I as noble a man as that? If this is true, I will not rest until I have put under my subjection the greater part of the world."

Said Merlin, "Certainly, you will not be hindered because you are not noble enough. But watch what you do. For if you are as noble as your father was, you will not lose any land in conquering more."

"And what," said the king, "was my father's name? That you must tell me."

"Certainly," said Merlin, "he was called Uther Pendragon, and was king of all this land."

Then said the king, "In the name of God! If he was my father, I cannot fail to be a nobleman. For I have heard so much of him that I know very well he was so noble he could not possibly have had bad heirs, unless marvels should happen. If this is indeed true, the nobles of this land will be very glad to hear it."

Said Merlin. "I will let them know. Before this month has passed they will all be certain—they will know the truth, that you are the son of Uther Pendragon and Queen Igerne."

Said the king, "You tell me such marvels, I can hardly believe you. And I will tell you why. If I was the son of who you say, they could not have placed me in the hands of such a minor vassal as the man who raised me, and I would not be as unknown as I am. For it could not be that the man who raised me would not know who I was—but he himself told me he was not my father, and that he did not know whose son I was. And you—you are a stranger here. How could you would know better than the man I have been around all my life?"

Said Merlin, "If I have not told you the truth about whose son you are, then do not give me what you owe me. But you should know that I am not telling you any of this to shame you or out of hatred, but because I love you. And if I have told you what I never should have revealed, then be certain I will conceal it as well as you do yourself—I mean, the sin with your sister with whom you lay carnally, as I told you. But I will not hide this sin so much out of love for you, as out of love for your father, who loved me greatly and did much for me, and I for him."

"Is what you say now true?"

Said Merlin, "Oh yes, certainly."

"In the name of God," said the king, "if you had said this before, I would not have believed anything you told me. You are not old enough to have ever seen my father—if he was Uther Pendragon. He could not have done anything for you, or you for him. Now I command you to leave this place, for after that blatant lie you would have me take for truth, I do not desire any more to have your company."

When Merlin heard this, he acted as if he were very angry and hastily left the king. He went into the thickest part of the forest and changed his appearance, taking on the form of an old man, eighty years old and so feeble-looking it seemed he could hardly walk. And he was dressed in a gray robe.

In this disguise he went before the king, looking like a wise man. He greeted the king as if he did not know him and said, "God save you, sir knight, and bring your cares quickly to good end. For it seems to me that you are not well at ease."

"So be it, noble sir," said the king, "for certainly I have great need of that. Come sit down with me, if you will, until my squire returns."

So Merlin sat down beside him and they began to talk of many things. The king found Merlin so knowledgeable about all the things he asked him that he was amazed.

And then Merlin said to him, "What were you thinking so deeply about when I arrived?"

"Noble sir," said the king, "no man of my age has seen so many marvels in such a short time, nor heard what I have heard, both sleeping and awake, since yesterday evening. And what I take to be the greatest marvel is that an infant only a few years old came by just now and told me things I would not have believed any mortal man but I alone could know."

"Sire," said the nobleman, "that should not amaze you, for there is nothing so secret that it cannot be discovered. If it happens on earth, then, it is true, it will be known on earth."

Then Merlin said to the king, "Sir, for God's sake, do not be so ill-at-ease, do not worry so, but tell me what it is. I will counsel you so that you will quickly be assured about all the things that are troubling you."

The king looked at the old man, and he seemed to him to be a very wise man. And he liked him and liked what he was saying, so he thought that he would tell him part of his thoughts and keep part hidden. So he began to tell him his dream, just as the tales have described it. And he told the truth about the beast and the knight.

When Arthur had told the old man all that he wanted to, Merlin replied, "Sire, with this dream I will help you, in so far as I can do so without harming myself. Know that you will fall into ruin and woe because of a knight who has been begotten but is not yet born. And all this kingdom will be destroyed, and the noblemen and the good knights of the realm of Logres will be slaughtered and killed. And the kingdom will be orphaned of good knights. This you will see in your time, and this land will remain deserted through the works of this sinner."

Said the king, "If this should happen, it would be an outrageous shame. It would be much better, and in my opinion it would be the greater charity, if this evil person in this evil body were to be destroyed as soon as he is born, since he will cause such great destruction. And since you have told me so much already, it cannot be that you do not know when he will be born and of whom. I pray you, tell me—for as soon as he is born into the earth I will have him burned, if it pleases Our Lord that I know the truth of his birth."

"Never," said Merlin, "never, if God pleases, will this creature of Our Lord receive evil through me. For even though he will be treacherous by the end, yet while he is innocent, the one who killed him would be villainous. I tell you, I feel so charged with my own sins and so guilty before Our Lord that never, if God wills, will I act so vilely that an infant, no matter how harmful a creature, will receive death by my counsel. Do not command it of me, for this I will refuse to do."

"Then," said the king, "you hate this realm mortally. And I will show you why. You say, and I truly believe it, that by one knight all the realm of Logres will be destroyed. Would it not be better if he who is to cause this great woe were himself destroyed, than that so many people died because of him?"

"Yes, truly," said Merlin, "his death is worth more than his life."

"Then I say to you," said the king, "it would be better to tell us whose son he will be than to hide it from us, for through the revealing this land will be saved, but through the concealing, it will be lost."

"Sire," said Merlin, "I truly believe that the revelation would be worth more and that it would save the glory of the realm. But I would lose more than the realm would gain—for I would lose my soul, which is worth more to me than all this land. Because of this, I will keep it a secret from you. I would rather save my soul than the land."

"At the least," said the king, "you can tell me when he will be born and in what place."

And Merlin began to smile and said, "With that you believe you can find him. But it cannot be, for it is not Our Lord's will."

Said the king, "Certainly, I will do it. If I know the hour of his birth and the country in which he will be born, this land will never be destroyed by him, for I will outstrip him."

Said Merlin, "I will tell you this, and this is all I will say. He will be born the first day of May in the realm of Logres."

Said the king, "Is that true?"

"Yes," said Merlin, "you know it is."

"Then," said the king, "now I will keep quiet and not ask you any more about it. But now advise me more of all that I ask you, you must instruct me." [*Merlin then told the king that the strange beast had to do with the Quest for the Holy Grail, and that all would be explained to him by Perceval, who would be the son of the knight chasing the beast.*] "In the name of God," said the king, "I have much to look forward to, if it is as you say."

Said Merlin, "It will be so."

"And you know it?" said the king. "Are you then certain that these things will happen in the future?"

"Yes," said Merlin, "I am certain. This gift God granted me of his mercy."

Then the king said, "If you are certain of things to come, you must know even more about something that happened in your lifetime."

"Surely," said Merlin, "I know it. Few things that can be spoken of have been done in this land since I was born that I do not know of."

"Then tell me," said the king, "tell me something I greatly desire to know."

"I will tell you," said Merlin, "for I know very well what you want to ask me."

"You know?" said the king. "But I have not yet asked it. How can that be?"

"You will see that I know it," said Merlin. "Now be quiet a little and listen."

Then he said, "You want to ask me, 'Who was my father?' And you believe no one could know this since you yourself do not know. But there is one. And that one will tell you what I tell you. And to the people of this realm I will make known who your father was, for they are doubting."

The king raised his hand and crossed himself on hearing this great marvel, and he said to Merlin, "You make me marvel at your words, for you tell me what I am thinking—and I did not believe that any man before God could do that. For this, if it pleases you, suffer that I may know you. Tell me your name. If it pleases you to remain in my company, there is nothing you might want that I will not do for you because of the great wisdom that you possess."

"King," said Merlin, "I am one who will never hide himself from you. Know that I am Merlin, the good wizard, of whom you have heard spoken many times." [*Arthur was overjoyed to meet Merlin. Told again that Uther Pendragon and Queen Igerne were his parents, this time he believed him. He asked how to hide his great sin, but Merlin said it could not be hidden. Many months later Arthur would command every child born on May Day to be sent to him, and would set 712 of them adrift in a pilotless boat. Mordred and his escorts, however, would shipwreck on their way to Arthur's court, Mordred alone being saved by a fisherman. The 712*] *children washed ashore, unharmed, by the castle of King Oriant, known as "Le Laid Hardi." Merlin appeased the knights by telling them their children were safe and would return to them in ten years.*]

The Didot-Perceval

The Esplumoir Merlin

(pp. 301–302 in Cerquiglini)

And so Arthur was taken to Avalon, but he told his men to wait for him, for he would return. The Britons returned to Carduel and waited more than forty years before choosing a king, because they believed Arthur would return. And surely you know that they often saw him hunting in the forests and heard his dogs: because of this they hoped for a long time that he truly would return.

Now when all these events were over, Merlin went to Blaise and told him everything just as it had happened. After Blaise had put it all down in writing, Merlin took him to Perceval, who guarded the Grail and lived such a sainted life that the Holy Spirit often descended to him. Blaise told Perceval the whole adventure of Arthur: how he was spirited away to Avalon and how Gawain was killed and how the knights of the Round Table met their ends. Perceval cried for pity while he listened and prayed Our Lord to have mercy on their souls, for he had deeply loved them.

Afterward Merlin came to Perceval and to his master Blaise and took his leave of them, saying that Our Lord no longer wished him to show himself to men, but neither could he die before the end of the world: "But then will I have eternal joy," he said. "And I would like to build a hermitage beside your house, where I will live, prophesying what Our Lord commands me to. And everyone who sees my hermitage will call it the Esplumoir [*esplumoir*: a cage to hold a moulting falcon or other hunting bird] of Merlin."

At that Merlin went away and built his Esplumoir and went inside and was never seen in the world again. The stories tell no more of Merlin and the Grail, only that Merlin prayed to Our Lord to grant mercy to all those who hear his book, and to all those who have it written down so as to remember his works. And all of it has been told to you: Amen.

Here ends the book of Merlin and the Grail.

chapter 6

MIDDLE ENGLISH ROMANCES

Peter Goodrich

G I V E N   T H E   great popularity of the intricate vernacular romances of Robert de Boron and his continuators, it was inevitable that they should inspire Middle English translations and adaptations between the beginning of the thirteenth century and the end of the fifteenth. While none of these equals the brilliance and originality of Thomas Malory's *Le Morte Darthur*, they deserve more than the obscurity they have suffered. Nevertheless, habitual scholarly concentration on original compositions and early sources at the expense of subsequent adaptations has left many Arthurian texts largely unappreciated by modern readers, and even vilified by their editors. Admittedly, most lengthy versions of the French Merlin romances in Middle English are aesthetically inferior to their sources, but they played a significant role in the development of an English vernacular style that flowered in Malory's work, and in the English conception of Merlin himself.

The three Middle English texts excerpted here serve to illustrate this development and, together with the previous selections from French sources, the variety of Merlin's medieval roles as wonder child, wild man, magician, seer, strategist, diplomat, educator, and lover. The earliest adaptation of the French Merlin romances was the anonymous *Of Arthour and of Merlin*, written in the second half of the thirteenth century. The author was someone from the London area, who worked the early narrative of the prose *Merlin* of de Boron and its Vulgate versions into a verse romance of eight-syllable couplets with four stresses per line. This was the general technique of the time, a compromise between the developing prose style of French romances and the earlier epic verse styles of the *chansons de geste* and Anglo-Saxon poetry. In fact the author carefully condensed the intricate plot of his French source to emphasize the heroic, warlike, and dynastic interests of the Norman rulers. Later, in the dynastic wars between the houses of York and Lancaster, Malory's work was to exhibit similar tendencies. The epic approach to the involved romantic tradition of King Arthur proved so popular that even after Malory new versions of *Arthour and Merlin* were produced. The late version included here and named *Merline* in the Percy manuscript collection uses a Middle English with much more modern linguistic forms, but still retains the original's heroic flavor and demonstrates that the story of Merlin's early years offered sufficient appeal to survive Malory's redefinition of his roles in Arthurian romance.

The Middle English prose *Merlin*, written about 1450 by another anonymous translator, is a much more literal rendition of the French *Estoire de Merlin*. Henry Lovelich, a versifier who attempted (but never came close to finishing) a translation of the entire Vulgate cycle, had produced a lengthy translation of half the *Estoire* about 1425. However, the prose *Merlin* is more accurate and aesthetically pleasing than Lovelich's work and was probably available to Malory. It was certainly known to at least one circle of aristocratic literary patrons, which included the Guildfords of Kent, who owned and annotated a copy early in the 1500s (Meale, pp. 100ff.). The annotator, who signed her name Elyanor Guldeford, appeared most interested in the courtly liaisons of important female characters—in which Merlin frequently plays a part. (Malory omits several of them, including the enchantment of Ban and Agravadain's daughter.) Such an interest in the French tradition of the wizard, and on the part of female as well as male readers, suggests that the Middle English romances prior to *Le Morte Darthur* had a continuing influence on English conceptions of the wizard. Furthermore, as Karen Stern suggests, it is likely "that these stories formed part of the literary heritage of the most esteemed medieval English romance writers" (p. 122), were appreciated by literate middle-class readers as well as the aristocracy, and exemplified the gradual absorption of French literary material and narrative styles into the developing English vernacular.

Malory's focus on the events of Arthur's life and reign is therefore an authorial choice that does not necessarily imply any actual diminution of audience interest in the figure of Merlin. His foreshortening of Merlin's role to that of agent and chief counselor for Arthur's early years results from that choice, which values the linear over the episodic and interlaced plots of the French romances, and the concept of Christian kingship over the magical or miraculous manipulation of social progress. It is also possible that Malory was not quite certain how to accommodate such a puissant wizard in his narrative without eclipsing Arthur, and distrusted Merlin's *deus ex machina* solutions to human problems. If true, this would certainly help us to understand why Nyneve (or Nimue) shuffles Merlin off the stage so rapidly and unceremoniously.

Malory's conception, however, indisputably became the chief influence on later ages, just as his prose and vision of English chivalry attained a richness and majesty and that surpassed earlier romancers. And it is partly through his influence and the powerful convention of the wise man outwitted by a woman that Merlin's own decline was ensured. The wizard's burial in the vast scheme of chivalric adventures that he helps to create and foretell is also metaphorically appropriate, for his fate in the *Suite du Merlin* and *Le Morte Darthur* is remarkably similar to the one from which he saves his mother: being "dolven" or buried alive for the sin of fornication. By the seventeenth century he is seen no longer as a master of history and society, but as a mere tributary to the chivalric order he had supposedly brought about through King Arthur—as a mystical prophet or devil's son and purveyor of magical machinations, far more a creature of popular imagination than of the compelling secular and religious concerns of powerful landowners, aristocrats, and their retinues.

In editing the texts that follow, I have tried to preserve as much of the Middle English flavor as possible. Only in this way, it seems to me, can these romances be fairly compared with each other. Readers who are encountering Middle English for the first time may find it intimidating for the first few pages, but increasingly easy to understand thereafter. I have adopted a number of minor changes to facilitate clarity and ease of reading without obscuring the writers' idiom. Modern letters have been substituted for obsolete equivalents and occasionally a modern spelling where the text's spelling creates particular confusion. The spelling of the characters' proper names and some place-names has been regularized, and doubled consonants at the beginning of words (such as "ffor") eliminated. Capitalization and punctuation have also been regularized, and I have used paragraphing to signify stages in both dialogue and action. Obsolete words whose meanings are undefined by the context have been glossed in the margin (for poetry) or square brackets (for prose). In a very few cases I have adopted a reading from a source other than the base edition. Otherwise I have left the Middle English syntax, vocabulary, and spelling unaltered.

Bibliographic note: The text for *Merline* is based on the edition in Volume 1 of *Bishop Percy's Folio Manuscript: Ballads and Romances*, ed. John W. Hales and Frederick J. Furnivall, 3 vols. (London: Trübner, 1867–1868), pp. 417–496. I am also greatly indebted to O.D. Macrae-Gibson's edition of the Auchinleck and Lincoln manuscripts, *Of Arthour and of Merlin*, 2 vols., Early English Text Society O.S. 268, 279 (London: Oxford University Press, 1973, 1979). A translation by Samuel Rosenberg of the *Estoire de Merlin* birth story is available in *The Romance of Arthur II*, ed. James J. Wilhelm (New York: Garland, 1986), pp. 214–222.

The only full manuscript of the Middle English prose *Merlin* is Cambridge UL. FF. III. ii., and the selections below are based on the edition of Henry B. Wheatley with additional scholarly essays by William Edward Mead, D.W. Nash, and J.S. Stuart Glennie in *Merlin; or The Early History of King Arthur: A Prose Romance*, 4 vols., Early English Text Society O.S. 10, 21, 36, 112 (London: Kegan Paul, Trench, Trübner, 1865, 1866, 1869, 1899), reprinted in two volumes (New York: Greenwood, 1969). Important essays on the text, its reception, and the problems of its interpretation are Carol M. Meale, "The Manuscripts and Early Audience of the Middle English *Prose Merlin*," pp. 112–122, and Karen Stern, "The Middle English *Prose Merlin*," pp. 123–136, both in *The Changing Face of Arthurian Romance*, ed. Alison Adams, Armel H. Diverres, Karen Stern, and Kenneth Varty (Woodbridge, Suffolk: Boydell, 1986). Samuel Rosenberg's translation of the *Suite du Merlin's* version of the Merlin-Nimiane story is in *The Romance of Arthur II*, pp. 252–266.

The texts from Malory's *Le Morte Darthur* are based upon H. Oskar Sommer's *Le Morte Darthur by Syr Thomas Malory: The Original Edition of William Caxton*, 2 vols. (London: David Nutt, 1890); also invaluable have been the modern editions of William Matthews and James Spisak (Berkeley: University of California Press, 1986), and Eugene Vinaver (Oxford: Clarendon, 1969). Of the voluminous criticism devoted to Malory, several articles focus on Merlin's problematic nature and on Nyneve/Nimue: Wendy Tibbetts Greene, "Malory's Merlin: An Ambiguous Magician?" *Arthurian Interpretations* 1.2 (Spring 1987): 56–63; Sue Ellen Holbrook, "Nymue, The Chief Lady of the Lake, in Malory's *Le Morte Darthur*," *Speculum* 53 (1978): 761–777; and Arthur Stanley Kimball, "Merlin's Miscreation and the Repetition Compulsion in Malory's *Morte Darthur*," *Literature and Psychology* 25 (1975): 27–33. Two important general studies of Malory are Larry D. Benson, *Malory's Morte Darthur* (Cambridge: Harvard University Press, 1976), and Robert M. Lumiansky, *Malory's Originality* (Baltimore: Johns Hopkins University Press, 1964).

Merline (Of Arthour and of Merlin, Percy MS.)

Of Arthour and of Merlin was the first English romance to incorporate the wizard after his "sea-change" in French Arthurian literature. The oldest and most complete version is the Auchinleck MS of 9,938 lines, but its longevity is attested by other, partial versions, such as the Percy MS from which *Merline* comes. The fact that five manuscripts date from the mid- to late fifteenth century indicates a revival of interest in this poem at the very time that Henry Lovelich and the writer of the prose *Merlin* were undertaking new translations from the French and Malory was writing his tales. Caxton's contemporary Wynkyn de Worde also printed a version of the romance called *Marlyn* (the surviving copy is dated 1510), so it was still in circulation after *Le Morte Darthur* appeared.

Merline itself dates from the seventeenth century, providing a counterpart to contemporary chronicle-based and antiquarian productions like Thomas Heywood's *The Life of Merlin*. It includes material missing from the Auchinleck MS and continues beyond the ending point of the Lincoln's Inn MS from 1450, its closest analogue and a likely source. The brief descriptions of battle, omitting the lengthy battle scenes that dominate the second half of *Arthour and Merlin*, suggest that the marvelous was of greater interest to its unknown scribe. His termination of the romance before Arthur's conception also indicates that his likely purpose was to provide the elements left out of Malory's first tale.

The writer updates Middle English for seventeenth-century readers, but his work is not technically skilled: the poem's rhymes tend to be predictable and repetitive, its rhythm monotonous, and its meter faulty. These flaws are typical of most Middle English verse romances, but in this case at least partly caused by the writer's attempt to translate obsolete wording into the vocabulary current in the seventeenth century. Despite these shortcomings as poetry, *Merline* has important structural virtues: the narrative is lively, direct, and skillfully paced, and it contains full versions of all the main episodes in Merlin's early life. It is a complete romance in its own right, and its inclusion in the Percy collection underlies the close relationship between verse romance and popular ballad forms.

Merline's 2,391 verses are divided into nine parts, covering the legendary period from Constantine's reign and Vortigern's usurpation of the throne to Pendragon's burial at Glastonbury (rather than Stonehenge). Like the other versions of *Arthour and Merlin*, the story of Merlin's birth is postponed until Vortigern's messengers are dispatched to find a child with no father; this story takes up parts three and four of the Percy text and follows Robert de Boron's version, in which the mage is conceived in a demonic plot to create the Antichrist. This plot was a brilliant innovation for the purpose of increasing Merlin's prestige and incorporating his actions into the developing Grail legend. De Boron and his continuators reconceived the mage in terms of Christian mysticism as the flawed counterpart to Christ, not merely a sage of dubious origin, and they defined his ultimate role as that of Grail prophet, who prepares the way for the Arthurian court to achieve its greatest quest and to leave behind the record by which we know of it. Furthermore, their innovation sharpens his ambivalence as a not quite demonic, angelic, *or* human figure.

How Merlin Was Begotten and Born

David the prophet, and Moyses,
wittenesse and saith how itt was
that God had made thorrow his Might
heaven full of Angells bright:
the joy that they hadden then,
forsooth no tounge tell can,
till Lucifer, with guilt of pryde,
and all that held with him that tyde,
such vengeance God on them can take
that they are now feinds blake.
And I find in holy ritt,
they fell from heaven to hell pitt
Six dayes and seven knights,
as thicke as hayle in thunder lights;

and when it was our Ladye's will,
heaven closed againe full still.
The feendes that I told of ere,
fellen out of heaven with Lucifer;
those that bidden on the ayre on haight,   [*live in*]
fell they beene, stronge and sleight;
of the ayre they take their light,
and have great strength and might
after man to make a bodye
fayre of coulour and rudye,
discending downe among mankind
to tise men to deadlye sinne.
All they wist well beforne
that Jesu wold on Mary be borne;
therto the feendes hadden envye,
and said to the earth they wolden hye
to neigh on earth a maiden mild,   [*have intercourse with*]
and begett on her a child.
Thus they wend the world to have filed,   [*thought, defiled*]
but att the last they were beguiled.
I shall you tell how itt was;
now yee may heere a wonderous case.
        In that time, I undestand,
a rich man was in England,
and had a good woman to his wiffe,
and lived together a cleane liffe;
a sonne they had, and daughters three,
the fairest children that might bee.
Anon a feende that I of told,
that woonen in the ayre soe bold;   [*lived*]
and for to tempt that good woman
he light on the earth then,
and in her body had great might,
and brought her into striffe and fight,
and made her after with egar moode
to cursse her child as shee was woode.
Upon a day att even late,
thorrow the feend, with great hate
with her sonne she gan to grame,   [*became angry*]
and curst him fast by his name,
and to the devill shee him behight
with all her power and her might.
Then was the feende glad and blythe,
and thought to doe him shame swithe;
and when it was come to night,
the feende went to her house right,
and strangled her sonne where he lay.

The wiffe rose up when it was day,
and found her sonne dead att morrow,
and went and strangled herselfe for sorrowe;
and when her lord heard this,
anon swithe for sorrow I-wis
sodainlye he dyed thoe
without shrift or houzell alsoe.   *[confession and/or eucharist]*
The folke of the cuntrye that tyde,
that wooned there neere beside,
came together then to see,
and had ruth and great pittye,
and many a man that day
weeped, and sayd "well-awaye"
for that good man and his wiffe
that had lived soe good a liffe!
    An hermitt that wooned there beside,
came to see them there that tyde—
Blasye forsooth his name was—
and oft for them he sayd "alas!"
that it was befallen soe.
In his heart he was full woe,
and said it was verament   *[really or truly]*
thorrow the feende's incomberment.
The daughters he found there alive;
the hermitt hee can them shrive;   *[confess]*
and when he had done and sayd,
fayre penance on them he layd;
and when hee had done soe,
home again can he goe.
Then the maydens all in fere   *[together]*
served God with blythe cheere.
    In all England then was the usage,
if any woman did outrage
(but if itt were in her spousage),
if any man old or younge
might it witt of that countrye,
all quicke shee shold dolven bee,   *[she should be buried alive]*
but if it were a light woman called
to all men that aske her wold.
Soe the feend that had might,
that wooned in the ayre light,
into the earth he light downe then,
and went unto an old woman,
and hight her both gold and fee
to wende to the sisters three,   *[go]*
the eldest mayden to enchant,
some younge man's body to enfante;   *[fornicate with]*

and shee might bring her therto,
he hett her gold for ever-more.   [*promised*]
That old queane was full glad,
and did as the devill her badde,
and went to the sisters three.
As soone as shee might them see,
to the eldest sister soone she saiyd,
"Alas, my deere sweete mayd!
thou hast fayre feete and hande,
a gentle body for to sounde,
white hayre and long arme;
I-wise it is much harme
that thy bodye might not assay
with some younge man for to play,
that yee might find in every place
game, mirth, and great solace."
      "Certaine," said the maiden then,
"If that I take any man,
but if it were in spousing,
any man either old or younge,
and itt were knowen in this countrye,
all quicke I shold dolven bee."
      "Nay, certaine," said the old queane,
"yee may it doe without dean   [*noise or reproach*]
both in bower and in bedd,
although noe man doe you wedd;
and therfore dread thee nought,
for it needs never be forth brought;
and if thou wilt doe by my rede,
thou diddest never a better deede."
      Soe thorrow the queane's inchantment
and the feend's incumberment,
the eldest sister, the sooth to say,
lett a young man with her play;
and when shee liked best the game,
it turned her to much shame,
for shee was taken and forth drawen,
and of her game shee was knowen,
and for that worke dolven was.
Many a man sayd for her "alas!"
      The feende yett another while
the other sister he can beguile,
and made her to love a faire young man,
and after was his lemman then.   [*mistress*]
Shee was taken forth-wise,
and brought before the Hye Justice
her judgment to understand,

as itt was the law of the land.
The Justice opposed her thoe   [*examined*]
wherfore shee had done soe;
shee answered as shee was taught,
and said shee forsooke itt nought,
and said shee was a light woman
to all that wold come to her common;
and soe shee scaped them away,
soe that her followed all that day
of harlotts a great race
to 'fyle her body for that case.
      Yett the feende in that while
the third sister can beguile.
Then was the youngest sister soe woe
that nye her hart burst in two,
for her mother had hang'd herselfe,
and her one sister quicke was delfe,
and for that her father dyed amisse,
and her brother was strangled I-wis,
her other sister a whore stronge,
that harlotts was ever among.
Almost for sorrow and for thought
in wan-hope shee was brought.
To the hermitt shee went then,
to that hight Blassye, that good man,
and told him all the sooth beforne,
how all her kindred were forlorne.
The hermitt had wonder great;
on God's 'halfe he her besett,
"I bid thee have God in thy mind,
and let be the lore of the feende,"
and bade her forsake in any wise
pryde, hate, and covetise,
alsoe sloth and envye,
and man's flesh in lecherye,
all such workes for to flee;
and bade her God's servant bee,
and bade her to take good keepe
that shee layd her not downe to sleepe,
and namelye not in the night,
unlesse shee had a candle light,
and windowes and dores in that stond   [*stand*]
to be spurred to roafe and ground,   [*bolted*]
and make there againe with good noyce
the signe of the holy crosse.
And when he had taught her soe,
home againe can shee goe,

and served God with hart glad,
and did as the hermitt her bade.
And yett the feend thorrow envye
beguiled her with treacherye,
and brought her into a dreerye cheere:
I shall you tell in what manner.
      Upon a day verament
with neighbors to ale shee went;
long shee sate, and did amisse
that drunken shee was I-wis.
Her other sister that I of told,
that was a whore stout and bold,
came thither that same day
with many harlotts for to play,
and missaide her sister as shee was wood,   [*was mad*]
and called her other then good.
Soe long shee chidd in a resse,   [*rage*]
the whore start up without lesse,
and went to her sister in a rage,
and smote her on the visage.
Then home to her chamber shee can goe,
and made to the dores betweene them tow,
and cryed out; and neighbors came,
and the whore soone they name   [*took*]
and droven her away anon,
and the harlotts everye one.
When they were driven away,
the maid that in the chamber lay
all made, as shee were woode,
weeped and fared as shee were with ill moode.
And when it was come to night,
upon the bed shee fell downe right,
all both shodd and cladde;
shee fell on sleepe, and all was madd,
and forgott her howse unblessed,
as the hermitt had her 'vised.
Then was the feende glad and blythe,
and thought to doe her shame swithe;   [*great shame (with puns on*
over all well he might,   *rapidly and burning)*]
for there was noe crosse made that night.
And to the mayd anon he went,
and thought all Christendome to have shent.   [*undone*]
A traine of a childe he put in her thoe,   [*consequence (with a pun*
and passed away where hee cam froe.   *on treachery)*]
And when that woman was awaked,
and found her body lying naked,
and shee grope with her honde,

and some seed there shee found,
wherby shee wend witterlye   [*knew for certain*]
that some man had lyen her by.
Then shee rose up in hast,
and found her dore sparred fast.
When shee found that it was soe,
in her hart shee was full woe,
and thought it was some wicked thinge
that wold her to shame bringe.
    All the night shee made great sorrowe,
and to the hermitt shee went att morrowe,
and told him all the case.
The hermitt sayd, "Alas! alas!"
that shee had broken her pennance;
and said it was the feend's combrance.
    "A! good father!" said shee thoe,
"what if itt be fallen soe
that a child be on me gotten,
and any man may it witten;
then shall I be delven anon
all quicke, both bodye and bone."
    "Certaine," said the good man,
"my deere daughter, after then
I shall you helpe with all my might
till of itt I have sight.
Goe home, daughter now mine,
and have God's blessing and mine,
for He may—and His will bee—
out of thy sorrow bringe thee."
Home shee went with drerye moode,
and served God with hart good;
and everye day after then
her wombe will greater began
soe that shee might it not hyde,
but itt was perceived in that tyde.
    Then was shee taken forsoothe I-wisse,
and brought afore the Hye Justice.
The Justice opposed her thoe
why shee had done soe;
and for shee wrought against the law,
he judged her for to be slowe.   [*slain*]
And shee answered and said, "Nay,
I wrought never against the law,"
and sware by him that dyed on tree,
"was never man that neighed mee
with fleshly lust or lecherye,
nor kissed my body with villanye."

The Justice answered anon,
"Dame, thou lyest, by St. John!
Thy words beene false and wylde,
when men may see thou art with childe!
In this world was never childe borne
but man's seede there was beforne,
save Jesu Christ thorrow his might
was borne of a mayden bright.
Now many thou for shame then
say thou had never part of any man,
when I myselfe the soothe may see
that a child is gotten of thee?"
  "Certaine, Sir," shee said then,
"I goe with child without any man.
By Him," shee said, "that made this day,
there was never [man] that by me lay;
but as I sleeped one night,
by mee lay a selcoth wight;   [*strange man*]
but I wist never what it was,
therfore I doe me in thy grace."
  The Justice said withouten fayle,
"I never hard of such a marveil!
Today nay shall the woman be delfe
till I have asked wiffes twelve
if any child may be made
without getting of manhood;
and if they say itt may soe bee,
all quitt shalt thou goe, and free;
And if they say that it may nay,
all quicke men shall delfe thee today."
On twelve wives shee did her anon,
and they answered every one,
that never child was borne of maiden
but Jesu Christ, they all saydden.
  Blasye the hermitt upstart then,
to answer the Justice he began,
"Sir Justice," he sayd thoe,
"hear me in a word or tow:
that this woman hath told eche deale,
certes I beleve itt weele;
and yee beleeven her right nought.
By God that all this world wrought,
I have her shriven and taught the law,
to mee wold shee never aknow
that any man for any meede   [*reward*]
neighed her body with fleshlye deede;
therfore it is against the law

that shee dolven shold be this day.
Iff shee have served for to spilt,   [*has deserved to die*]
the chylde in her wombe hath not gilt;
therfore, sir, doe by my reade,
and put her not this time to dead,   [*advice*]
but doe her in warde before
till the childe be bore;
and then," he sayd, "God itt wott,
two yeere keepe it shee motte,
and peradventure," he sayd, "then
the child may prove a good man."
        Then said the Justice,
"Hermitt, thy words are full wise;
therfore by thy doome I will;
noe man today shall her spill."
The Justice commanded anon
to lead her to a tower of stone,
and that noe wight shold with her goe
but a midswiffe, and noe moe.
The tower was strong and hye,
that noe man might come her nye.
A window there was made thoe,
and a cord tyed therto
to draw therein all thinke,   [*things*]
fire and water, meate and drinke.
And when the time was comen,
shee bare a selcoth soune.
        Right faire shape he had then,
all the forme that fell for a man;
blacke he was without lase   [*lying*]
and rough as a swine he was.
Then the midwiffe anon-right
was afeard of that sight;
and for he was soe rough of hyde,
full well shee wist that tyde
that he was never gotten by any man,
and full faine shee wold then
in hell that he had beene her froe,
that never man had seene him moe.
The hermitt that hight Blassye
wist full well sikerlye
The time the child shold be borne,
and to the tower he came att morne,
and called upward to them yare,
and asked them how they did fare.
The midwiffe said without lesse
a knave child there borne was.

"Take him me," he sayd then,
"and I shall make him a Christen man;
whether he dye, or live abyde,
the fairer grace he may betyde."
    Full glad was the midwiffe,
and caught the chyld belive,   [*immediately*]
and by a cord shee lett him downe,
and Blassy gave him his benison,
and bare him home with merry moode,
and baptized him in the holy floode,
and called him to his Christendome,
and named him Merlyn in God's name.
Thorrow that name, I you tell,
all the feends that were in hell
were agreeved, and that full sore;
therfore was their power lore.
And when he had christened him soe,
home againe he bare him thoe,
and in the cord he gan him laine;
the midwiffe drew him up againe,
and he bade her without blame
call him Merlyne by his name.
    The midwiffe bare him anon-right
to the fyer that was bright,
and as shee warmed him by the fyer
shee beheld his lodlye cheere: [*ugly face*]
"Alas," said shee, "art thou Merlyn?
Whence art thou, of what kinne?
Who whas thy father by night or day,
that noe man i-witt itt may.   [*understand*]
It is great ruth, by heaven's King,
that for thy love, thou foule thinge,
thy mother shalbe slaine with woe!
Alas the time it shalbe soe!
I wold thow were farr in the sea,
that thy mother might scape free!"
    When Merlyn hard her speake soe,
he bradde open his eyen towe,
and lodlye on her can hee looke,
and his head on her hee shooke,
and gan to cry with lowd dinne,
"Thou lyest," he sayd, "thou foule queane!
My mother," he sayd, "shall noe man quell
for nothing that men can tell;
whilest I may speak or gone,
mauger them that wold her slone,   [*slay*]
I shall save her liffe for this;

that you shall see and heare I-wis."
    When the midwife, shee heard that,
shee fell downe almost flatt;
shee gan to quake as shee were wood,
and had rather then any good
that shee had beene farr away.
Soe had his mother where she lay;
soe sore they were of him agast,
thy blessed them, and that full fast,
and cryed on him in God's name
that he shold doe them noe shame;
and fast on him they can crye
in God's name and St. Marye
he shold them tell what hee were,
and what misdaventure brought him there.
He did lye and held him still,
and lett them crye all their fill;
and if they shold have slaine him tho,
he wold not speake a word moe.
    And the three lived there
with much sorrow and with care;
and for after halfe a yeare,
as shee held him by the fyer,
rufullye shee gan to greete,
and said to him, "My sonne sweete,
for thy love, withouten weene,
all quicke dolve shall I beene."
    He answered and said, "Nay,
Dame, thou gables by this day;   *[gabbles (speak without sense)]*
there is neither man nor justice
that shall yee deeme in noe wise
then whilest I may either goe or speak,
in earth thy body for to wreak."
Then was his mother a blythe woman,
and everye day after then
he made her gladd and bold,
and mervelous tales to her he told.
    When he cold speake and gone,
the Justice was ready anon,
and bade bring forth anon then
befor him that ilke woman   *[same]*
for to receive her judgment.
And when shee came in present,
the Justice forgatt itt nought,
but egerlye he said his thought,
and sware anon by heaven's Queene
all quicke shee shold dolven beene.

Then the child answered with words bold—
and he was but two yeeres old—
he sayd to the Justice with egar moode,
"Sir Justice! thou can but litle goode
to doe my mother to the dead,
and wotts not by what reade,
save a chance that to her fell;
therfore thou dost not to her well;
for everye man will wott well then
that against chance may be noe man,
and thorrow chance I was begott;
therfore everye man may well wott
that my mother ought nought
for my love to death be brought."
        Great wonder had both old and younge
of the child's answering.
Then the Justice was full wrath,
and on loud sware an oathe
all quicke shee shold dolven bee.
"Nay!" said Merlyn, "soe mote I thee,
thou shalt her never bring therto
for ought that ever thou canst doe!
It shall not goe as thou wilt,
for shee hath done to guiltt,
and I shall prove itt through skill,
mauger of them that wold her spill.
My father that begatt mee
is a feende of great potencye,
and is in the ayre above the light,
and tempts men both day and night;
and therfore to my mother he went,
and wend all Christendome to have shent,
and gott mee on her without leasinge,   [*lying*]
and shee therof wist no thing.
And for shee wist not when it was,
I prove that shee is guiltless;
for all the feends wenden by mee
to have shent all Christentye,
and had of me a wicked foode.   [*child or imp*]
But God hath turned me to goode;
for now I am of God sende
for to helpe all Englande;
and forsoothe," hee said then,
"pardie, tell you I can
all that ever was and now is.
I can you tell well I-wis
thou dost not wott, Justice then,

who was thy father that thee wanne;
and therfore I prove that mother thine
rather to be dolven then mine."
    Hearken now all the striffe,
how Merlyne saved his mother's liffe!
Then was the Justice in hart woe,
and to Merlyne he said thoe,
"Thou lyest!" he sayd, "thou glutton!
My father was a good barron,
and my mother a layde free;
yett on live thou may her see."
    "Sir," said Merlyne then anon,
"send after her full soone,
and I shall make her to be knowen,
or else hange me on todrawen."
    The Justice after his mother sent,
and when shee was comen present,
the Justice before them all
to Merlyn can he call.
He said to him, "Belamye,
be now sow bold and hardye
to prove thy tale, if thou can,
that thou saidest of this woman."
    Merlyn said to the Justice,
"Sir, thy words be not wise;
if I tell theese folke beforne
how thow was gotten and borne,
then shold it spring wyde and broad,
and thou shold lose thy manhood;
then shall thy mother dolven bee,
and all were for the love of thee."
    The Justice then understood
that Merlyn cold mikle good.
Then to a chamber can they goe,
he and Merlyne, and noe moe.
Merlyn," he said, "I pray thee,
what was that man that begatte me?"
    "Sir," he said, "by St. Simon,
it was the parson of the towne!
Hee thee gott, by St. Jame,
upon this woman that is thy dame."
    The lady said, "Thow fowle thinge!
Thou hast made a starke leasinge!
His father was a noble baron,
and a man holden of great renowne;
and thou art a misebegott wretch;
I pray thee God, devill thee feitch!

[i.e., your father is not who you think]

[or draw and quarter me]

[good friend]

[knew much]

[lie]

In wyld fyer thou shalt be brent,
for with wronge thou hast me shent."
        "Dame," sayd Merlyn, "hold thee still,
for itt were both right [and] skill,
for I wott withouten weene
thou deserve dolven to beene;
for sithe thou was to this world brought,
all the worke that thou hast wrought,
I can tell itt everye word
better then thou, by our Lord,
how thy sonne was begotten.
Dame, if thou have forgotten,
I can tell you all the case,
how, and where, and when itt was,
and thou shalt be ashamed sore;
thee were better speak noe more."
        The Lady was sore dismay'd,
and Merlyn forth his tale sayd:
"Dame," he said verament,
"That time thy Lord to Carlile went—
itt was by night and not by day—
the parson in thy bed lay;
att thy chamber dore thy lord can knocke,
and thou didest on thy smocke
and was sore afrayd that tyde,
and undidst a windowe wyde,
and there the parson thou out lett,
and he ran away full tyte.   [*full-tilt*]
Dame," he said, "that ilke night
was begotten thy sonne the knight.
Dame," he sayd, "lye I ought?"
Shee stood still and sayd nought.
        Then was the Justice wrath and woe,
and to his mother he sayd thoe,
"Dame," hee sayd, "how goeth this?"
        "Sonne," shee said, "all sooth, I-wis!
For if thou hand me with a corde,
hee belyeth me never a word."
The Justice for shame waxes redd,
and on his mother shooke his head,
and bade her in hast wend home
with much shame as shee come.
        "Belyve," sayd Merlyn, "send after a spye,
for to the parson shee will her hye,
and all the sooth shee will him saine
how that I have them betraine;
and when the parson hath hard this,

anon for shame and sorrowe I-wis
to a bridge he will flee,
and after noe man shall him see;
into the watter start he will,
liffe and soule for to spill.
And but itt be sooth that I say,
boldlye hang me today."
    The Justice withouten fayle
did after Merlyn's counsayle.
He sent after a spye bold,
and found itt as Merline told;
and the Justice, for Merlin's sake,
him and his mother he lett take,
and lett them goe quitt and free
before the folke of that countrye.
And when Merlin was seven yeere old,
he was both stout and bold;
his mother he did a nun make,
and blacke habitt he let her take,
and from that time verament
shee served God with good entent.

Middle English Prose Merlin

    Like *Of Arthour and of Merlin* and Henry Lovelich's *Merlin*, the Middle English prose *Merlin* translated the Vulgate *Estoire* for English readers. Although thoroughly disparaged by its nineteenth-century editor Henry Wheatley, it is not unskilled but suffers by comparison with Malory and from the conventional expectation of a linear narrative. Now that modern readers have become able to appreciate nonlinear forms of narration with fragmented plot lines and seemingly discontinous sensory impressions, it no longer seems that "the fragments ... sweep along confusedly, like blocks of drift-ice in a river" (Wheatley, Vol. 1, p. ccxliv). We may still object to prolixity, of which both the anonymous translator and his French source are certainly guilty, but we now realize that the complex interlace of medieval romances is a flexible and highly artistic pattern.

    The episodes below provide good examples of medieval narrative practice as well as entertaining embellishments upon Merlin's traditional roles. The romancer treats traditional Arthurian story as a framework that can be filled in or expanded by new episodes, such as Merlin's visit to Rome and his first encounter with Nimiane. Moreover, these interpolated episodes themselves incorporate traditional story materials: Merlin as a wild man or stag, his journey as prisoner to a king's court, his sardonic laughter and prophecies. These materials derive from the Welsh tradition and ultimately from Near Eastern or oriental sources. The savage man living in the wilderness, for example, was not only (in less fanciful form) an actual feature of the medieval landscape, but a recurring feature in ancient literature. The motif of the wild man captured by a woman is present in the epic of Gilgamesh; the male harem is common in oriental literature; the woman disguised as a man and the wise man outwitted by a woman are so frequent that they need no comment. Immediate sources were also available; like the tale of Lailoken and Meldred and the *Vita Merlini*'s story of Merlin and Rhydderch, the Grisandol story is a variant of Solomon's encounter with Asmodeus, in which Asmodeus plays the part of Merlin. These traditional features also refresh significant motifs and prefigure future adaptations of them: the vergier or pleasure garden that Merlin creates for Nimiane is analogous to Eden, Elysium, and the fair tower in which she eventually immures him; and his masque has analogues in the burlesque entertainments he creates for Vortigern in Heywood's *Life of Merlin*, and Prospero's masque for Ferdinand and Miranda in *The Tempest*. Such popular features are "too good" to be used only once!

Not only do interpolated stories allow further experimentation with traditional themes and motifs, but they also build upon the significance of earlier episodes and help to develop the framing legend itself. Like medieval theologians who interpreted episodes in the Old Testament as *figura* or preenactments of significant events in the life of Christ, the repetition of traditional elements in medieval romance was intended to reinforce the meaning of the narrative—the overarching pattern of divine will and human frailty, the cyclical nature of aspiration, sin, and mortality that can somehow be ordered with other contemporaneously occurring events toward an ultimate goal. In this way the interlace of courtly romance is not merely repetitive or haphazard, but inventive and sophisticated, exploring metaphorical as well as structural connections between events and motifs. With his ability to know all things and participate in widely scattered plots, Merlin is at the center of the process symbolized by the book that he dictates to his mentor Blaise.

The story of Grisandol, therefore, is more than just another recapitulation of Merlin's magical roles and an oriental fabliau: it reconfirms his elemental nature, his involvement in sexual intrigues, his prophetic foresight, and the similarity in feudal culture between good stewards and good wives; it also prefigures his "capture" by Nimiane, comments upon Arthur's marriage to the noble Gonnore, prepares the reader for Arthur's conflict with Rome, and expands upon the hidden corruption of royal courts that ultimately brings down even Arthur's. The relation of Merlin's first meeting with Nimiane and eventual imprisonment by her also displays his own activity as a courtly lover. The ending of their affair follows the much gentler version of the Vulgate *Estoire* rather than the earlier story of de Boron's continuators and the *Suite du Merlin*, which Malory used. Here the great mage is not lustfully senile or outwitted, but isolated by love from deeds.

Merlin's First Meeting with Nimiane

Merlin . . . wente to se a maiden of grete bewte, and was right yonge, and was in a manor that was right feire and delitable and right riche, in a valee under a mounteyne rounde side be side to the Forest of Brioke, that was full delitable and feire for to hunte at hertes and at hyndes and bukke and doo and wilde swyn. This mayden of whom I speke was the doughter of a vavasor of right high lynage, and his name was cleped [*called*] Dionas, and many tymes Diane com to speke with hym that was the goddesse, and was with hym many dayes, for he was hir godsone; and whan she departed she gaf hym a gefte that plesed hym wele.

"Dionas," quod Diane, "I graunte the, and so doth the god of the see and of the sterres shull ordeyne, that the firste childe that thow shalt have female shall be so moche coveyted of the wisest man that ever was erthly or shall be after my deth, whiche in the tyme of Kynge Vortiger of the Bloy Mountayne shall begynne for to regne—that he shall hir teche the moste parte of his witte and connynge by force of nygremauncye, in soche manere that he shall be so desirouse after the tyme that he hath hir seyn that he shall have no power to do nothinge agein hir volunte [*will or desire*], and alle thinges that she enquereth he shall hir teche."

Thus gaf Diane to Dionas hir gefte, and whan Dionas was grete he was right a feire knyght and a goode, of high prowesse of body, and he was moche and longe, and longe tyme served a Duke of Burgoyne, that to hym gaf his nyece to ben his wif, that was right a feire maiden and a wise.

This Dionas loved moche the deduyt [*pleasures*] of the wode and the river while that he was yonge, and the Duke of Burgoyne hadde a parte in the Foreste of Brioke, so that was his the halvendell [*half*] all quyte, and that other half was the Kynge Ban's. Whan the Duke hadde maried his nyece he gaf to Dionas his part of this foreste and londe that he hadde aboute grete plente, and whan Dionas wente it for to se, it plesed hym wele, and he lete make a maner to repeire to that was right feire and riche by the vyvier [*fishpond*], and whan it was made he com thider to be ther for the deduyt of the wode and the river that was nygh. And ther aboode Dionas longe tyme, and repeired ofte to the court of Kynge Ban, hym served with nine knyghtes, and in his servise he yede [*went*] at many a grete nede agein the Kynge Claudas, to whom he dide many a grete damage till that the Kynge Ban and the Kynge Boors hadden hym in grete love, for thei knewe hym so noble a knyght and so trewe. And the Kynge Ban to hym graunted his part of this foreste in heritage to hym and to his heyres, and londe and rentys grete foyson [*plenty*]. And the Kynge Boors gaf hym also a town and men and londe, for the grete trouthe that he saugh in hym, and he was so graciouse that alle tho[se] that aboute hym repeyred loved hym above all thinge.

Thus dwelled Dionas in that londe longe tyme, till that he gat upon his wif a doughter of excellent bewte, and hir name was cleped Nimiane, and it is a name of Hebrewe, that seith in Frensch "ment neu ferai"—that is to sey in English "I shall not lye"—and this turned upon Merlin as ye shall here herafter. This mayden wax till she was twelve yere of age whan Merlin com

to speke with Leonces of Paerne, and Merlin spedde hym so that he com to
the Foreste of Brioke, and than he toke a semblaunce of a feire yonge squyre,
and drowgh hym down to a welle whereof the springes were feire and the
water clere, and the gravell so feire that it semed of fyn silver. To this
fountayn ofte tyme com Nimiane for to disporte, and the same day that
Merlin com thider was she come; and whan Merlin hir saugh he behilde hir
moche and avised [*studied*] hir well er he spake eny worde, and thought that
a moche fole were he yef he slepte so in his synne to lese his witte and his
connynge for to have the deduyt [*joy*] of a mayden, and hym-self shamed, and
God to lese and displese.

And whan he hadde longe thought, he hir salued, and she ansuerde wisely
and seide that Lorde that alle thoughtes knoweth sende hym soche volunte
[*good will*] and soche corage [*inclination*] that hym be to profite, and hym not
greve ne noon other, and the same welthe and the same honour hym sende
as he wolde to other. And when Merlin herde the maide thus speke, he sett
hym down upon the brinke of the welle and asked hir what she was; and she
seide she was of this contrey, the daughter of a vavasour, a grete gentilman
that was at a manior therynne.

And what be ye, feire swete frende?" quod she.

"Damesell," quod Merlin, "I am a squyer traveillinge that go for to seche
my maister, that was wonte me for to teche, and moche he is for to preise."

"And what maister is that?" seide the maiden.

"Certes," quod he, "he taught me so moche that I cowde here reyse a
castell, and I cowde make withoute peple grete plente that it sholde assaile,
and withynne also peple that it sholde defende; and yet I sholde do mo
maistries, for I cowde go upon this water and not wete my feet, and also I
cowde make a river whereas never hadde be water."

"Certes," seide the'maiden, "these be queynte craftes, and fayn wolde I
that I cowde do soche disportes."

"Certes," seid the squyer, "yet can I mo delitable pleyes for to rejoise
every high astate more than these ben, for noon can devise nothinge but that
I shall it do and make it to endure as longe as I will."

"Certes," seid the maiden, "yef it were to yow no gref, I wolde se somme
pleyes by covenaunt that I sholde ever be youre love."

"Certes," seid Merlin, "ye seme to me so plesaunt and deboneir that for
youre love I shal shewe yow a party of my pleyes, by covenaunt that youre
love shall be myn, for other thinge will I not aske." And she hym graunted
that noon evell ne thought [*without any evil thought*], and Merlin turned hym
apart and made a cerne [*circle*] with a yerde [*clearing*] in myddell of the launde
[*glade*], and than returned to the maiden and satte agein down by the
fountayn, and anoon the mayden beheilde and saugh come oute of the
Foreste of Brioke ladyes and knyghtes and maydons and squyres, eche
holdinge other by the hondes, and com singinge and made the grettest joye
that ever was seyn in eny londe. And before the maiden com jogelours and
tymbres and tabours [*players of timbrels and tabors*], and com before the cerne
that Merlin hadde made, and whan thei were withynne, thei begonne the
caroles and the daunces so grete and so merveilouse that oon myght not sey
the fourthe parte of the joye that ther was made. And for that the launde was

so grete, Merlin lete rere vergier [*pleasure garden*], whereynne was all maner of fruyt and alle maner of flowres, that gaf so grete swetnesse of flavour that merveile it were for to telle. And the maiden that all this hadde seyn was abaisshed of the merveile that she saugh, and was so at ese that sche ne atended to nothinge but to beholde and entende what songe thei seiden, saf that thei seiden in refreite [*refrain*] of her songe, "Vraiement comencent amours en joye, et fynissent en dolours." [*Truly love begins in joy, yet ends in pain.*]

Quod the maiden, "How know ye that I am a clerke?"

"Damesell," quod Merlin, "I knowe it well, for my maister hath me so well taught that I knowe alle thinges that oon doth."

"Certes," seide the mayden, "that is the moste connynge that ever I herde, and moste myster [*skill, art*] were therof in many places, and that I wolde faynest lerne. And of thinges that be to come, knowe ye ought?"

"Certes," quod he, "swete love, yee, a grete part."

"God mercy!" quod the mayden, "what go ye than sechynge?"

"Truly," quod Merlin, "of that ye moste yet abide yef it be youre plesier."

And while the mayden and Merlin helde this parlement, assembled agein the maidenes and the ladyes and wente daunsinge and bourdinge toward the foreste fro whens thei were come firste; and whan thei were nygh thei entred in so sodaynly, that oon ne wiste where thei were become; but the orcharde abode stille ther longe tyme for the maiden that swetly therof hym praide, and was cleped ther by name "the repeire of joye and of feeste." And whan Merlin and the maiden hadde be longe togeder, Merlin seyde at the laste, "Ffeire maiden, I go, for I have moche to do in other place than here."

"How," quod the maiden, "feire frende, shull ye not teche me firste some of youre pleyes?"

"Damesell," quod Merlin, "ne haste yow not sore, for ye shull know enowe all in tyme, for I moste have therto grete leyser and grete sojour, and on that other side I have yet no suerte of youre love."

"Sir," quod she, "what suerte wolde ye aske? Devise ye, and I shall it make."

"I will," quod Merlin, "that ye me ensure that youre love shall be myn, and ye also for to do my plesier of what I will."

"And the maiden her bethought a litill, and than she seide, "Sir," quod she, "with goode will by soche forwarde, that after that ye have me taught all the things that I shall yow aske, and that I can hem werke." And Merlin seide that so it plesed hym well. Than he asured the maiden to holde covenaunt like as she hadde devised, and he toke hir surete.

Than he taught hir ther a pley that she wrought after many tymes, for he taught hir to do come a grete river over all ther as her liked, and to abide as longe as she wolde; and of other games enowe, whereof she wrote the wordes in perchemyn [*parchment*] soche as he hir devised, and she it cowde full well bringe it to ende. And whan he hadde abiden ther till evesonge tyme, he comaunded hir to God and she hym. But er he departed the maiden hym asked whan he sholde come agein, and he seide on Seint Johne's Even, and thus departed that oon fro that other.

The Story of Grisandol

Julyus Cesar hadde a wif that was of grete bewte, and she hadde with hir twelve yonge men araied in gise of wymen, with whom she lay at alle tymes that the Emperour was oute of hir companye, for she was the most lecherouse woman of all Rome. And for the dredde that theire beerdes sholde growe, she lete anoynte ther chynnes with certeyn oynementes made for the nones [*purpose*], and thei were clothed in longe traylinge robes, and theire heer longe waxen in gise of maydenes and tressed at theire bakkes, that alle that hem saugh wende wele thei were wymen; and longe thei endured with the Empresse unknowen.

In this tyme that the Emperesse ledde this lif, it fill that a mayden com to the Emperour's court that was the doughter of a prince, and the name of this prince was Matan, Duke of Almayne. This mayden com in semblance of a squyer, and this Matan the Duke Frolle hadde disherited and driven out of his londe; and she com to serve the Emperour, for she wiste not where her fader ne moder were becomen. And she was moche and semly and well shapen, and demened hir well in all maners that a man ought, saf only eny vylonye, and never was she knowen but for a man by no semblante, and so a-boode with the Emperour, and was of grete prowesse and peyned tendirly to serve well the Emperour, and plesed hym so well that she was lorde and governour of hym and his housolde. And the Emperour hir loved so well that he made hir knyght atte a feeste of Seint John with other yonge squyers, wherof were mo than two hundred, and after made hir stiward of all his londe. Than the newe knyghtes reised a quyntayne [*target for jousting*] in the mede [*meadow*] of Noiron, and begonne the bourdinge [*games*] grete and huge, and many ther were that dide right wele. But noon so well as dide Grisandol, for so she lete hir be cleped [*named*]; but in bapteme her name was Avenable. This bourdinge endured all day on ende till evesonge that thei departed, and Grisandol bar awey the pris amonge all other, and whan the Emperour saugh Grisandol of so grete prowesse, he made hym stiward of all his londe and comaunder above alle that ther weren, and Grisandol was well beloved of riche and pore.

And upon a nyght after it fill that the Emperour lay in his chamber with the Emperesse; and whan he was aslepe he hadde a vision that hym thought he saugh a sowe in his court that was right grete before his paleys, and he hadde never seyn noon so grete ne so huge, and she hadde so grete bristelis on her bakke that it trayled on the grounde a fadome large [*fathom long*], and hadde upon hir heed a cercle that semed of fyn golde, and whan the Emperour avised hym wele hym thought that he hadde seyn hir other tymes, and that he hadde hir norisshed up; but he durste not sey of trouthe that she were hys. And while he entended to avise hym on this thinge he saugh come oute of his chamber twelve lyonsewes, and com in to the courte to the sowe, and assailed hir oon after another. Whan the Emperour saugh this merveile he asked his barouns what sholde he do with this sowe by whom these lyonsewes hadde thus leyn, and thei seide she was not worthi to be conversaunt amonge peple, ne that no man sholde ete nothinge that of hir come, and juged hir to be brente and also the lyonsewes togeder; and than awooke the Emperour sore affraied and pensif of this avision. Ne never to man ne to wif wolde he it telle, for he was full of grete wisdom.

On the morowe as soone as he myght se the day, he aroos and yede to the mynster [*church*] to here messe, and whan he was come agein he fonde the barouns assembled, and hadde herde messe at the mynster and the mete was all redy; and whan thei hadde waisshen thei satte to mete, and were well served. Than fill that the Emperour fill in to a grete stodye, wherfore all the courte was pensif and stille, and ther was noon that durste sey a worde for sore thei dredde for to wrathe the Emperour. But now we moste turne a litill to Merlin that was come in to the foreste of Rome to certefie these thinges and these avisiouns.

While that the Emperour satte at his mete amonge his barouns thus pensif, Merlin come in to the entre of Rome and caste an enchauntement merveilouse, for he becom an herte [*male deer*], the gretteste and the moste merveilouse that eny man hadde seyn, and hadde oon of his feet before white, and hadde five braunches in the top, the grettest that ever hadde be seyn, and than he ran thourgh Rome so faste as all the worlde hadde hym chaced. And whan the peple saugh hym so renne, and saugh how it was an herte the noyse aroos, and the cry on alle partyes, and ronne after grete and small with staves and axes and other wepen, and chaced hym thourgh the town, and he com to the maister gate of the paleys whereas the Emperour satte at his mete, and whan thei that served herde the noyse of the peple, thei ronne to the wyndowes to herkene what it myght be, and anoon thei saugh come rennynge the herte and all the peple after. And whan the herte com to the maister paleys he drof in at the gate sodeynly, and than he ran thourgh the tables abandon and tombled mete and drynke all on an hepe, and began therin a grete trouble of pottis and disshes. And whan the herte hadde longe turned therynne he com before the Emperour, and kneled and seide, "Julius Cesar, Emperour of Rome, wheron thinkest thow, lete be thi stodyinge for it availeth nought, for never of thyne avision shalt thow not knowe the trouthe before that man that is savage thee certefie, and for nought is it that thow stodyest theron eny more."

Than the herte hym dressed and saugh the gate of the paleyse cloos, and he caste his enchauntement that alle the dores and gates of the paleise opened so rudely that thei fly alle in peces; and the herte lept oute and fledde thourgh the town, and the chace began agein after hym longe till that he com oute into the playn feeldes; and than he dide vanysshe that noon sey where he becom. And than thei returned agein, and whan the Emperour wiste the herte was ascaped he was wroth and lete crye thourgh the londe that who that myght brynge the savage man or the herte sholde have his feire doughter to wif, and half his reame yef that he were gentill of birthe, and after his deth have all; and lepe to horse many a vailaunt knyght and squyer of pris, and serched and sought thourgh many contrees; but all was for nought, for never cowde thei heere no tidinges of that thei sought, and whan thei myght no more do thei returned agein. But ever Grisandol serched thourgh the forests, oon hour foreward, another bakke, that so endured eight dayes full.

And on a day as Grisandol was alight under an oke for to praye oure Lorde to helpe and to spede for to fynde that he sought, and as he was in his prayours the herte that hadde ben at Rome com before hym and seide, "Avenable, thow chacest folye, for thow maist not spede of thy queste in no maner, but I shall telle the what thow shalt do. Purchese flessh newe and salt, and mylke and hony, and hoot breed newe bake, and bringe with the foure felowes, and a boy to turne the spite till it be enough rosted, and com in to this foreste by the moste uncouthe weyes that thow canste fynde, and sette a table by the fier, and the breed and the mylke and the hony upon the table, and hide the and thi companye a litile thens, and doute the nought that the savage man will come."

Than ran the herte a grete walope thourgh the foreste, and Grisandol lept to horse and thought well on that the herte hadde seide, and thought in his corage [*heart*] that it was somme spirituell thinge that by hir right name hadde hir cleped, and thought well that of this thinge sholde come some merveile. And Grisandol rode forth to a town nygh the forest seven myle, and toke ther that was myster [*needed*], and com in to the foreste ther as he hadde spoke with the herte as soon as he myght, and roode into the deepe of the foreste whereas he fonde a grett oke full of leves. And the place semed delitable, and he alight and sette theire horse fer thens, and made a grete fier and sette the flesshe to roste, and the smoke and the savour spredde thourgh the foreste that oon myght fele the savour right fer, and than sette the table be the fier, and whan all was redy thei hidde hem in a bussh. And Merlin that all this knewe and that made all this to be don covertly that he were not knowen, drough that wey that he were not knowen with a grete staffe in his nekke [*grasp*] smytinge grete strokes from oke to oke, and was blakke and rough for rympled and longe berde, and barfoote, and clothed in a rough pilche [*animal pelt*].

And so he com to the fier ther as the flessh was rosted, and whan the boy saugh hym come he was so aferde that he fledde nygh out of his witte. And he this com to the fier and began to chacche and frote [*putter and poke*] aboute the fier, and saugh the mete and than loked all aboute hym and began to rore lowde as a man wood [*demented*] oute of mynde, and than beheilde and saugh the cloth spredde and soche mete theron as ye have herde; and after he beheilde towarde the fier and saugh the flesshe that the knave hadde rosted that was tho enough, and raced it of with his hondes madly and rente it asonder in peces, and wette it in mylke, and after in the hony, and ete as a wood man that nought ther lefte of the flesh; and than he eete of the hoot breed and hony that he was full and swollen grete, and somwhat was it colde, and he lay down by the fier and slept. And whan Grisandol saugh he was on slepe she and hir felowes com as softely as thei myght and stale awey his staffe, and than thei bounde hym with a cheyne of iren streytely aboute the flankes, and than delyvered hym to oon of the companye by the tother ende of the cheyne. And whan he was so well bounde he awooke and lept up lightly, and made semblaunt to take his staff as a wilde man, and Grisandol griped hym in his armes right sore and hilde hym stille. And whan he saugh hym so bounde and taken, he hilde hym as shamefaste and mate [*shamed and overcome*]; and than the horse were brought forth, and he was sette upon oon of hem and bounden to the sadell with two bondes, and a man sette behynde hym that was bounde to hym and enbraced hym by the myddill. And so thei rode forth her wey, and the savage man loked on Grisandol that rode by hym and began to laugh right harde; and whan Grisandol saugh hym laughe he approched ner and rode side by side, and aqueynted with hym the beste that he myght and enquered and asked many thinges. But he ne wolde nought ansuere, and Grisandol asked why he lough, but he wolde not telle saf that he seide, "Creature formed of nature chaunged into other forme, fro hensforth begilynge alle thinges venimouse as serpent, holde thi pees, for nought will I telle the till that I com before the Emperour."

With that the savage man hilde his pees and spake no more, and rode forth togeder, and Grisandol of this that he hadde seide spake to his companye, and thei seide that he was wiser than he shewed, and that som grete merveile sholde falle in the londe. Thus thei ride spekynge of many thinges till thei passede before an abbey, and saugh before the gate moche pore peple abidinge almesse, and than the savage man lowgh right lowde; and than Grisandol com toward hym and swetly praide hym to telle wherefore he lough, and he loked proudly on traverse [*sideways*], and seide, "Ymage repaired and disnatured fro kynde, holde thy pees, ne enquere no mo thinges for nought will I telle the but before the Emperour." And whan Grisandol this undirstode, he lete hym be at that tyme and no more thinge hym asked, and hereof spake thei in many maners.

Thus thei ride forth all day till nyght, and on the morowe till the hour of prime [*sunrise or 6 A.M.*], and fill that thei passed byfore a chapell where a preste was toward masse, and fonde a knyght and a squyer heringe the servyse; and whan Grisandol saugh this, thei alight alle the companye and entred in to here the masse. And whan the knyght that was in the chapell saugh the man bounde with chaynes he hadde merveile what it might be; and while the knyght beheilde the man that was savage, the squyer that was in an angle behynde the chapel dore come agein his lorde, and lifte up his hande and gaf hym soche a slap that alle thei in the chapell myght it here, and than returned thider as he com fro all shamefaste [*ashamed*] of that he hadde don. And whan he was come in to his place he ne rofte [*cared*] nothinge, for the shame lasted no lenger but while he was in returnynge. And whan the savage man saugh this he began to laugh right harde, and the knyght that was so smyten was so abaisshed that he wiste not what to sey but suffred; and Grisandol and the other companye merveiled sore what it myght be. Anoon after the squyer com agein to his lorde and gaf hym soche another stroke as he dide before, and wente agein into his place, and the savage man hym behilde and began to laughe right harde. And yef the knyght before were abaisshed, he was than moche more, and the squyer that hadde hym smyten returned sorowfull and pensif to the place that he com fro, and hilde hymself foule disceyved of that he hadde don, and whan he was in his place he rought [*cared*] never, and Grisandol and the companye merveiled right sore, and herden oute the service be leyser. And in the mene while that thei thoughten upon these thinges that thei hadde seyn, the squyer com the thridde tyme

and smote his lorde sorer than he hadde don before, and therat lowgh the
wilde man sore, and be that was the masse at an ende. And than Grisandol
and alle wente oute of the chapell, and the squyer that hadde smyten his
lorde com after and asked Grisandol what man it was that thei hadde so
bounde, and thei seide that thei were with Julius Cesar, Emperour of Rome,
and ledde to hym that savage man that thei hadde founded in the foreste, for
to certefie of a vision that was shewed hym slepinge.

"But sir," seide Grisandol, "tell me wherefore hath this squyer yow
smyten thre tymes an ye ne spake no worde agein; have ye soche a custome?"
And the knyght ansuerde that he sholde it wite in tyme comynge.

Than the knyght cleped [*called*] his squyer and asked hym before Grisandol
wherefore he hadde hym smyten, and he was shamefaste and seide he wiste
never, but so it fill in his corage [*heart*]; and the knyght hym asked yef he
hadde now eny talent [*inclination*] hym for to smyte, and the squyer seide he
hadde lever be deed, "but that," quod he, "it fill in my mynde that I myght
not kepe me therfro," and Grisandol lough of the merveile.

Than seide the knyght that he wolde go to court with hem for to here what
the savage man wolde sey, and with that thei rode forth on her wey, and
Grisandol by the savage manne's side. And whan thei hadde awhile riden,
he asked the wilde man wherfore he lough so thre tymes whan the squyer
smote his lorde, and he loked on hir a traverse and seide, "Ymage repeyred
semblaunce of creature wherby men ben slayn and diffouled, rasour
trenchaunt [*razor sharp*] fountayne coraunt [*a running and violent dance*] that
never is full of no springes [*a pun on Grisandol's true sex is intended: (fountain
= spring or source; springe = fountain or leap: "dangerous cause of a dance (love-
making) that has no leaping"*], holde thy pees and nothinge of me enquere but
before the Emperour, for nought will I telle the."

And whan that Grisandol undirstode the fell wordes that he spake, he was
all abaisshed and pensef and durste not no more enquere, and rode forth till
thei come to Rome. And whan thei entred in to the town and the peple hem
parceyved, thei wente all ageins hym for to se the man that was savage, and
the noyse was grete of the peple that folowed and behilde his facion [*face*] as
longe as thei myght; and so thei conveyed hym to the paleise. And whan the
Emperour herde the tidinges, he com hem ageins and mette with hem
comynge upon the greces [*over the grass*], and than com Grisandol before the
Emperour and seide, "Sir, have here the man that is savage that I to yow here
yelde, and kepe ye hym fro hensforth, for moche peyne have I hadde with
hym." And the Emperour seide he wolde hem well guerdon [*reward*] and the
man sholde be well kepte, and than he sente to seche a smyth to bynde hym
in chaynes and feteres, and the savage man badde hym therof not to
entermete [*bother*], "for wite it right well," quod he, "I will not go withoute
youre leve." And the Emperour hym asked how he therof sholde be sure, and
he seide he wolde hym asure by his Cristyndome.

Quod the Emperour, "Art thow than Cristin?" and he seide, "Ye, withoute
faile."

"How were thow than baptized," seide the Emperour, "whan thow art so
wilde?"

"That shall I telle yow," quod he. "This is the trouthe that my moder on a day com from the market of a town, and it was late whan she entred into the Foreste of Brocheland [*Broceliande*] and wente oute her way so fer that the same nyght behoved hir to lye in the foreste. And whan she saugh she was so alone be hirself she was afeerde and lay down under an oke and fill aslepe, and than com a savage man oute of the foreste and by hir lay, because she was sool by hirself. Durste she not hym diffende, for a woman aloone is feerfull, and that nyght was I begeten on my moder. And whan she was repeired hom, she was full pensif longe tyme till that she knewe verily that she was with childe, and bar me so till I was born into this worlde and was baptised in a fonte, and dide me norishe till I was grete. And as soone as I cowde lyve withouten hir I wente in to the grete forestes, for by the nature of my fader behoveth me thider to repeire, and for that he was savage I am thus wilde. Now have ye herde what I am."

"So God me helpe," seide the Emperour, "never for me shalt thow be putte in feteres ne in irenes, seth thow wilt me graunte that thow will not go withoute my leve."

Than tolde Grisandol how he dide laugh before the abbey, and in the chapell for the squyer that hadde smyten his maister, and the dyverse wordes that he hadde spoken whan he asked wherefore he dide laugh. "And he seide that never wolde he nought sey till he com before yow, and now is he here, and therfore aske hym why he hath so often laughed by the wey." And than the Emperour hym asked, and he seide he sholde it knowe all in tyme. "But sendeth first for all youre barouns, and than shall I telle yow that and other thinges."

With that entred the Emperour in to his chamber and the savage man and his prive counseile, and ther thei rested and disported and spake of many thinges; and on the morowe the Emperour sente to seche his barouns, hem that he supposed sonest to fynde, and than thei come anoon bothe oon and other from alle partyes.

On the fourthe day after the savage man was comen, where that the lordes were assembled in the maister paleise, and the Emperour brought in this savage man and made hym to sitte down by hym, and whan the barouns hadde enough hym beholden thei asked why he hadde for hem sente, and he tolde hem for a vision that hym befill in his slepynge, "for I will that it be expowned before yow." And thei seide that the significacion wolde thei gladly heren. Than the Emperour comaunded this man to telle the cause why that he was sought, and he ansuerde and seide that he wolde nothinge telle till that the Emperesse and hir twelve maydones were comen, and she com anon with gladde semblaunce as she that gaf no force of nothinge that myght befalle.

Whan the Emperesse and hir twelve maydones were come amonge the barouns, the lordes roos agein hir and dide hir reverence, and as soone as the savage man hir saugh comynge he turned his need in traverse and began to laughe as in scorne. And whan he hadde awhile laughed he loked on the Emperour stadfastly, and than on Grisandol, and than on the Emperesse, and than on hir twelve maydenys that weren with hir, and than he turned toward the barouns and began to laughe right lowde as it were in dispite [*scorn*]. Whan the Emperour saugh hym so laughe he preied hym to telle that he hadde in covenaunt, and whi that he lough now and other tymes.

With that he stode up and seide to the Emperour so lowde that all myght it heren, "Sir, yef ye me graunte as trewe Emperour before youre barouns that ben here that I shall not be in the werse ne no harme to me therfore shall come, and that ye will geve me leve as soone as I have yow certefied of youre avision, I shall telle yow the trewe significacion."

And the Emperour hym ansuerde and graunted that noon harme ne annoye to hym sholde be done, ne that he sholde come hym no magre [*receive no blame*], to telle hym that he was so desirouse for to heren, and that he sholde have leve to go whan hym liste. "But I praye the telle me myn avision in audience of alle my barouns what it was, and than shall I the better beleve the significacion whan thow haste me tolde of that I never spake to no creature," and he ansuerde as for that sholde hym not greve, and therfore wolde he not lette, and than he began the avision.

"Sir," seide the savage man to the Emperour, "it fill on a nyght that ye lay by youre wif that is here, and whan ye were aslepe ye thought ye saugh before yow a sowe that was feire and smothe, and the heer that she hadde on her bakke was so longe that it trailed to grounde more than a fadome, and on hir heed she hadde a cercle of goolde bright shynynge, and yow semed that ye hadde norisshed that sowe in youre house, but ye cowde it not verily knowe, and therwith yow semed that ye hadde hir othir tymes sein. And whan ye hadde longe thought on this thinge ye saugh come oute of youre chamber twelve lyonsewes full feire and smothe; and thei com by the halle thourgh the courte to the sowe and lay by hir oon after another, and whan thei hadde do that thei wolde thei wente agein into youre chamber. Than com ye to youre barouns and hem asked what sholde be do with this sowe that ye saugh thus demened, and the barouns and alle the peple seide she was nothinge trewe, and thei juged to be brent bothe the sowe and the twelve lyonsewes. And than was the fier made redy grete and merveillouse in this courte, and therynne was the sowe brente and the twelve lyonsewes. Now have ye herde youre swevene in the same forme as ye it saugh in your slepinge, and yef ye se that I have eny thinge mystaken, sey it before your barouns." And the Emperour seide he hadde of nothinge failed.

"Sir Emperour," seide the barouns, "seth that he hath seide what was youre avision, hit is to beleve the significacion yef he will it telle, and it is a thinge that wolde gladly heren."

"Certes," seide the man, "I shall it delcare to yow so openly that ye may it se, and knowe apertly that I yow shall sey. The grete sowe that he saugh signifieth my lady the Emperesse, youre wif, that is ther; and the longe her that she hadde on hir bakke betokeneth the longe robes that she is ynne iclothed; and the sercle that ye saugh on her heed shynynge betokeneth the crowne of goolde that ye made her with to be crowned; and yef it be youre plesier I will no more sey at this tyme."

"Certes," seide the Emperour, "yow behoveth to sey all as it is yef ye will be quyte of youre promyse."

"Certes," seide man, "than shall I telle yow. The twelve lyonsewes that ye saugh come oute of a chamber betokeneth the twelve maydenes that be ther with the Emperesse; and knowe it for very trouthe that thei be no wymen for it be men, and therefore make hem be dispoiled, and ye shull se the trouthe; and as ofte as ye go oute of the town she maketh hem serve in hir chamber and in hir bedde. Now have ye herde youre avision and the significacion, and ye may se and knowe yef that I have seide to yow the soth."

Whan the Emperour understode the untrouthe that his wif hadde don, he was so abaisshed that he spake no worde a longe while; and then he spake and seide that that wolde he soone knowe, and than he cleped Grisandol and seide, "Dispoile me tho dameseles, for I will that alle the barouns that be hereynne knowe the trouthe." And anoon Grisandol and other lept forth and dispoiled hem before the Emperour and his barouns, and fonde hem formed alle as other men weren; and than the Emperour was so wroth that he wiste not what to do. Than he made his oth that anoon ther sholde be do justice soche as was right to be awarded; and the barouns juged seth she hadde don hir lorde soche untrouthe that she sholde be brente and the harlottes hanged, and some seide that thei sholde be flayn all quik; but in the ende thei acorded that thei sholde be brente in a fier. And anoon as the Emperour herde the jugement of the barouns he comaunded to make the fier in the place, and anoon it was don, and thei were bounde hande and foot, and made hem to be caste in to the brynynge fier, and in short tyme thei were alle brent, for the fier was grete and huge. Thus toke Emperour vengaunce of his wif, and grete was the renomede [*praise*] that peple of hym spake whan it was knowen.

Whan the Emperesse was brente, and thei that she hadde made hir maydenes, the barouns returned agein to the Emperour and seide oon to another that the savage man was right wise and avisee, "for yet shall he sey some other thinges wherof shall come some grete merveile us, and to all the worlde." And the Emperour hymself seide that he hadde seide his avision as it was in trouthe. Thus wiste the Emperour the lyvinge of his wif, and than the Emperour hym called and asked yef he wolde sey eny more, and he seide ye, yef he asked hym whereof.

"I wolde wite," quod he, "wherefore thow didist laughe whan thow were in the foreste, and loked on Grisandol, and also whan thow were ledde before an abbey, and in the chapell whan the squyer smote his lorde, and why thow seidest tho wordes to my stiwarde whan he asked why thow loughe; and after telle me what betokeneth the laughter hereynne whan thow saugh the Emperesse come."

"Sir," seide the savage man, "I shall telle yow enowgh. I do yow to wite that the firste laughter that I made was for that a woman hadde me taken by her engyn [*ingenuity*], that no man cowde not do; and wite ye well that Grisandol is the beste maiden and the trewest withynne youre reame, and therefore was it that I lough. And the laughter that I made before the abbey was for ther is under erthe before the gate the grettest tresour hidde that eny man knoweth, and therfore I lough for that it was under feet of hem that aboode after the almesse, for more richesse is in that tresour than alle the monkes beth worth, and all the abbey and all that therto belongeth, and the pore peple that theron stoden cowde it not take. And Avenable youre stywarde, that Grisandol doth her clepen, saugh that I lowgh and asked me wherefore, and the coverte wordes that I to hir spake was for that she was chaunged into the fourme of man, and hadde take anothir habite than hir owne. And alle the wordes that I spake thei ben trewe, for by woman is many a man disceyved; and therefore I cleped hir disceyaunt, for by women ben many townes sonken and brent, and many a riche londe wasted and exiled, and moche peple slayn. But I sey it not for noon evell that is in hir, and thow thyself maist well perceyve that by women be many worthi men shamed and wratthed that longe have loved togeder yef it were not for debate of women. But now rech [*care*] the not for thy wif that thou haste distroied, for she hath it well deserved; and have therfore no mystrust to other, for as longe as the worlde endureth it doth but apeire, and all that cometh to hem be the grete synne of luxure that in hem is closeth. For woman is of that nature and of that disire that whan she hath the moste worthi man of the worlde to hir lorde, she weneth she have the werste, and wite he fro whens this cometh of the grete fragelite that is in hem; and the foule corage [*lust*] and the foule thought that thei have where thei may beste hir volunte acomplish. But therfor be not wroth, for ther ben in the worlde [many] that ben full trewe, and yef thow have be desceyved of thyn, yet shall thow have soche oon that is worthy to be Emperesse and to resceyve that high dignite, and yef thow wilt it beleve thow shalt wynne theron more than thowe shalt lese. [*Merlin digresses to prophesy that a dragon from Rome will come to destroy Britain and battle against a crowned lion, but that it will be killed by a bull.*]

"The tother laughter that I made in the chapell was not for the buffetes that the squyer gaf his lorde, but for the betokenynges that therynne ben. In the same place ther the squyer stode was entred, and yet ther is undir his feet a merveillouse tresour. The firste buffet that the squyer gaf his lorde signifieth that for avoure [*because of wealth and property*] the worlde becometh so prowde that he douteth nother God ne his soule, no more than the squyer douted to smyte his maister, but the riche wolde oppresse the pore under theire feet; and that make these untrewe riche peple whan enythinge cometh to hem be myschaunce thei swere and stare and sey maugre have God for his geftes, and wite ye what maketh this: nothinge but pride of richesse. The seconde buffet betokeneth the riche userer that deliteth in his richesse and goth scornynge his pore nyghebours that be nedy whan thei come to hym ought for to borough, and the userer so leneth hem litill and litill that at laste thei moste selle theire heritage to hym that so longe hath it coveyted. The thridde buffet signifieth these false pletours [*advocates*], men of lawe that sellen and apeire theire neyghbours behinde here bakke for covetise and envye of that thei se hem thrive, and for thei be not in her daungier. For whan these laweers sen that her neighbours don hem not grete reverence and servise, thei thenken and aspien how thei may hem anoyen in eny wise and to make hem lese that thei have, and therfor men seyn an olde sawe: who hath a goode neighbour hath goode morowe. Now have ye herde the significaciouns why the buffetes were goven, but the squyer delited nothinge therynne whan that he smote his maister, but he wiste not fro whens this corage to hym com. But God that is Almyghty wolde have it to be shewed in exsample that men sholde not be prowde for worldly richesse, for to the covetouse theire richesse doth hem but harme that slepen in averice, and foryete God and don the werkes of the devell that ledeth hem to everlastinge deth, and all is for the grete delite that thei have in richesse.

"But now shall I telle you whi I lough today whan I saugh the Emperesse comynge and hir lechours. I do yow to wite that it was but for dispite, for I saugh that she was youre wif, and hadde oon of the worthiest men of the worlde that eny man knoweth of youre yowthe, and she hadde take these twelve harlottes and wende ever for to have ledde this foly all hir lif; and therfore hadde I grete dispite for the love of yow and of youre doughter—for she is youre doughter withoute doute, and draweth litill after hir moder. Now have ye herde alle the laughtres and wherefore thei were, and therfore may I go yef it be youre plesier."

"Now a-bide a litill," seide the Emperour, "and telle us the trouthe of Grisandol, and also we shull sende to digge after the tresour for I will wite yef it be trewe," and he therto dide assent. Than the Emperour comaunded that Grisandol were sought, and so she was founden oon of the feirest maydenes that neded to enquere in eny londe, and whan the Emperour knewe that Grisandol his stiwarde that longe hadde hym served was a woman, he blissed hym for the wonder that he therof hadde. Than he asked the savage man counseile what he sholde do of that he hadde promysed to geve his doughter and half his reame, for loth he was to falsen his promyse of covenaunt.

"I shall telle yow," quod the man, "what ye shull do yef ye will do my counseile; and wite it well, it is the beste that eny man can geven."

"Sey on, than," seide Emperour, "for what counseile that thow gevest I shall it well beleve, for I have founde thy seyinge trewe."

Than seide the savage man, "Ye shall take Avenable to be yowre wif, and wite ye whos doughter she is. She is doughter to the Duke Matan that the Duke Frolle hath disherited and driven oute of his londe for envye with grete wronge. And he and his wif be fledde, and his sone, that is a feire yonge squyer, into Provence into a riche town that is called Monpellier. And sende to seche hem and yelde hem her heritage that thei have loste with wronge, and make the mariage of youre doughter and Avenable's brother that is so feire, and ye may her no better be setten."

And whan the barouns undirstode that the savage man seide, thei spoke moche amonge hem and seiden in the ende that the Emperour myght do no better after theire advis. And than the Emperour asked his name and what he was, and the hert that so pertly spake unto hym, and than seide he, "Sir, of that enquere no more, for it is a thinge the more ye desire to knowe the lesse shall ye witen."

[*Merlin speaks again of his prophecy about the dragon, asks the Emperor never to go against Avenable's will, and takes his leave.*] And the Emperour betaught hym to God seth it myght no better be, and therwith he wente on his wey, and whan he com to the halle dore he wrote letteres on the lyntell of the dore in grewe [*engraved*] that seide, "Be it knowe to alle tho that these letteres reden, that the savage man that spake to the Emperour and expounded his dreme, hit was Merlin of Northumberlande—and the hert Brancus with fifteen braunches that spake to hym in his halle at mete amonge alle his knyghtes and was chaced though the citee of Rome, that spake to Avenable in the foreste whan he tolde hir how she sholde fynde the man savage. And lete the Emperour well wite that Merlin is maister counseller to Kynge Arthur of the Grete Breteyne." And than he departed and spake no mo wordes.

[*The Emperor does as Merlin advises, marrying Avendable's brother Patrick to his daughter and Avenable to himself. Later a messenger discovers the letters that Merlin has engraved upon the lintel.*] And whan the Emperour undirstode these wordes he merveiled sore, and than befill a grete merveile whereof alle that were therynne hadde wonder, and the Emperour hymself; for as soon as the Emperour herde what the letteres mente, anoon the letteres vanysshed so sodeynly that no man wiste how, and therof hadde thei grete wonder, and moche it was spoken of thourgh the contrey. But now cesseth the tale of the Emperour of Rome that abode in his paleise gladde and myry with his wif Avenable, and ledde goode lif longe tyme, for bothe were thei yonge peple, for the Emperour was but twenty-eight yere of age at that hour and his wif was twenty-two, and yef thei ledde myri lif, yet Patrik and Soldate, the doughter of the Emperour, lyved in more delite.

Merlin's Imprisonment

[*After living with King Arthur and the Knights of the Round Table for a long time, Merlin commends them to God and leaves to visit his master Blaise. He relates everything that has happened since his last visit and his master writes it down in his book, by which we have knowledge of it.*] Whan Merlin hadde be ther eight dayes he toke leve of Blase and seide, "This is the laste tyme that I shall speke with yow eny more, for fro hensforth I shall sojourne with my love, ne never shall I have power hir for to leve ne to come ne go."

Whan Blase undirstode Merlin, he was full of sorowe, and seide, "Dere frende, seth it is so that ye may not departe, cometh not ther."

"Me behoveth for to go," quod Merlin, "for so have I made hir covenaunt, and also I am so supprised with hir love that I may me not withdrawen. And I have her taught and lerned all the witte and connynge that she can, and yet shall she lerne more, for I may not hir withsein ne it disturue [*prevent*]."

Than departed Merlin from Blase, and in litill space com to his love, that grete joye of hym made and he of hir, and dwelled togeder longe tyme; and ever she enquered of his craftes, and he hir taught and lerned so moche that after he was holden a fooll and yet is. And she hem well undirstode and put hem in writinge, as she that was well expert in the seven artes. Whan that he hadde hir taught all that she cowde aske, she bethought hir how she myght hym withholde forevermore; than began she to glose [*cajole, flatter*] Merlin more than ever she hadde do ever beforn, and seide, "Sir, yet can I not oon thinge that I wolde fain lerne, and therfore I pray you that ye wolde me enforme."

And Merlin that well knewe her entent seid, "Madame, what thinge is that?"

"Sir," quod she, "I wolde fain lerne how I myght oon shet in a tour withouten walles, or withoute eny closure be enchauntement, so that never he sholden go oute withouten my licence." And whan Merlin it herde he bowed down the heed and began to sigh; and she it aparceived, she asked whi he sighed.

"Madame," seide Merlin, "I shall telle yow I knowe well what ye thinke, and that ye will me withholde, and I am so supprised with love that me behoveth to do youre plesier."

And than she caste hir armes aboute his nekke and hym kiste, and seide that wele he ought to be hirs seth that she was all his. "Ye knowe wele that the grete love that I have to you hath made me forsake alle other for to have yow in myn armes nyght and day, and ye be my thought and my desire, for withoute yow have I neither joye ne welthe. In you have I sette all my hope, and I abide noon other joye but of yow; and seth that I love you, and also ye love me, is not right than that ye do my volunte and I yours?"

"Certes, yesse," seide Merlin, "Now sey than what ye will."

"I will" quod she, "ye teche me a place feire and covenable [*suitable*], that I myght enclose by art in soche wise that never myght be undon, and we shull be ther, ye and I in joye and disporte whan that yow liketh."

"Madame," seide Merlin, "that shall I well do."

"Sir," quod she, "I will not that ye it make, but lerne it to me that I may it do, and I shall make it than more at my volunte."

"Well," seide Merlin, "I will do youre plesire." Than he began to devise the crafte unto hir, and she it wrote all that he seide; and whan hadde alle devised, the damesell hadde grete joye in herte, and he hir loved more and more, and she shewed hym feirer chere than beforn.

And so thei sojourned togeder longe tyme, till it fill on a day that thei wente thourgh the forest hande in hande, devisinge and disportinge, and this was in the Foreste of Brochelonde, and fonde a bussh that was feire and high of white hawthorne full of floures, and ther thei satte in the shadowe; and Merlin leide his need in the damesel's lappe, and she began to taste [*caress him*] softly till he fill on slepe. And whan she felt that he was on slepe she aroos softly and made a cerne [*circle*] with hir wymple all aboute the bussh and all aboute Merlin, and began hir enchauntementz soche as Merlin hadde hir taught, and made the cerne nine tymes, and nine tymes hir enchauntementes; and after that she wente and satte down by hym and leide his heed in hir lappe, and hilde hym ther till he dide awake. And than he loked aboute hym, and hym semed he was in the feirest tour of the worlde and the moste strong, and fonde hym leide in the feirest place that ever he lay beforn. And than he seide to the damesell, "Lady, thou hast me disceived but yef ye will abide with me, for noon but ye may undo this enchauntementes."

And she seide, "Feire swete frende, I shall often tymes go oute, and ye shull have me in youre armes, and I yow; and fro hensforth shull ye do alle youre plesier." And she hym hilde wele covenaunt, for fewe hours ther were of the nyght ne of the day but she was with hym. Ne never after com Merlin oute of that fortresse that she hadde hym in sette; but she wente in and oute whan she wolde.

Sir Thomas Malory: Le Morte Darthur

The earlier selections in this chapter concentrate upon aspects of Merlin's character and deeds that Malory has omitted or altered to fit his own conception of the mage. It is no denigration of Malory to observe that he downplays the wizard's power and authority in comparison with his French sources and Middle English counterparts, for that authoritative role is not fully conducive to the kind of romance he is developing. Malory's own title, which Caxton replaced with *Le Morte Darthur*, was *The Whole Book of King Arthur and of His Knights of the Round Table*. This book is after all not a work about Merlin, or the Grail-related conception of history, though they are important elements in it, but specifically about Arthur and his fellowship. Fate, not Merlin, is sufficient constraint upon their free will.

Consequently, Merlin is less a featured character with his own fully developed story than a subordinate to Arthur and ennabler to his knights. In Malory Merlin affects the action as much by his absence or inaction as by his presence at crucial tests; so long as he controls the decision-making there can be little suspense or room for characters to develop their own destinies. The selections that follow incorporate traditional elements of the wild man, prophet, magician, and lover, but emphasize most of all Merlin's value as a counselor and tutor. He is in the tale primarily to teach the king and lend the imprimatur of destiny; in the twentieth century T.H. White emphasizes the same two elements.

Nevertheless, Merlin's wisdom in Malory apparently does not extend to the courtly treatment of women, as it does in the Middle English prose *Merlin* excerpts. He warns Arthur against marrying Guinevere, but understands only that although he can show the king women enough he may not gainsay Arthur's wish for her. He plays little part in the quests of Gawain, Tor, and Pellinore at the wedding feast other than to identify the participants (so I have omitted these episodes), yet the primary purpose of their quests is to generate a radically new, chivalric code of conduct toward women. For his part Merlin acknowledges filial responsibility rather than chivalry in rebuking Pellinore for abandoning his daughter; and his lustful pursuit of Nyneve is purely atavistic, opposed to the true courtly love shared by even adulterous couples such as Tristram and Iseult or Lancelot and the Queen.

Although the exact identity of the author, a knight and prisoner, is still not certain, the likeliest candidate still appears to be the Thomas Malory of Newbold Revel in Warwickshire, who was born in 1416 and died in 1471. A wealthy landowner, this Malory had access to many works of romance, both in French and in Middle English. About 1450 he suddenly became a murderer, rapist, and thief (although these charges could have been trumped up during the general unrest that accompanied the War of the Roses). Imprisoned in 1452, he was freed in 1460 by the Yorkist faction. Apparently his political sympathies changed, for by the end of the decade he was again in prison, and freed by the Lancastrian side in 1470. Clearly his experiences can account for his work's intense concern with a monarchial and social ideal that is overcome by human imperfections.

The man who published his work is less mysterious, but no less unusual. William Caxton (1422–1491) was originally a textile merchant, then a diplomat in Bruges, where he learned the new printing trade and opened his first shop. Like Malory, his favorite literature was chivalric romance. He established the first English press at Westminster, and completed the first edition of *Le Morte Darthur* on July 31, 1485.

Malory's primary source for the early tales that include Merlin is the thirteenth-century *Suite du Merlin*—although his brief summary of the wizard's death is modeled upon that of the prose *Lancelot*, which also identifies Cornwall as the site. His work exists in both printed and manuscript forms. The two remaining copies of Caxton's first edition are in the Pierpont Morgan Library in New York and the John Rylands University Library in Manchester. The sole manuscript copy was discovered in 1934 at Winchester College and edited by Eugene Vinaver. The printed and manuscript copies differ in a number of ways, but marks on the manuscript show that it was in Caxton's possession while he was working on *Le Morte Darthur*; for some reason the printer chose not to follow it. Since Caxton's exemplar is missing, there is disagreement about his role in revising and editing the book; some scholars agree with Vinaver in regarding him as responsible for the differences between the manuscript and printed versions (against his usual practice), while others believe that Malory himself revised the book for printing. It seems impossible to be certain which version is closer to Malory's intentions, so I have used Caxton's text because it has had incomparably greater historical impact. The spaces correspond to chapter divisions in Sommer's edition.

The War Against the Rebel Kings

Thenne the kyng remeved in to Walys and lete crye a grete feste that it shold be holdyn at Pentecost after the incoronacion of hym at the Cyte of Carlyon. Unto the fest come Kyng Lott of Lowthean and of Orkeney with fyve hundred knyghtes with hym. Also ther come to the feste Kynge Uryens of Gore with four hundred knyghtes with him; also ther come to that feeste Kyng Nayntres of Garloth with seven hundred knyghtes with hym; also ther came to the feest the Kynge of Scotland with sixe honderd knyghtes with him, and he was but a yong man; also ther came to the feste a kyng that was called the Kyng with the Honderd Knyghtes, but he and his men were passyng wel bisene at al poyntes; also ther cam the Kyng of Cardos with fyve honderd knyghtes.

And Kyng Arthur was glad of their comynge, for he wende [*thought*] that al the kynges and knyghtes had come for grete love and to have done hym worship at his feste, wherfor the kyng made grete joye and sente the kynges and knyghtes grete presentes. But the kynges wold none receyve, but rebuked the messagers shamefully and said they had no joye to receyve no geftes of a berdles boye that was come of lowe blood, and sente him word they wold none of his geftes, but that they were come to gyve him geftes with hard swerdys betwixt the neck and the sholders. And therfore they came thyder, so they told to the messagers playnly, for it was grete shame to all them to see suche a boye to have a rule of soo noble a reaume as this land was. With this ansuer the messagers departed and told to Kyng Arthur this ansuer, wherfor by the advys of his barons he took hym to a strong towre with five hundred good men with him. And all the kynges aforesaid in a maner leyd a syege tofore hym, but Kyng Arthur was well vytailled.

And within fifteen dayes ther came Merlyn amonge hem into the Cyte of Carlyon. Thenne all the kynges were passyng gladde of Merlyn, and asked him, "For what cause is that boye Arthur made your kynge?"

"Syres," said Merlyn, "I shalle telle yow the cause, for he is Kynge Uther Pendragon's sone, borne in wedlok, goten on Igrayne, the duke's wyf of Tyntigail."

"Thenne is he a bastard," they said al.

"Nay," said Merlyn. "After the deth of the duke more than thre houres was Arthur begoten, and thirteen dayes after Kyng Uther wedded Igrayne, and therfor I preve him he is no bastard. And, who saith nay, he shal be kyng and overcome alle his enemyes, and or he deye he shalle be long Kynge of all Englond and have under his obeyssaunce Walys, Irland, and Scotland, and moo reames than I will now reherce."

Some of the kynges had merveyl of Merlyn's wordes and demed well that it shold be as he said, and som of hem lough hym to scorne, as Kyng Lot and mo other called hym a wytche. But thenne were they accorded with Merlyn that Kynge Arthur shold come oute and speke with the kynges, and to come sauf and to goo sauf; suche suraunce ther was made. So Merlyn went unto Kynge Arthur and told hym how he had done, and badde hym fere not but come oute boldly and speke with hem, and spare hem not, but ansuere them as their kynge and chyvetayn: "For ye shal overcome hem all whether they wille or nylle."

Thenne Kynge Arthur came oute of his tour and had under his gowne a jesseraunte of double maylle, and ther wente with hym the Archebisshop of Caunterbury, and Syr Baudewyn of Bretayne, and Syr Kay, and Syre Brastias; these were the men of moost worship that were with hym. And whan they were mette there was no mekenes, but stoute wordes on bothe sydes; but alweyes Kynge Arthur ansuerd them and said he wold make them to bowe and he lyved, wherfore they departed with wrath. And Kynge Arthur badde kepe hem wel, and they bad the kynge kepe hym wel. Soo the kynge retorned hym to the toure ageyne and armed hym and alle his knyghtes.

"What will ye do?" said Merlyn to the kynges. "Ye were better for to stynte, for ye shalle not here prevaille though ye were ten times so many."

"Be we wel avysed to be aferd of a dreme reder?" said Kynge Lot.

With that Merlyn vanysshed aweye and came to Kynge Arthur, and bad hym set on hem fiersly. And in the menewhyle there were thre honderd good men of the best that were with the kynges that wente streyghte unto Kynge Arthur, and that comforted hym gretely.

"Syr," said Merlyn to Arthur, "fyghte not with the swerde ye had by myracle [*the sword from the stone*] til that ye see ye go unto the wers; thenne drawe it out and do your best."

So forthwithalle Kynge Arthur sette upon hem in their lodgyng. And Syre Bawdewyn, Syre Kay, and Syr Brastias slewe on the right hand and on the lyfte hand that it was merveylle, and alweyes Kynge Arthur on horsback leyd on with a swerd and dyd merveillous dedes of armes, that many of the kynges had grete joye of his dedes and hardynesse. Thenne Kynge Lot brake out on the bak syde, and the Kyng with the Honderd Knyghtes, and Kyng Carados, and sette on Arthur fiersly behynd hym. With that Syre Arthur torned with his knyghtes and smote behynd and before, and ever Sir Arthur was in the formest prees tyl his hors was slayne undernethe hym, and therwith Kynge Lot smote doune Kyng Arthur. With that, his four knyghtes receyved hym and set hym on horsback. Thenne he drewe his swerd Excalibur, but it was so bryght in his enemyes' eyen that it gaf light lyke thirty torchys, and therwith he put hem on bak and slewe moche peple. And thenne the comyns of Carlyon aroos with clubbis and stavys and slewe many knyghtes, but alle the kynges helde them togyders with her knyghtes that were lefte on lyve, and so fled and departed. And Merlyn come unto Arthur and counceilled hym to folowe hem no further.

So after the feste and journeye Kynge Arthur drewe hym unto London, and soo by the counceil of Merlyn the kynge lete calle his barons to counceil. For Merlyn had told the kynge that the sixe kynges that made warre upon hym wold in al haste be awroke [*avenged*] on hym and on his landys, wherfor the kyng asked counceil at hem al. They coude no counceil gyve, but said they were bygge ynough.

"Ye saye wel," said Arthur. "I thanke you for your good courage, but wil ye al that loveth me speke with Merlyn? Ye knowe wel that he hath done

moche for me and he knoweth many thynges, and whan he is afore you I wold
that ye prayd hym hertely of his best avyse."

Alle the barons sayd they wold pray hym and desyre hym, soo Merlyn was
sente for and fair desyred of al the barons to gyve them best counceil.

"I shall say you," said Merlyn; "I warne yow al, your enemyes are passyng
strong for yow and they are good men of armes as ben on lyve, and by thys
tyme they have goten to them four kynges mo and a myghty duke. And
onlesse that our kyng have more chyvalry with hym than he may make within
the boundys of his own reame, and he fyghte with hem in batail he shal be
overcome and slayn."

"What were best to doo in this cause?" said al the barons.

"I shal telle you," said Merlyn, "myne aduys. There ar two bretheren
beyond the see and they be kynges bothe and merveillous good men of her
handes. And that one hyghte Kynge Ban of Benwyck, and that other hyght
Kyng Bors of Gaule; that is, Fraunce. And on these two kynges warrith a
myghty man of men, the Kynge Claudas, and stryveth with hem for a castel,
and grete werre is betwixt them. But this Claudas is so myghty of goodes
wherof he geteth good knyghtes, that he putteth these two kynges moost
parte to the werse. Wherfor this is my counceil: that our kyng and soverayne
lord sende unto the kynges Ban and Bors by two trusty knyghtes with letters
wel devysed, that they wil come and see Kynge Arthur and his courte, and
so helpe hym in his warrys that he wil be sworne unto them to helpe them
in their warrys ageynst Kynge Claudas. Now what saye ye unto this counceill?"
said Merlyn.

"Thys is wel couneilled," said the kynge and alle the barons. Right so in
alle haste ther were ordeyned to goo two knyghtes on the message unto the
two kynges. Soo were there made letters in the plesaunt wyse accordyng
unto Kyng Arthur's desyre. Ulfyus and Brastias were made the messagers
and so rode forth wel horsed and wel armed.

[*After crossing the channel and skirmishing with Claudas's knights, Ulfyus and
Brastias are welcomed by King Ban and King Bors. The two kings agree to help
Arthur, who upon his messengers' return prepares a feast and tournament to honor
them at Allhallowmas. Arthur and the two kings plan how to counter the next attack,
together with Merlyn, the "wise clerk" Gwenbaus who is brother to Ban and Bors, and
the two kings' stewards Gracian and Placidas.*]

At the last they were concluded that Merlyn shold goo with a token of
Kyng Ban (and that was a rynge) unto his men and Kynge Bors's, and Gracian
and Placidas sholde goo ageyne and kepe theire castles and her countreyes,
as for Kynge Ban of Benwick and Kynge Bors of Gaule had ordeyned hem.
And so [they] passed the see and came to Benwyck. And whan the peple
sawe Kyng Ban's rynge and Gracian and Placidas, they were glad and asked
how the kynges ferd, and made grete joye of their welfare and cordyng
[*accord with Arthur*]. And accordynge unto the soverayne lordes' desyre, the
men of warre made hem redy in al hast possyble so that they were fifteen
thousand on hors and foot, and they had grete plente of vytaylle with hem
by Merlyn's provysyon. But Gracian and Placidas were lefte to furnysshe and

garnysshe the castels for drede of Kynge Claudas.

Ryght so Merlyn passed the see wel vytailled bothe by water and by land, and whan he came to the see he sente home the footemen ageyne and took no mo with hym but ten thousand men on horsbak, the moost parte men of armes, and so shypped and passed the see into Englond and londed at Dover. And thorow the wytte of Merlyn he had the hoost northward the pryvyest wey that coude by thoughte unto the Foreist of Bedegrayne, and there in a valey he lodged hem secretely.

Thenne rode Merlyn unto Arthur and two kynges and told hem how he had sped, wherof they had grete merveylle that man on erthe myghte spede so soone, and goo and come. So Merlyn told them ten thousand were in the forest of Bedegrayne wel armed at al poyntes. Thenne was there no more to saye, but to horsbak wente all the hoost as Arthur had afore purveyed. So with twenty thousand he passed by nyghte and day, but ther was made suche an ordenaunce afore by Merlyn that ther shold no man of werre ryde nor go in no countrey on this side Trent Water but yf he had a token from Kynge Arthur, where thorow the kynge's enemyes durste not ryde as they dyd tofore to aspye.

[*The combined forces of Arthur, Ban, and Bors gather at the Castle of Bedegrayne. The six kings who fought against Arthur at Caerleon are joined by five more rebels: the Duke of Candebenet, King Brandegoris of Strangore, King Idres of Cornwall, King Cardelmans of North Wales, and King Agwysaunce of Ireland. (One of the initial six, the King of Scotland, is replaced in this list by King Claryvous of Northumberland.) Numbering fifty thousand men on horseback and ten thousand on foot, they move toward Bedegrayne.*]

So by Merlyn's advys ther were sente forerydars to skumme the countreye, and they mette with the forerydars of the north and made hem to telle whiche wey the hooste cam, and thenne they told it to Arthur, and by Kyng Ban's and Bors's counceill they lete brenne and destroye alle the contrey afore them there they shold ryde.

The Kynge with the Honderd Knyghtes mette a wonder dreme two nyghtes afore the bataille, that ther blewe a grete wynde and blewe down her castels and her townes, and after that cam a water and bare hit all awey. Alle that herd of the sweven [*dream*] said it was a token of grete batayll. Thenne by counceill of Merlyn whan they wist whiche way the eleven kynges wold ryde and lodge that nyghte, at mydnyght they sette upon them as they were in theyr pavelyons. But the scoute watche by her hoost cryed, "Lordes, att armes! for here be your enemyes at your hand!"

Thenne Kynge Arthur and Kynge Ban and Kynge Bors with her good and trusty knyghtes set on hem so fyersly that he made them overthrowe her pavelions on her hedys, but the eleven kynges by manly prowesse of armes tooke a fayre champayne [*fared well on the field*]. But there was slayne that morowe tyde ten thousand good mennys bodyes; and so they had afore hem a strong passage, yet were they fyfty thousand of hardy men. Thenne it drewe toward day.

"Now shalle ye doo by myne advys," said Merlyn unto the thre kynges. "I wold that Kynge Ban and Kynge Bors with her felauship of ten thousand men were put in a wood here besyde in an enbusshement, and kepe them prevy, and that they be leid or the lyght of the daye come and that they stere not tyll ye and your knyghtes have foughte with hem longe. And whanne hit is dayelyght dresse your bataille even afore them, and the passage that they may see alle your hooste. For thenne wyl they be the more hardy when they see yow but aboute twenty thousand, and cause hem to be the gladder to suffre yow and youre hoost to come over the passage."

All the thre kynges and the hoole barons sayde that Merlyn said passyngly wel, and it was done anone as Merlyn had devysed. Soo on the morn whan eyther hoost sawe other, the hoost of the north was well comforted. Thenne to Ulfyus and Brastias were delyverd thre thowsand men of armes, and they sette on them fyersly in the passage and slewe on the ryght hand and on the lyft hand that it was wonder to telle.

[*The battle continues all day with great deeds of arms on both sides. The ambush turns the struggle against the rebels, and Arthur, Ban, and Bors especially distinguish themselves. Eventually the rebel kings are forced to retreat.*]

With that came Merlyn on a grete black hors and said unto Arthur, "Thow hast never done! Hast thou not done ynough? Of thre score thousand this day hast thow lefte on lyve but fifteen thousand, and it is tyme to saye 'ho' for God is wrothe with the that thow wolt never have done. For yonder eleven kynges at this tyme will not be overthrowen, but and thow tary on them ony lenger thy fortune wille torne and they shall encreace. And therfor withdrawe yow unto your lodgyng and reste you as soone as ye may and rewarde your good knyghtes with gold and with sylver, for they have wel deserved hit. There may no rychesse be too dere for them, for of so fewe men as ye have ther were never men dyd more of prowesse than they have done today, for ye have matched this day with the beste fyghters of the world."

"That is trouthe," said Kyng Ban and Bors.

"Also," said Merlyn, "withdrawe yow where ye lyst, for this thre yere I dar undertake they shalle not dere yow. And by than ye shalle here newe tydynges." And thenne Merlyn said unto Arthur, "These eleven kynges have more on hand than they are ware of, for the Sarasyns [*Saxons*] are londed in their countreyes: mo than forty thousand that brenne and slee, and have leid syege att the Castel Wandesborow and make grete destruction. Therfore drede yow not this thre yere. Also, syre, al the goodes that ben goten at this bataill, lete it be serched. And whanne ye have it in your handys lete it be gyven frely unto these two kynges, Ban and Bors, that they may rewarde theyr knyghtes withall, and that shalle cause straungers to be of better wyll to do yow servyse at nede. Also ye be able to reward youre owne knyghtes of your owne goodes whansomever it lyketh you."

"It is wel said," quod Arthur, "and as thow hast devysed, so shal it be done." Whanne it was delyverd to Ban and Bors, they gaf the goodes as frely to their knyghtes—as frely as it was geven to them.

Thenne Merlyn took his leve of Arthur and of the two kynges for to go and see his mayster Bleyse that dwelde in Northumberland. And so he departed and cam to his maister that was passyng glad of his comynge, and there he tolde how Arthur and the two kynges had sped at the grete batayll and how it was ended, and told the names of every kyng and knyght of worship that was there. And soo Bleyse wrote the bataill word by word as Merlyn told hym how it began and by whome, and in lyke wyse how it was endyd and who had the worst. All the batails that were done in Arthur's dayes Merlyn dyd his maister Bleyse do wryte; also he did do wryte all the batails that every worthy knyght dyd of Arthur's courte.

After this, Merlyn departed from his mayster and came to Kynge Arthur that was in the castel of Bedegrayne, that was one of the castels that stondyn in the forest of Sherewood. And Merlyn was so disguysed that Kynge Arthur knewe hym not, for he was al befurred in black shepeskynnes, and a grete payre of bootes, and a bowe and arrowes in a russet gowne, and broughte wild gyse in his hand. And it was on the morne after Candelmas day, but Kyng Arthur knewe hym not.

"Syre," said Merlyn unto the kynge, "wil ye gyve me a gefte?"

"Wherfor," said Kyng Arthur, "Shold I gyve the a gefte, chorle?"

"Sir," said Merlyn, "ye were better to gyve me a gefte that is not in your hand than to lese grete rychesse, for here in the same place there the grete bataill was is grete tresour hyd in the erthe."

"Who told the so, chorle?" said Arthur.

"Merlyn told me so," said he.

Thenne Ulfyus and Brastias knew hym wel ynough and smyled. "Syre," said these two knyghtes, "it is Merlyn that so speketh unto yow!"

Thenne Kyng Arthur was gretely abasshed and had merveyll of Merlyn, and so had Kynge Ban and Kynge Bors, and soo they had grete dysport at hym.

Soo in the meanewhyle there cam a damoysel that was an erly's doughter. His name was Sanam and her name was Lyonors, a passynge fair damoysel; and so she cam thyder for to do homage as other lordes dyd after the grete bataill. And Kyng Arthur sette his love gretely upon her and so dyd she upon hym, and the kyng had adoo with her and gat on her a child: his name was Borre, that was after a good knyghte and of the Table Round.

Thenne ther cam word that the Kyng Ryence of Northern Walys maade grete werre on Kynge Lodegreance of Camylyard, for the whiche thyng Arthur was wroth for he loved hym wel, and hated Kyng Ryence for he was alwey ageynst hym. So by ordenaunce of the thre kynges ther were sente home unto Benwyck alle they wold departe, for drede of Kynge Claudas, and Pharyaunce and Anthemes and Gracian and Lyonses [of] Payarne were the leders of tho that shold kepe the kynges' landys.

And thenne Kynge Arthur and Kynge Ban and Kyng Bors departed with her felaushyp a twenty thousand and came within six dayes into the countrey of Camylyard, and there rescowed Kynge Lodegreance and slewe ther moche people of Kynge Ryence unto the nombre of ten thousand men, and put hym to flyghte. And thenne had these thre kynges grete chere of Kyng

Lodegreance, that thanked them of their grete goodnesse that they wold
revenge hym of his enemyes. And there hadde Arthur the fyrst syght of
Gwenever, the kynge's doughter of Camylyard, and ever after he loved her.
After, they were weddyd as it telleth in the booke.

Soo brevely to make an ende, they took theyr leve to goo into theyre own
countreyes, for Kynge Claudas dyd grete destruction on their landes.
Thenne said Arthur, "I wille goo with yow."

"Nay," said the kynges, "ye shalle not at this tyme, for ye have moche to
doo yet in these landes. Therfore we wille departe, and with the grete goodes
that we have goten in these landes by youre geftes we shalle wage good
knyghtes and withstande the Kynge Claudas's malyce, for by the grace of
God and we have nede, we wille sende to yow for youre socour. And yf ye
have nede, sende for us and we wille not tary by the feythe of our bodyes."

"Hit shalle not," saide Merlyn, "nede that these two kynges come ageyne
in the wey of werre. But I knowe wel Kynge Arthur maye not be longe from
yow, for within a yere or two ye shalle have grete nede, and thenne shalle he
revenge yow on youre enemyes as ye have done on his. For these eleven
kynges shal deye all in a day by the grete myghte and prowesse of armes of
two valyaunt knyghtes." As it telleth after, her names ben Balyn le Saveage
and Balan his broder, that ben merveillous good knyghtes as ben ony lyvyng.

The Finding of Excalibur

[*A squire arrives at court with his mortally wounded master and asks for
vengeance against a knight (Pellinore) who has set his pavilion by a fountain in the
forest. Arthur knights a squire named Gryflet, whom the stranger defeats and seriously
wounds. Then twelve aged knights arrive from Rome to demand that King Arthur pay
tribute to the Emperor. Angered by Gryflet's injury and the Roman Emperor's
haughty demand, Arthur defies the ambassadors and arms himself to go alone into the
forest.*]

And so Arthur roode a softe paas tyll it was day, and thenne was he ware
of thre chorles chacynge Merlyn, and wold have slayne hym. Thenne the
kyng rode unto them and bad them, "Flee, chorles!" Thenne were they
aferd whan they sawe a knyght, and fled.

"O Merlyn," said Arthur, "here haddest thou be slayne for all thy craftes
had I not byn."

"Nay," said Merlyn, "not soo, for I coude save myself and I wold. And
thou arte more nere thy deth than I am, for thow gost to the dethward and
God be not thy frend."

So as they wente thus talkyng, they came to the fontayne and the ryche
pavelione there by hit. Thenne Kyng Arthur was ware where sat a knyght
armed in a chayer. "Syr knyght," said Arthur, "for what cause abydest thow
here, that ther maye no knyght ryde this wey but yf he juste wyth the?" said
the kynge. "I rede the leve that custome," said Arthur.

"This customme," saide the knyght, "have I used and wille use, magre who saith nay, and who is greved with my custome, lete hym amende hit that wol."

"I wil amende it," said Arthur.

"I shal defende the," said the knyght. Anon he toke his hors and dressid his shylde and toke a spere, and they met so hard either in other's sheldes that al to-shevered their sperys. Therwith anone Arthur pulled oute his swerd.

"Nay, not so," said the knyght. "It is fayrer," said the knyght, "that we tweyne renne more togyders with sharp sperys."

"I wille wel," said Arthur, "and I had ony mo sperys."

"I have ynow," said the knyght. So ther cam a squyer and brought in good sperys, and Arthur chose one and he another. So they spored their horses and cam togyders with al the myghtes that eyther brak her speres to her handes. Thenne Arthur sette hand on his swerd.

"Nay," said the knyght, "ye shal do better. Ye are a passynge good juster as ever I mette withal, and ones for the love of the hyghe ordre of knyghthode lete us juste ones ageyn."

"I assente me," said Arthur. Anone there were brought two grete sperys, and every knyght gat a spere and therwith they ranne togyders that Arthur's spere al to-shevered. But the other knyghte hyt hym so hard in myddes of the shelde that horse and man felle to the erthe, and therwith Arthur was egre, and pulled oute his swerd and said, "I will assay the, syr knyghte, on foote, for I have lost the honour on horsbak."

"I will be on horsbak," said the knyght.

Thenne was Arthur wrothe and dressid his sheld toward hym with his swerd drawen. Whan the knyght sawe that, he alyghte, for hym thought no worship to have a knyght at suche availle: he to be on horsbak and he on foot. And so he alyght and dressid his sheld unto Arthur, and ther began a strong bataille with many grete strokes, and soo hewe with her swerdes that the cantels [*pieces of the shields*] flewe in the feldes and moche blood they bledde bothe, that al the place there as they faught was overbledde with blood. And thus they fought long and rested hem, and thenne they wente to the batayl ageyne and so hurtled togyders lyke two rammes that eyther felle to the erthe. So at the last they smote togyders that both her swerdys met even togyders, but the swerd of the knyght smote Kyng Arthur's swerd in two pyeces, wherfor he was hevy.

Thenne said the knyghte unto Arthur, "Thow arte in my daunger whether me lyst to save the or slee the, and but thou yelde the as overcome and recreaunt thow shalt deye."

"As for deth," said Kyng Arthur, "welcome be it whan it cometh. But to yelde me unto the as recreaunt I had lever dye than to be soo shamed." And therwithal the kynge lepe unto Pellinore and tooke hym by the myddel and threwe hym doune and raced of his helme. Whan the knyght felt that, he was adrad, for he was a passynge bygge man of myghte. And anone he broughte Arthur under hym and reaced of his helme, and wold have smyten of his hede.

Therwithall came Merlyn and sayd, "Knyghte, hold thy hand! For and thow slee that knyghte, thou puttest this reame in the gretest dammage that ever was reame, for this knyght is a man of more worship than thou wotest of."

"Why, who is he?" said the knyghte.

"It is Kyng Arthur."

Thenne wold he have slayn hym for drede of his wrathe, and heve up his swerd, and therwith Merlyn cast an enchauntement to the knyghte that he felle to the erthe in a grete slepe. Thenne Merlyn tooke up Kyng Arthur and rode forth on the knyghte's hors.

"Allas," said Arthur, "what hast thou done, Merlyn? Hast thow slayne this good knyghte by thy craftes? There lyveth not soo worshipful a knyghte as he was. I had lever than the stynte of my land a yere that he were on lyve."

"Care ye not," sayd Merlyn, "for he is holer than ye, for he is but on slepe and will awake within thre houres. I told you," said Merlyn, "what a knyghte he was. Here had ye be slayn had I not ben. Also ther lyveth not a bygger knyght than he is one, and he shal hereafter do yow ryght good servyse, and his name is Pellinore. And he shal have two sones that shal be passyng good men; sauf one, they shalle have no felawe or prowesse and of good lyvynge, and her names shal be Persyval of Walys and Lamerak of Walys. And he shal telle yow the name of your own sone bygoten of your syster that shal be the destruction of alle this royame."

Ryght so the kyng and he departed and wente untyl an ermyte that was a good man and a grete leche. Soo the heremyte serched all his woundys and gaf hym good salves; so the kyng was there thre days and thenne were his woundes wel amendyd that he myght ryde and goo, and so departed. And as they rode Arthur said, "I have no swerd."

"No force," said Merlyn. "Hereby is a swerd that shalle be yours and I may." Soo they rode tyl they came to a lake, the whiche was a fayr water and brood. And in the myddes of the lake Arthur was ware of an arme clothed in whyte samyte, that held a fayr swerd in that hand.

"Loo," said Merlyn, "yonder is that swerd that I spake of. " With that they sawe a damoisel goyng upon the lake.

"What damoysel is that?" said Arthur.

"That is the Lady of the Lake," said Merlyn. "And within that lake is a roche, and theryn is as fayr a place as ony on erthe and rychely besene. And this damoysell wylle come to yow anone, and thenne speke ye fayre to her that she will gyve yow that swerd."

Anone withall came and damoysel unto Arthur and salewed hym, and he her ageyne. "Damoysel," said Arthur, "what swerd is that that yonder the arme holdeth above the water? I wold it were myne, for I have no swerd."

"Syr Arthur, Kynge," said the damoysell, "that swerd is myn. And yf ye will gyve me a gefte whan I aske it yow, ye shal have it."

"By my feyth," said Arthur, "I will geve yow what gefte ye will aske."

"Wel," said the damoisel, "go ye into yonder barge and rowe yourself to the swerd, and take it and scaubart with yow, and I will aske my gefte whan I see my tyme." So Syr Arthur and Merlyn alyght and tayed their horses to two trees, and so they went into the ship. And whanne they came to the swerd that the hand held, Syre Arthur toke it up by the handels and toke it with hym, and the arme and the hand went under the water, and so come unto the lond and rode forth.

And thenne Syr Arthur sawe a ryche pavelion. "What sygnyfyeth yonder pavelion?"

"That is the knyghte's pavlion," seid Merlyn, "that ye fought with last, Syr Pellinore. But he is out; he is not there. He hath adoo with a knyght of yours that hyght Egglame, and they have foughten togyder; but at the last Egglame fledde and els he had ben dede, and he hath chaced hym even to Carlyon. And we shal mete with hym anon in the hyghwey."

"That is wel sayd," said Arthur. "Now have I a swerd; now wille I wage bataill with hym and be avenged on hym."

"Sir, ye shal not so," sayd Merlyn, "for the knyght is wery of fyghtyng and chacyng, so that ye shal have no worship to have ado with hym. Also he will not be lyghtly matched of one knyght lyvyng; and therfor it is my counceil lete hym passe, for he shal do you good servyse in shorte tyme, and his sones after his dayes. Also ye shal see that day in short space ye shal be right glad to geve him your sister to wedde."

"Whan I see hym, I wil doo as ye advyse," sayd Arthur.

Thenne Syre Arthur loked on the swerd and lyked it passynge wel. "Whether lyketh yow better," sayd Merlyn, "the suerd or the scaubard?"

"Me lyketh better the swerd," sayd Arthur.

"Ye are more unwyse," sayd Merlyn, "for the scaubard is worth ten of the swerdys. For whyles ye have the scaubard upon yow ye shalle never lese no blood, be ye never so sore wounded. Therfor kepe wel the scaubard alweyes with yow."

So they rode unto Carlyon, and by the way they met with Syr Pellinore. But Merlyn had done suche a crafte that Pellinore sawe not Arthur, and he past by withoute ony wordes.

"I merveylle," sayd Arthur, "that the knyght wold not speke."

"Syr," said Merlyn, "he sawe yow not, for and he had sene yow ye had not lyghtly departed." Soo they come unto Carlyon, wherof his knyghtes were passynge glad, and whanne they herd of his aventures they merveilled that he wold jeoparde his persone soo alone. But alle men of worship said it was mery to be under suche a chyvetayne, that wolde put his persone in aventure as other poure knyghtes dyd.

The Wedding of Arthur and Guenever

In the begynnynge of Arthur after he was chosen kyng by adventure and by grace—for the most party of the barons knewe not that he was Uther Pendragon's sone, but as Merlyn made it openly knowen. But yet many kynges and lordes helde grete werre ayenst hym for that cause, but wel Arthur overcame hem alle. For the mooste party the days of his lyf he was ruled moche by the counceil of Merlyn.

Soo it fell on a tyme Kyng Arthur sayd unto Merlyn, "My barons wille lete me have no rest but nedes I muste take a wyf, and I wylle none take but by thy counceill and by thyne advys."

"It is wel done," said Merlyn, "that ye take a wyf, for a man of your bounte and noblesse shold not be without a wyf. Now is ther ony that ye love more than another?"

"Ye," said Kyng Arthur, "I love Gwenever, the kynge's doughter Lodegreance of the land of Camylyd, the whiche holdeth in his hows the Table Round that ye told he had of my fader Uther. And this damoysel is the moost valyaunt and fayrest lady that I knowe lyvynge, or yet that ever I coude fynde."

"Syre," sayd Merlyn, "as of her beaute and fayrenes, she is one of the fayrest on lyve; but and ye loved her not so wel as ye doo, I shold fynde yow a damoysel of beaute and of goodenesse that shold lyke yow and plese yow, and your herte were not sette. But there as a man's herte is set he wylle be lothe to retorne [*turn back*]."

"That is trouth," said Kyng Arthur. But Merlyn warned the kynge covertly that Gwenever was not holsome for hym to take to wyf, for he warned hym that Launcelot shold love her and she hym ageyne; and so he torned his tale to the aventures of Sancgreal. Thenne Merlyn desyred of the kynge for to have men with hym that shold enquere of Gwenever, and so the kyng graunted hym, and Merlyn wente forth unto Kyng Lodegreance of Camylyerd and told hym of the desyre of the kyng that he wold have unto his wyf Gwenever his doughter.

"That is to me," sayd Kyng Lodegreance, "the best tydynges that ever I herd, that so worthy a kyng of prowesse and noblesse wille wedde my doughter! And os for my landes, I wylle gyve hym wyst I it myght please hym, but he hath londes ynowe; hym nedeth none. But I shalle sende hym a gyfte shalle please hym moche more, for I shalle gyve hym the Table Round, the whiche Uther Pendragon gave me, and whan it is ful complete ther is an hundred knyghtes and fyfty. And as for on hundred good knyghtes I have myself, but I fawte [*lack*] fifty, for so many have ben slayne in my dayes." And so Lodegreance delyverd his doughter Gwenever unto Merlyn, and the Table Round with the hundred knyghtes, and so they rode fresshly with grete royalte, what by water and what by land, tyl that they came nyghe unto London.

Whenne Kyng Arthur herd of the comyng of Gwenever and the hundred knyghtes with the Table Round, thenne Kyng Arthur maade grete joye for her comyng and that ryche presente, and said openly, "This fair lady is passyng welcome unto me, for I have loved her longe, and therfore ther is nothyng so lyef to me. And these knyghtes with the Round Table pleasen me more than ryght grete rychesse." And in alle hast the kynge lete ordeyne for the maryage and the coronacyon in the moost honorable wyse that coude by devysed.

"Now Merlyn," said Kyng Arthur, "goo thow and aspye me in al this land fifty knyghtes whiche ben of most prowesse and worship." Within short tyme Merlyn had founde suche knyghtes that shold fulfylle twenty and eight knyghtes, but no mo he coude fynde. Thenne the Bisshop of Caunterbury was fette [*fetched*] and he blessid the syeges [*seats*] with grete royalte and devoycyon, and there sette the eight and twenty knyghtes in her syeges.

And whan this was done Merlyn said, "Fayr syrs, ye must al aryse and come to Kyng Arthur for to doo hym homage; he will have the better wil to mayntene yow." And so they arose and dyd their homage, and when they were gone Merlyn fond in every syeges letters of gold that told the knyghtes' names that had sytten therin. But two fyeges were voyde.

The Interment of Merlin

It felle so that Merlyn felle in a dottage on the damoisel that Kyng Pellinore broughte to the Courte, and she was one of the damoysels of the lake, that hyght Nyneve. But Merlyn wold lete have her no rest, but alweyes he wold be with her; and ever she maade Merlyn good chere tyl she had lerned of hym al maner thynge that she desyred, and he was assoted upon her that he myghte not be from her. Soo on a tyme he told Kynge Arthur that he sholde not dure longe, but for al his craftes he shold be put in the erthe quyck. And so he told the kynge many thynges that shold befall; but allewayes he warned the kynge to kepe wel his swerd and the scaubard, for he told hym how the swerd and the scaubard shold be stolen by a woman from hym that he most trusted. Also he told Kynge Arthur that he shold mysse hym: "Yet had ye lever than al your landes to have me ageyne."

"A," sayd the kynge, "syn ye knowe of your adventure, purvey for hit and put awey by your craftes that mysaventure!"

"Nay," said Merlyn, "it wylle not be." Soo he departed from the kynge, and within a whyle the damoysel of the lake departed. And Merlyn wente with her evermore wheresomever she wente, and oftymes Merlyn wold have had her pryvely awey by his subtyle craftes. Thenne she made hym to swere that he shold never do none enchauntement upon her yf he wold have his wylle, and so he sware.

So she and Merlyn wente over the see unto the land of Benwyck, thereas Kynge Ban was kynge, that had grete warre ageynst Kynge Claudas. And there Merlyn spake with Kynge Ban's wyf, a fair lady and a good, and her name was Elayne; and there he sawe yonge Launcelot. There the quene made grete sorowe for the mortal werre that Kyng Claudas made on her lord and on her landes.

"Take none hevynesse," said Merlyn, "for this same child within this twenty yere shall revenge yow on Kynge Claudas, that all Crystendom shalle speke of it. And this same child shalle be the moost man of worship of the world, and his fyrst name is Galahad. That knowe I wel," said Merlyn, "and syn ye have confermed hym Launcelot."

"That is trouthe," said the quene. "His fyrst name was Galahad. O Merlyn," said the quene, "shalle I lyve to see my sone suche a man of prowesse?"

"Ye, lady, on my parel [*word of honor*] ye shal see hit, and lyve many wynters after." And soo sone after the lady and Merlyn departed, and by the waye Merlyn shewed her many wondres, and cam into Cornewaille. And alweyes Merlyn lay aboute the lady to have her maydenhode, and she was ever passynge wery of hym and fayne wold have ben delyverd of hym, for she was aferd of hym by cause he was a devyl's sone, and she coude not beskyfte [*get rid of*] hym by no meane.

And soo on a tyme it happed that Merlyn shewed to her in a roche whereas was a greete wonder, and wroughte by enchauntement that wente under a grete stone. So by her subtyle wyrchynge she maade Merlyn to goo under that stone to lete her wete of the merveilles there, but she wroughte so ther for hym that he came never oute for alle the crafte he coude doo. And so she departed and lefte Merlyn.

IV.

MERLIN IN
THE RENAISSANCE

chapter 7

EDMUND SPENSER:
THE FAERIE QUEENE
(BOOK III, CANTO 3)

T H E P R O D U C T I O N of new prose romances declined after the fifteenth century; nevertheless, medieval romances continued to be popular into the sixteenth century, revitalized by the printing press and distributed to audiences to whom they had previously been unavailable. The print revival of these complicated and lengthy tales of knights and ladies, together with the longevity of verse epics like the *Chanson de Roland* and verse romances about heroes like Alexander the Great, William of Palerne, and others both historical and imaginary, all inspired a new genre of epic verse romance. In particular, the Italian poets Pulci, Boiardo, Tasso, and Ariosto transformed the literary tradition of Charlemagne and his knights into magnificent fantasies of the Crusading era, replete with noble Saracens and Christians, distressed damsels and female knights-errant, sorcerers, monsters, and marvels. Their adventures expressed both the fancy and the developing materialism of aristocratic culture, as well as the sense of a rapidly expanding and exotic world.

King Arthur and his knights also remained well known, although increasingly at the popular rather than aristocratic level of taste. And for many readers romance and history remained indistinguishable—the marvels seemingly corroborated by the material solidity of print. Therefore both medieval romance and Italian epic were available as models to Edmund Spenser for the great romantic epic of Elizabethan England. *The Faerie Queene*, which Spenser crafted between 1579 and 1596, both reflects and reconciles the dichotomies of the age. It answers the artistic decline of medieval romance, which had become stereotypical and overblown, by adopting the aristocratic verse epic fashion, and it builds upon the imaginative appeal of romance by inventing new marvels and adventures. It furnishes the highly particularized description that was usually lacking, except for the occasional stylized set-piece, in the medieval attention to narrative. Yet Spenser's epic romance endows each detail with rich symbolic associations that contribute to the action rather than standing in splendid, static isolation. It comments upon the relationship between the actuality of history and the idealism of romance and Christianity by creating alternative but occasionally intersecting realities: the world of Arthurian and Elizabethan England, and the world of Faerie, ruled by Elizabeth I's counterpart the Faerie Queene.

In Spenser's conception King Arthur reigned first in the historical world but was then transported by Merlin's art (via Avalon, perhaps?) to the world of Faerie. Similarly, his half-brother Artegall (a Spenserian invention) is a human changeling, stolen by a fairy from the "historical" world of Arthurian England. This concept of contrasting realities that may once have been united but gradually become separated is a commonplace of fairy lore and an archetype for alternative universes in science fiction and in modern fantasies like those of White, Lewis, and Tolkien. By it, author and reader can acknowledge the fundamental difference between physical and imagined realities while exploring the intellectual and emotional vitality of both.

The Faerie Queene serves as a profound commentary on the spiritual values and potential of a fallen humanity living through history. Each of its six books examines the nature of a cardinal virtue—Holiness, Temperance, Chastity, Friendship, Justice, and Courtesy—through the adventures of its personifying hero or heroes. These are carefully chosen to be social as well as individual virtues, and point toward cultural perfection as well as personal salvation. Therefore the Arthurian legend of a reconstituted Golden Age becomes more than a national theme, and fundamentally more appropriate to Spenser's allegorical purposes than the Carolingian theme of colliding cultures. Furthermore, Spenser's method implicitly balances the barren, adulterous love that was Arthur's downfall in the human world with the fertile, chaste love that will exist between Britomart (the knight of Chastity and heroine of Book III) and Arthur's half-brother Artegall (the knight of Justice). Britomart's chastity does not mean sexual abstinence, although she defends her virginity against all kinds of temptation and attack in Book III. It does mean sexual commitment to one person as the physical emblem of a fulfilled love. This kind of loyalty was in fact a goal of *fine amour* or courtly love, especially when such love could exist in matrimony (which was not always possible given the political and economic nature of aristocratic marriages). Merlin's prophecy concerning the progeny of Britomart and Artegall illustrates that even this fulfilling love, which Arthur and Guinevere's marriage traditionally lacked, does not bring the Britons a lasting triumph. Human fortunes are endlessly mutable within the lines fixed by the divine will, and must be worked out individually within each generation.

While not an active player in the adventures, Spenser's Merlin is central as an example by which we can measure the corruptness of sorcerers like Archimago and Busirane. Although a devil's son and commander of devils, he does not make pacts with them. He is a model of the Renaissance magus or natural philosopher: his magic does not conceal truth, but either destroys illusion or uses illusion to reveal truth. He fashions Arthur's arms and armor, tutors him, and transports him into Faerie to be healed of the wounds suffered at Camlan. Merlin is also an historical figure who becomes imprisoned in Faerie—as Spenser's contemporary Michael Drayton wrote in his chronicle *Poly-Olbion* (1612) "by loving of an Elfe." Drayton combines Spenser's influence with Malory's:

> For, walking with his Fay, her to the Rocke hee brought,
> In which he oft before his Nigromancies wrought:
> And going in thereat his Magiques to have showne,
> Shee stopt the Caverns mouth with an inchanted stone:
> Whose cunning strongly crost, amaz'd whilst he did stand,
> Shee captive him convay'd unto the Fairie Land [Song 4,
> ll. 337–342].

Spenser's Merlin is not technically a dealer in dead spirits, however; his thaumaturgical powers are wholly in the service of good and he summons spirits yet to come. "The Ruines of Time," published a year after Books I–III of *The Faerie Queene*, epitomizes Spenser's purpose by referring to Merlin as creator of an earthly paradise. The canto printed here names him not as necromancer or sorcerer, but as "the Dreadful Mage," "the wisard," "the Prophet," and "Magician." Stanza 14 of the canto, where he is introduced binding demons, contrasts deliberately with III, xii, stanza 31, where "the vile Enchaunter" Busirane is first encountered "Figuring straunge characters of his art,/ With living bloud he those characters wrate." And Merlin's purpose in the canto is to encourage a noble love that will produce a great lineage; Busirane's is solely to satisfy his lust.

As an artificer, Merlin's most notable creation in *The Faerie Queene* is the magic "mirror" or globe that, like the wall of brass, was a popular image of Renaissance magic. It complements Arthur's impenetrable diamond shield, which defeats magical attack, by revealing what is happening or will happen elsewhere in the world: "What ever foe had wrought, or frend had fayn'd,/ Therein discovered was, ne ought mote pas,/ Ne ought in secret from the same remayn'd;/ For thy it round and hollow shaped was,/ Like to the world it selfe, and seem'd a world of glas" (III, ii, 19). Not only does it show who are one's friends and foes, but it reveals true or false love (like the mirror in Chaucer's *Squire's Tale*) and signifies "fragile marital harmony" (Hamilton, p. 320). Furthermore, it symbolizes both "the poet's ability to reveal the truth" and "a world free of illusion and error" (Blackburn, p. 190). Merlin had made the globe for King Ryence (surprisingly, for he is one of Arthur's most formidable early foes in medieval romance!). Britomart, whose name means "warlike Britoness," sees Artegall in it and falls in love with him. She becomes so afflicted that she sets out, with her nurse Glauce, to seek advice from Merlin about where to find him. Her encounter with Merlin marks her entry to fairy land in quest of Artegall.

Britomart's and Glauce's visit to Merlin's tomb is modeled on the third book and canto of Ariosto's *Orlando Furioso* (first published in 1516), where the maiden knight Bradamante is foretold her destiny and offspring with the Saracen knight Ruggiero. Bradamante is dropped from a cliff by the false knight Pinabello, but survives unhurt to discover at its foot a resplendent

tomb in Renaissance style. There Merlin's body is embalmed in a marble
stone, and attended by a seeress named Melissa. Sir John Harington's
famous translation, which appeared the year after *The Faerie Queene*'s first three
books, describes it (III, 8, 16):

> This was a church most solemne and devout,
>   Standing on marble pillers small and round,
>   Rais'd by great art on arches all about,
>   That made ech voice to yeeld a double sound.
>   A lightsome lampe that never goeth out,
>   Burned on an altar sta[n]ding in the ground. . . .
> Whether it be the nature of some stone,
>   A darksome place with lightsomnes to fill,
>   Or were it done by magike art alone,
>   Or else by helpe of Mathematike skill,
>   To make transparencies to meete in one,
>   And to convay the sunne beames where you will.
>   But sure it was most curious to behold
>   Set forth with carved workes and guilt with gold.

Merlin's voice issues from this "flaming" tomb, prophesying Bradamánte's
union with Ruggiero and their illustrious offspring (most of them named in
Geoffrey of Monmouth's *Historia*). Melissa then summons the likenesses of
their descendants and foretells their fates. In contrast, Spenser adopts
Ariosto's grotto, but relocates it from southern France to Carmarthen. He
does not describe its architecture, but instead portrays a living and unattended
Merlin. Ariosto's wizard is a disembodied voice; Spenser's seems as active as
in life.

His prophecy to Britomart echoes the tradition that the Britons are
descended from a Trojan band led by Aeneas's son Brutus. Its narrative
begins with Artegall's birth and kidnapping to the land of Faerie, foretells
the future fate of the Britons, who will be led by the offspring of Britomart
and Artegall, and concludes with a vision of Queen Elizabeth. Spenser
generally follows the pattern created by Geoffrey of Monmouth, but dispenses
with most of the allegorical animal imagery that characterizes the *Prophetiae
Merlini*. Occasionally he makes changes in the chronicle tradition to improve
the lot or character of the British kings after Arthur, but he does not change
the gradual decline of British power.

The prophecies may be divided into three sections of eight stanzas each.
The first (stanzas 26–33) describes the feats of Artegall, his (and Britomart's)
son Conan, grandson Vortipore, great-grandson Malgo, and great-great-
grandson Careticus, but ends with the triumph of the Norwegian king
Gormond. The second (34–41) foretells a resurgence of British power under
Cadwan and especially Cadwallin until, growing too proud late in
Cadwallader's reign, the Britons are decimated by plague and yield again.
The third (stanzas 42–49) describes the triumph of the Saxons and thralldom
of the Britons (relieved only partially by the deeds of several British princes),

the eventual fall of the Saxons to new invaders from Denmark, and finally the conquest by William I, whose Tudor descendant Henry VII unifies both British and English peoples. At the end of the canto Britomart herself symbolizes this future union by donning the armor of Angela, a warrior queen of the Saxons, and acquiring the spear of Bladud, a legendary British king. Harry Berger discerns in Merlin's prophecies "the familiar Spenserian pattern: early ascendancy followed by some kind of failure which leads to a phase of captivity, withdrawal, or exile" (p. 48). This is a fundamental pattern in Old Testament chronicle and medieval romance, too—and, of course, a capsule summary of Arthur's legend.

Edmund Spenser was born in London about 1552 and attended the Merchant Taylor's, an influential school of the English Renaissance. He took a Master's degree from Pembroke College, Cambridge, and briefly served the Earl of Leicester before leaving for Ireland in 1580 as secretary to Lord Grey of Wilton, who became the model for Artegall. Except for two visits to England, one with Sir Walter Raleigh, Spenser remained in Ireland and in 1586 was given Kilcolman Castle, Munster, after its previous owner, the Earl of Desmond, had been stripped of his property for rebellion. Ireland was a wild and unruly country beyond the English Pale around Dublin, and some of this quality entered into the adventures of *The Faerie Queene*, which Spenser had begun in 1579. The native Irish were reduced almost to savagery by the hardships of the Tudor occupation and continual insurrection, and Spenser was forced out of Kilcolman by the O'Neill rebellion in 1598. After taking a dispatch to London, he died in January 1599 and was buried near Chaucer in Westminster Cathedral.

Bibliographic note: The poetic meter and language of Spenser's epic set it apart from all other English poetry. Spenser read the Italian epic poets in Italian but adopted a new stanza form for his poem, rhyming *ababbcbcc*, with eight lines of ten syllables concluded by a twelve-syllable alexandrine. The diction is based more on English than on Latin words, and is deliberately archaic: Spenser wanted to give the impression, if not of "long ago and far away," then at least of a significant medieval Neverland. He coined many words as well as using older forms, so that Ben Jonson complained he "writ no language" in affecting an ancient style. Even so, *The Faerie Queene* is not difficult to read and can be enjoyed today, like many of Chaucer's *Canterbury Tales*, for a good tale brilliantly told.

Because these linguistic features are important and intentional, I have not modernized vocabulary and spelling beyond glossing the most difficult terms and converting *u* and *v*, which printers of the time often interchanged, to their "correct" forms. I have also regularized the use of some punctuation: providing apostrophes for possessives and in contractions of *-ed* (as in *pour'd*), but not where *t* is substituted for *-ed* (as in *encompast*). The first edition of Books I–III appeared in 1590, but without Welsh names, while Spenser was in London with Raleigh. I have based this text upon the second edition of 1592, published for William Ponsonbie, which supplies the names. For additional checking and explanatory notes I have referred to *The Faerie Queene*,

Book Three, ed. Frederick Morgan Padelford, *The Works of Edmund Spenser: A Variorum Edition* (Baltimore: Johns Hopkins University Press, 1966) and A.C. Hamilton's fine edition of *The Faerie Queene* in the Annotated English Poets Series (London and New York: Longman, 1977). The passage by Michael Drayton comes from *Poly-Olbion*, The Works of Michael Drayton, Vol. 4, ed. J. William Hebel (Oxford: Shakespeare Head Press, 1933; rpt. Blackwell, 1961); that by Lodovico Ariosto is from *Orlando Furioso in English Heroical Verse*, trans. John Harington, facsimile ed. (Amsterdam and New York: Da Capo, 1970). Spenser scholarship is a field as vast and complex as *The Faerie Queene* itself; however, two essays are particularly informative about Merlin's role in the poem. They are Harry Berger, Jr., "The Structure of Merlin's Chronicle in *The Faerie Queene* III, (iii)," *Studies in English Literature, 1500–1900* 9 (Winter 1969): 39–51, and William Blackburn, "Spenser's Merlin," *Renaissance and Reformation* 4 (Fall 1980): 179–198. A broader context is provided by Berger's "*The Faerie Queene*, Book III: A General Description," in *Essential Articles for the Study of Edmund Spenser*, ed. A.C. Hamilton (Hamden, Conn.: Archon, 1972), pp. 395–424, and Charles Bowie Millican's *Spenser and the Table Round: A Study in the Contemporaneous Background for Spenser's Use of the Arthurian Legend* (Cambridge: Harvard University Press, 1932).

Edmund Spenser: The Faerie Queene

The III. Booke of the Cant. III.

Merlin bewrays to Britomart,
the state of Artegall.
And shewes the famous Progeny
which from them springen shall.

1

Most sacred fire, that burnest mightily
    In living brests, ykindled first above,
    Emongst th'eternall spheres and lamping sky,
    And thence pour'd into men, which men call Love;
    Not that same, which doth base affections move
    in brutish minds, and filthy lust inflame,
    But that sweet fit, that doth true beautie love,
    And chooseth vertue for his dearest Dame,
Whence spring all noble deeds and never dying fame:

2

Well did Antiquitie a God thee deeme,
   That over mortall minds hast so great might,
   To order them as best to thee doth seeme,
   And all their actions to direct aright;
   The fatall purpose of divine foresight,
   Thou doest effect in destined descents,
   Through deepe impression of thy secret might,
   And stirredst up th' Heroes' high intents,
Which the last world admyres for wondrous moniments.

3

But thy dread darts in none do triumph more,
   Ne braver proofe in any, of thy powre
   Shew'dst thou, then in this royall Maid of yore,
   Making her seeke an unknowne Paramoure,
   From the world's end, through many a bitter stowre: [*struggle*]
   From whose two loynes thou afterwards did rayse
   Most famous fruits of matrimoniall bowre,
   Which through the earth have spred their living prayse,
That fame in trompe of gold eternally displayes.

4

Begin then, O my dearest sacred Dame,
   Daughter of *Phoebus* and of *Memorie*,
   That dost ennoble with immortall name
   The warlike Worthies, from antiquitie,
   In thy great volume of Eternitie:
   Begin, O *Clio*, and recount from hence
   My glorious Soveraine's goodly auncestrie,
   Till that by due degrees and long protense,   [*extended time*]
Thou have it lastly brought unto her Excellence.

5

Full many wayes within her troubled mind,
   Old *Glauce* cast, to cure this Ladie's griefe:
   Full many waies she sought, but none could find,
   Nor herbes, nor charmes, nor counsell that is chiefe
   And choisest med'cine for sicke hart's reliefe:
   For thy great care she tooke, and greater feare,
   Least that it should her turne to foule repriefe,
   And sore reproch, when so her father deare
Should of his dearest daughter's hard misfortune heare.

6

At last she her avis'd, that he, which made
   That mirrhour, wherein the sicke Damosell

So straungely vewed her straunge lover's shade,
To weet, the learned *Merlin*, well could tell,
Under what coast of heaven the man did dwell,
And by what meanes his love might best be wrought:
For though beyond the *Africk Ismaell*,   [*North Africa*]
Or th'Indian *Peru* he were, she thought
Him forth through infinite endevour to have sought.

7

Forthwith themselves disguising both in straunge
And base attyre, that none might them bewray:
To *Maridunum*, that is now by chaunge
Of name *Cayr-Merdin* cald, they tooke their way:
There the wise *Merlin* whylome wont (they say)
To make his wonne, low underneath the ground,   [*home*]
In a deepe delve, fare from the vew of day,
That of no living wight he mote be found,
When so he counsel'd with his sprights encompast round.

8

And if thou ever happen that same way
To travell, goe to see that dreadfull place:
It is an hideous hallow cave (they say)
Under a rocke that lyes a litle space
From the swift *Barry*, tombling downe apace,
Emongst the woodie hilles of *Dynevowre*.
But dare thou not, I charge, in any cace,
To enter into that same balefull Bowre,
For feare the cruell Feends should thee unwares devowre.

9

But standing high aloft, low lay thine eare
And there such ghastly noise of yron chaines,
And brasen Caudrons thou shalt rombling heare,
Which thousand sprights with long enduring paines
Do tosse, that it will stonne thy feeble braines,
And oftentimes great grones, and grievous stounds,   [*pains or roars*]
When too huge toile and labour them constraines:
And oftentimes loud strokes, and ringing sounds
From under that deepe Rocke most horribly rebounds.

10

The cause some say is this: A litle while
Before that *Merlin* dyde, he did intend,
A brasen wall in compas to compile
About *Cairmardin*, and did it commend

Unto these Sprights, to bring to perfect end.
During which worke the Ladie of the Lake,
Whom long he lov'd, for him in hast did send,
Who thereby forst his workemen to forsake,
Them bound till his returne, their labour not to slake.

11

In the meane time through that false Ladie's traine,   [*treachery*]
    He was surpris'd, and buried under beare,   [*bier (in his tomb)*]
    Ne ever to his worke return'd againe:
    Nath'lesse those feends may not their worke forbeare,
    So greatly his commaundement they feare,
    But there do toyle and travell day and night,
    Untill that brasen wall they up doe reare:
    For *Merlin* had in Magicke more insight,
Then ever him before or after living wight.

12

For he by words could call out of the sky
    Both Sunne and Moone, and make them him obay:
    The land to sea, and sea to maineland dry,
    And darkesome night he eke could turne to day:
    Huge hostes of men he could alone dismay,
    And hostes of men of meanest things could frame,
    When so him list his enimies to fray:
    That to this day for terror of his fame,
The feends do quake, when any him to them does name.

13

And sooth, men say that he was not the sonne
    Of mortall Syre, or other living wight,
    But wondrously begotten, and begonne
    By false illusion of a guilefull Spright,
    On a faire Ladie Nonne, that whilome hight
    Matilda, daughter to *Pubidius*,
    Who was the Lord of *Mathravall* by right,
    And coosin unto king *Ambrosius*:
Whence he indued was with skill so marvelous.

14

They here ariving, staid a while without,
    Ne durst adventure rashly in to wend,
    But of their first intent gan make new dout
    For dread of daunger, which it might portend:
    Untill the hardie Mayd (with love to frend)
    First entering, the dreadfull Mage there found

Deepe busied bout worke of wondrous end,
And writing strange characters in the ground,
With which the stubborn feends he to his service bound.

15

He nought was moved at their entrance bold:
　　For of their comming well he wist afore,
　　Yet list them bid their businesse to unfold,
　　As if aught in this world in secret store
　　Were from him hidden, or unknowne of yore.
　　Then *Glauce* thus, Let not it thee offend,
　　That we thus rashly through thy darkesome dore,
　　Unwares have prest: for either fatall end,
Or other mightie cause us two did hither send.

16

He bad tell on; And then she thus began
　　Now have three Moones with borrow'd brothers light,
　　Thrice shined faire, and thrice seem'd dim and wan,
　　Sith a sore evill, which this virgin bright
　　Tormenteth, and doth plonge in dolefull plight,
　　First rooting tooke; but what thing it mote bee,
　　Or whence it sprong, I cannot read aright:
　　But this I read, that but if remedee
Thou her afford, full shortly I her dead shall see.

17

Therewith th'Enchaunter softly gan to smyle
　　At her smooth speeches, weeting inly well,   [*knowing*]
　　That she to him dissembled womanish guyle,
　　And to her said, Beldame, by that ye tell,
　　More need of leach-craft hath your Damozell,
　　Then of my skill: who helpe may have elsewhere,
　　In vaine seekes wonders out of Magicke spell.
　　Th'old woman wox half blanck, those words to heare;   [*became half*
And yet was loth to let her purpose plaine appeare.   *pale*]

18

And to him said, If any leache's skill,
　　Or other learned meanes could have redrest
　　This my deare daughter's deepe engraffed ill,   [*gripping or grafted*]
　　Certes I should be loth thee to molest:
　　But this sad evill, which doth her infest,
　　Doth course of naturall cause farre exceed,
　　And housed is within her hollow brest,
　　That either seemes some cursed witche's deed,

Or evill spright, that in her doth such torment breed.

19

The wisard could no lenger beare her bord,   [*dissembling nonsense*]
　　But brusting forth in laughter, to her sayd;
　　Glauce, what needs this colourable word,
　　To cloke the cause, that hath it selfe bewray'd?
　　Ne ye fair *Britomartis*, thus aray'd,
　　More hidden are, then Sunne in cloudy vele;
　　Whom thy good fortune, having fate obay'd,
　　Hath hither brought, for succour to appele:
The which the powres to thee are pleased to revele.

20

The doubtfull Mayd, seeing her selfe descryde,
　　Was all abasht, and her pure ivory
　　Into a cleare Carnation suddeine dyde;
　　As faire *Aurora* rising hastily,
　　Doth by her blushing tell, that she did lye
　　All night in old *Tithonus's* frosen bed,
　　Whereof she seemes ashamed inwardly.
　　But her old Nourse was nought dishartened,
But vauntage made of that, which *Merlin* had aread.

21

And sayd, Sith then thou knowest all our griefe,
　　(For what doest not thou know?) of grace I pray,
　　Pitty our plaint, and yield us meet reliefe.
　　With that the Prophet still awhile did stay,
　　And then his spirite thus gan forth display;
　　Most noble Virgin, that by fatall lore
　　Hast learn'd to love, let no whit thee dismay
　　The hard begin, that meets thee in the dore,
And with sharpe fits thy tender hart oppresseth sore.

22

For so must all things excellent begin,
　　And eke enrooted deepe must be that Tree,
　　Whose big embodied braunches shall not lin,   [*cease*]
　　Till they to heavens hight forth stretched bee.
　　For from thy wombe a famous Progenie
　　Shall Spring, out of the auncient *Troian* blood,
　　Which shall revive the sleeping memorie
　　Of those same antique Peers, the heavens brood,
Which *Greeke* and *Asian* rivers stained with their blood.

23

Renowned kings, and sacred Emperours,
    Thy fruitfull Ofspring, shall from thee descend,
    Brave Captaines, and most mighty warriours,
    That shall their conquests through all lands extend,
    And their decayed kingdomes shall amend:
    The feeble Britons, broken with long warre,
    They shall upreare, and mightily defend
    Against their forrein foe, that comes from farre,
Till uniuersall peace compound all civill iarre.   [*war or ire*]

24

It was not, *Britomart*, thy wand'ring eye,
    Glauncing unwares in charmed looking glas,
    But the streight course of heavenly destiny,
    Led with eternall providence, that has
    Guided thy glaunce, to bring his will to pas:
    Ne is thy fate, ne is thy fortune ill,
    To love the prowest knight, that ever was.   [*best and bravest*]
    Therefore submit thy wayes unto his will,
And do by all due meanes thy destiny fulfill.

25

But read (said *Glauce*) thou Magitian
    What meanes shall she out seeke, or what wayes take?
    How shall she know, how shall she find the man?
    Or what needs her to toyle, sith fates can make
    Way for themselves, their purpose to partake?
    Then *Merlin* thus; Indeed the fates are firme,
    And may not shrinck, though all the world do shake:
    Yet ought men's good endevours them confirme,
And guide the heavenly causes to their constant terme.

26

The man whom heavens have ordaynd to bee
    The spouse of *Britomart* is *Arthegall*:
    He wonneth in the land of *Fayeree*,
    Yet is no *Fary* borne, ne sib at all   [*kin*]
    To Elfes, but sprong of seed terrestriall,
    And whilome by false *Faries* stolne away,
    Whiles yet in infant cradle he did crall;
    Ne other to himselfe is knowne this day,
But that he by an Elfe was gotten of a *Fay*.

27

But sooth he is the sonne of *Gorlois*,
    And brother vnto *Cador* Cornish king,
    And for his warlike feates renowned is,

From where the day out of the sea doth spring,
Untill the closure of the Evening.
From thence, him firmely bound with faithfull band,
To this his native soyle thou backe shalt bring,
Strongly to aid his countrey, to withstand
The powre of forrein Paynims, which invade thy land.

28

Great aid thereto his mighty puissuance,
    And dreaded name shall give in that sad day:
    Where also proofe of thy prow valiaunce
    Thou then shalt make, t'increase thy lover's pray.   *[spoils of war and*
    Long time ye both in armes shall beare great sway,   *praise or shame]*
    Till thy wombe's burden thee from them do call,
    And his last fate him from thee take away,
    Too rathe cut off by practise criminall   *[soon]*
Of secret foes, that him shall make in mischiefe fall.

29

With thee yet shall he leave for memory
    Of his late puissaunce, his Image dead,   *[the image of the dead Artegall]*
    That living him in all activity
    To thee shall represent. He from the head
    Of his coosin *Constantius* without dread
    Shall take the crowne, that was his father's right,
    And therewith crowne himselfe in th'others stead:
    Then shall he issew forth with dreadfull might,
Against his Saxon foes in bloudy field to fight.

30

Like as a Lyon, that in drowsie cave
    Hath long time slept, himselfe so shall he shake,
    And comming forth, shall spred his banner brave
    Over the troubled South, that it shall make
    The warlike *Mertians* for feare to quake:
    Thrise shall he fight with them, and twise shall win,
    But the third time shall faire accordaunce make:
    And if he then with victorie can lin,   *[leave off or desist]*
He shall his dayes with peace bring to his earthly In.   *[end (in the sense*
                                            of harvest)]

31

His sonne, hight *Vortipore*, shall him succeede
    In kingdome, but not in felicity;
    Yet shall he long time warre with happy speed,
    And with great honour many battels try:
    But at the last to th'importunity

Of froward fortune shall be forst to yield.
But his sonne *Malgo* shall full mightily
Avenge his father's losse, with speare and shield,
And his proud foes discomfit in victorious field.

32

Behold the man, and tell me *Britomart*,
    If ay more goodly creature thou didst see;
    How like a Gyaunt in each manly part
    Beares he himselfe with portly maiestee,
    That one of th'old *Heroes* seemes to bee:
    He the six Islands, comprovinciall
    In auncient times unto great Britainee,
    Shall to the same reduce, and to him call
Their sundry kings to do their homage severall.

33

All which his sonne *Careticus* awhile
    Shall well defend, and *Saxon's* powre suppresse,
    untill a straunger king from unknowne soyle
    Arriving, him with multitude oppresse;
    Great *Gormond*, having with huge mightinesse
    Ireland subdew'd, and therein fixt his throne,
    Like a swift Otter, fell through emptinesse,
    Shall overswim the sea with many one
Of his Norueyses, to assist the Briton's sone.   [*Norwegians*]

34

He in his furie all shall overrunne,
    And holy Church with faithlesse hands deface,
    That thy sad people utterly fordonne,
    Shall to the utmost mountaines fly apace:
    Was never so great wast in any place,
    Nor so fowle outrage done by living men:
    For all thy Cities they shall sacke and race,   [*raze*]
    And the greene grasse, that groweth, they shall bren,
That even the wild beast shall dy in starved den.

35

Whiles thus thy Britons do in languour pine,
    Proud *Etheldred* shall from the North arise,
    Serving th'ambitious will of *Augustine*,
    And passing *Dee* with hardy enterprise,
    Shall backe repulse the valiaunt *Brockwell* twise,
    And *Bangor* with massacred Martyrs fill;
    But the third time shall rew his foolhardise:

> For *Cadwan* pittying his people's ill,
> Shall stoutly him defeat, and thousand *Saxons* kill.

36

But after him, *Cadwallin* mightily
    On his sonne *Edwin* all those wrongs shall wreake;
    Ne shall availe the wicked sorcery
    Of false *Pellite*, his purposes to breake,
    But him shall slay, and on a gallowes bleake
    Shall give th'enchaunter his unhappy hire:
    Then shall the Britons, late dismay'd and weake,
    From their long vassalage gin to respire,
And on their Paynim foes avenge their ranckled ire.

37

Ne shall he yet his wrath so mitigate
    Till both the sonnes of *Edwin* he have slaine,
    Offricke and *Osricke*, twinnes unfortunate,
    Both slaine in battell upon Layburne plaine,
    Together with the king of *Louthiane*,
    Hight *Adin*, and the king of *Orkeny*,   *[named]*
    Both joynt partakers of their fatall paine:
    But *Penda*, fearefull of like desteny,
Shall yield him selfe his liegeman, and sweare fealty.

38

Him shall he make his fatall Instrument,
    T'afflict the other *Saxons* unsubdew'd;
    He marching forth with fury insolent
    Against the good king *Oswald*, who indew'd
    With heavenly powre, and by Angels reskew'd,
    All holding crosses in their hands on hye,
    Shall him defeate withouten bloud imbrew'd   *[staining them]*
    Of which, that field for endlesse memory,
Shall *Hevenfield* be cal'd to all posterity.

39

Where at *Cadwallin* wroth, shall forth issew,
    And an huge hoste into Northumber lead,
    With which he godly *Oswald* shall subdew,
    And crowne with martyrdome his sacred head.
    Whose brother *Oswin*, daunted with like dread,
    With price of silver shall his kingdome buy,
    And *Penda*, seeking him adowne to tread
    Shall tread adowne, and do him fowly dye,
But shall with gifts his Lord *Cadwallin* pacify.

40

Then shall *Cadwallin* dye, and then the raine
    Of *Britons* eke with him attonce shall dye;
    Ne shall the good *Cadwallader* with paine,
    Or powre, be able it to remedy,
    When the full time prefixt by destiny,
    Shalbe expir'd of *Britons'* regiment.
    For heaven it selfe shall their successe envy,
    And them with plagues and murrins pestilent   [*diseases*]
Consume, till all their warlike puissaunce be spent.

41

Yet after all these sorrowes, and huge hills
    Of dying people, during eight yeares space,
    Cadwallader not yielding to his ills,
    From *Armoricke*, where long in wretched cace
    He liv'd, returning to his native place,
    Shalbe by vision staid from his intent:
    For th' heavens have decreed, to displace
    The *Britons*, for their sinnes' dew punishment,
And to the *Saxons* over-give their government.

42

Then woe, and woe, and everlasting woe,
    Be to the Briton babe, that shalbe borne,
    To live in thraldome of his father's foe;
    Late King, now captive, late Lord, now forlorne,
    The world's reproch, the cruell victour's scorne,
    Banisht from Princely bowre to wastfull wood: [*desolate*]
    O who shall helpe me to lament, and mourne
    The royall seed, the antique *Troian* blood,
Whose Empire lenger here, then ever any stood.

43

The Damzell was full deepe empassioned,
    Both for his griefe, and for her people's sake,
    Whose future woes so plaine he fashioned,
    And sighing sore, at length him thus bespake;
    Ah but will heaven's fury never slake,
    Nor vengeaunce huge relent it selfe at last?
    Will not long misery late mercy make,
    But shall their name for ever be defast,
And quite from off the earth their memory be rast?

44

Nay but the terme (said he) is limited,
    That in this thraldome *Britons* shall abide,
    And the just revolution measured,
    That they as Straungers shalbe notifide.
    For twise foure hundreth yeares shalbe supplide,
    Ere they to former rule restor'd shalbee,
    And their importune fates all satisfide:
    Yet during this their most obscuritee,
Their beames shall oft breake forth, that men them faire may see.

45

For *Rhodoricke*, whose surname shalbe Great,
    Shall of him selfe a brave ensample shew,
    That Saxon kings his friendship shall intreat;
    And *Howell Dha* shall goodly well indew
    The salvage minds with skill of just and trew;
    Then *Griffyth Conan* also shall up reare
    His dreaded head, and the old sparkes renew
    Of native courage, that his foes shall feare,
Least backe againe the kingdome he from them should beare.

46

Ne shall the Saxon's selves all peaceably
    Enjoy the crowne, which they from Britons wonne
    First ill, and after ruled wickedly:
    For ere two hundred yeares be full outronne,
    There shall a Raven far from rising Sunne,   [*=Denmark*]
    With his wide wings upon them fiercely fly,
    And bid his faithlesse chickens overronne   [*the heathen Danes*]
    The fruitfull plaines, and with fell cruelty,
In their avenge, tread downe the victours' surquedry.   [*arrogance*]

47

Yet shall a third both these, and thine subdew;
    There shall a Lyon from the sea-bord wood
    Of *Neustria* come roring, with a crew   [*William the Conqueror,*
Of hungry whelpes, his battailous bold brood,   *from Normandy*]
    Whose clawes were newly dipt in cruddy blood,   [*clotted*]
    That from the Daniske Tyrant's head shall rend
    Th'usurped crowne, as if that he were wood,   [*mad with rage*]
    And the spoile of the countrey conquered
Emongst his young ones shall divide with bountyhed.

48

Tho when the terme is full accomplishid,

There shall a sparke of fire, which hath long-while
Bene in his ashes raked up, and hid,
Be freshly kindled in the fruitful Ile
Of *Mona*, where it lurked in exile;
Which shall breake forth into bright burning flame,
And reach into the house, that beares the stile   [*title*]
Of royall maiesty and soveraigne name;
So shall the Briton bloud their crowne againe reclame.

49

Thenceforth eternall union shall be made
Betweene the nations different afore,
And sacred Peace shall lovingly perswade
The warlike minds, to learne her goodly lore,
And civile armes to exercise no more:
Then shall a royall virgin raine, which shall
Stretch her white rod over the *Belgicke* shore,
And the great Castle smite so sore with all,
That it shall make him shake, and shortly learne to fall.

50

But yet the end is not. There *Merlin* stay'd,
As overcomen of the spirite's powre,
Or other ghastly spectacle dismay'd,
That secretly he saw, yet note discoure: [*could not reval*]
Which suddein fit, and half extatick stoure
When the two fearefull women saw, they grew
Greatly confused in behavioure;
At last the fury past, to former hew
Hee turn'd againe, and chearefull looks as earst did shew.

51

Then, when them selves they well instructed had
Of all, that needed them to be inquir'd,
They both conceiving hope of comfort glad,
With lighter hearts unto their home retir'd;
Where they in secret counsell close conspir'd,
How to effect so hard an enterprize,
And to possesse the purpose they desir'd:
Now this, now that twixt them they did devise,
And diverse plots did frame, to maske in strange disguise.

52

At last the Nourse in her foolhardy wit
Conceiv'd a bold devise, and thus bespake;
Daughter, I deeme that counsell aye most fit,
That of the time doth dew advauntage take;

Ye see that good king *Uther* now doth make
Strong warre vpon the Paynim brethren, hight
Octa and *Oza*, whom he lately brake
Beside *Cayr Verolame*, in victorious fight,
That now all *Britanie* doth burne in armes bright.

53

That therefore nought our passage may empeach,   [*impede*]
Let us in feigned armes our selves disguize,
And our weake hands (whom need new strength shall teach)
The dreadfull speare and shield to exercize:
Ne certes daughter that same warlike wize
I weene, would you misseeme; for ye bene tall,
And large of limbe, t'atchieve an hard emprize,
Ne ought ye want, but skill, which practize small
Will bring, and shortly make you a mayd Martiall.

54

And sooth, it ought your courage much inflame,
To heare so often, in that royall house,
From whence to none inferiour ye came,
Bards tell of many women valorous
Which have full many feats adventurous
Perform'd, in paragone of proudest men:
The bold *Bunduca*, whose victorious
Exploits made *Rome* to quake, stout *Guendolen*,
Renowned *Martia*, and redoubted *Emmilen*.

55

And that, which more then all the rest may sway,
Late dayes ensample, which these eyes beheld,
In the last field before *Menevia*
Which *Uther* with those forrein Pagans held,
I saw a *Saxon* Virgin, the which fel'd
Great *Ulfin* thrise upon the bloudy plaine,
And had not *Carados* her hand withheld
From rash revenge, she had him surely slaine,
Yet *Carados* himselfe from her escapt with paine.

56

Ah read, (quoth *Britomart*) how is she hight
Faire *Angela* (quoth she) men do her call,
No whit lesse faire, then terrible in fight:
She hath the leading of a Martiall
And mighty people, dreaded more then all
The other *Saxons*, which do for her sake

And love, themselves of her name *Angles* call.
Therefore faire Infant her ensample make
Unto thy selfe, and equall courage to thee take.

57

Her harty words so deepe into the mynd
    Of the young Damzell sunke, that great desire
    Of warlike armes in her forthwith they tynd,   [*kindled*]
    And generous stout courage did inspire,
    That she resolv'd, unweeting to her Sire,
    Advent'rous knighthood on her selfe to don,
    And counsel'd with her Nourse, her Maide's attire
    To turne into a massy habergeon,
And bad her all things put in readinesse anon.

58

Th'old woman nought, that needed, did omit;
    But all things did conveniently purvay:
    It fortuned (so time their turne did fit)
    A ban of Britons ryding on forray
    Few dayes before, had gotten a great pray   [*booty or plunder*]
    Of Saxon goods, emongst the which was seene
    A goodly Armour, and full rich aray,
    which long'd to *Angela* the Saxon Queene,
All fretted round with gold, and goodly well beseene.

59

The same, with all the other ornaments,
    King *Ryence* caused to be hanged hy
    In his chiefe Church, for endlesse moniments
    Of his successe and gladfull victory:
    Of which her selfe avising readily,
    In th'evening late old *Glauce* thither led
    Faire *Britomart*, and that same Armory
    Downe taking, her therein appareled,
Well as she might, and with brave bauldrick garnished.

60

Beside those armes there stood a mighty speare,
    Which *Bladud* made by Magick art of yore,
    And us'd the same in battell aye to beare;
    Sith which it had bin here preserv'd in store,
    For his great vertues proved long afore:
    For never wight so fast in sell could sit,   [*saddle*]
    But him perforce unto the ground it bore:
    Both speare she tooke, and shield, which hong by it:
Both speare and shield of great powre, for her purpose fit.

61

Thus when she had the virgin all aray'd,
    Another harnesse, which did hang thereby,   [*suit of armor*]
    About her selfe she dight, that the young Mayd
    She might in equall armes accompany,
    And as her Squire attend her carefully:
    Tho to their ready Steeds they clombe full light,
    And through back wayes, that none might them espy,
    Covered with secret cloud of silent night,
Themselves they forth convay'd, and passed forward right.

62

Ne rested they, till that to Faery lond
    They came, as *Merlin* them directed late:
    Where meeting with his *Redcrosse* knight, she fond
    Of diverse things discourses to dilate,
    But most of *Arthegall*, and his estate.
    At last their wayes so fell, that they mote part:
    Then each to other well affectionate,
    Friendship professed with unfained hart,
The *Redcrosse* knight diverst, but forth rode *Britomart*.   [*diverged or turned aside*]

chapter 8

THOMAS HEYWOOD:
THE LIFE OF MERLIN

WHILE WRITERS early in the English Renaissance presented Merlin at his dignified peak, the general trend was toward the popular ironic traditions in which the mage was not so august. Although Ben Jonson used Merlin to enunciate the role of the poet as a counselor of kings in the masque presented at Prince Henry's investiture as the Prince of Wales in 1610, this was one of the few occasions between Spenser and Tennyson where the wizard represents profoundly aristocratic values and obligations. Much more typical of the seventeenth and eighteenth centuries is the marvelous but tainted spellcaster pictured by William D'Avenant's 1637 masque *Britannia Triumphans*, which, like Jonson's, featured scenery and costumes by Inigo Jones. The stage directions provide an unusually picturesque description: "Merlin the prophetic magician enters apparel'd in a gown of light purple down to his ankles, slackly girt, with wide sleeves turned up with powdered ermines, and a roll on his head of the same, with a tippet hanging down behind; in his hand a silvered rod" (*Dramatic Works*, Vol. 2, p. 272).

Such sensational and dandified images also flavored burlesque portrayals of the wizard, like William Rowley's play *The Birth of Merlin; or, The Childe hath found his Father* (written about 1620 and published 1662; Rowley's authorship is now disputed). However, Merlin and his prophecies remained as much a touchstone as his legendary association with antique marvels like Stonehenge, and crises in English history seldom failed to bring out references to them.

Thomas Heywood's *The Life of Merlin*, which went through two editions in 1641 and 1651, demonstrates how the traditions were revived for popular consumption. The tract is based upon Geoffrey of Monmouth's *Historia Regum Britanniae* and *Prophetiae Merlini* and its preface refers to subsequent chroniclers who used Geoffrey's material: Holinshed, Higden, Fabyan, and Speed. Heywood boasts of his ability to encapsulate these sources in "pocket" size: "For in the stead of a large study book, and huge voluminous tractate, able to take up a whole year in reading, and to load and tire a porter in carrying, thou hast here a small manuel, containing all the pith and marrow of the greater" (ii). It is not an original work: long passages are borrowed directly from printed sources available to Heywood, notably Alanus de Insulis's edition of Geoffrey, *Prophetia Anglicana Merlini Ambrosii Britanni* (Frankfort, 1603) and Fabyan's *The Chronicles of England and France* (1516).

Nevertheless, Heywood's work shows how influential Geoffrey had remained, and is more entertaining than most seventeenth-century works invoking Merlin. In addition to recounting the British travails with the Saxons leading up to Arthur's birth, and interpreting the prophecies uttered to Vortigern in the light of British history, Heywood introduced a few charming touches of his own, like the marvels conjured for the disconsolate Vortigern, and he treats the conception of Arthur with more than usual imaginative detail. The entertainments for Vortigern recall not only tidbits from English chroniclers and D'Avenant's masque (and perhaps other dramatic presentations of the period that have been lost), but the visions Merlin creates to woo Viviane in French romance and the Middle English prose *Merlin*. They are, however, considerably less courtly—as we would expect from a tract intended for popular distribution.

Heywood himself is an interesting figure, although one about whom, like his near-contemporary Shakespeare, we know relatively little. Unlike Shakespeare, Heywood was not averse to referring to himself in his works. He often did so anonymously, as when he recycled some of *The Life of Merlin* material in two other pamphlets, *Brightman's Predictions and Prophecies* and *A Revelation of Mr. Brightman's Revelation* (both 1641). These pretended to recount predictions made by Thomas Brightman (1562–1607), a Puritan preacher who wrote *Revelation of Revelations* in 1615. It appears that Heywood liked to cover his literary bets; people who found the figure of Merlin too tainted or incredible might be more inclined to trust a Puritan divine for the same prognostications!

What we know about Heywood's life and voluminous output can be summarized as follows. He was nearly of an age with Ben Jonson; the exact dates of his birth and death are uncertain, but likely to have been 1573–1641. His works mention several times that he was from Lincolnshire; he is thought to have been the son of Robert, a parish priest in Rothwell or Ashby, and Elizabeth Heywood. He entered Cambridge and may have become a graduate fellow at Peterhouse, or left the university without a degree after his father died in 1591. By 1596 he was acting and writing plays for the London theater with the Lord Admiral's Men and later the Queen's players. He also served the earls of Southampton and Worcester. Writing occupied him constantly; nearly all of it is mediocre or sentimental, and haphazardly constructed. His prose and poetry include *An Apology for Actors* (1612), *Nine Books of Various History concernynge Women* (1624), and *The Hierarchie of the Blessed Angells. Their Names, Orders, and Offices* (1635). The preface to one of his better plays, *The English Traveller* (1633) claims "an entire hand or at least a main finger" in 220 plays. All but two dozen of them are lost, and he is known primarily for one masterpiece, the domestic tragedy *A Woman Killed with Kindness* (1607). One of his collaborators, and a possible source for his knowledge of Merlin, was William Rowley.

According to Arthur Clark, "Heywood's interest in Merlin's prophecies was partly temperamental, for he was as credulous as a child of the strange and wonderful, partly in the way of business" (p. 184). The willingness to believe in marvels was shared by many—after all, it was also the period of religious eccentricity, of John Dee's notorious conversations with spirits and Robert Fludd's alchemical investigations, of King James I's *Demonologie* and Marlowe's *Doctor Faustus*. Furthermore, the increasing power of Puritanism, and the growing conflicts between the Stuart kings and Parliament that reached a climax in 1641 and the civil wars of the following years, seemed to imply the opening of a new and apocalyptic age. This political and social instability encouraged the tendency to credit marvels, and translated into a wave of astrological handbooks and prophecies lasting into the eighteenth century, "with Merlin's name as a guarantee on the title page" (Clark, p. 185). Even so famous a writer as Jonathan Swift was to take a turn in his satirical *A Famous Prediction of Merlin, the British Wizard, Written Above a Thousand Years ago, and Relating to the Present Year 1709*. Therefore it must have been natural for Heywood, one of the earliest people to make a living by his writing, to accommodate the trend by furnishing the legend of the earliest and greatest British seer.

The bulk of *The Life of Merlin* elaborates prophecies translated in the chapter on Geoffrey of Monmouth. Since Heywood's interpretation of them will be uninteresting to most people who are not thoroughly conversant with British history, I have selected the portions that justify Merlin's abilities to the reader and relate his activities up to Arthur's conception and Uther's marriage with Igraine. Heywood's prose style is discursive and his punctuation idiosyncratic, but his story attains in these portions a flow of events and enlivening embellishments that make it worth reading even for those who know Geoffrey.

Bibliographic note: The first edition was *The Life of Merlin, Sirnamed Ambrosius, His Prophecies, and Predictions Interpreted; and their truth made good by our English Annalls* (London: J. Okes, 1641); the second reproduces the text with a slightly different title, *Merlin's Prophecies and Predictions Interpreted, and their truth made good by our English Annalls, with The Life of Merlin* (London: Thomas Pierrepoint, 1651). I have taken my selections from the 1812 edition printed in Carmarthen by J. Evans, which also included several of the Welsh Myrddin poems. This edition has recently been reprinted in facsimile by the Welsh Dragon, Annapolis, Maryland (1987). The Evans text is a careful one for its day; it modernizes spelling, regularizes Heywood's idiosyncratic punctuation as best it can, and corrects several obvious misprints in the 1641 and 1651 editions. However, it occasionally introduces an error of its own, as when Publius Vergilius Maro (the author of the *Aeneid*) is dismembered into three people! I have compared it with the earlier editions, silently corrected these errors, and further modernized the spelling and punctuation where needed to facilitate comprehension. Since Heywood's diction is not intentionally anachronistic, I have occasionally replaced an obsolete word by a modern equivalent. Wherever the first edition reading is better, I have adopted it.

A fascinating sidelight on the privileged status that prophetic discourse still retained in 1812 (and even holds for many in today's mystical revival) is the publisher's footnote after the first direct verse quote of Merlin's prophecies to Vortigern. It reads, "Observe. All the prophecies are here inserted in their original orthography." And except for a few minor oversights, they are indeed scrupulously identical to the first edition. Further reading about Heywood may be found in two critical biographies, Arthur Melville Clark's *Thomas Heywood: Playwright and Miscellanist* (Oxford: Oxford University Press, 1931; New York: Columbia University Press, 1958, and Russell & Russell, 1967), and F. S. Boas's *Thomas Heywood* (Oxford: Oxford University Press, 1950; rpt. New York: Phaeton, 1974).

The Life of Merlin

Of the birth of Merlin, surnamed Ambrosius; whether he was a Christian or nods, and by what spirit he prophecied.

To prophets there be several attributes given; some are called *prophetae*, some *vates*, others *videntes*: that is, prophets, predictors and seers, and these have been from all antiquity. The name of prophets was and ought to be peculiar to those that dealt only in divine mysteries, and spake to the people the words which the Almighty did dictate unto them concerning those things which should futurely happen, and such also are called in the holy text seers. But *vates* was a title promiscuously conferred on prophets and poets, as belonging to them both: of the first were Moses, Samuel, David, Isaiah, Jeremiah, Daniel, and the rest, whose divine oracles were extant in the old Testament. Others there were in the time of the gospel, as John the Baptist, of whom our Savior himself witnesseth, that he was not only a prophet, but more than a prophet; and we read in the Acts of the Apostles, Chap. 11, 27, "*And in those days also came prophets from Jerusalem to Antiochia. And there stood up one of them called Agabus, and signified by the spirit, that there should be great famine in all the world, which came to pass under Claudius Caesar.*" Of the vatical or prophetical poets among the Greeks were Orpheus, Linus, Homer, Hesiod, &c. and amongst the Latins, Publius Virgilius Maro, with others.

But, before I come to enquire in which of those lists this our countryman Merlin, whose surname was Ambrosius, ought to be filed, it is needful that I speak something of his birth and parents—his mother being certain, but his father doubtful, (for so our most ancient Chronologers have left them) that is, whether he were according to nature begot by a man and a woman, or according to his mother's confession, that he was conceived by the compression of a fantastical spiritual creature, without a body, which may be easily believed to be a mere fiction, or excuse to mitigate her fault (being a royal Virgin, the daughter of King Demetius), or to conceal the person of her sweetheart, by disclosing of whose name she had undoubtedly exposed him to imminent danger, and this is most probable. And yet we read that the other fantastical congression is not impossible; for Speusippus, the son of Plato's sister, and Elearchus the Sophist, and Amaxilides, in the second book of his philosophy, affirm in the honour of Plato that his mother, Perictione, having congression with the imaginary shadow of Apollo, conceived and brought into the world him who proved to be the prince of philosophers.

Apuleius also, in his book, intitled *De Socratis Daemonio*, of Socrates his Daemon, or Genius, writes at large that betwixt the moon and the earth spirits inhabit, called Incubi, of which opinion Plato was also, who saith that their harbour was between the moon and the earth, in the moist part of the air—a kind of Daemons which he thus defines: a living creature, moist, rational, immortal and passible, whose property is to envy men; because to that place from whence they were precipitated by their pride, man by his humility is preferred; and of these, some are so libidinous and luxurious, that sometimes taking human shape upon them, they will commix themselves with women and generate children, from whence they have the name of Incubi, whom the Romans called *Fauni*, and *Sicarii*; and of such St. Augustine, in his book *De civitate Dei*, makes mention.

It further may be questioned whether he was a Christian or a Gentile? as also by what spirit he prophesied? a Pythonick or Divine; that is, by the devil, who spake delusively in the oracle of Apollo, or by holy and celestial revelation? For the first, it is not to be doubted but he was a Christian, as being of the British nation: this kingdom having for the space of 200 and odd years before his birth received the Gospel under King Lucius, the first king of this land, by the substitutes of Pope Eleutherius—by whose preaching the king and a great part of his people quite renounced all pagan idolatry and were baptized into the Christian faith. But by what spirit he so truly predicted is only known to the God of all spirits, who in every nation and language pick'd out some choice persons by whose mouths he would have uttered things which should futurely happen to posterity, according to his divine will and pleasure; and amongst these was this our Merlin. . . .

[Here follow two pages of references to classical and biblical prophets, such as the Sibyl of Cumae and Moses.]

But whosoever shall make question of the true events of his prophecies, I shall refer him to the reading of that most excellent orator Polyhistor, and theologist of his time Alanus de Insulis, a German doctor, for his admirable and multifarious learning, sirnamed Universalis and rector of the Parisian academy, in his explanation or comment upon Merlin's Prophecies: the original being extracted out of Jeffery of Monmouth. Part of his words are these: "In all his prophecies I find nothing dissonant, incongruous, or absurd, nor any thing foreign, or averse from truth. And those who shall live in ages to come, shall find those his predictions as constantly to happen in their days (according to the limit of time) as we have hitherto found them certain and infallible, even to the age in which we now live." And for these signs and tokens which before the consummation of the world shall appear, he divineth and foretelleth of them in the sun and moons, and the other five planets Juno [=Jupiter?], Mars, Mercury, Venus, Saturn, and other stars— how they shall confound and alter their courses which they had in the creation, according to that in the holy evangelist Saint Luke, chap. 21. v. 25: "Then there shall be signs in the sun and the moon, and in the stars; and upon the earth trouble amongst the nations with perplexity, the sea and the waters shall roar, and men's hearts shall fail them for fear, and for looking after those things which shall come in the world, for the powers of heaven shall be shaken, &c." But of the new heaven and the new earth, and the resurrection of the dead to new life, how truly he spake according to the prophetical, evangelical, and apostolical traditions. It is manifest that he no way deviated or erred from the orthodoxal Christian faith; and so much Doctor Alanus concerning the truth of his prophecies, with whom I conclude this first chapter.

[*Like Geoffrey of Monmouth, Heywood recounts Vortigern's murder of Constantine and usurpation of the throne, invitation to Saxon mercenaries led by Hengist and Horsa, and marriage to Hengist's daughter Rowena. The Britons depose Vortigern in favor of his son Vortimer, who nearly drives the Saxons out before Rowena poisons him. Vortigern is recalled, but captured at the massacre on Salisbury plain. After deeding southeastern England to Hengist, he is released and retreats to Wales, where he starts to build a castle called Generon, or Gwayneren, at the west side of the River Grana, upon a hill called Cloaricus. Since the castle's foundations will not stand, his soothsayers advise him to cement them with the blood of a fatherless boy. Satisfied with this advice, Vortigern sends his agents to seek the child.*]

One of them amongst the rest happened to come to a town or city called Caer-Merlin, which implies Merlin's town or Merlin's borough, which there is no doubt is the same which we call to this day Caermarthen, but my author terms it a city; at whose gates the messengers of the king arriving, it happened that a great many young lads were sporting themselves without the walls; and of the company, two of them in gaming fell out, the one young Merlin, the other called Dinabutius, who, amongst other breathing words cast into Merlin's teeth that he was but some moon-calf, as born of a mother who knew not his father. The servant, taking notice of this language, presently demanded what he was and who were his parents, who returned him answer that for any father he had, they knew none, but his mother was daughter to King Demetius and lived a votaress in that city, in a nunnery belonging to the church of St. Peter. [The servant] presently went to the chief magistrates and shewed his commission from the king, which they obeying, sent both the mother and son under his conduct to attend the pleasure of his Majesty.

Of whose coming the king was exceeding joyful, and when they appeared before him (both ignorant of the occasion why they were sent for) the king first asked her if that were her natural son, who replied that he was, and born of her own body. He then desired to know by what father he was begot, to which she likewise answered that she never had the society of any one mortal or human; only a spirit assuming the shape of a beautiful young man had many times appeared unto her, seeming to court her with no common affection, but when any of her fellow-virgins came in he would suddenly disappear and vanish, by whose many and urgent importunities being at last overcome, I yielded, saith she, to his pleasure, and was comprest by him, and when my full time of teeming came, I was delivered of this son (now in your presence) whom I caused to be called Merlin. Which words were uttered with such modesty and constancy, considering withal the royalty of her birth, and the strictness of the order (in which she now lived) that the king might the more easily be induced to believe that whatsoever she spoke was truth.

When, casting his eye upon Merlin, he began to apprehend strange promising things in his aspect, as having a quick and piercing eye, an ingenious and gracious countenance, and in his youthful face a kind of austerity and supercilious gravity, which took in him such deep impression, that he thought his blood too noble to be mingled with the dust and rubbish of the earth. And therefore instead of sentencing him to death, and commanding him to be slain, he opened unto him the purpose he had to build this castle, and the strange and prodigious impediments which hindred the work, then his assembly of the bards and wisards and what answer they returned him of his demand, but bade him withal be of comfort, for he prized his life (being a Christian) above ten such citadels, though erected and perfected with all the cost and magnificence that human art or fancy could devise.

To which words, Merlin (who had all this while stood silent and spoke not a word) thus replied, "Royal Sir, blind were your bards, witless your wisards, and silly and simple your soothsayers; who shewed themselves averse to art and altogether unacquainted with the secrets of nature, as altogether ignorant that in the brest of this hill lies a vast moat, or deep pool, which hath ingurgitated and swallowed all these materials thrown into the trenches. Therefore command them to be digged deeper, and you shall discover the water in which your squared stones have been washed, and in the bottom of the lake you shall find two hollow rocks of stone, and in them two horrible dragons fast asleep." Which having uttered, he with a low obeisance made to the king, left speaking.

[Vortigern] instantly commanded pioneers with pickaxes, mattocks, and shovels, to be sent for; who were presently employed to dig the earth deep, where the pond was found and all the water drained so that the bottom thereof was left dry. Then were discovered the two hollow rocks, which being opened, out of them issued two fierce and cruel dragons, the one red, the other white, and made betwixt them a violent and terrible conflict; but in the end the white dragon prevailed over the red. At which sight the king, being greatly stupified and amazed, demanded of Merlin what this their combat might portend; who fetching a great sigh, and tears in abundance issuing from his eyes, with a prophetical spirit made him this following answer:

"Woe's me for the red Dragon, for alach,
The time is come, hee hasteth to his mach:
The bloudy Serpent, (yet whose souls are white)
Implys that Nation, on which thy delight
Was late sole-fixt, (the *Saxons*) who as friends
Came to thee first, but ayming at shrewd ends
They shall have power over the drooping *red*,
In which the British Nation's figured:
Drive shall he them into caves, holes, and dens,
To barren Mountains, and to moorish fens,
Hills shall remove to where the valleyes stood,
And all the baths and brooks shall flow with blood.
The worship of the holy God shall cease.
For in thilk dayes the Kirke shall have no peace:
The Panims (woe the while) shall get the day,
And with their Idols mawmetry [*heathenism*] beare sway,
And yet in fine shee that was so opprest,
Shal mount, & in the high rocks build her nest
For out of *Cornwall* shall proceed a Bore,
Who shall the Kerk to pristine state restore,
Bow shall all *Britaine* to his kingly beck,
And tread he shall on the white Dragon's neck."

Then casting a sad look upon the king, as reading his fate in his forehead, he muttered to himself and said,

"But well-away for thee, to *Britaine* deere,
For I fore-see thy sad disaster's neere."

Which accordingly happened, and that within a few years after, for Vortigern having builded this castle and fortified it, making it defensible against any foreign opposition, the two sons of Constantine, whom Vortigern had before caused to be slain, assisted by their near kinsman Pudentius, king of Armorica or little Britain (where they had been liberally fostered and cherished), passed the sea with a compleat Army and landed at Totness, whereof when the Britains who were dispersed in many provinces understood, they crept out of their holes and corners and drew unto their host, which was no small encouragement to the two brothers Ambrosius Aurelius and Uter-Pendragon, who now finding their forces to be sufficiently able both in strength and number, made their speedy expedition towards Wales with purpose to distress Vortigern the usurper.

Who having notice of their coming, and not able in regard of the paucity of his followers to give them battle, he made what provision he could for the strengthening of his castle to endure a long siege and to oppose the rage of any violent battery till he might send for supply elsewhere. But such was the fury of the assailants that after many fierce and dangerous attempts finding the walls and gates to be impregnable, casting into the castle balls of wild fire with other incendiaries they burnt him and his people alive, amongst whom not one escaped. Of him it is reported that he should have carnal society with his own daughter, in hope that kings should issue from them; thus died he most miserably when he had reigned, since his last inauguration, nine years and some odd months. The explanation of the rest of [Merlin's] prophecy I will leave to the chapter following.

Merlin's former prophecy explained; with sundry prodigious acts done by him to delight the king. His prophecy of the king's death, and bringing Stonehenge from Ireland.

You have heard what the red and white dragons figured: namely, the British and Saxon people. We will now punctually examine the truth of his predictions in the rest. The caverns, corners, mountains, and moorish places express into what sundry distresses the natives were driven into by the merciless cruelty of the strangers; by the hills and valleys, shifting places, that there was no difference amongst the poor Britains, between the courtier and the cottager, the peer and the peasant; by the rivers flowing with blood, the many battles fought between the two nations; and that in those days religion and the true worship of God was supprest, happened under Hengist and Horsus and their posterity: Octa the son of Hengist, who succeeded his father in the kingdom of Kent, Tosa, Pascentius, and Colgrinus—all pagans and princes of the Saxons. For the Britains from the time of Eleutherius, whom the Romists write was the fourteenth pope after the blessed St. Peter, had received the Christian faith under King Lucius of glorious memory, and had continued it for many years unto that time.

The Saxons, after coming into the land, being then miscreants, laboured by all means to suppress the same, and in the stead thereof to plant their pagan idolatry, which they accomplished even to the coming of St. Augustine, sent hither by Pope Gregory; in whose time again it began to flourish and get the upper hand in the reign of Aurelius Ambrose and his brother Uter-pendragon (which is by interpretation "the head of the dragon"), who succeeded him. By the boar which should come out of Cornwall and tread upon the neck of the white dragon is meant the invincible King Arthur, who vanquished the Saxons and subdued them in many battles, and was a great maintainer and exalter of the true Christian religion. Of whose begetting and birth, in this our History of Merlin, we shall have occasion to speak hereafter.

As Merlin was plentifully endued with the spirit of divination, so by some authors it is affirmed of him that he was skilful in dark and hidden arts, as magic, necromancy, and the like; and relate of him that when King Vortigern lived solitary in his late erected castle, forsaken of the greatest part of his followers and friends and quite sequestered from all kingly honours, he grew into a deep and dumpish melancholy, delighting only (if any delight can be taken therein) in solitude and want of company. To expel which sad fits from him, which might be dangerous to impair his health, [Merlin] would devise for his recreation and disport many pleasant fancies to beget mirth and sometimes laughter by solacing his ear with several strains of music, both courtly and rural—the sound heard, but the persons not seen, as with the harp, bagpipes, cymbal, and tabret, and sometimes again with the lute, orphorian, viol, sackbut, cornet and organ. Then, to recreate his eyes, he would present him with stately masks and anti-masks; and again, for variety sake, with rustick dances presented by swines and shepherdesses. And when these grew stale or tedious to his eye or ear, he would take him up into the top of one of his turrets, whereon he should see eagles and hawks fly after sundry games, and what fowl the king liked, they would strike it into his lap to add to his slender provision for dinner and supper, which gave the king so small contentment.

Sometimes he would have an hare or hart hunted and chased by a pack of dogs in the air—the game flying, the hounds, with open and audible mouths, pursuing, with huntsmen winding their horns and following the chase with all the indents and turnings, losses and recoveries; the champaign plains, the woods and coverts appearing as visible and natural as if the sport had been upon the firm and solid earth.

Upon a time, being in the king's summer parlour, who was desirous to be partaker of some novelty which he had never seen, there instantly appeared upon the table a pair of butts and whites [*archery targets*] in the middle to shoot at, where suddenly came in six dapper and pert fellows like archers, in stature not above a foot high, and all other members accordingly proportioned. Their bows were of the side bones of an overgrown pike, their strings of a small slivy [*filament of*] silk no bigger than the thread of a cobweb, their arrows less than pick-tooths, feathered with the wings of small flies and headed with the points of Spanish needles—who made a show as if they were to shoot a match three to three, and roundly they went about it. In the middle of their game there was a shot which rested doubtful; which, as it appeared, the gamesters could not well decide. Then Merlin called to one of the servants (who had somewhat a big nose) that stood by, and bade him measure to the mark and give it to the best; to which, while he stooped and inclined his face, the better to umpire the matter, one of the pigmy archers who had an arrow to shoot delivered it from his bow and shot him quite through the nose, at which he started, and the king heartily laughed (for there was no room to be seen), and the butts with the archers together disappeared.

But when Merlin knew the king's fate to draw nigh, and [was] not willing to partake in his disaster, he fained occasions abroad and though with much difficulty, had at length leave to depart, leaving behind him a paper which he put into the king's closet, where, upon occasion, he might easily find and read this ensuing prophecy.

> "Fly from these fatall severall fires o King,
> Which from less *Britain* the two exiles bring:
> Now are their ships a rigging, now forsake
> Th' *Armoricke* shoares, and towards *Albion* make,
> To avenge their murdered brothers bloud on thee;
> In *Totnesse* road to morrow they will bee.
> The *Saxon* Princes shall contend in vain,

> For young *Aurelius* having *Hengist* slain
> Shall peaceably possesse the *British* throne,
> Striving the opposite Nations to attone.
> He the true faith shall seek to advance on high,
> But in the quest thereof, by poyson die.
> The Dragons head his brother shall succeed,
> And after many a brave heroick deed,
> By him perform'd, the fates shall strive to waft
> His soule ore *Styx*, by a like poysnous draught.
> But those who sent them to th' *Elizian* bower,
> His sonne the Bore of *Cornwall* shall devoure."

This history needs no comment, being so plain in itself by the success thereof; only this much let me entreat the reader to bear in memory, that that Arthur figured under the name of Aper Cornubiae, that is, the Boar of Cornwall, was son to Uter-pendragon, here called the head of the Dragon.

Amongst many brave heroical acts done by this Aurelius Ambrose after the death of Vortigern, he maintained the middle part of the kingdom of Britain, with all Cambria and Wales, endeavouring to repair all the ruined places in the land, as forts, castles, and citadels, but especially the temples which were much defaced by the pagan idolators, and [he] caused divine service to be every where said in them, and after that encountered the Saxons in the hill of Baden or Badove, where he slew many of them and utterly routed their whole army. After which defeat another Saxon prince named Porthe, with his two sons, landed at an haven in Sussex, after whom, as some authors affirm, the place is called Portsmouth unto this day. Others landed also in several parts of the kingdom, so that Aurelius had with them many conflicts and battles in which he sped diversly, being for the most part conqueror, and yet at some times repulsed and overset.

Our English chronicles and others say that he, by the help of Merlin, caused the great stones which stand till this day on the plain of Salisbury to be brought in a whirl-wind one night out of Ireland, and caused them to be placed where they now stand in remembrance of the British lords there slain and after buried in the time of the pretended treaty and communication had betwixt Vortigern and Hengist, as formerly touched, but Polychronicon and others ascribe the honour of their transportage to his brother Uter-pendragon, at whose request to Merlin that miraculous conveyance was performed; which if by art he was able to do, no question [is] to be made of the truth of those former prestigious feats, in this chapter before remembered.

Uter-pendragon succeedeth his brother Aurelius; he is enamoured of Igerna, wife of the duke of Cornwall, whom by the art of Merlin, he enjoys; of whom he begot king Arthur the Worthy. Merlin's prophecy of him before his birth.

Aurelius Ambrose in the prime of his age and honour being taken away by poison, his brother Uter-pendragon, by the general suffrage both of the clergy, peers, and people, was made king; who pursuing his brother's former victories gave the Saxons many battles in which he came off with great honour and victory, as awing them so far that they durst not once approach his confines and territories. Afterwards he began to repair the decayed and ruinated churches and to provide that God should be carefully worshipped, restoring to his people all those goods and possessions which by the enemy had been extorted from them. And afterwards, having slain Pascentius the son of Hengist in battle, with Guillamore king of Ireland, who came to his assistance, who had with great tyranny afflicted his subjects of the north with fire, sword, and sundry direptions [*plunderings*] and spoils; and having taken Octa (who was also the son of Hengist) and Cosa his nephew, and put them in prison, [Uter-pendragon] made a great solemnity at the feast of Easter, to which he invited all his nobility and gentry with their wives and daughters, to gratulate with him his former victories. Among the rest of his peers was then present Gorlais, duke of Cornwall, with his most beautiful Igerna, who was held to be the prime paramount of the whole English nation. [*That is, Gorlais was considered the foremost ruler of the British after Uter-pendragon; Heywood is using the word "English" in the sense of his own historical period.*]

With whose beauty and demeanor the king was so infinitely taken, that all other his most necessary affairs neglected, he could not restrain or bridle his extraordinary affection, but he must needs court and kiss her openly in the presence of her husband, at which he, incensed with the rage of jealousy, presently, without any leave taken of the king or the rest of his fellow peers, rose from the table, and taking his wife with him along by no persuasion could be moved to stay, but instantly posted with her into his country, which the king (being perditely enamoured of his lady) took in such ill part that he sent for them back, pretending they must use his council in matters of state, to make his speedy return. But he, more prizing his lady than all his other fortunes (whether favourable or disastrous) which way soever they should happen, disobeyed the king's command, with a peremptory answer *that he would not come.* At which the king, more enraged, sent him word that if he persisted in his obstinacy he would invade his dukedom and beat his towers and turrets (to which he trusted) about his ears, but vain were his menaces, for loath to lose so sweet a bed-fellow, he set the king at public defiance.

To chastise whose pride (as he pretended), Uter-pendragon gathered a strong army and invaded his country with fire and sword, but Gorlais, perceiving himself unable to oppose so potent a prince, attended with such multitudes of experienced and tried soldiers, he betook himself to a strong castle then called Dimilioch; and there fortified himself, daily expecting forces from Ireland. But because he would not hazard all his estate in one bottom, he like a wise merchant sent his wife to another impregnable fort called Tindagol, being round environed with the sea, and one way leading into it which three men elbowing one another could not pass at once. A few days being past in the besieging of that former castle which the duke maintained against him, [Uter-pendragon] grew still the more besotted with the love of the lady, insomuch that he could neither enter nor escape. At length he uttered the impatience of his affection to one whom he had amongst many others chosen for his familiar friend, whose name was Ulphin of Caer-Caradoc [*Urfin of Ricaradoch in the first edition*]; who when he had truly pondered the whole that the king had delivered unto him, he returned him answer that he could perceive small hope for the king to attain his amourous ends in regard that the fort in which she resided, by reason of the situation of the place (munified both by art and nature) was altogether inaccessible. For three armed men (so straight was the passage) might keep out his whole army; one refuge only remained, that if the prophet Merlin, who was then in the army, would undertake the business, it might be accomplished, but otherwise not.

The king, being attentive to his language, presently caused Merlin to be sent for, and told him how ardently he was affected to the countess, without enjoying whose person he was not able to subsist alive, aggravating the trouble and perplexity of his mind, with much paleness in his face, many deep suspires and extraordinary passion; which Merlin commiserating, he told his majesty that to compass a thing so difficult as that was, being but a little degree from impossibility, he must make proof of art mystical and unknown, by which he would undertake by such unctions and medicaments as he would apply, to metamorphose his highness into the true figure and resemblance of Duke Gorlais; his friend Ulphin into Jordan of Tintegell, his familiar companion and counsellor; and himself would make the third in the adventure, changing himself into Bricel [*Bricot in the first edition*], a servant that waited of him in his chamber; and they three thus disguised would in the twilight of the evening, whilst the duke in one place was busied in the defence of his castle against the assailants, command their entrance into the other fort in the name and person of the duke, where they should be undoubtedly received.

This prestigious plot much pleased the king, who, impatient of delay, gave order to his chief captains and commanders concerning the siege, excusing to them his absence for some certain hours. He, in the mean time, the same night committed himself to the charge and art of Merlin; who, disguised as aforesaid, knocked at the gates of Tindagol, to whom the porter (thinking he had heard his lord's voice demanding entrance) instantly opened the gate, and meeting him with Ulphin and Merlin, taking them for Jordan and Bricel, so that the king was presently conducted to the chamber of Igerna, who gladly and lovingly received him as her lord and husband, where he was bountifully feasted, and bedding with her he freely enjoyed her most loving embraces to the full satiating of his amorous desires, where betwixt them that night was begot the noble prince Arthur, who for his brave facinourous [*deeds*], and high and heroical achievements, made his name glorious and venerable through the face of the whole earth. Of whom Merlin, long before his begetting or birth, thus prophesied.

"The *Cornish Bore* shall fill with his devotion,
The Christian World: the Islands of the Ocean,
He shall subdue: the Flower de Lyces plant
In his own Garden, and prove Paramant;
The two-neckt *Roman* Eagle hee shall make

To flag her plumes, and her faint feathers quake.
Pagans shal strive in vain to bend or break him,
Who shall be meat to all the mouths that speake him;
Yet shall his end be doubtfull: Him six Kings
Shall orderly succeed, but when their wings
Art clipt by death, a *German* Worme shall rise
Who shall the *British* State anatomise.
Him shall a Sea-Wolfe waited on by Woods
From *Africke* brought to passe Saint *Georges* floods
Advance on high: then shall Religion faile,
And then shall *London's* Clergie honour vaile
To *Dorobernia*: he that seventy shall sit
In th' *Eborucensick* Sea; he forc'd to flit
Into *Armorica*: *Menevia* sad
Shall with the Legion Cities Pall be clad,
And they that in thilk days shall live, may see
That all these changes in the Kirke shall bee."

But before I come to the opening of this prophecy, which to the ignorant may appear rather a rhyming riddle, then to be grounded on truth or reason it is necessary that I look back to where I late left, and proceed with the history which thus followeth. The king more ecstasied in the embraces of his sweet and desired bedfellow, his soldiers, without any commission by him granted, made a strange and terrible assault upon the other fort, in which Gorlais was besieged; who being of a high and haughty spirit, scorning to be long immured and cooped up without making some expression of his magnanimity and valour, issued out of the castle and with great rage and resolution set upon the camp, in hopes with his handful of men to have dislodged and routed a multitude. But it fell out far contrary to his expectation, for in the hottest brunt of the first encounter he himself was slain, and all his soldiers—without mercy offered or quarter given—most cruelly put to the sword, the castle entered and seized, and the spoil divided amongst the soldiers.

Early in the morning before the king or the countess were ready in their wearing habits and ornaments, some of the besieged who had escaped the massacre bounced at the gates of Tindagol, and being known to be of the duke's party were received; who told the porter and the rest that they brought heavy news along which they must first deliver to their lady; of which she, having notice and knowing they came from that castle, caused them to be admitted into her presence, and demanding of them what news, they made answer: the tidings they brought was sad and disastrous, that the fort was the preceding night robustuously assaulted by the enemy, whom the duke her husband valiantly encountered without the gates, that all their fellow-soldiers were put to the sword, the castle taken and rifled, and that the general her lord and husband, by his over hardiness was the first man slain in the conflict. At the relation of the first part of their news she seemed wondrously disconsolate and dejected, but casting her eyes upon the king she was again somewhat solaced in the safety of her husband.

They also, when they saw the king, taking him for the duke their general, began to blush at their report of his death, being wondrously astonished that him, whom to their thinking they had left wounded and breathless in the field, they now see living and in health, musing withal that [the duke and his attendants] posting thither with so much speed, would arrive thither before them, being altogether ignorant of the admirable transformation that Merlin's art had wrought upon them. In this anxiety and diversity of thoughts, the king, more glad of the duke's fate than the rifling of his fort, thus bespoke to the duchess, "Most beautiful and my best beloved Igerna, I am not as these report dead, but as thou seest yet alive; but much grieved both for the surprisal of my castle and the slaughter of my soldiers, upon which victory it may be feared that the king, animated by his late success, may raise his army thence and endanger us here in our fort of Tindagol. Therefore, my best and safest course is to leave this place for the present and to submit myself to the king in his camp, of whose acceptance and grace I make no question, as knowing him to be of a disposition flexible and merciful. Then be you of comfort, for not after many hours you may expect to hear from me with all things answerable to your desires and wishes." With which words, Igerna was much pleased and fully satisfied.

So with a loving kiss they parted, she to her chamber and he with his two followers towards the camp; who no sooner from the sight of the citadel, but Merlin began to uncharm and dissolve his former incantations and spells, so that the king was no more Gorlais but Uter-pendragon, and his friend ceased to be Jordan of Tindagol but Ulphin of Caer-Caradoc; and the mage who had made this transformation left the shape of Bricel and turned again to be Merlin. And the king, being now arived at his army, first caused the body of Gorlais to be searched for amongst the slain soldiers, afterwards to be embalmed and honourably interred, and first acquainting Igerna by letters with all the former passages, how they stood, and how much he had hazarded his person for the fruition of her love, he invited her to her lord's funeral, at which the king and she both mourned; but after the celebration thereof ended, he the second time courted her, and in a few days made her his queen of a duchess, by whom he had Arthur and Anna, by which match the fame of Merlin spread far abroad.

V.

MERLIN IN THE NINETEENTH CENTURY

chapter 9

ALFRED, LORD TENNYSON: "MERLIN AND VIVIEN"

T H E   F I G U R E of Merlin reemerged in the 1800s after two centuries of exile as an antiquarian curiosity. Although the Romantic poets' reviving interest in Arthurian legend did not produce any great poetry or prose, isolated forays, such as Wordsworth's "The Egyptian Maid" (1835), prefigured the Victorian revival of the legends during the second half of the century. Preparing the way for this interest were new editions of older works; among the most influential were Bishop Thomas Percy's *Reliques of Ancient English Poetry* (1765) and Robert Southey's edition of Malory, *The Byrth, Lyf, and Actes of King Arthur* (1817), which in a footnote paraphrases the French Vulgate version of Merlin's imprisonment.

Victorian poets from Matthew Arnold to Algernon Charles Swinburne retold the tale of Merlin and his love in widely differing ways, but unquestionably the finest and most famous version belongs to Alfred, Lord Tennyson. Born in 1809 and appointed Poet Laureate after Wordsworth's death in 1850, Tennyson had been enchanted by Arthurian legend since as a boy he discovered Malory, and he had attempted Arthurian subjects from 1830 on with poems like "The Lady of Shalott" (written 1832, published 1842). He began work on the Arthurian cycle that was to become *Idylls of the King* with the seduction of Merlin as his first subject in 1856, completed the structure in 1885 with the insertion of "Balin and Balan" before "Merlin and Vivien," and continued to revise it until his death in 1892. Among modern writers only T.H. White's portrayal of the wizard begins to approach the popularity and influence of Tennyson's.

One reason for Tennyson's importance may be his deep imaginative identification with the character. He used "Merlin" as a pseudonym in 1852, and posed wearing wizard's robes for photographs by Julia Margaret Cameron that were published in the edition of 1875. The late poem "Merlin and the Gleam" (1889) makes clear his conception of the mage as the personification of his poetic vocation. Another reason, stemming from Tennyson's lifelong fascination with the legends and over thirty-year forging of the *Idylls*, is the creativity and symbolic density of the poems themselves. They represent all of Tennyson's poetic concerns, from idealism to carnality, individuality to social obligation, and imagination to historic inevitability. Merlin himself is perhaps the best figuration of these concerns, although he is so consistently portrayed that at first glance he appears uncomplex.

The wizard is presented as knower of all arts and builder (to music) of Camelot—yet also, in some indefinable way, constrained or limited. At the coronation in the first Idyll, "The Coming of Arthur," he is part of the tableau framing the king (ll. 279–284):

> And there I saw mage Merlin, whose vast wit
> And hundred winters are but as the hands
> Of loyal vassals toiling for their liege.
>   And near him stood the Lady of the Lake,
> Who knows a subtler magic than his own—
> Clothed in white samite, mystic, wonderful.

He is almost, in Fred Kaplan's words, "the Kubla Khan of this Arthurian Xanadu" (p. 287). Yet by the sixth Idyll—the one that bears his name—the Lady of the Lake's feminine wisdom has been supplanted by the feminine wiles of Vivien. If Merlin is so great and so wise, why does he fall to Vivien's transparent seduction? Readers of the poem must ponder whether her magic is also "subtler" and how Merlin fails to repulse the evil he recognizes in her. It is not an easy puzzle.

Most interpreters have tended to allegorize Tennyson's Merlin as the intellect, the artistic imagination, or aesthetic sensuality—all cerebral but linked progressively closer to the flesh. Compounding this tendency has been the predominance since Malory of a fabliau interpretation of his love affair with the Lady of the Lake's damsel: a simple matter of the old man's lust for a youthful woman. While intellect can clearly fall victim to carnal urges, the romantic tendency is to involve art increasingly with sensation, and in this development Tennyson mirrors his century. Vivien's seduction of Merlin is not simple, but possesses many twists and turns that expose the erotic nerve of a society (either medieval or Victorian) whose conventions attempt to suppress or sublimate sensuality.

Merlin is "an agent of the controlling order" (Stevenson, p. 15) and thus the object of Vivien's attack after she fails to tempt Arthur. He refutes the tradition that he is a devil's son (ll. 495–498) and lives, in the idyll's refrain, for "use and name and fame." To him the most important of these is use, for by it are earned both name and fame. Although Merlin considers the last to be the most ephemeral, it is his fame that attracts Vivien to him and to which she attaches her hopes, "fancying that her glory would be great/ According to his greatness whom she quench'd" (ll. 215–216). Nevertheless, it is his use to the moral and social order of Arthur's court that she destroys.

Merlin's tolerance, a virtue necessary to keep any society from becoming tyrannical, contributes to his downfall. He views Vivien's less attractive characteristics as kittenish, in contrast to the serpentlike imagery associated with her. Less Eve than Lilith, she appears in "Balin and Balan" as cohabitor with Garlon, the invisible raper of women and slayer of knights. Her slurs against Lancelot and the Queen and betrayal of Balin foreshadow the role she adopts in the next idyll as Mark's agent in Camelot. Although she "cannot brook to gaze upon the dead" ("Balin and Balan" l. 575), she was born "among the dead and sown upon the wind—" ("Merlin and Vivien" l. 43) and represents mortality in its most sensual and destructive aspects. To her the essential nature of humanity is "That old true filth, and bottom of the well,/ Where Truth is hidden" (ll. 48–49). Her carnal nature is Merlin's polar opposite, although the two are linked by a shared sensuality. In this way, Merlin's nature can be seen as ultimately "doomed by its own sensibility" (Stevenson, p. 19), and by the mortality of wisdom or judgment itself.

Vivien can even be seen as a "projection of the magician" and her defeat of him, "overtalk'd and overworn," as one consequence of the romantic imagination (Kaplan, pp. 285, 286). She is also a projection of the Victorian male fear, shared by Tennyson, of female sexuality. In a broader sense she represents that "imp of the perverse" which fascinated Poe in the period immediately before Tennyson began the *Idylls*, a "little pitted speck in garner'd fruit,/ That rotting slowly inward moulders all" (ll. 392–393). Tennyson's son Hallam pronounced her "the evil genius of the Round Table," and many readers strongly objected to the character's "harlotry" and the poem's disturbing sexual entendres; Tennyson withdrew the trial edition of *Enid and Nimue* partly because of these objections.

Does Vivien's intense sexuality too blatantly personify evil or abuse femininity? She does not simply do evil for its own sake, but is both horrified and fascinated by death (Rosenberg, p. 115), and possibly compelled by evil because it is all too powerfully her own experience of war and love—the twin preoccupations of chivalric society. Corrupt as her view of life seems in Tennyson's poem, it has been corroborated by numerous ironic treatments of the legend in the late twentieth century, notably Thomas Berger's *Arthur Rex* (1978) and Robert Nye's *Merlin* (1979). She insinuates herself so easily into Guinevere's entourage because her envious and erotic "evil" is inescapably part of the truth about Arthur's court.

"The Holy Grail" tells of the Siege Perilous, "fashion'd by Merlin ere he passed away,/ And carven with strange figures; and in and out/ The figures, like a serpent, ran a scroll/ Of letters in a tongue no man could read" (ll. 168–171). Although the mage warns that anyone who sits there will lose himself, he sits there himself "by misadvertence." What seems at first to be a competing version of Merlin's death metaphorically extends Vivien's sexual "scroll" or spell, for the secret of imprisonment that she learns from Merlin is part of the commentary on a magic text that even he cannot read. With such mysterious letters and texts at the core of Arthur's court, and such limits on human knowledge and experience, is it any wonder that even the forest's final echo in "Merlin and Vivien" is ambiguous as to just who is "fool"?

Bibliographic note: The earliest version of the poem appeared in a trial edition, *Enid and Nimue: The True and the False* (London: Edward Moxon, 1857), and was revised and renamed "Vivien" in *The True and the False: Four Idylls of the King* (London: Edward Moxon, 1859). In *The Idylls of the King* (London: Strahan, 1869) it appeared with its final name. The poet's conception of both Merlin and Vivien continued to grow along with the other idylls, and his revisions can be consulted in John Pfordresher's *A Variorum Edition of Tennyson's "Idylls of the King"* (New York: Columbia University Press, 1973). The final version of the text, approved by Tennyson's family, is the Eversley Edition edited by Hallam, Lord Tennyson (London: Macmillan, 1908), and this is the text printed below. The most recent edition of the *Idylls* with complete commentary is *Alfred, Lord Tennyson: Idylls of the King*, ed. J.M. Gray, The English Poets (New Haven: Yale University Press, 1983).

Among Tennyson's many sources for the evolving "Merlin and Vivien" were Southey's edition of Malory with its references to "the old *Romance of Merlin*" or Vulgate version of the French prose *Merlin*; W.D. Nash's "Merlin the Enchanter, Merlin the Bard," printed in Volume 1 of *Merlin, or The Early History of King Arthur*, ed. Henry B. Wheatley, 4 vols., Early English Text Society (London: Kegan Paul, Trench, Trübner, 1865, 1866, 1869, 1899) and given to him by James Knowles in 1866; and Edward Davies's *The Mythology and Rites of the British Druids* (London, 1809).

The sheer volume of criticism devoted to the *Idylls* clearly indicates how influential they have been. Books that devote considerable discussion to "Merlin and Vivien" include William E. Buckler, *Man and His Myths: Tennyson's Idylls of the King in Critical Context* (New York: New York University Press, 1984), which includes not only Buckler's interpretation but a selection from others; J. Phillip Eggers, *King Arthur's Laureate* (New York: New York University Press, 1971); John R. Reed, *Perception and Design in Tennyson's "Idylls of the King"* (Athens: Ohio University Press, 1969); John D. Rosenberg, *The Fall of Camelot: A Study of Tennyson's "Idylls of the King"* (Cambridge: Harvard University Press, 1973); and David Staines, *Tennyson's Camelot: "The Idylls of the King" and Its Medieval Sources* (Waterloo, Ont.: Wilfred Laurier University Press, 1983). Some additional articles that repay consultation are Thomas P. Adler, "The Uses of Knowledge in Tennyson's *Merlin and Vivien*," *Texas Studies in Literature and Language* 11 (1970): 1397–1403; J. Martin Gray, "Arthurian Invention in 'Merlin and Vivien,'" *Tennyson Research Bulletin* 2.1 (1972): 36; Gordon S. Haight, "Tennyson's Merlin," *Studies in Philology* 44.3 (July 1947): 549–566; Fred Kaplan, "Woven Paces and Waving Hands: Tennyson's Merlin as Fallen Artist," *Victorian Poetry* 7.4 (Winter 1969): 285–298; and Catherine Barnes Stevenson, "Druids, Bards, and Tennyson's Merlin," *Victorian Newsletter* 57 (Spring 1980): 14–23.

"Merlin and Vivien"

A storm was coming, but the winds were still,
And in the wild woods of Broceliande,
Before an oak, so hollow, huge and old
It look'd a tower of ivied masonwork,
At Merlin's feet the wily Vivien lay.   5

    For he that always bare in bitter grudge
The slights of Arthur and his Table, Mark
The Cornish King, had heard a wandering voice,
A minstrel of Caerleon by strong storm
Blown into shelter at Tintagil, say   10
That out of naked knightlike purity
Sir Lancelot worshipt no unmarried girl
But the great Queen herself, fought in her name,
Sware by her—vows like theirs, that high in heaven
Love most, but neither marry, nor are given   15
In marriage, angels of our Lord's report.

    He ceased, and then—for Vivien sweetly said
(She sat beside the banquet nearest Mark),
'And is the fair example follow'd, Sir,
In Arthur's household?'—answer'd innocently: 20

    'Ay, by some few—ay, truly—youths that hold
It more beseems the perfect virgin knight
To worship woman as true wife beyond
All hopes of gaining, than as maiden girl.
They place their pride in Lancelot and the Queen.   25
So passionate for an utter purity
Beyond the limit of their bond, are these,
For Arthur bound them not to singleness.
Brave hearts and clean! and yet—God guide them—young.'

    Then Mark was half in heart to hurl his cup   30
Straight at the speaker, but forbore: he rose
To leave the hall, and, Vivien following him,
Turn'd to her: 'Here are snakes within the grass;
And you methinks, O Vivien, save ye fear
The monkish manhood, and the mask of pure   35
Worn by this court, can stir them till they sting.'

    And Vivien answer'd, smiling scornfully,
'Why fear? because that foster'd at *thy* court

I savour of thy—virtues? fear them? no.
As Love, if Love be perfect, casts out fear,   40
So Hate, if Hate be perfect, casts out fear.
My father died in battle against the King,
My mother on his corpse in open field;
She bore me there, for born from death was I
Among the dead and sown upon the wind—   45
And then on thee! and shown the truth betimes,
That old true filth, and bottom of the well,
Where Truth is hidden. Gracious lessons thine
And maxims of the mud! "This Arthur pure!
Great Nature thro' the flesh herself hath made   50
Gives him the lie! There is no being pure,
My cherub; saith not Holy Writ the same?"—
If I were Arthur, I would have thy blood.
Thy blessing, stainless King! I bring thee back,
When I have ferreted out their burrowings,   55
The hearts of all this Order in mine hand—
Ay—so that fate and craft and folly close,
Perchance, one curl of Arthur's golden beard.
To me this narrow grizzled fork of thine
Is cleaner-fashion'd—Well, I loved thee first,   60
That warps the wit.'

               Loud laugh'd the graceless Mark.
But Vivien, into Camelot stealing, lodged
Low in the city, and on a festal day
When Guinevere was crossing the great hall
Cast herself down, knelt to the Queen, and wail'd.   65

     'Why kneel ye there? What evil have ye wrought?
Rise!' and the damsel bidden rise arose
And stood with folded hands and downward eyes
Of glancing corner, and all meekly said,
'None wrought, but suffer'd much, an orphan maid!   70
My father died in battle for thy King,
My mother on his corpse—in open field,
The sad sea-sounding wastes of Lyonesse—
Poor wretch—no friend!—and now by Mark the King
For that small charm of feature mine, pursued—   75
If any such be mine—I fly to thee.
Save, save me thou—Woman of women—thine
The wreath of beauty, thine the crown of power,
Be thine the balm of pity, O Heaven's own white
Earth-angel, stainless bride of stainless King—   80
Help, for he follows! take me to thyself!
O yield me shelter for mine innocency
Among thy maidens!'

Here her slow sweet eyes
Fear-tremulous, but humbly hopeful, rose
Fixt on her hearer's, while the Queen who stood   85
All glittering like May sunshine on May leaves
In green and gold, and plumed with green replied,
'Peace, child! of overpraise and overblame
We choose the last. Our noble Arthur, him
Ye scarce can overpraise, will hear and know.   90
Nay—we believe all evil of thy Mark—
Well, we shall test thee farther; but this hour
We ride a-hawking with Sir Lancelot.
He hath given us a fair falcon which he train'd;
We go to prove it. Bide ye here the while.'   95

She past; and Vivien murmur'd after 'Go!
I bide the while.' Then thro' the portal-arch
Peering askance, and muttering broken-wise,
As one that labours with an evil dream,
Beheld the Queen and Lancelot get to horse.   100

'Is that the Lancelot? goodly—ay, but gaunt:
Courteous—amends for gauntness—takes her hand—
That glance of theirs, but for the street, had been
A clinging kiss—how hand lingers in hand!
Let go at last!—they ride away—to hawk   105
For waterfowl. Royaller game is mine.
For such a supersensual sensual bond
As that gray cricket chirpt of at our hearth—
Touch flax with flame—a glance will serve—the liars!
Ah little rat that borest in the dyke   110
Thy hole by night to let the boundless deep
Down upon far-off cities while they dance—
Or dream—of thee they dream'd not—nor of me
These—ay, but each of either: ride, and dream
The mortal dream that never yet was mine—   115
Ride, ride and dream until ye wake—to me!
Then, narrow court and lubber King, farewell!
For Lancelot will be gracious to the rat,
And our wise Queen, if knowing that I know,
Will hate, loathe, fear—but honour me the more.'   120

Yet while they rode together down the plain,
Their talk was all of training, terms of art,
Diet and seeling, jesses, leash and lure.
'She is too noble' he said 'to check at pies,
Nor will she rake: there is no baseness in her.'   125
Here when the Queen demanded as by chance

'Know ye the stranger woman?' 'Let her be,'
Said Lancelot and unhooded casting off
The goodly falcon free; she tower'd; her bells,
Tone under tone, shrill'd; and they lifted up   130
Their eager faces, wondering at the strength,
Boldness and royal knighthood of the bird
Who pounced her quarry and slew it. Many a time
As once—of old—among the flowers—they rode.

But Vivien half-forgotten of the Queen   135
Among her damsels broidering sat, heard, watch'd
And whisper'd: thro' the peaceful court she crept
And whisper'd: then as Arthur in the highest
Leaven'd the world, so Vivien in the lowest,
Arriving at a time of golden rest,   140
And sowing one ill hint from ear to ear,
While all the heathen lay at Arthur's feet,
And no quest came, but all was joust and play,
Leaven'd his hall. They heard and let her be.

Thereafter as an enemy that has left   145
Death in the living waters, and withdrawn,
The wily Vivien stole from Arthur's court.

She hated all the knights, and heard in thought
Their lavish comment when her name was named.
For once, when Arthur walking all alone,   150
Vext at a rumour issued from herself
Of some corruption crept among his knights,
Had met her, Vivien, being greeted fair,
Would fain have wrought upon his cloudy mood
With reverent eyes mock-loyal, shaken voice,   155
And flutter'd adoration, and at last
With dark sweet hints of some who prized him more
Than who should prize him most; at which the King
Had gazed upon her blankly and gone by:
But one had watch'd, and had not held his peace: 160
It made the laughter of an afternoon
That Vivien should attempt the blameless King.
And after that, she set herself to gain
Him, the most famous man of all those times,
Merlin, who knew the range of all their arts,   165
Had built the King his havens, ships, and halls,
Was also Bard, and knew the starry heavens;
The people call'd him Wizard; whom at first
She play'd about with slight and sprightly talk
And vivid smiles, and faintly-venom'd points   170

Of slander, glancing here and grazing there;
And yielding to his kindlier moods, the Seer
Would watch her at her petulance, and play,
Ev'n when they seem'd unloveable, and laugh
As those that watch a kitten; thus he grew   175
Tolerant of what he half disdain'd, and she,
Perceiving that she was but half disdain'd,
Began to break her sports with graver fits,
Turn red or pale, would often when they met
Sigh fully, or all-silent gaze upon him   180
With such a fixt devotion, that the old man,
Tho' doubtful, felt the flattery, and at times
Would flatter his own wish in age for love,
And half believe her true: for thus at times
He waver'd; but that other clung to him,   185
Fixt in her will, and so the seasons went.

        Then fell on Merlin a great melancholy;
He walk'd with dreams and darkness, and he found
A doom that ever poised itself to fall,
An ever-moaning battle in the mist,   190
World-war of dying flesh against the life,
Death in all life and lying in all love,
The meanest having power upon the highest,
And the high purpose broken by the worm.

        So leaving Arthur's court he gain'd the beach;   195
There found a little boat, and stept into it;
And Vivien follow'd, but he mark'd her not.
She took the helm and he the sail; the boat
Drave with a sudden wind across the deeps,
And touching Breton sands, they disembark'd   200
And then she follow'd Merlin all the way,
Ev'n to the wild woods of Broceliande.
For Merlin once had told her of a charm,
The which if any wrought on anyone
With woven paces and with waving arms,   205
The man so wrought on ever seem'd to lie
Closed in the four walls of a hollow tower,
From which was no escape for evermore;
And none could find that man for evermore,
Nor could he see but him who wrought the charm   210
Coming and going, and he lay as dead
And lost to life and use and name and fame.

And Vivien ever sought to work the charm
Upon the great Enchanter of the Time,

As fancying that her glory would be great   215
According to his greatness whom she quench'd.

    There lay she all her length and kiss'd his feet,
As if in deepest reverence and in love.
A twist of gold was round her hair; a robe
Of samite without price, that more exprest   220
Than hid her, clung about her lissome limbs,
In colour like the satin-shining palm
On sallows in the windy gleams of March:
And while she kiss'd them, crying, 'Trample me,
Dear feet, that I have follow'd thro' the world,   225
And I will pay you worship; tread me down
And I will kiss you for it,' He was mute:
So dark a forethought roll'd about his brain,
As on a dull day in an Ocean cave
The blind wave feeling round his long sea-hall   230
In silence: wherefore, when she lifted up
A face of sad appeal, and spake and said,
'O Merlin, do ye love me?' and again,
'O Merlin, do ye love me?' and once more,
'Great master, do ye love me?' He was mute.   235
And lissome Vivien, holding by his heel,
Writhed toward him, slided up his knee and sat,
Behind his ankle twined her hollow feet
Together, curved an arm about his neck,
Clung like a snake; and letting her left hand   240
Droop from his mighty shoulder, as a leaf,
Made with her right a comb of pearl to part
The lists of such a beard as youth gone out
Had left in ashes: then he spoke and said,
Not looking at her, 'Who are wise in love   245
Love most, say least,' and Vivien answer'd quick,
'I saw the little elf-god eyeless once
In Arthur's arras hall at Camelot:
But neither eyes nor tongue—O stupid child!
Yet you are wise who say it; let me think   250
Silence is wisdom: I am silent then,
And ask no kiss;' then adding all at once,
'And lo, I clothe myself with wisdom,' drew
The vast and shaggy mantle of his beard
Across her neck and bosom to her knee,   255
And call'd herself a gilded summer fly
Caught in a great old tyrant spider's web,
Who meant to eat her up in that wild wood
Without one word. So Vivien call'd herself,
But rather seem'd a lovely baleful star   260

Veil'd in gray vapour; till he sadly smiled:
'To what request for what strange boon,' he said
'Are these your pretty tricks and fooleries,
O Vivien, the preamble? yet my thanks,
For these have broken up my melancholy.'   265

        And Vivien answer'd smiling saucily,
'What, O my Master, have ye found you voice?
I bid the stranger welcome. Thanks at last!
But yesterday you never open'd lip,
Except indeed to drink: no cup had we: 270
In mine own lady palms I cull'd the spring
That gather'd trickling dropwise from the cleft,
And made a pretty cup of both my hands
And offer'd you it kneeling: then you drank
And knew no more, nor gave me one poor word;   275
O no more thanks than might a goat have given
with no more sign of reverence than a beard.
And when we halted at that other well,
And I was faint to swooning, and you lay
Foot-gilt with all the blossom-dust of those   280
Deep meadows we had traversed, did you know
That Vivien bathed your feet before her own?
And yet no thanks: and all thro' this wild wood
And all this morning when I fondled you:
Boon, ay, there was a boon, one not so strange—   285
How had I wrong'd you? surely ye are wise,
But such a silence is more wise than kind.'

        And Merlin lock'd his hand in hers and said:
'O did ye never lie upon the shore,
And watch the curl'd white of the coming wave   290
Glass'd in the slippery sand before it breaks?
Ev'n such a wave, but not so pleasurable,
Dark in the glass of some presageful mood,
Had I for three days seen, ready to fall.
And then I rose and fled from Arthur's court   295
To break the mood. You follow'd me unask'd;
And when I look'd, and saw you following still,
My mind involved yourself the nearest thing
In that mind-mist: for shall I tell you truth?
You seem'd that wave about to break upon me   300
And sweep me from my hold upon the world,
My use and name and fame. Your pardon, child.
Your pretty sports have brighten'd all again.
And ask your boon, for boon I owe you thrice,
Once for wrong done you by confusion, next   305

For thanks it seems till now neglected, last
For these your dainty gambols: wherefore ask;
And take this boon so strange and not so strange.'

    And Vivien answer'd smiling mournfully:
'O not so strange as my long asking it,   310
Not yet so strange as you yourself are strange,
Nor half so strange as that dark mood of yours.
I ever fear'd ye were not wholly mine;
And see, yourself have own'd ye did me wrong.
The people call you prophet: let it be: 315
But not of those that can expound themselves.
Take Vivien for expounder; she will call
That three-days-long presageful gloom of yours
No presage, but the same mistrustful mood
That makes you seem less noble than yourself,   320
Whenever I have ask'd this very boon,
Now ask'd again: for see you not, dear love,
That such a mood as that, which lately gloom'd
Your fancy when ye saw me following you,
Must make me fear still more you are not mine,
Must make me yearn still more to prove you mine,   325
And make me wish still more to learn this charm
Of woven paces and of waving hands,
As proof of trust. O Merlin, teach it me.
The charm so taught will charm us both to rest.   330
For, grant me some slight power upon your fate,
I, feeling that you felt me worthy trust,
Should rest and let you rest, knowing you mine.
And therefore be as great as ye are named,
Not muffled round with selfish reticence.   335
How hard you look and how denyingly!
O, if you think this wickedness in me,
That I should prove it on you unawares,
That makes me passing wrathful; then our bond
Had best be loosed for ever: but think or not,   340
By Heaven that hears I tell you the clean truth,
As clean as blood of babes, as white as milk:
O Merlin, may this earth, if ever I,
If these unwitty wandering wits of mine,
Ev'n in the jumbled rubbish of a dream,   345
Have tript on such conjectural treachery—
May this hard earth cleave to the Nadir hell
Down, down, and close again, and nip me flat,
If I be such a traitress. Yield my boon,
Till which I scarce can yield you all I am;   350
And grant my re-reiterated wish,

The great proof of your love: because I think,
However wise, ye hardly know me yet.'

    And Merlin loosed his hand from hers and said,
'I never was less wise, however wise,   355
Too curious Vivien, tho' you talk of trust,
Than when I told you first of such a charm.
Yea, if ye talk of trust I tell you this,
Too much I trusted when I told you that,
And stirr'd this vice in you which ruin'd man   360
Thro' woman the first hour; for howsoe'er
In children a great curiousness be well,
Who have to learn themselves and all the world,
In you, that are no child, for still I find
Your face is practised when I spell the lines,   365
I call it,—well, I will not call it vice:
But since you name yourself the summer fly,
I well could wish a cobweb for the gnat,
That settles, beaten back, and beaten back
Settles, till one could yield for weariness: 370
But since I will not yield to give you power
Upon my life and use and name and fame,
Why will ye never ask some other boon?
Yea, by God's rood, I trusted you too much.'

    And Vivien, like the tenderest-hearted maid   375
That ever bided tryst at village stile,
Made answer, either eyelid wet with tears:
'Nay, Master, be not wrathful with your maid,
Caress her: let her feel herself forgiven
Who feels no heart to ask another boon.   380
I think ye hardly know the tender rhyme
Of "trust me not at all or all in all."
I heard the great Sir Lancelot sing it once,
And it shall answer for me. Listen to it.

    "In Love, if Love be Love, if Love be ours,   385
Faith and unfaith can ne'er be equal powers:
Unfaith in aught is want of faith in all.

    "It is the little rift within the lute,
That by and by will make the music mute,
And ever widening slowly silence all.   390

    "The little rift within the lover's lute
Or little pitted speck in garner'd fruit,
That rotting inward slowly moulders all.

"It is not worth the keeping: let it go:
But shall it? answer, darling, answer, no.   395
And trust me not at all or all in all."

O Master, do ye love my tender rhyme?'

And Merlin look'd and half believed her true,
So tender was her voice, so fair her face,
So sweetly gleam'd her eyes behind her tears   400
Like sunlight on the plain behind a shower:
And yet he answer'd half indignantly:

'Far other was the song that once I heard
By this huge oak, sung nearly where we sit:
For here we met, some ten or twelve of us,   405
To chase a creature that was current then
In these wild woods, the hart with golden horns
It was the time when first the question rose
About the founding of a Table Round,
That was to be, for love of God and men   410
And noble deeds, the flower of all the world.
And each incited each to noble deeds.
And while we waited, one, the youngest of us,
We could not keep him silent, out he flash'd,
And into such a song, such fire for fame,   415
Such trumpet-blowings in it, coming down
To such a stern and iron-clashing close,
That when he stopt we long'd to hurl together,
And should have done it; but the beauteous beast
Scared by the noise upstarted at our feet,   420
And like a silver shadow slipt away
Thro' the dim land; and all day long we rode
Thro' the dim land against a rushing wind,
That glorious roundel echoing in our ears,
And chased the flashes of his golden horns   425
Until they vanish'd by the fairy well
That laughs at iron—as our warriors did—
Where children cast their pins and nails, and cry,
"Laugh, little well!" but touch it with a sword,
It buzzes fiercely round the point; and there   430
We lost him: such a noble song was that.
But, Vivien, when you sang me that sweet rhyme,
I felt as tho' you knew this cursed charm,
Were proving it on me, and that I lay
And felt them slowly ebbing, name and fame.'   435

And Vivien answer'd smiling mournfully:
'O mine have ebb'd away for evermore,

And all thro' following you to this wild wood,
Because I saw you sad, to comfort you.
Lo now, what hearts have men! they never mount   440
As high as woman in her selfless mood.
And touching fame, howe'er ye scorn my song,
Take one verse more—the lady speaks it—this:

    '"My name, once mine, now thine, is closelier mine,
For fame, could fame be mine, that fame were thine,   445
And shame, could shame be thine, that shame were mine.
So trust me not at all or all in all."

    'Says she not well? and there is more—this rhyme
Is like the fair pearl-necklace of the Queen,
That burst in dancing, and the pearls were spilt;   450
Some lost, some stolen, some as relics kept.
But nevermore the same two sister pearls
Ran down the silken thread to kiss each other
On her white neck—so is it with this rhyme:
It lives dispersedly in many hands,   455
And every minstrel sings it differently;
Yet is there one true line, the pearl of pearls:
"Man dreams of Fame while woman wakes to love."
Yea! Love, tho' Love were of the grossest, carves
A portion from the solid present, eats   460
And uses, careless of the rest; but Fame,
The Fame that follows death is nothing to us;
And what is Fame in life but half-disfame,
And counterchanged with darkness? ye yourself
Know well that Envy calls you Devil's son,   465
And since ye seem the Master of all Art,
They fain would make you Master of all vice.'

    And Merlin lock'd his hand in hers and said,
'I once was looking for a magic weed,
And found a fair young squire who sat alone,   470
Had carved himself a knightly shield of wood,
And then was painting on it fancied arms,
Azure, an Eagle rising or, the Sun
In dexter chief; the scroll "I follow fame."
And speaking not, but leaning over him,   475
I took his brush and blotted out the bird,
And made a Gardener putting in a graff,
With this for motto, "Rather use than fame."
You should have seen him blush; but afterwards
He made a stalwart knight. O Vivien,   480
For you, methinks you think you love me well;

For me, I love you somewhat; rest: and Love
Should have some rest and pleasure in himself,
Not ever be too curious for a boon,
Too prurient for a proof against the grain   485
Of him ye say ye love: but Fame with men,
Being but ampler means to serve mankind,
Should have small rest or pleasure in herself,
But work as vassal to the larger love,
That dwarfs the petty love of one to one.   490
Use gave me Fame at first, and Fame again
Increasing gave me use. Lo, there my boon!
What other? for men sought to prove me vile,
Because I fain had given them greater wits:
And then did Envy call me Devil's son: 495
The sick weak beast seeking to help herself
By striking at her better, miss'd, and brought
Her own claw back, and wounded her own heart.
Sweet were the days when I was all unknown,
But when my name was lifted up, the storm   500
Brake on the mountain and I cared not for it.
Right well know I that Fame is half-disfame,
Yet needs must work my work. That other fame,
To one at least, who hath not children, vague,
The cackle of the unborn about the grave,   505
I cared not for it: a single misty star,
Which is the second in a line of stars
That seem a sword beneath a belt of three,
I never gazed upon it but I dreamt
Of some vast charm concluded in that star   510
To make fame nothing. Wherefore, if I fear,
Giving you power upon me thro' this charm,
That you might play me falsely, having power,
However well ye think ye love me now
(As sons of kings loving in pupilage   515
Have turn'd to tyrants when they came to power)
I rather dread the loss of use than fame;
If you—and not so much from wickedness,
As some wild turn of anger, or a mood
Of overstrain'd affection, it may be,   520
To keep me all to your own self,—or else
A sudden spurt of woman's jealousy,—
Should try charm on whom ye say ye love.'

        And Vivien answer'd smiling as in wrath:
'Have I not sworn? I am not trusted. Good!   525
Well, hide it, hide it; I shall find it out;
And being found take heed of Vivien.

A woman and not trusted, doubtless I
Might feel some sudden turn of anger born
Of your misfaith; and your fine epithet   530
Is accurate too, for this full love of mine
Without the full heart back may merit well
Your term of overstrain'd. So used as I,
My daily wonder is, I love at all.
And as to woman's jealousy, O why not?   535
O to what end, except a jealous one,
And one to make me jealous if I love,
Was this fair charm invented by yourself?
I well believe that all about this world
Ye cage a buxom captive here and there,   540
Closed in the four walls of a hollow tower
From which is no escape for evermore.'

       Then the great Master merrily answer'd her:
'Full many a love in loving youth was mine;
I needed then no charm to keep them mine   545
But youth and love; and that full heart of yours
Whereof ye prattle, may now assure you mine;
So live uncharm'd. For those who wrought it first,
The wrist is parted from the hand that waved,
The feet unmortised from their ankle-bones   550
Who paced it, ages back: but will ye hear
The legend as in guerdon for your rhyme?

       'There lived a king in the most Eastern East,
Less old than I, yet older, for my blood
Hath earnest in it of far springs to be.   555
A tawny pirate anchor'd in his port,
Whose bark had plunder'd twenty nameless isles;
And passing one, at the high peep of dawn,
He saw two cities in a thousand boats
All fighting for a woman on the sea.   560
And pushing his black craft among them all,
He lightly scatter'd theirs and brought her off,
With loss of half his people arrow-slain;
A maid so smooth, so white, so wonderful,
They said a light came from her when she moved: 565
And since the pirate would not yield her up,
The King impaled him for his piracy;
Then made her Queen: but those isle-nurtured eyes
Waged such unwilling tho' successful war
On all the youth, they sicken'd; councils thinn'd,   570
And armies waned, for magnet-like she drew
The rustiest iron of old fighters' hearts;

And beasts themselves would worship; camels knelt
Unbidden, and the brutes of mountain back
That carry kings in castles, bow'd black knees   575
Of homage, ringing with their serpent hands,
To make her smile, her golden ankle-bells.
What wonder, being jealous, that he sent
His horns of proclamation out thro' all
The hundred under-kingdoms that he sway'd   580
To find a wizard who might teach the King
Some charm, which being wrought upon the Queen
Might keep her all his own: to such a one
He promised more than ever king has given,
A league of mountain full of golden mines,   585
A province with a hundred miles of coast,
A palace and a princess, all for him:
But on all those who tried and fail'd, the King
Pronounced a dismal sentence, meaning by it
To keep the list low and pretenders back,   590
Or like a king, not to be trifled with—
Their heads should moulder on the city gates.
And many tried and fail'd, because the charm
Of nature in her overbore their own:
And many a wizard brow bleach'd on the walls: 595
And many weeks a troop of carrion crows
Hung like a cloud above the gateway towers.'

        And Vivien breaking in upon him, said:
'I sit and gather honey; yet, methinks,
Thy tongue has tript a little: ask thyself.   600
The lady never made *unwilling* war
With those fine eyes: she had her pleasure in it,
And made her good man jealous with good cause.
And lived there neither dame nor damsel then
Wroth at a lover's loss? were all as tame,   605
I mean, as noble, as their Queen was fair?
Not one to flirt a venom at her eyes,
Or pinch a murderous dust into her drink,
Or make her paler with a poison'd rose?
Well, those were not our days: but did they find   610
A wizard? Tell me, was he like to thee?'

        She ceased, and made her lithe arm round his neck
Tighten, and then drew back, and let her eyes
Speak for her, glowing on him, like a bride's
On her new lord, her own, the first of men.   615

        He answer'd laughing, 'Nay, not like to me.
At last they found—his foragers for charms—

A little glassy-headed hairless man,
Who lived alone in a great wild on grass;
Read but one book, and ever reading grew   620
So grated down and filed away with thought,
So lean his eyes were monstrous; while the skin
Clung but to crate and basket, ribs and spine.
And since he kept his mind on one sole aim,
Nor ever touch'd fierce wine, nor tasted flesh,   625
Nor own'd a sensual wish, to him the wall
That sunders ghosts and shadow-casting men
Became a crystal, and he saw them thro' it,
And heard their voices talk behind the wall,
And learnt their elemental secrets, powers   630
And forces; often o'er the sun's bright eye
Drew the vast eyelid of an inky cloud,
And lash'd it at the base with slanting storm;
Or in the noon of mist and driving rain,
When the lake whiten'd and the pinewood roar'd,   635
And the cairn'd mountain was a shadow, sunn'd
The world to peace again: here was the man.
And so by force they dragg'd him to the King.
And then he taught the King to charm the Queen
In such-wise, that no man could see her more,   640
Nor saw she save the King, who wrought the charm,
Coming and going, and she lay as dead,
And lost all use of life: but when the King
Made proffer of the league of golden mines,
The province with a hundred miles of coast,   645
The palace and the princess, that old man
Went back to his old wild, and lived on grass,
And vanish'd, and his book came down to me.'

      And Vivien answer'd smiling saucily:
'Ye have the book: the charm is written in it: 650
Good: take my counsel: let me know it at once:
For keep it like a puzzle chest in chest,
With each chest lock'd and padlock'd thirty-fold,
And whelm all this beneath as vast a mound
As after furious battle turfs the slain   655
On some wild down above the windy deep,
I yet should strike upon a sudden means
To dig, pick, open, find and read the charm:
Then, if I tried it, who should blame me then?'

      And smiling as a master smiles at one   660
That is not of his school, nor any school
But that where blind and naked Ignorance

Delivers brawling judgments, unashamed,
On all things all day long, he answer'd her:

    'Thou read the book, my pretty Vivien!   665
O ay, it is but twenty pages long,
But every page having an ample marge,
And every marge enclosing in the midst
A square of text that looks a little blot,
The text no larger than the limbs of fleas;   670
And every square of text an awful charm,
Writ in a language that has long gone by.
So long, that mountains have arisen since
With cities on their flanks—thou read the book!
And every margin scribbled, crost, and cramm'd   675
With comment, densest condensation, hard
To mind and eye; but the long sleepless nights
Of my long life have made it easy to me
And none can read the text, not even I;
And none can read the comment but myself;   680
And in the comment did I find the charm.
O, the results are simple; a mere child
Might use it to the harm of anyone,
And never could undo it: ask no more:
For tho' you should not prove it upon me,   685
But keep that oath ye sware, ye might, perchance,
Assay it on some one of the Table Round,
And all because ye dream they babble of you.'

    And Vivien, frowning in true anger, said:
'What dare the full-fed liars say of me?   690
They ride abroad redressing human wrongs!
They sit with knife in meat and wine in horn!
They bound to holy vows of chastity!
Were I not woman, I could tell a tale.
But you are man, you well can understand   695
The shame that cannot be explain'd for shame.
Not one of all the drove should touch me: swine!'

    Then answer'd Merlin careless of her words:
'You breathe but accusation vast and vague,
Spleen-born, I think, and proofless. If ye know,   700
Set up the charge ye know, to stand or fall!'

    And Vivien answer'd frowning wrathfully:
'O ay, what say ye to Sir Valence, him
Whose kinsman left him watcher o'er his wife
And two fair babes, and went to distant lands;   705

Was one year gone, and on returning found
Not two but three? there lay the reckling, one
But one hour old! What said the happy sire?
A seven-months' babe had been a truer gift.
Those twelve sweet moons confused his fatherhood.'   710

    Then answer'd Merlin, 'Nay, I know the tale.
Sir Valence wedded with an outland dame:
Some cause had kept him sunder'd from his wife:
One child they had: it lived with her: she died:
His kinsman travelling on his own affair   715
Was charged by Valence to bring home the child.
He brought, not found it therefore: take the truth.'

    'O ay,' said Vivien, 'overtrue a tale.
What say ye then to sweet Sir Sagramore,
That ardent man? "To pluck the flower in season,"   720
So says the song, "I trow it is no treason."
O Master, shall we call him overquick
To crop his own sweet rose before the hour?'

    And Merlin answer'd, 'Overquick art thou
To catch a loathly plume fall'n from the wing   725
Of that foul bird of rapine whose whole prey
Is man's good name: he never wrong'd his bride.
I know the tale. An angry gust of wind
Puff'd out his torch among the myriad-room'd
And many-corridor'd complexities   730
Of Arthur's palace: then he found a door,
And darkling felt the sculptured ornament
That wreathen round it made it seem his own;
And wearied out made for the couch and slept,
A stainless man beside a stainless maid;   735
And either slept, nor knew of other there;
Till the high dawn piercing the royal rose
In Arthur's casement glimmer'd chastely down,
Blushing upon them blushing, and at once
He rose without a word and parted from her: 740
But when the thing was blazed about the court,
The brute world howling forced them into bonds,
And as it chanced they are happy, being pure.'

    'O ay,' said Vivien, 'that were likely too.
What say ye then to fair Sir Percivale   745
And of the horrid foulness that he wrought,
The saintly youth, the spotless lamb of Christ,
Or some black wether of St. Satan's fold.

What, in the precincts of the chapel-yard,
Among the knightly brasses of the graves,   750
And by the cold Hic Jacets of the dead!'

And Merlin answer'd careless of her charge,
'A sober man is Percivale and pure;
But once in life was fluster'd with new wine,
Then paced for coolness in the chapel-yard;   755
Where one of Satan's shepherdesses caught
And meant to stamp him with her master's mark;
And that he sinn'd is not believable;
For, look upon his face!—but if he sinn'd,
The sin that practice burns into the blood,   760
And not the one dark hour which brings remorse,
Will brand us, after, of whose fold we be:
Or else were he, the holy king, whose hymns
Are chanted in the minster, worse than all.
But is your spleen froth'd out, or have ye more?'   765

And Vivien answer'd frowning yet in wrath:
'O ay; what say ye to Sir Lancelot, friend
Traitor or true? that commerce with the Queen,
I ask you, is it clamour'd by the child,
Or whisper'd in the corner? do ye know it?'   770

To which he answer'd sadly, 'Yea, I know it.
Sir Lancelot went ambassador, at first,
To fetch her, and she watch'd him from her walls:
A rumour runs, she took him for the King,
So fixt her fancy on him: let them be.   775
But have ye no one word of loyal praise
For Arthur, blameless King and stainless man?'

She answer'd with a low and chuckling laugh:
'Man! is he man at all, who knows and winks?
Sees what his fair bride is and does, and winks?   780
By which the good King means to blind himself,
And blinds himself and all the Table Round
To all the foulness that they work. Myself
Could call him (were it not for womanhood)
The pretty, popular name such manhood earns,   785
Could call him the main cause of all their crime;
Yea, were he not crown'd King, coward, and fool.'

Then Merlin to his own heart, loathing, said:
'O true and tender! O my liege and King!
O selfless man and stainless gentleman,   790
Who wouldst against thine own eye-witness fain

Have all men true and leal, all women pure;
How, in the mouths of base interpreters,
From over-fineness not intelligible
To things with every sense as false and foul   795
As the poach'd filth that floods the middle street,
Is thy white blamelessness accounted blame!'

    But Vivien, deeming Merlin overborne
By instance, recommenced, and let her tongue
Rage like a fire among the noblest names,   800
Polluting, and imputing her whole self,
Defaming and defacing, till she left
Not even Lancelot brave, nor Galahad clean.

Her words had issue other than she will'd.
He dragg'd his eyebrow bushes down, and made   805
A snowy penthouse for his hollow eyes,
And mutter'd in himself, 'Tell *her* the charm!
So, if she had it, would she rail on me
To snare the next, and if she have it not
So will she rail. What did the wanton say?   815
"Not mount as high"; we scarce can sink as low:
For men at most differ as Heaven and earth,
But women, worst and best, as Heaven and Hell.
I know the Table Round, my friends of old;
All brave, and many generous, and some chaste.   815
She cloaks the scar of some repulse with lies;
I well believe she tempted them and fail'd,
Being so bitter: for fine plots may fail,
Tho' harlots paint their talk as well as face
With colours of the heart that are not theirs.   820
I will not let her know: nine tithes of times
Face-flatterer and backbiter are the same.
And they, sweet soul, that most impute a crime
Are pronest to it, and impute themselves,
Wanting the mental range; or low desire   825
Not to feel lowest makes them level all;
Yea, they would pare the mountain to the plain,
To leave an equal baseness; and in this
Are harlots like the crowd, that if they find
Some stain or blemish in a name of note,   830
Not grieving that their greatest are so small,
Inflate themselves with some insane delight,
And judge all nature from her feet of clay,
Without the will to lift their eyes, and see
Her godlike head crown'd with spiritual fire,   835
And touching other worlds. I am weary of her.'

He spoke in words part heard, in whispers part,
Half-suffocated in the hoary fell
And many-winter'd fleece of throat and chin.
But Vivien, gathering somewhat of his mood,   840
And hearing 'harlot' mutter'd twice or thrice,
Leapt from her session on his lap, and stood
Stiff as a viper frozen; loathsome sight,
How from the rosy lips of life and love,
Flash'd the bare-grinning skeleton of death!   845
White was her cheek; sharp breaths of anger puff'd
Her fairy nostril out; her hand half-clench'd
Went faltering sideways downward to her belt,
And feeling; had she found a dagger there
(For in a wink the false love turns to hate)   850
She would have stabb'd him; but she found it not:
His eye was calm, and suddenly she took
To bitter weeping like a beaten child,
A long, long weeping, not consolable.
Then her false voice made way, broken with sobs: 855

    'O crueller than was ever told in tale,
Or sung in song! O vainly lavish'd love!
O cruel, there was nothing wild or strange,
Or seeming shameful—for what shame in love,
So love be true, and not as yours is—nothing   860
Poor Vivien had not done to win his trust
Who call'd her what he call'd her—all her crime,
All—all—the wish to prove him wholly hers.'

    She mused a little, and then clapt her hands
Together with a wailing shriek, and said: 865
'Stabb'd through the heart's affections to the heart!
Seethed like the kid in its own mother's milk!
Kill'd with a word worse than a life of blows!
I thought that he was gentle, being great:
O God, that I had loved a smaller man!   870
I should have found in him a greater heart.
O, I, that flattering my true passion, saw
The knights, the court, the King, dark in your light,
Who loved to make men darker than they are,
Because of that high pleasure which I had   875
To seat you sole upon my pedestal
Of worship—I am answer'd, and henceforth
The course of life that seem'd so flowery to me
With you for guide and master, only you,
Becomes the sea-cliff pathway broken short,   880
And ending in a ruin—nothing left,

But into some low cave to crawl, and there,
If the wolf spare me, weep my life away,
Kill'd with inutterable unkindliness.'

    She paused, she turn'd away, she hung her head,   885
The snake of gold slid from her hair, the braid
Slipt and uncoil'd itself, she wept afresh,
And the dark wood grew darker toward the storm
In silence, while his anger slowly died
Within him, till he let his wisdom go   890
For ease of heart, and half believed her true:
Call'd her to shelter in the hollow oak,
'Come from the storm,' and having no reply,
Gazed at the heaving shoulder, and the face
Hand-hidden, as for utmost grief or shame;   895
Then thrice essay'd, by tenderest-touching terms,
To sleek her ruffled peace of mind, in vain.
At last she let herself be conquer'd by him,
And as the cageling newly flown returns,
The seeming-injured simple-hearted thing   900
Came to her old perch back, and settled there.
There while she sat, half-falling from his knees,
Half-nestled at his heart, and since he saw
The slow tear creep from her closed eyelid yet,
About her, more in kindness than in love,   905
The gentle wizard cast a shielding arm.
But she dislink'd herself at once and rose,
Her arms upon her breast across, and stood,
A virtuous gentlewoman deeply wrong'd,
Upright and flush'd before him: then she said: 910

    'There must be now no passages of love
Betwixt us twain henceforward evermore;
Since, if I be what I am grossly call'd,
What should be granted which your own gross heart
Would reckon worth the taking? I will go.   915
In truth, but one thing now—better have died
Thrice than have ask'd it once—could make me stay—
That proof of trust—so often ask'd in vain!
How justly, after that vile term of yours,
I find with grief! I might believe you then,   920
Who knows? once more. Lo! what was once to me
Mere matter of the fancy, now hath grown
The vast necessity of heart and life.
Farewell; think gently of me, for I fear
My fate or folly, passing gayer youth   925
For one so old, must be to love thee still.
But ere I leave thee let me swear once more

That if I schemed against thy peace in this,
May yon just heaven, that darkens o'er me, send
One flash, that, missing all things else, may make   930
My scheming brain a cinder, if I lie.'

        Scarce had she ceased, when out of heaven a bolt
(For now the storm was close above them) struck,
Furrowing a giant oak, and javelining
With darted spikes and splinters of the wood   935
The dark earth round. He raised his eyes and saw
The tree that shone white-listed thro' the gloom.
But Vivien, fearing heaven had heard her oath,
And dazzled by the livid-flickering fork,
And deafen'd with the stammering cracks and claps   940
That follow'd, flying back and crying out,
'O Merlin, tho' you do not love me, save
Yet save me!' clung to him and hugg'd him close;
And call'd him dear protector in her fright,
Nor yet forgot her practice in her fright,   945
But wrought upon his mood and hugg'd him close.
The pale blood of the wizard at her touch
Took gayer colours, like an opal warm'd.
She blamed herself for telling hearsay tales:
She shook from fear, and for her fault she wept   950
Of petulancy; she call'd him lord and liege,
Her seer, her bard, her silver star of eve,
Her God, her Merlin, the one passionate love
Of her whole life; and ever overhead
Bellow'd the tempest, and the rotten branch   955
Snapt in the rushing of the river-rain
Above them; and in change of glare and gloom
Her eyes and neck glittering went and came;
Till now the storm, its burst of passion spent,
Moaning and calling out of other lands,   960
Had left the ravaged woodland yet once more
To peace; and what should not have been had been,
For Merlin, overtalk'd and overworn,
Had yielded, told her all the charm, and slept.

        Then, in one moment, she put forth the charm   965
Of woven paces and of waving hands,
And in the hollow oak he lay as dead,
And lost to life and use and name and fame.

        Then crying 'I have made his glory mine,'
And shrieking out 'O fool!' the harlot leapt   970
Adown the forest, and the thicket closed
Behind her, and the forest echo'd 'fool.'

chapter 10

MARK TWAIN:
A CONNECTICUT YANKEE
IN KING ARTHUR'S COURT

K N I G H T S I N armor have been as fascinating to Americans as cowboys and Indians to Europeans, and writers as perceptive as Mark Twain have not failed to make the connection. However, it would be difficult to find a more striking contrast in Arthurian visions than between Tennyson's *Idylls of the King* and Twain's burlesque novel *A Connecticut Yankee in King Arthur's Court.* This is hardly surprising considering the contrast between the authors themselves—the august Poet Laureate of England and the sharp-tongued humorist from Hannibal, Missouri. Twain gleefully satirizes not only the Arthurian tradition but Tennyson and the British reverence for that tradition. One of the things he could have had in mind when he praised Daniel Beard's illustrations for his book was Beard's use of Tennyson as the model for Merlin and probably the "Dirty Monk" as well.

For their part the British did not receive this American's irreverent version of Camelot very favorably. The reviewer for London's *Daily Telegraph* drew the line unmistakably: "The stories of King Arthur that have come down to us represent in legendary form not any historical fact, but an ideal of kingship and knighthood which had birth in the hearts and aspirations of mediaeval men. This was their ideal of what a King amongst his warriors ought to be, and the beautiful image has fired the thoughts and purified the imagination of millions of men and women for many generations. Will this shrine in human souls be destroyed because a Yankee scribe chooses to fling pellets of mud upon the high altar?" (Anderson, p. 161, rpt. Ensor, p. 329). The more discerning William T. Stead selected *A Connecticut Yankee* as Novel of the Month in the February 1890 *Review of Reviews*, but also had reservations: "Tennyson sang the idyls [sic] of the King, and as long as the world lasts Sir Thomas Malory's marvellous old Romance will fill the hearts and imaginations of men with some far-off reflection of the splendours and the glories of that child-like age. But truly he sang 'the old order changeth, giving place to the new,' of which can we have a more notable and even brutal illustration than the apparition of this vulgar Yankee realist, with his telephones and his dynamite, his insufferable slang and his infinite self-conceit, in the midst of King Arthur's Court, applying to all the knighthood of the Round Table the measure of his yardstick,—the welfare of the common man?" (Anderson, p. 169; Ensor, pp. 333–334). Twain was wonderful when he wrote about American life, and even a book like *The Prince and the Pauper* could be condoned, but this was too much.

Twain himself anticipated this response, and explained to his British publisher Andrew Chatto that "it was written for England. So many Englishmen have done their sincerest best to teach us something for our betterment, that it seems to me high time... to pry up the English nation to a little higher level of manhood in turn" (Anderson, p. 333). Nevertheless, this successor to *The Adventures of Huckleberry Finn* was not conceived as an attempt to mock British institutions, but as a contrast that would do homage to the power of Arthurian legend while exposing the disservices to humanity of monarchy and Church.

The book began in 1884 with Twain's discovery (or rediscovery) of Malory. That year the Twain household in Hartford, Connecticut, purchased a copy of Sidney Lanier's *The Boy's King Arthur* (1880), and George Washington Cable, an author friend, got him a copy of Malory during a reading tour they shared in November and December. Soon Twain was making notes from dreams about the discomforts of armor and imagined fights between modern soldiers and mounted knights, and the Yankee first encounters Merlin boring Arthur's court to sleep by reciting the story of Excalibur, which Twain quotes from Sir Edmund Strachey's Globe Edition of Malory (1868). But as time went on, the book changed from a whimsical pastime to a purposeful contrast between democratic "low culture" and aristocratic "high culture," the industrial future and the romantic past. While Twain was writing it, he became increasingly outraged by the social injustices he was discovering through his reading in sources like W.E.H. Lecky's *History of European Morals from Augustus to Charlemagne* (1872) and George Standring's *The People's History of the English Aristocracy* (1887), and adopted a tone as scathing as it was high-spirited.

His conception of the book's message also became increasingly ambivalent as he worked on it. David Ketterer notices four contrasting "realms of experience" in the novel: the nostalgia for the chivalric experience, the "actual living conditions" of medieval times, the Yankee's utopian vision, and the "dehumanized Armageddon" that his confrontation with the forces opposed to him finally brings about (p. 1106; Ensor, pp. 421–422). These realms are never fully integrated by Twain; both the romantic and the technological world view contain the seeds of their own abuses and destruction. Twain's ambivalence must also have been influenced by his disastrous experience with the Paige typesetting machine, which he thought would make him a millionaire many times over but ended up losing him over $200,000.

While critical attention to this novel has focused on Hank Morgan, the nineteenth-century Hartford engineer and entrepreneur who is catapulted into the sixth century by a dint on the head with a crowbar, very little has been devoted to Merlin. Nevertheless, Merlin is Hank's medieval counterpart and chief rival. As Twain himself expressed the contrast at a reading in 1888, "Take a practical man, thoroughly equipped with the scientific [magic] enchantments of our day & set him down alongside of Merlin the head magician of Arthur's time, & what sort of a show would Merlin stand?" (Smith, pp. 84–85; Ensor, pp. 412–413). Because Hank narrates the story, Merlin's role is underlined by his portrayal as a charlatan—devious, jealous, and repeatedly ineffectual. Hank's dislike of the magician is initially motivated by Merlin's order to strip him naked before Arthur's court and to have him burned at the stake. But the Yankee's technological know-how and historical hindsight prevail in contest after contest, from eclipse to apocalypse.

Hank is in fact Merlin in modern guise. If Merlin is the "architect of Camelot" in Tennyson's *Idylls*, Hank is its engineer in Twain. Both of them are loners and *ex machina* influences on the Arthurian society. This doubling of character is one of the novel's finest devices, and particularly notable in the five chapters here, which relate four of their magical duels. Hank relies upon the mechanism of gunpowder in the first two, lasso and revolver in the third. Finally Merlin weaves his only successful spell and true magical feat by putting Hank to sleep for thirteen centuries, shortly before electrocuting himself in the midst of a triumphant wicked-witch cackle. The ambivalence of Twain's contrast between old and new societies is nowhere more evident than in this ending.

Even more than "the life of knight-erranty" is at stake. Writing about the Yankee's hyperbolic anticipation of his fight with the knights, Henry Nash Smith raises an interesting problem: "The most obvious meaning is of course that Merlin is a only a fraud, with no real power, whereas the Yankee wields the true power of science, which is magical only in the eyes of ignorant spectators. But the Yankee implies that he and Merlin are almost evenly matched. . . " (p. 96). If they are, as Clarence's postscript seems to confirm, then which is the fraud, and what does their equivalence imply about magic and science?

Bibliographic note: These chapters are from the first edition by Charles L. Webster, Twain's own company, in 1879. A text with corrections from both the manuscript and excerpts published by Twain in *Century Magazine*, November 1889, was edited by Bernard L. Stein for The Mark Twain Library (Berkeley: University of California Press, 1979). The major study of the novel is Henry Nash Smith, *Mark Twain's Fable of Progress: Political and Economic Ideas in "A Connecticut Yankee"* (New Brunswick, N.J.: Rutgers University Press, 1964) and its reception is fully documented in *Mark Twain: The Critical Heritage*, ed. Frederick Anderson (New York: Barnes & Noble, 1971), pp. 148–181. Excerpts from these two books and David Ketterer's detailed exploration of Hank's "magic"—"Epoch-Eclipse and Apocalypse: Special 'Effects' in *A Connecticut Yankee*," *PMLA* 88.5 (October 1973): 1104–1114—also appear in Allison R. Ensor's Norton Critical Edition (New York: Norton, 1982), which includes other important background material and criticism.

A Connecticut Yankee in King Arthur's Court

Merlin's Tower

Inasmuch as I was now the second personage in the kingdom, as far as political power and authority were concerned, much was made of me. My raiment was of silks and velvets and cloth-of-gold, and by consequence was very showy, also uncomfortable. But habit would soon reconcile me to my clothes; I was aware of that. I was given the choicest suite of apartments in the castle, after the king's. They were aglow with loud-colored silken hangings, but the stone floors had nothing but rushes on them for a carpet, and they were misfit rushes at that, being not all of one breed. As for conveniences, properly speaking, there weren't any. I mean *little* conveniences; it is the little conveniences that make the real comfort of life. The big oaken chairs, graced with rude carvings, were well enough, but that was the stopping-place. There was no soap, no matches, no looking-glass— except a metal one, about as powerful as a pail of water. And not a chromo [*inexpensive colored print produced by chrome lithograph*]. I had been used to chromos for years, and I saw now that without my suspecting it a passion for art had got worked into the fabric of my being, and was become a part of me. It made me homesick to look around over this proud and gaudy but heartless barrenness and remember that in our house in East Hartford, all unpretending as it was, you couldn't go into a room but you would find an insurance-chromo, or at least a three-color God-Bless-Our-Home over the door; and in the parlor we had nine. But here, even in my grand room of state, there wasn't anything in the nature of a picture except a thing the size of a bedquilt, which was either woven or knitted (it had darned places in it), and nothing in it was the right color or the right shape; and as for proportions, even Raphael himself couldn't have botched them more formidably, after all his practice on those nightmares they call his "celebrated Hampton Court cartoons." Raphael was a bird. We had several of his chromos; one was his "Miraculous Draught of Fishes," where he puts in a miracle of his own—puts three men into a canoe which wouldn't have held a dog without upsetting. I always admired to study R.'s art, it was so fresh and unconventional.

There wasn't even a bell or a speaking-tube in the castle. I had a great many servants, and those that were on duty lolled in the anteroom; and when I wanted one of them I had to go and call for him. There was no gas, there were no candles; a bronze dish half full of boarding-house butter with a blazing rag floating in it was the thing that produced what was regarded as light. A lot of these hung along the walls and modified the dark, just toned in down enough to make it dismal. If you went out at night, your servants carried torches. There were no books, pens, paper or ink, and no glass in the openings they believed to be windows. It is a little thing—glass is—until it is absent, then it becomes a big thing. But perhaps the worst of all was, that there wasn't any sugar, coffee, tea, or tobacco. I saw that I was just another Robinson Crusoe cast away on an uninhabited island, with no society but some more or less tame animals, and if I wanted to make life bearable I must do as he did—invent, contrive, create, reorganize things; set brain and hand to work, and keep them busy. Well, that was in my line.

One thing troubled me along at first—the immense interest which people took in me. Apparently the whole nation wanted a look at me. It soon transpired that the eclipse had scared the British world almost to death; that while it lasted the whole country, from one end to the other, was in a pitiable state of panic, and the churches, hermitages, and monkeries overflowed with praying and weeping poor creatures who thought the end of the world was come. Then had followed the news that the producer of this awful event was a stranger, a mighty magician at Arthur's court; that he could have blown out the sun like a candle, and was just going to do it when his mercy was purchased, and he then dissolved his enchantments, and was now recognized and honored as the man who had by his unaided might saved the globe from destruction and its peoples from extinction. Now if you consider that everybody believed that, and not only believed it, but never even dreamed of doubting it, you will easily understand that there was not a person in all Britain that would not have walked fifty miles to get a sight of me. Of course I was all the talk—all other subjects were dropped; even the king became suddenly a person of minor interest and notoriety. Within twenty-four hours the delegations began to arrive, and from that time onward for a fortnight they kept coming. The village was crowded, and all the country-side. I had to go out a dozen times a day and show myself to these reverent and awestricken multitudes. It came to be a great burden, as to time and trouble, but of course it was at the same time compensatingly agreeable to be so celebrated and such a center of homage. It turned Brer Merlin green with envy and spite, which was a great satisfaction to me. But there was one thing I couldn't understand—nobody had asked for an autograph. I spoke to Clarence about it. By George! I had to explain to him what it was. Then he said nobody in the country could read or write but a few dozen priests. Land! think of that.

There was another thing that troubled me a little. Those multitudes presently began to agitate for another miracle. That was natural. To be able to carry back to their far homes the boast that they had seen the man who could command the sun, riding in the heavens, and be obeyed, would make them great in the eyes of their neighbors, and envied by them all; but to be able to also say they had seen him work a miracle themselves—why, people would come a distance to see *them*. The pressure got to be pretty strong. There was going to be an eclipse of the moon, and I knew the date and hour, but it was too far away. Two years. I would have given a good deal for license to hurry it up and use it now when there was a big market for it. It seemed a great pity to have it wasted so, and come lagging along at a time when a body wouldn't have any use for it, as like as not. If it had been booked for only a month away, I could have sold it short; but as matters stood, I couldn't seem to cipher out any way to make it do me any good, so I gave up trying. Next, Clarence found that old Merlin was making himself busy on the sly among those people. He was spreading a report that I was a humbug, and that the reason I didn't accommodate the people with a miracle was because I couldn't. I saw that I must do something. I presently thought out a plan.

By my authority as executive I threw Merlin into prison—the same cell I had occupied myself, and I didn't thin out the rats any for his accommodation. Then I gave public notice by herald and trumpet that I should be busy with affairs of state for a fortnight, but about the end of that time I would take a moment's leisure and blow up Merlin's stone tower by fires from heaven; in the meantime, whoso listened to evil reports about me, let him beware. Furthermore, I would perform but this one miracle at this time, and no more; if it failed to satisfy and any murmured, I would turn the murmurers into horses, and make them useful. Quiet ensued.

I took Clarence into my confidence, to a certain degree, and we went to work privately. I told him that this was a sort of miracle that required a trifle of preparation, and that it would be sudden death to ever talk about these preparations to anybody. That made his mouth safe enough. Clandestinely we made a few bushels of first-rate blasting-powder, and I superintended my armorers while they constructed a lightning-rod and some wires. This old stone tower was very massive—and rather ruinous, too, for it was Roman, and four hundred years old. Yes, and handsome, after a rude fashion, and clothed with ivy from base to summit, as with a shirt of scale mail. It stood on a lonely eminence, in good view from the castle, and about half a mile away.

Working by night, we stowed the powder in the tower—dug stones out, on the inside, and buried the powder in the walls themselves, which were fifteen feet thick at the base. We put in a peck at a time, in a dozen places. We could have blown up the Tower of London with these charges. When the thirteenth night was come we put up our lightning-rod, bedded it in one of the batches of powder, and ran wires from it to the other batches. Everybody had shunned that locality from the day of my proclamation, but on the morning of the fourteenth I thought best to warn the people, through the heralds, to keep clear away—a quarter of a mile away. Then added, by command, that at some time during the twenty-four hours I would consummate the miracle, but would first give a brief notice; by flags on the castle towers if in the daytime, by torch-baskets in the same places if at night.

Thunder-showers had been tolerably frequent of late, and I was not much afraid of a failure; still, I shouldn't have cared for a delay of a day or two; I should have explained that I was busy with affairs of state yet, and the people must wait.

Of course, we had a blazing sunny day—almost the first one without a cloud for three weeks; things always happen so. I kept secluded, and watched the weather. Clarence dropped in from time to time and said the public excitement was growing and growing all the time, and the whole country filling up with human masses as far as one could see from the battlements. At last the wind sprang up and a cloud appeared—in the right quarter, too, and just at nightfall. For a little while I watched that distant cloud spread and blacken, then I judged it was time for me to appear. I ordered the torch-baskets to be lit, and Merlin liberated and sent to me. A quarter of an hour later I ascended the parapet and there found the king and the court assembled and gazing off in the darkness toward Merlin's Tower. Already the darkness was so heavy that one could not see far; these people and the old turrets, being partly in deep shadow and partly in the red glow from the great torch-baskets overhead, made a good deal of a picture.

Merlin arrived in a gloomy mood. I said:

"You wanted to burn me alive when I had not done you any harm, and latterly you have been trying to injure my professional reputation. Therefore I am going to call down fire and blow up your tower, but it is only fair to give you a chance; now if you think you can break my enchantments and ward off the fires, step to the bat, it's your innings."

"I can, fair sir, and I will. Doubt it not."

He drew an imaginary circle on the stones of the roof, and burnt a pinch of powder in it, which sent up a small cloud of aromatic smoke, whereat everybody fell back and began to cross themselves and get uncomfortable. Then he began to mutter and make passes in the air with his hands. He worked himself up slowly and gradually into a sort of frenzy, and got to thrashing around with his arms like the sails of a windmill. By this time the storm had about reached us; the gusts of wind were flaring the torches and making the shadows swash about, the first heavy drops of rain were falling, the world abroad was black as pitch, the lightning began to wink fitfully. Of course, my rod would be loading itself now. In fact, things were imminent. So I said:

"You have had time enough. I have given you every advantage, and not interfered. It is plain your magic is weak. It is only fair that I begin now."

I made about three passes in the air, and then there was an awful crash and that old tower leaped into the sky in chunks, along with a vast volcanic fountain of fire that turned night to noonday, and showed a thousand acres of human beings groveling on the ground in a general collapse of consternation. Well, it rained mortar and masonry the rest of the week. This was the report; but probably the facts would have modified it.

It was an effective miracle. The great bothersome temporary population vanished. There were a good many thousand tracks in the mud the next morning, but they were all outward bound. If I had advertised another miracle I couldn't have raised an audience with a sheriff.

Merlin's stock was flat. The king wanted to stop his wages; he even wanted to banish him, but I interfered. I said he would be useful to work the weather, and attend to small matters like that, and I would give him a lift now and them when his poor little parlor magic soured on him. There wasn't a rag of his tower left, but I had the government rebuild it for him, and advised him to take boarders; but he was too high-toned for that. And as for being grateful, he never even said thank you. He was a rather hard lot, take him how you might; but then you couldn't fairly expect a man to be sweet that had been set back so.

The Holy Fountain

The pilgrims were human beings. Otherwise they would have acted differently. They had come a long and difficult journey, and now when the journey was nearly finished, and they learned that the main thing they had come for had ceased to exist, they didn't do as horses or cats or angle-worms would probably have done—turn back and get at something profitable—no, anxious as they had before been to see the miraculous fountain, they were as much as forty times as anxious now to see the place where it had used to be. There is no accounting for human beings.

We made good time; and a couple of hours before sunset we stood upon the high confines of the Valley of Holiness, and our eyes swept it from end to end and noted its features. That is, its large features. These were the three masses of buildings. They were distant and isolated temporalities shrunken to toy constructions in the lonely waste of what seemed a desert—and was. Such a scene is always mournful, it is so impressively still, and looks so steeped in death. But there was a sound here which interrupted the stillness only to add to its mournfulness; this was the faint far sound of tolling bells which floated fitfully to us on the passing breeze, and so faintly, so softly, that we hardly knew whether we heard it with our ears or with our spirits.

We reached the monastery before dark, and there the males were given lodging, but the women were sent over to the nunnery. The bells were close at hand now, and their solemn booming smote upon the ear like a message of doom. A superstitious despair possessed the heart of every monk and published itself in his ghastly face. Everywhere, these black-robed, soft-sandaled, tallow-visaged specters appeared, flitted about and disappeared, noiseless as the creatures of a troubled dream, and as uncanny.

The old abbot's joy to see me was pathetic. Even to tears; but he did the shedding himself. He said:

"Delay not, son, but get to thy saving work. An we bring not the water back again, and soon, we are ruined, and the good work of two hundred years must end. And see thou do it with enchantments that be holy, for the Church will not endure that work in her cause be done by devil's magic."

"When I work, Father, be sure there will be no devil's work connected with it. I shall use no arts that come of the devil, and no elements not created by the hand of God. But is Merlin working strictly on pious lines?"

"Ah, he said he would, my son, he said he would, and took oath to make his promise good."

"Well, in that case, let him proceed."

"But surely you will not sit idle by, but help?"

"It will not answer to mix methods, Father; neither would it be professional courtesy. Two of a trade must not underbid each other. We might as well cut rates and be done with it; it would arrive at that in the end. Merlin has the contract; no other magician can touch it till he throws it up."

"But I will take it from him; it is a terrible emergency and the act is thereby justified. And if it were not so, who will give law to the Church? The Church giveth law to all; and what she wills to do, that she may do, hurt whom it may. I will take it from him; you shall begin upon the moment."

"It may not be, Father. No doubt, as you say, where power is supreme, one can do as one likes and suffer no injury; but we poor magicians are not so situated. Merlin is a very good magician in a small way, and has quite a neat provincial reputation. He is struggling along, doing the best he can, and it would not be etiquette for me to take his job until he himself abandons it."

The abbot's face lighted.

"Ah, that is simple. There are ways to persuade him to abandon it."

"No-no, Father, it skills not, as these people say. If he were persuaded against his will, he would load that well with a malicious enchantment which would balk me until I found out its secret. It might take a month. I could set up a little enchantment of mine which I call the telephone, and he could not find out its secret in a hundred years. Yes, you perceive, he might block me for a month. Would you like to risk a month in a dry time like this?"

"A month! The mere thought of it maketh me to shudder. Have it thy way, my son. But my heart is heavy with this disappointment. Leave me, and let me wear my spirit with weariness and waiting, even as I have done these ten long days, counterfeiting thus the thing that is called rest, the prone body making outward sign of repose where inwardly is none."

Of course, it would have been best, all round, for Merlin to waive etiquette and quit and call it half a day, since he would never be able to start that water, for he was a true magician of the time; which is to say, the big miracles, the ones that gave him his reputation, always had the luck to be performed when nobody but Merlin was present; he couldn't start this well with all this crowd around to see; a crowd was as bad for a magician's miracle in that day as it was for a spiritualist's miracle in mine; there was sure to be some skeptic on hand to turn up the gas at the crucial moment and spoil everything. But I did not want Merlin to retire from the job until I was ready to take hold of it effectively myself; and I could not do that until I got my things from Camelot, and that would take two or three days.

My presence gave the monks hope, and cheered them up a good deal; insomuch that they ate a square meal that night for the first time in ten days. As soon as their stomachs had been properly reinforced with food, their spirits began to rise fast; when the mead began to go round they rose faster. By the time everybody was half-seas over, the holy community was in good shape to make a night of it; so we stayed by the board and put it through on that line. Matters got to be very jolly. Good old questionable stories were told that made the tears run down and cavernous mouths stand wide and the round bellies shake with laughter; and questionable songs were bellowed out in a mighty chorus that drowned the boom of the tolling bells.

At last I ventured a story myself; and vast was the success of it. Not right off, of course, for the native of those islands does not, as a rule, dissolve upon the early applications of a humorous thing; but the fifth time I told it, they began to crack in places; the eighth time I told it, they began to crumble; at the twelfth repetition they fell apart in chunks; and at the fifteenth they disintegrated, and I got a broom and swept them up. This language is figurative. Those islanders—well, they are slow pay at first, in the matter of return for your investment of effort, but in the end they make the pay of all other nations poor and small by contrast.

I was at the well next day betimes. Merlin was there, enchanting away like a beaver, but not raising the moisture. He was not in a pleasant humor; and every time I hinted that perhaps this contract was a shade too hefty for a novice he unlimbered his tongue and cursed like a bishop—French bishop of the Regency days, I mean.

Matters were about as I expected to find them. The "fountain" was an ordinary well, it had been dug in the ordinary way, and stoned up in the ordinary way. There was no miracle about it. Even the lie that had created its reputation was not miraculous; I could have told it myself, with one hand tied behind me. The well was in a dark chamber which stood in the center of a cut-stone chapel, whose walls were hung with pious pictures of a workmanship that would have made a chromo feel good; pictures historically commemorative of curative miracles which had been achieved by the waters when nobody was looking. That is, nobody but angels; they are always on deck when there is a miracle to the fore—so as to get put in the picture, perhaps. Angels are as fond of that as a fire company; look at the old masters.

The well-chamber was dimly lighted by lamps; the water was drawn with a windlass and chain by monks, and poured into troughs which delivered it into stone reservoirs outside in the chapel—when there was water to draw, I mean—and none but monks could enter the well-chamber. I entered it, for I had temporary authority to do so, by courtesy of my professional brother and subordinate. But he hadn't entered it himself. He did everything by incantations; he never worked his intellect. If he had stepped in there and used his eyes, instead of his disordered mind, he could have cured the well by natural means, and then turned it into a miracle in the customary way; but no, he was an old numskull, a magician who believed in his own magic; and no magician can thrive who is handicapped with a superstition like that.

I had an idea that the well had sprung a leak; that some of the wall stones near the bottom had fallen and exposed fissures that allowed the water to escape. I measured the chain—ninety-eight feet. Then I called in a couple of monks, locked the door, took a candle, and made them lower me in the bucket. When the chain was all paid out, the candle confirmed my suspicion; a considerable section of the wall was gone, exposing a good big fissure.

I almost regretted that my theory about the well's trouble was correct, because I had another one that had a showy point or two about it for a miracle. I remembered that in America, many centuries later, when an oil-well ceased to flow, they used to blast it out with a dynamite torpedo. If I should find this well dry and no explanation of it, I could astonish these people most nobly by having a person of no especial value drop a dynamite bomb into it. It was my idea to appoint Merlin. However, it was plain that there was no occasion for the bomb. One cannot have everything the way he would like it. A man has no business to be depressed by a disappointment, anyway; he ought to make up his mind to get even. That is what I did. I said to myself, I am in no hurry, I can wait; that bomb will come good yet. And it did, too.

When I was above ground again, I turned out the monks, and let down a fish-line; the well was a hundred and fifty feet deep, and there was forty-one feet of water in it! I called in a monk and asked:

"How deep is the well?"

"That, sir, I wit not, having never been told."

"How does the water usually stand in it?"

"Near to the top, these two centuries, as the testimony goeth, brought down to us through our predecessors."

It was true—as to recent times at least—for there was witness to it, and better witness than a monk; only about twenty or thirty feet of the chain showed wear and use, the rest of it was unworn and rusty. What had happened when the well gave out that other time? Without doubt some practical person had come along and mended the leak, and then had come up and told the abbot he had discovered by divination that if the sinful bath were destroyed the well would flow again. The leak had befallen again now, and these children would have prayed, and processioned, and tolled their bells for heavenly succor till they all dried up and blew away, and no innocent of them all would ever have thought to drop a fish-line into the well or go down in it and find out what was really the matter. Old habit of mind is one of the toughest things to get away from in the world. It transmits itself like physical form and feature; and for a man, in those days, to have had an idea that his ancestors hadn't had, would have brought him under suspicion of being illegitimate. I said to the monk:

"It is a difficult miracle to restore water in a dry well, but we will try, if my brother Merlin fails. Brother Merlin is a very passable artist, but only in the parlor-magic line, and he may not succeed; in fact, is not likely to succeed. But that should be nothing to his discredit; the man that can do *this* kind of miracle knows enough to keep hotel."

"Hotel? I mind not to have heard—"

"Of hotel? It's what you call hostel. The man that can do this miracle can keep hostel. I can do this miracle; I shall do this miracle; yet I do not try to conceal from you that it is a miracle to tax the occult powers to the last strain."

"None knoweth that truth better than the brotherhood, indeed; for it is of record that aforetime it was parlous difficult and took a year. Natheless, God send you good success, and to that end will we pray."

As a matter of business it was a good idea to get the notion around that the thing was difficult. Many a small thing has been made large by the right kind of advertising. That monk was filled up with the difficulty of this enterprise; he would fill up the others. In two days the solicitude would be booming.

On my way home at noon, I met Sandy. She had been sampling the hermits. I said:

"I would like to do that myself. This is Wednesday. Is there a matinée?"

"A which, please you, sir?"

"Matinée. Do they keep open afternoons?"

"Who?"

"The hermits, of course."

"Keep open?"

"Yes, keep open. Isn't that plain enough? Do they knock off at noon?"

"Knock off?"

"Knock off?—yes, knock off. What is the matter with knock off? I never saw such a dunderhead; can't you understand anything at all? In plain terms, do they shut up shop, draw the game, bank the fires—"

"Shut up shop, draw—"

"There, never mind, let it go; you make me tired. You can't seem to understand the simplest thing."

"I would I might please thee, sir, and it is to me dole and sorrow that I fail, albeit sith I am but a simple damsel and taught of none, being from the cradle unbaptized in those deep waters of learning that do anoint with a sovereignty him that partaketh of that most noble sacrament, investing him with reverend state to the mental eye of the humble mortal, who by bar and lack of that great consecration seeth in his own unlearned estate but a symbol of that other sort of lack and loss which men do publish to the pitying eye with sackcloth trappings whereon the ashes of grief do lie bepowdered and bestrewn, and so, when such shall in the darkness of his mind encounter these golden phrases of high mystery, these shut-up-shops, and draw-the-game, and bank-the-fires, it is but by the grace of God that he burst not for envy of the mind that can beget, and tongue that can deliver so great and mellow-sounding miracles of speech, and if there do ensue confusion in that humbler mind, and failure to divine the meanings of these wonders, then if so be this miscomprehension is not vain but sooth and true, wit ye well it is the very substance of worshipful dear homage and may not lightly be misprized, nor had been, an ye had noted this complexion of mood and mind and understood that that I would I could not, and that I could not I might not, nor yet nor might *nor* could, nor might-not nor could-not, might be by advantage turned to the desired *would*, and so I pray you mercy of my fault, and that ye will of your kindness and your charity forgive it, good my master and most dear lord."

I couldn't make it all out—that is, the details—but I got the general idea; and enough of it, too, to be ashamed. It was not fair to spring those nineteenth-century technicalities upon the untutored infant of the sixth and then rail at her because she couldn't get their drift; and when she was making the honest best drive at it she could, too, and no fault of hers that she couldn't fetch the home plate; and so I apologized. Then we meandered pleasantly away toward the hermit holes in sociable converse together, and better friends than ever.

I was gradually coming to have a mysterious and shuddery reverence for this girl; nowadays whenever she pulled out from the station and got her train fairly started on one of those horizonless transcontinental sentences of hers, it was borne in upon me that I was standing in the awful presence of the Mother of the German Language. I was so impressed with this, that sometimes when she began to empty one of these sentences on me I unconsciously took the very attitude of reverence, and stood uncovered; and if words had been water, I had been drowned, sure. She had exactly the German way; whatever was in her mind to be delivered, whether a mere remark, or a sermon, or a cyclopedia, or the history of a war, she would get it into a single sentence or die. Whenever the literary German dives into a sentence, that is the last you are going to see of him till he emerges on the other side of his Atlantic with his verb in his mouth.

We drifted from hermit to hermit all the afternoon. It was a most strange menagerie. The chief emulation among them seemed to be, to see which could manage to be the uncleanest and most prosperous with vermin. Their manner and attitudes were the last expression of complacent self-righteousness. It was one anchorite's pride to lie naked in the mud and let the insects bite him and blister him unmolested; it was another's to lean against a rock, all day long, conspicuous to the admiration of the throng of pilgrims, and pray; it was another's to go naked and crawl around on all fours; it was another's to drag about with him, year in and year out, eighty pounds of iron; it was another's to never lie down when he slept, but to stand among the thorn-bushes and snore when there were pilgrims around to look; a woman, who had the white hair of age, and no other apparel, was black from crown to heel with forty-seven years of holy abstinence from water. Groups of gazing pilgrims stood around all and every of these strange objects, lost in reverent wonder, and envious of the fleckless sanctity which these pious austerities had won for them from an exacting heaven.

By and by we went to see one of the supremely great ones. He was a mighty celebrity; his fame has penetrated all Christendom; the noble and the renowned journeyed from the remotest lands on the globe to pay him reverence. His stand was in the center of the widest part of the valley; and it took all that space to hold his crowds.

His stand was a pillar sixty feet high, with a broad platform on the top of it. He was now doing what he had been doing every day for twenty years up there—bowing his body ceaselessly and rapidly almost to his feet. It was his way of praying. I timed him with a stop-watch, and he made twelve hundred and forty-four revolutions in twenty-four minutes and forty-six seconds. It seemed a pity to have all this power going to waste. It was one of the most useful motions in mechanics, the pedal movement; so I made a note in my memorandum-book, purposing some day to apply a system of elastic cords to him and run a sewing-machine with it. I afterward carried out that scheme, and got five years' good service out of him; in which time he turned out upward of eighteen thousand first-rate tow-linen shirts, which was ten a day. I worked him Sundays and all; he was going, Sundays, the same as week-days, and it was no use to waste the power. These shirts cost me nothing but just the mere trifle for the materials—I furnished those myself, it would not have been right to make him do that—and they sold like smoke to pilgrims at a dollar and a half apiece, which was the price of fifty cows or a blooded race-horse in Arthurdom. They were regarded as a perfect protection against sin, and advertised as such by my knights everywhere, with the paint-pot and stencil-plate; insomuch that there was not a cliff or a boulder or a dead wall in England but you could read on it at a mile distance:

"Buy the only genuine St. Stylite; patronized by the Nobility. Patent applied for."

There was more money in the business than one knew what to do with. As it extended, I brought out a line of goods suitable for kings, and a nobby thing for duchesses and that sort, with ruffles down the forehatch and the running-gear clewed up with a feather-stitch to leeward and then hauled aft with a back-stay and triced up with a half-turn in the standing rigging forward of the weather-gaskets. Yes, it was a daisy.

But about that time I noticed that the motive power had taken to standing on one leg, and I found that there was something the matter with the other one; so I stocked the business and unloaded, taking Sir Bors de Ganis into camp financially along with certain of his friends; for the works stopped within a year, and the good saint got him to his rest. But he had earned it. I can say that for him.

When I saw him that first time—however, his personal condition will not quite bear description here. You can read it in the *Lives of the Saints*.[1]

Restoration of the Fountain

Saturday noon I went to the well and looked on awhile. Merlin was still burning smoke-powders, and pawing the air, and muttering gibberish as hard as ever, but looking pretty downhearted, for of course he had not started even a perspiration in that well yet. Finally I said:

"How does the thing promise by this time, partner?"

"Behold, I am even now busied with trial of the powerfulest enchantment known to the princes of the occult arts in the lands of the East; an it fail me, naught can avail. Peace, until I finish."

He raised a smoke this time that darkened all the region, and must have made matters uncomfortable for the hermits, for the wind was their way, and it rolled down over their dens in a dense and billowy fog. He poured out volumes of speech to match, and contorted his body and sawed the air with his hands in a most extraordinary way. At the end of twenty minutes he dropped down panting, and about exhausted. Now arrived the abbot and several hundred monks and nuns, and behind them a multitude of pilgrims and a couple of acres of foundlings, all drawn by the prodigious smoke, and all in a grand state of excitement. The abbot inquired anxiously for results. Merlin said:

"If any labor of mortal might break the spell that binds these waters, this which I have but just essayed had done it. It has failed; whereby I do now know that that which I had feared is a truth established; the sign of this failure is, that the most potent spirit known to the magicians of the East, and whose name none may utter and live, has laid his spell upon this well. The mortal does not breathe, nor ever will, who can penetrate the secret of that spell, and without that secret none can break it. The water will flow no more forever, good Father. I have done what man could. Suffer me to go."

Of course this threw the abbot into a good deal of a consternation. He turned to me with the signs of it in his face, and said:

"Ye have heard him. Is it true?"

"Part of it is."

"Not all, then, not all! What part is true?"

"That that spirit with the Russian name has put his spell upon the well."

"God's wownds, then are we ruined!"

"Possibly."

"But not certainly? Ye mean, not certainly?"

"That is it."

"Wherefore, ye also mean that when he saith none can break the spell—"

---

[1]   All the details concerning the hermits, in this chapter, are from Lecky—but greatly modified. This book not being a history but only a tale, the majority of the historian's frank details were too strong for reproduction in it.—EDITOR.

"Yes, when he says that, he says what isn't necessarily true. There are conditions under which an effort to break it may have some chance—that is, some small, some trifling chance—of success."

"The conditions—"

"Oh, they are nothing difficult. Only these: I want the well and the surroundings for the space of half a mile, entirely to myself from sunset today until I remove the ban—and nobody allowed to cross the ground but by my authority."

"Are these all?"

"Yes."

"And you have no fear to try?"

"Oh, none. One may fail, of course; and one may also succeed. One can try, and I am ready to chance it. I have my conditions?"

"These and all others ye may name. I will issue commandment to that effect."

"Wait," said Merlin, with an evil smile. "Ye wit that he that would break this spell must know that spirit's name?"

"Yes, I know his name."

"And wit you also that to know it skills not of itself, but ye must likewise pronounce it? Ha-ha! Knew ye that?"

"Yes, I knew that, too."

"You had that knowledge! Art a fool? Are ye minded to utter that name and die?"

"Utter it? Why certainly. I would utter it if it was Welsh."

"Ye are even a dead man, then; and I go to tell Arthur."

"That's all right. Take your gripsack and get along. The thing for *you* to do is to go home and work the weather, John W. Merlin."

It was a home shot, and it made him wince; for he was the worst weather failure in the kingdom. Whenever he ordered up the danger-signals along the coast there was a week's dead calm, sure, and every time he prophesied fair weather it rained brickbats. But I kept him in the weather bureau right along, to undermine his reputation. However, that shot raised his bile, and instead of starting home to report my death, he said he would remain and enjoy it.

My two experts arrived in the evening, and pretty well fagged, for they had traveled double tides. They had pack-mules along, and had brought everything I needed—tools, pump, lead pipe, Greek fire, sheaves of big rockets, roman candles, colored fire sprays, electric apparatus, and a lot of sundries—everything necessary for the stateliest kind of a miracle. They got their supper and a nap, and about midnight we sallied out through a solitude so wholly vacant and complete that it quite overpassed the required conditions. We took possession of the well and its surroundings. My boys were experts in all sorts of things, from the stoning-up of a well to the constructing of a mathematical instrument. An hour before sunrise we had that leak mended in shipshape fashion, and the water began to rise. Then we stowed our fireworks in the chapel, locked up the place, and went home to bed.

Before the noon mass was over, we were at the well again; for there was a deal to do yet, and I was determined to spring the miracle before midnight,

for business reasons: for whereas a miracle worked for the Church on a week-
day is worth a good deal, it is worth six times as much if you get it in on a
Sunday. In nine hours the water had risen to its customary level; that is to say,
it was within twenty-three feet of the top. We put in a little iron pump, one
of the first turned out by my works near the capital; we bored into a stone
reservoir which stood against the outer wall of the well-chamber and inserted
a section of lead pipe that was long enough to reach to the door of the chapel
and project beyond the threshold, where the gushing water would be visible
to the two hundred and fifty acres of people I was intending should be
present on the flat plain in front of this little holy hillock at the proper time.

   We knocked the head out of an empty hogshead and hoisted this
hogshead to the flat roof of the chapel, where we clamped it down fast,
poured in gunpowder till it lay loosely an inch deep on the bottom, then we
stood up rockets in the hogshead as thick as they could loosely stand, all the
different breeds of rockets there are; and they made a portly and imposing
sheaf, I can tell you. We grounded the wire of pocket electrical battery in that
powder, we placed a whole magazine of Greek fire on each corner of the
roof—blue on one corner, green on another, red on another, and purple on
the last—and grounded a wire in each.

   About two hundred yards off, in the flat, we built a pen of scantlings, about
four feet high, and laid planks on it, and so made a platform. We covered it
with swell tapestries borrowed for the occasion, and topped it off with the
abbot's own throne. When you are going to do a miracle for an ignorant race,
you want to get in every detail that will count; you want to make all the
properties impressive to the public eye; you want to make matters comfortable
for your head guest; then you can turn yourself loose and play your effects
for all they are worth. I know the value of these things, for I know human
nature. You can't throw too much style into a miracle. It costs trouble, and
work, and sometimes money; but it pays in the end. Well, we brought the
wires to the ground at the chapel, and then brought them under the ground
to the platform, and hid the batteries there. We put a rope fence a hundred
feet square around the platform to keep off the common multitude, and that
finished the work. My idea was, doors open at ten-thirty, performance to
begin at eleven-twenty-five sharp. I wished I could charge admission, but of
course that wouldn't answer. I instructed my boys to be in the chapel as early
as ten, before anybody was around, and be ready to man the pumps at the
proper time, and make the fur fly. Then we went home to supper.

   The news of the disaster to the well had traveled far by this time; and now
for two or three days a steady avalanche of people had been pouring into the
valley. The lower end of the valley was become one huge camp; we should
have a good house, no question about that. Criers went the rounds early in
the evening and announced the coming attempt, which put every pulse up
to fever-heat. They gave notice that the abbot and his official suite would
move in state and occupy the platform at ten-thirty, up to which time all the
region which was under my ban must be clear; the bells would then cease
from tolling, and this sign should be permission to the multitudes to close in
and take their places.

   I was at the platform and all ready to do the honors when the abbot's solemn procession hove in sight—which it did not do till it was nearly to the rope fence, because it was a starless black night and no torches permitted. With it came Merlin, and took a front seat on the platform; he was as good as his word for once. One could not see the multitudes banked together beyond the ban, but they were there, just the same. The moment the bells stopped, those banked masses broke and poured over the line like a vast black wave, and for as much as a half-hour it continued to flow, and then it solidified itself, and you could have walked upon a pavement of human heads to—well, miles.

We had a solemn stage-wait, now, for about twenty minutes—a thing I had counted on for effect; it is always good to let your audience have a chance to work up its expectancy. At length, out of the silence a noble Latin chant— men's voices—broke and swelled up and rolled away into the night, a majestic tide of melody. I had put that up, too, and it was one of the best effects I ever invented. When it was finished I stood up on the platform and extended my hands abroad, for two minutes, with my face uplifted—that always produces a dead hush—and then slowly pronounced this ghastly word with a kind of awfulness which caused hundreds to tremble, and many women to faint:

Constantinopolitanischerdudelsackspfeifenmachersgesellschafft!"

Just as I was moaning out the closing hunks of that word, I touched off one of my electric connections, and all that murky world of people stood revealed in a hideous blue glare! It was immense—that effect! Lots of people shrieked, women curled up and quit in every direction, foundlings collapsed by platoons. The abbot and the monks crossed themselves nimbly and their lips fluttered with agitated prayers. Merlin held his grip, but he was astonished clear down to his corns; he had never seen anything to begin with that, before. Now was the time to pile in the effects. I lifted my hands and groaned out this word—as it were in agony:

**"Nihilistendynamitttheaterkaestchenssprengungs-
attentaetsversuchungen!"**

—and turned on the red fire! You should have heard that Atlantic of people moan and howl when that crimson hell joined the blue! After sixty seconds I shouted:

**"Transvaaltruppentropentransporttrampeltthier-
treibertrauungstthraenenrragoedie!"**

—and lit up the green fire! After waiting only forty seconds this time, I spread my arms abroad and thundered out the devastating syllables of this word of words:

**"Mekkamuselmannenmassenmenchenmoerder-
mohrenmuttermarmormonumentenmacher!"**

—and whirled on the purple glare! There they were, all going at once, red, blue, green, purple!—four furious volcanoes pouring vast clouds of radiant smoke aloft, and spreading a blinding rainbowed noonday to the furthest of that valley. In the distance one could see that fellow on the pillar standing rigid against the background of sky, his seesaw stopped for the first time in twenty years. I knew the boys were at the pump now and ready. So I said to the abbot:

"The time is come, Father. I am about to pronounce the dread name and command the spell to dissolve. You want to brace up, and take hold of something." Then I shouted to the people: "Behold, in another minute the spell will be broken, or no mortal can break it. If it break, all will know it, for you will see the sacred water gush from the chapel door!"

I stood a few moments, to let the hearers have a chance to spread my announcement to those who couldn't hear, and so convey it to the furthest ranks; then I made a grand exhibition of extra posturing and gesturing, and shouted:

"Lo, I command the fell spirit that possesses the holy fountain to now disgorge into the skies all the infernal fires that still remain in him, and straightway dissolve his spell and flee hence to the pit, there to lie bound a thousand years. By his own dread name I command it—BGWJJILLIGKKK!"

Then I touched off the hogshead of rockets, and a vast fountain of dazzling lances of fire vomited itself toward the zenith with a hissing rush, and burst in mid-sky into a storm of flashing jewels! One mighty groan of terror started up from the massed people—then suddenly broke into a wild hosannah of joy—for there, fair and plain in the uncanny glare, they saw the freed water leaping forth! The old abbot could not speak a word, for tears and the chokings in his throat; without utterance of any sort, he folded me in his arms and mashed me. It was more eloquent than speech. And harder to get over, too, in a country where there were really no doctors that were worth a damaged nickel.

You should have seen those acres of people throw themselves down in that water and kiss it, kiss it, and pet it, and fondle it, and talk to it as if it were alive, and welcome it back with the dear names they gave their darlings, just as if it had been a friend who was long gone away and lost, and was come home again. Yes, it was pretty to see, and made me think more of them than I had done before.

I sent Merlin home on a shutter. He had caved in and gone down like a landslide when I pronounced that fearful name, and had never come to since. He never had heard that name before—neither had I—but to him it was the right one. Any jumble would have been the right one. He admitted, afterward, that that spirit's own mother could not have pronounced that name better than I did. He never could understand how I survived it, and I didn't tell him. It is only young magicians that give away a secret like that. Merlin spent three months working enchantments to try to find out the deep trick of how to pronounce that name and outlive it. But he didn't arrive.

When I started to the chapel, the populace uncovered and fell back reverently to make a wide way for me, as if I had been some kind of superior being—and I was. I was aware of that. I took along a night shift of monks, and taught them the mystery of the pump, and set them to work, for it was plain that a good part of the people out there were going to sit up with the water all night; consequently it was but right that they should have all they wanted of it. To those monks that pump was a good deal of a miracle itself, and they were full of wonder over it; and of admiration, too, of the exceeding effectiveness of its performance.

It was a great night, an immense night. There was reputation in it. I could hardly get to sleep for glorying over it.

The Yankee's Fight with the Knights

Home again, at Camelot. A morning or two later I found the paper, damp from the press, by my plate at the breakfast-table. I turned to the advertising columns, knowing I should find something of personal interest to me there. It was this:

DE PAR LE ROI.

ẍnow that the great lord and illustrious Kni8ht, ЅIR SAGRAMOR LE
DESIẍOUS naving condescended to
meet the King's Minister, Hank Morgan, the which is surnamed The Boss,
for satisfgction of offence anciently given,
these wilL engage ín the lists by
Camelot about the fourth hour of the
morning of the sixteenth day of this
next succeeding month. The bɐttle
wiil be à l outrance, sith the said offence
was of a deadly sort, admitting of no
comPosition.

DE PAR LE ẍOẍ

[*At a tournament three or four years previously, Sir Sagramor had taken offense from a chance remark of the Yankee's, and challenged him to a duel to take place after the knight had returned from "holy grailing."*]

Clarence's editorial reference to this affair was to this effect:

It will be observed, by a gl7nce at our advertising columns, that the community is to be favored with a treat of unusual interest in the tournament line. The names of the artists are warrant of good entertainment. The box-office will be open at noon of the 13th; admission 3 cents, reserved seats 5; proceeds to go to the hospital fund The royal pair and all the Court will be present. With these exceptions, and the press and the clergy, the free list is strictly suspended. Parties are hereby warned against buying tickets of speculators; they will not be good at the door. Everybody knows and likes The Boss, everybody knows and likes Sir Sag.; come, let us give the lads a good send-off. ReMember, the proceeds go to a great and free charity, and one whose broad benevolence stretches out its helping hand, warm with the blood of a loving heart, to all that suffer, regardless of race, creed, condition or color—the only charity yet established in the earth which has no politico-religious stop-cock on its compassion, but says Here flows the stream; let *all* come and drink! Turn out, all hands! fetch along your doughnuts and your gum-drops and have a good time. Pie for sale on the grounds, and rocks to crack it with; also circus-lemonade—three drops of lime juice to a barrel of water.

N. B. *This is the first tournament under the new law, which allows each combatant to use any weapon he may prefer.* You want to make a note of that.

Up to the day set, there was no talk in all Britain of anything but this combat. All other topics sank into insignificance and passed out of men's thoughts and interest. It was not because a tournament was a great matter; it was not because Sir Sagramor had found the Holy Grail, for he had not, but had failed; it was not because the second (official) personage in the kingdom was one of the duelists; no, all these features were commonplace. Yet there was abundant reason for the extraordinary interest which this coming fight was creating. It was born of the fact that all the nation knew that this was not to be a duel between mere men, so to speak, but a duel between two mighty magicians; a duel not of muscle but of mind, not of human skill but of super-human art and craft; a final struggle for supremacy between the two master enchanters of the age. It was realized that the most prodigious achievements of the most renowned knights could not be worthy of comparison with a spectacle like this; they could be but child's play, contrasted with this mysterious and awful battle of the gods. Yes, all the world knew it was going to be in reality a duel between Merlin and me, a measuring of his magic powers against mine. It was known that Merlin had been busy whole days and nights together, imbuing Sir Sagramor's arms and armor with supernal powers of offense and defense, and that he had procured for him from the spirits of the air a fleecy veil which would render the wearer invisible to his antagonist while still visible to other men. Against Sir Sagramor, so weaponed and protected, a thousand knights could accomplish nothing; against him no known enchantments could prevail. These facts were sure; regarding them there was no doubt, no reason for doubt. There was but one question: might there be still other enchantments, *unknown* to Merlin, which could render Sir Sagramor's veil transparent to me, and make his enchanted mail vulnerable to my weapons? This was the one thing to be decided in the lists. Until then the world must remain in suspense.

So the world thought there was a vast matter at stake here, and the world was right, but it was not the one they had in their minds. No, a far vaster one was upon the cast of this die: *the life of knight-errantry.* I was a champion, it was true, but not the champion of the frivolous black arts; I was the champion of hard unsentimental common sense and reason. I was entering the lists to either destroy knight-errantry or be its victim.

Vast as the show-grounds were, there were no vacant spaces in them outside of the lists, at ten o'clock on the morning of the 16th. The mammoth grand-stand was clothed in flags, streamers, and rich tapestries, and packed with several acres of small-fry tributary kings, their suites, and the British aristocracy; with our own royal gang in the chief place, and each and every individual a flashing prism of gaudy silks and velvets—well, I never saw anything to begin with it but a fight between an Upper Mississippi sunset and the aurora borealis. The huge camp of beflagged and gay-colored tents at one end of the lists, with a stiff-standing sentinel at every door and a shining shield hanging by him for challenge, was another fine sight. You see, every knight was there who had any ambition or any caste feeling; for my feeling toward their order was not much of a secret, and so here was their chance. If I won my fight with Sir Sagramor, others would have the right to call me out as long as I might be willing to respond.

Down at our end there were but two tents; one for me, and another for my servants. At the appointed hour the king made a sign, and the heralds, in their tabards, appeared and made proclamation, naming the combatants and stating the cause of quarrel. There was a pause, then a ringing bugle-blast, which was the signal for us to come forth. All the multitude caught their breath, and an eager curiosity flashed into every face.

Out from his tent rode great Sir Sagramor, an imposing tower of iron, stately and rigid, his huge spear standing upright in its socket and grasped in his strong hand, his grand horse's face and breast cased in steel, his body clothed in rich trappings that almost dragged the ground—oh, a most noble picture. A great shout went up, of welcome and admiration.

And then out I came. But I didn't get any shout. There was a wondering and eloquent silence for a moment, then a great wave of laughter began to sweep along that human sea, but a warning bugle-blast cut its career short. I was in the simplest and comfortablest of gymnast costumes—flesh-colored tights from neck to heel, with blue silk puffings about my loins, and bareheaded. My horse was not above medium size, but he was alert, slender-limbed, muscled with watch-springs, and just a greyhound to go. He was a beauty, glossy as silk, and naked as he was when he was born, except for bridle and ranger-saddle.

The iron tower and the gorgeous bed-quilt came cumbrously but gracefully pirouetting down the lists, and we tripped lightly up to meet them. We halted; the tower saluted, I responded; then we wheeled and rode side by side to the grand-stand and faced our king and queen, to whom we made obeisance. The queen exclaimed:

"Alack, Sir Boss, wilt fight naked, and without lance or sword or—"

But the king checked her and made her understand, with a polite phrase or two, that this was none of her business. The bugles rang again; and we separated and rode to the ends of the lists, and took position. Now old Merlin stepped into view and cast a dainty web of gossamer threads over Sir Sagramor which turned him into Hamlet's ghost; the king made a sign, the bugles blew, Sir Sagramor laid his great lance in rest, and the next moment here he came thundering down the course with his veil flying out behind, and I went whistling through the air like an arrow to meet him—cocking my ear the while, as if noting the invisible knight's position and progress by hearing, not sight. A chorus of encouraging shouts burst out for him, and one brave voice flung out a heartening word for me—said:

"Go it, slim Jim!"

It was an even bet that Clarence had procured that favor for me—and furnished the language, too. When that formidable lance-point was within a yard and a half of my breast I twitched my horse aside without an effort, and the big knight swept by, scoring a blank. I got plenty of applause that time. We turned, braced up, and down we came again. Another blank for the knight, a roar of applause for me. This same thing was repeated once more; and it fetched such a whirlwind of applause that Sir Sagramor lost his temper, and at once changed his tactics and set himself the task of chasing me down.

Why, he hadn't any show in the world at that; it was a game of tag, with all the advantage on my side; I whirled out of his path with ease whenever I chose, and once I slapped him on the back as I went to the rear. Finally I took the chase into my own hands; and after that, turn, or twist, or do what he would, he was never able to get behind me again; he found himself always in front at the end of his manoeuver. So he gave up that business and retired to his end of the lists. His temper was clear gone now, and he forgot himself and flung an insult at me which disposed of mine. I slipped my lasso from the horn of my saddle, and grasped the coil in my right hand. This time you should have seen him come!—it was a business trip, sure; by his gait there was blood in his eye. I was sitting my horse at ease, and swinging the great loop of my lasso in wide circles about my head; the moment he was under way, I started for him; when the space between us had narrowed to forty feet, I sent the snaky spirals of the rope a-cleaving through the air, then darted aside and faced about and brought my trained animal to a halt with all his feet braced under him for a surge. The next moment the rope sprang taut and yanked Sir Sagramor out of the saddle! Great Scott, but there was a sensation!

Unquestionably, the popular thing in this world is novelty. These people had never seen anything of that cowboy business before, and it carried them clear off their feet with delight. From all around and everywhere, the shout went up:

"Encore! encore!"

I wondered where they got the word, but there was no time to cipher on philological matters, because the whole knight-errantry hive was just humming now, and my prospect for trade couldn't have been better. The moment my lasso was released and Sir Sagramor had been assisted to his tent, I hauled in the slack, took my station and began to swing my loop around my head again. I was sure to have use for it as soon as they could elect a successor for Sir Sagramor, and that couldn't take long where there were so many hungry candidates. Indeed, they elected one straight off—Sir Hervis de Revel.

Bzz! Here he came, like a house afire; I dodged: he passed like a flash, with my horse-hair coils settling around his neck; a second or so later, *fst!* his saddle was empty.

I got another encore; and another, and another, and still another. When I had snaked five men out, things began to look serious to the ironclads, and they stopped and consulted together. As a result, they decided that it was time to waive etiquette and send their greatest and best against me. To the astonishment of that little world, I lassoed Sir Lamorak de Galis, and after him Sir Galahad. So you see there was simply nothing to be done now, but play their right bower—bring out the superbest of the superb, the mightiest of the mighty, the great Sir Launcelot himself!

A proud moment for me? I should think so. Yonder was Arthur, King of Britain; yonder was Guinever; yes, and whole tribes of little provincial kings and kinglets; and in the tented camp yonder, renowned knights from many lands; and likewise the selectest body known to chivalry, the Knights of the

Table Round, the most illustrious in Christendom; and biggest fact of all, the very sun of their shining system was yonder couching his lance, the focal point of forty thousand adoring eyes; and all by myself, here was I laying for him. Across my mind flitted the dear image of a certain hello-girl of West Hartford, and I wished she could see me now. In that moment, down came the Invincible, with the rush of a whirlwind—the courtly world rose to its feet and bent forward—the fateful coils went circling through the air, and before you could wink I was towing Sir Launcelot across the field on his back, and kissing my hand to the storm of waving kerchiefs and the thunder-crash of applause that greeted me!

Said I to myself, as I coiled my lariat and hung it on my saddle-horn, and sat there drunk with glory, "The victory is perfect—no other will venture against me—knight-errantry is dead." Now imagine my astonishment—and everybody else's, too—to hear the peculiar bugle-call which announces that another competitor is about to enter the lists! There was a mystery here: I couldn't account for this thing. Next, I noticed Merlin gliding away from me; and then I noticed that my lasso was gone! The old sleight-of-hand expert had stolen it, sure, and slipped it under his robe.

The bugle blew again. I looked, and down came Sagramor riding again, with his dust brushed off and his veil nicely rearranged. I trotted up to meet him, and pretended to find him by the sound of his horse's hoofs. He said:

"Thou'rt quick of ear, but it will not save thee from this!" and he touched the hilt of his great sword. "An ye are not able to see it, because of the influence of the veil, know that it is no cumbrous lance, but a sword—and I ween ye will not be able to avoid it."

His visor was up; there was death in his smile. I should never be able to dodge his sword, that was plain. Somebody was going to die this time. If he got the drop on me, I could name the corpse. We rode forward together, and saluted the royalties. This time the king was disturbed. He said:

"Where is thy strange weapon?"

"It is stolen, sire."

"Hast another at hand?"

"No, sire, I brought only the one."

Then Merlin mixed in:

"He brought but the one because there was but the one to bring. There exists none other but that one. It belongeth to the king of the Demons of the Sea. This man is a pretender, and ignorant; else he had known that that weapon can be used in but eight bouts only, and then it vanisheth away to its home under the sea."

"Then is he weaponless," said the king. "Sir Sagramor, ye will grant him leave to borrow."

"And I will lend!" said Sir Launcelot, limping up. "He is as brave a knight of his hands as any that be on live, and he shall have mine."

He put his hand on his sword to draw it, but Sir Sagramor said:

"Stay, it may not be. He shall fight with his own weapons; it was his privilege to choose them and bring them. If he has erred, on his head be it."

"Knight!" said the king. "Thou'rt overwrought with passion; it disorders thy mind. Wouldst kill a naked man?"

"An he do it, he shall answer it to me," said Sir Launcelot.

"I will answer it to any he that desireth!" retorted Sir Sagramor hotly.

Merlin broke in, rubbing his hands and smiling his low-downest smile of malicious gratification:

"'Tis well said, right well said! And 'tis enough of parleying, let my lord the king deliver the battle signal."

The king had to yield. The bugle made proclamation, and we turned apart and rode to our stations. There we stood, a hundred yards apart, facing each other, rigid and motionless, like horsed statues. And so we remained, in a soundless hush, as much as a full minute, everybody gazing, nobody stirring. It seemed as if the king could not take heart to give the signal. But at last he lifted his hand, the clear note of a bugle followed, Sir Sagramor's long blade described a flashing curve in the air, and it was superb to see him come. I sat still. On he came. I did not move. People got so excited that they shouted to me:

"Fly, fly! Save thyself! This is murther!"

I never budged so much as an inch till that thundering apparition had got within fifteen paces of me; then I snatched a dragoon revolver out of my holster, there was a flash and a roar, and the revolver was back in the holster before anybody could tell what had happened.

Here was a riderless horse plunging by, and yonder lay Sir Sagramor, stone dead.

The people that ran to him were stricken dumb to find that the life was actually gone out of the man and no reason for it visible, no hurt upon his body, nothing like a wound. There was a hole through the breast of his chain-mail, but they attached no importance to a little thing like that; and as a bullet-wound there produces but little blood, none came in sight because of the clothing and swaddlings under the armor. The body was dragged over to let the king and the swells look down upon it. They were stupefied with astonishment, naturally. I was requested to come and explain the miracle. But I remained in my tracks, like a statue, and said:

"If it is a command, I will come, but my lord the king knows that I am where the laws of combat require me to remain while any desire to come against me."

I waited. Nobody challenged. Then I said:

"If there are any who doubt that this field is well and fairly won, I do not wait for them to challenge me, I challenge them."

"It is a gallant offer," said the king, "and well beseems you. Whom will you name first?"

"I name none, I challenge all! Here I stand, and dare the chivalry of England to come against me—not by individuals, but in mass!"

"What!" shouted a score of knights.

"You have heard the challenge. Take it, or I proclaim you recreant knights and vanquished, every one!"

It was a "bluff," you know. At such a time it is sound judgment to put on a bold face and play your hand for a hundred times what it is worth; forty-nine times out of fifty nobody dares to "call," and you rake in the chips. But just this once—well, things looked squally! In just no time, five hundred knights were scrambling into their saddles, and before you could wink a widely scattering drove were under way and clattering down upon me. I snatched both revolvers from the holsters and began to measure distances and calculate chances.

Bang! One saddle empty. Bang! another one. Bang—bang, and I bagged two. Well, it was nip and tuck with us, and I knew it. If I spent the eleventh shot without convincing these people, the twelfth man would kill me, sure. And so I never did feel so happy as I did when my ninth downed its man and I detected the wavering in the crowd which is premonitory of panic. An instant lost now could knock out my last chance. But I didn't lose it. I raised both revolvers and pointed them—the halted host stood their ground just about one good square moment, then broke and fled.

The day was mine. Knight-errantry was a doomed institution. The march of civilization was begun. How did I feel? Ah, you never could imagine it.

And Brer Merlin? His stock was flat again. Somehow, every time the magic of fol-de-rol tried conclusions with the magic of science, the magic of fol-de-rol got left.

[*After King Arthur dies in battle against Mordred, the Church seizes control of the country. The Yankee responds by declaring a republic and fortifying Merlin's cave to meet the Church's attack. His technological preparations annihilate what is left of Arthur's chivalry in the ensuing seige. The victory leaves him and his cadets masters of Britain, and at the same time dooms them. In despair, the Yankee leaves off the narrative he has been writing.*]

A Postscript by Clarence

I, Clarence, must write it for him. He proposed that we two go out and see if any help could be accorded the wounded. I was strenuous against the project. I said that if there were many, we could do but little for them; and it would not be wise for us to trust ourselves among them, anyway. But he could seldom be turned from a purpose once formed; so we shut off the electric current from the fences, took an escort along, climbed over the inclosing ramparts of dead knights, and moved out upon the field. The first wounded man who appealed for help was sitting with his back against a dead comrade. When The Boss bent over him and spoke to him, the man recognized him and stabbed him. That knight was Sir Meliagraunce, as I found out by tearing off his helmet. He will not ask for help any more.

We carried the Boss to the cave and gave his wound, which was not very serious, the best care we could. In this service we had the help of Merlin, though we did not know it. He was disguised as a woman, and appeared to be a simple old peasant goodwife. In this disguise, with brown-stained face and smooth-shaven, he had appeared a few days after the Boss was hurt, and offered to cook for us, saying her people had gone off to join certain new camps which the enemy were forming, and that she was starving. The Boss had been getting along very well, and had amused himself with finishing up his record.

We were glad to have this woman, for we were short-handed. We were in a trap, you see—a trap of our own making. If we stayed where we were, our dead would kill us; if we moved out of our defenses, we should no longer be invincible. We had conquered; in turn we were conquered. The Boss recognized this; we all recognized it. If we could go to one of those new camps and patch up some kind of terms with the enemy—yes, but the Boss could not go, and neither could I, for I was among the first that were made sick by the poisonous air bred by those dead thousands. Others were taken down, and still others. To-morrow—

To-morrow. It is here. And with it the end. About midnight I awoke, and saw that hag making curious passes in the air about the Boss's head and face, and wondered what it meant. Everybody but the dynamo-watch lay steeped in sleep; there was no sound. The woman ceased from her mysterious foolery, and started tiptoeing toward the door. I called out:

"Stop! What have you been doing?"

She halted, and said with an accent of malicious satisfaction:

"Ye were conquerors; ye are conquered! These others are perishing—you also. Ye shall all die in this place—every one—except *him.* He sleepeth now—and shall sleep thirteen centuries. I am Merlin!"

Then such a delirium of silly laughter overtook him that he reeled about like a drunken man, and presently fetched up against one of our wires. His mouth is spread open yet; apparently he is still laughing. I suppose the face will retain that petrified laugh until the corpse turns to dust.

The Boss has never stirred—sleeps like a stone. If he does not wake to-day we shall understand what kind of a sleep it is, and his body will then be borne to a place in one of the remote recesses of the cave where none will ever find it to desecrate it. As for the rest of us—well, it is agreed that if any one of us ever escapes alive from this place, he will write the fact here, and loyally hide this Manuscript with the Boss, our dear good chief, whose property it is, be he alive or dead.

VI.

MERLIN IN
THE TWENTIETH CENTURY

chapter 11

EDWIN ARLINGTON ROBINSON:
MERLIN

A V E R Y different American response to Tennyson's *Idylls* than Twain's *A Connecticut Yankee* was developed by Edward Arlington Robinson's three Arthurian poems *Merlin* (1917), *Lancelot* (1920), and *Tristram* (1927). Most early reviewers tended to dislike the first two, which Robinson intended to be read together and considered among his finest poems, but the third received a Pulitzer Prize—perhaps in tardy recognition of his achievement. Robinson's portrayal of Merlin's self-chosen exile in Broceliande against the backdrop of Camelot's inevitable fall has none of Twain's slapstick. Neither does it mock the abuses of monarchy and organized religion; it was written in an altogether darker time, two years into the First World War, when all of western society seemed embroiled in an endless bloodletting.

Merlin also departs firmly from the romance conventions of knightly combat and supernatural (or technological) marvels. Where Twain deliberately contrasted the medieval and the modern, Robinson is thoroughly modern: his Merlin is not a worker of magic, an engineer or a charlatan, but an exceptionally powerful and intelligent king-maker whose sole "supernatural" characteristic is his ability to see into the future. Nor is Vivian an enchantress—just an enchantingly beautiful, complex, and intelligent woman. Though the critics all marked this "realistic" characterization, only Stark Young found Vivian better portrayed here than anywhere else in literature (*The New Republic*, September 29, 1917: 250–251).

The poem is divided into seven sections: I–III concern Merlin's brief return to Camelot at Arthur's request after a ten-year absence in Broceliande, IV–V relate this idyllic sojourn with Vivian, VI describes his increasing unease during two years back in Broceliande, and VII depicts his final visit to the "wild and final rain on Camelot," after which he leaves both societies, accompanied only by Dagonet the fool. Nathan Comfort Starr accurately characterizes the generally somber narrative by Robinson's thematic "preoccupation with men faced by agonizing difficulties, losses of direction, failures of will, and paralyzing disillusionments" (p. 110).

Many touches in *Merlin* transform and interpret the *Idylls of the King*. The brooding storm that charges the atmosphere of "Merlin and Vivien" and breaks with the wizard's surrender also hovers over *Merlin*, together with the mage's recurring intimations of Camelot's destruction. Broceliande parallels Eden in both poems, providing a nature-culture contrast with Camelot. Robinson's Vivian shares her counterpart's Eve-like yet reptilian characteristics; she claims to be "cruel and cold," to like frogs and snakes, and to "love no man/ As I have seen him yet." She is self-willed, quick at repartee, and adjusts instantaneously, like Tennyson's "harlot," to Merlin's moods; both poems devote much space to their conversation.

The central theme is also similar. The *Idylls*'s dying Arthur remarks as his barge departs for Avalon, "The old order changeth, yielding place to new,/ And God fulfils himself in many ways,/ Lest one good custom should corrupt the world" ("The Passing of Arthur" ll. 408–410). In view of the slaughter taking place in Europe as Robinson wrote, this theme was especially poignant. In *Merlin* the mage finds that "his cold angel's name/ Was Change" and that despite his effort to live out of time in Broceliande, this angel must overtake him even as it does King Arthur and his kingdom. Similarly, the Victorian cultural values and social order had been stricken by the assassination at Sarajevo and pulverized by the guns of the Somme. The fate that Merlin sees looming over Camelot, but is powerless to prevent, is equally catastrophic for the chivalric and Edwardian societies.

It is not surprising, therefore, that Robinson's poem lacks Tennyson's moral certainty; the author himself called it both "immoral" and "entirely moral" (Davis, p. 92). The *Idylls*'s wizard perceives little conflict between love and duty. He tolerates Vivien because like Arthur he is too good to conceive the depth of her hatred; considering her a child, he also underestimates her sexual power and cunning. When his melancholy comes, "And he walked with dreams and darkness, and he found/ A doom that ever poised itself to fall," it does not seem that he truly understands why he must go to Broceliande. However, *Merlin*'s mage knows very well; he locates the cause in "two pits/ Of living sin,—so founded by the will/ Of one wise counsellor who loved the king." Because Tennyson's wizard lacks moral ambiguity, some readers find his surrender to Vivien unconvincing; yet this very lack, disguising the suppressed sensuality of Victorian culture, makes her conquest of him inevitable. Robinson's Merlin goes to Broceliande with his eyes open, knowing and accepting that it offers luxury and sensation, that his beard will be shorn like Samson's, and that beyond this he cannot yet see.

While Tennyson's Vivien despises life and uses her talents only to connive and destroy, Robinson's woman is more complexly motivated. She "hates" Arthur and Camelot only because they compete with her for Merlin, whom she truly loves. Possessive yet wise and compassionate, she gives Merlin his freedom within her forest and even the freedom to leave it. Her manipulation of him comes not from the ulterior motive of destroying Camelot, but from the conventional limitations placed upon women, which barred them from most occupations and left relationships with powerful men as the primary means of influence. She has spent most of her life waiting for

Merlin, "Whose love and service were to be her school,/ Her triumph, and her history." Vivian is a potentially emancipated woman in a society without female suffrage; Broceliande represents her isolation as well as her sensuality and mystery.

By leaving out the supernatural derring-do and making his characters more morally and psychologically complex, Robinson demythologizes the story of Merlin's imprisonment. In fact that "imprisonment" is metaphorical — both a private joke between Merlin and Vivian and a rationalization in Camelot for Merlin's apparent abandonment of Arthur. *Merlin* has been interpreted in terms of the conflict between love (for Vivian) and duty (to Arthur), built upon the conflict in medieval romance between *fine amour* and feudal loyalty. It has also been seen as an examination of "the failure of reason to sustain what it has created" (Thompson, p. 237). If both interpretations are at least partly correct, it is worth noting that Merlin goes to Broceliande *because* he "saw too far" and also that he does not stay there. He is no more captive in Vivian's kingdom than in Arthur's. Although he is powerless to save the Camelot he created or to defeat time with Vivian's love, Merlin does foresee the "two fires that are to light the world." That future redemption is to come from "the torch/ Of woman and the light that Galahad found"—the fires that have fulfilled and destroyed his world—is an insight worthy of the prophet and servant of change, and one that defeats simplistic interpretation.

Robinson (1869–1935) was born in Maine and studied at Harvard between 1891 and 1893. He found his vocation as writer early in life, and held several jobs briefly before Theodore Roosevelt appointed him to the Customs Office in New York in 1905—a sinecure he resigned just four years later. Although he is considered one of the finest American poets, his long poems earned more critical than popular appreciation. Three of his books received Pulitzers: *Collected Poems* in 1922, *The Man Who Died Twice* in 1924, and *Tristram* in 1927. Like his other long poems, *Merlin* is written in a plain and flexible blank-verse style based on iambic pentameter, which allowed him to develop complex thoughts without the restrictions usually imposed by traditional rhyme and metrical schemes.

Bibliographic note: In addition to Tennyson and (of course) Malory, Robinson's chief source for *Merlin* was S. Humphreys Gurteen's *The Arthurian Epic* (1895). By summarizing the Vulgate *Merlin*, Gurteen provided the poet with a far more sympathetic and idyllic love interest for Merlin than either of the first two sources. *Merlin* was begun in the spring of 1916, when Robinson borrowed Gurteen's book, and finished in November of that year. It was published by Macmillan in March 1917, and included in *Collected Poems of Edwin Arlington Robinson* (New York: Macmillan, 1921, 1927, 1929, and 1937). Among the most informative essays dealing with the poem are Charles T. Davis, "Robinson's Road to Camelot," pp. 88–105, and Nathan Comfort Starr, "The Transformation of Merlin," pp. 106–119, in *Edwin Arlington Robinson: Centenary Essays*, ed. Ellsworth Barnard (Athens: University of Georgia Press, 1969); W.R. Thompson, "Broceliande: E.A.

Robinson's Palace of Art," *New England Quarterly* 43 (June 1970): 231–249;
and three by Laurence Perrine: "Contemporary References of Robinson's
Arthurian Poems," *Twentieth Century Literature* 8 (April 1962): 74–82; "The
Sources of Robinson's *Merlin*," *American Literature* 44 (May 1972): 313–321;
and "Tennyson and Robinson: Legalistic Moralism vs. Situation Ethics,"
Colby Library Quarterly 8 (December 1968): 416–434.

Merlin

I

"Gawaine, Gawaine, what look ye for to see,
So far beyond the faint edge of the world?
D'ye look to see the lady Vivian,
Pursued by divers ominous vile demons
That have another king more fierce than ours?   5
Or think ye that if ye look far enough
And hard enough into the feathery west
Ye'll have a glimmer of the Grail itself?
And if ye look for neither Grail nor lady,
What look ye for to see, Gawaine, Gawaine?"   10

So Dagonet, whom Arthur made a knight
Because he loved him as he laughed at him,
Intoned his idle presence on a day
To Gawaine, who had thought himself alone,
Had there been in him thought of anything   15
Save what was murmured now in Camelot
Of Merlin's hushed and all but unconfirmed
Appearance out of Brittany. It was heard
At first there was a ghost in Arthur's palace,
But soon among the scullions and anon   20
Among the knights a firmer credit held
All tongues from uttering what all glances told—
Though not for long. Gawaine, this afternoon,
Fearing he might say more to Lancelot
Of Merlin's rumor-laden resurrection   25
Than Lancelot would have an ear to cherish,
Had sauntered off with his imagination
To Merlin's Rock, where now there was no Merlin
To meditate upon a whispering town
Below him in the silence.—Once he said   30
To Gawaine: "You are young; and that being so,
Behold the shining city of our dreams

And of our King."—"Long live the King," said Gawaine.—
"Long live the King," said Merlin after him;
"Better for me that I shall not be King;   35
Wherefore I say again, Long live the King,
And add, God save him, also, and all kings—
All kings and queens. I speak in general.
Kings have I known that were but weary men
With no stout appetite for more than peace   40
That was not made for them."—"Nor were they made
For kings," Gawaine said, laughing.—"You are young,
Gawaine, and you may one day hold the world
Between your fingers, knowing not what it is
That you are holding. Better for you and me,   45
I think, that we shall not be kings."

                    Gawaine,
Remembering Merlin's words of long ago,
Frowned as he thought, and having frowned again,
He smiled and threw an acorn at a lizard:
"There's more afoot and in the air to-day   50
Than what is good for Camelot. Merlin
May or may not know all, but he said well
To say to me that he would not be King.
Nor more would I be King." Far down he gazed
On Camelot, until he made of it   55
A phantom town of many stillnesses,
Not reared for men to dwell in, or for kings
To reign in, without omens and obscure
Familiars to bring terror to their days;
For though a knight, and one as hard at arms   60
As any, save the fate-begotten few
That all acknowledged or in envy loathed,
He felt a foreign sort of creeping up
And down him, as of moist things in the dark,—
When Dagonet, coming on him unawares,   65
Presuming on his title of Sir Fool,
Addressed him and crooned on till he was done:
"What look ye for to see, Gawaine, Gawaine?"

"Sir Dagonet, you best and wariest
Of all dishonest men, I look through Time,   70
For sight of what it is that is to be.
I look to see it, though I see it not.
I see a town down there that holds a king,
And over it I see a few small clouds—
Like feathers in the west, as you observe;   75
And I shall see no more this afternoon

Than what there is around us every day,
Unless you have a skill that I have not
To ferret the invisible for rats."

"If you see what's around us every day,   80
You need no other showing to go mad.
Remember that and take it home with you;
And say tonight, 'I had it of a fool—
With no immediate obliquity
For this one or for that one, or for me.'"   85
Gawaine, having risen, eyed the fool curiously:
"I'll not forget I had it of a knight,
Whose only folly is to fool himself;
And as for making other men to laugh,
And so forget their sins and selves a little,   90
There's no great folly there. So keep it up,
As long as you've a legend or a song,
And have whatever sport of us you like
Till havoc is the word and we fall howling.
For I've a guess there may not be so loud   95
A sound of laughing here in Camelot
When Merlin goes again to his gay grave
In Brittany. To mention lesser terrors,
Men say his beard is gone."

                         "Do men say that?"
A twitch of an impatient weariness   100
Played for a moment over the lean face
Of Dagonet, who reasoned inwardly:
"The friendly zeal of this inquiring knight
Will overtake his tact and leave it squealing,
One of these days."—Gawaine looked hard at him: 105
"If I be too familiar with a fool,
I'm on the way to be another fool,"
He mused, and owned a rueful qualm within him:
"Yes, Dagonet," he ventured, with a laugh,
"Men tell me that his beard has vanished wholly,   110
And that he shines now as the Lord's anointed,
And wears the valiance of an ageless youth
Crowned with a glory of eternal peace."

Dagonet, smiling strangely, shook his head:
"I grant your valiance of a kind of youth   115
To Merlin, but your crown of peace I question;
For, though I know no more than any churl
Who pinches any chambermaid soever
In the King's palace, I look not to Merlin

For peace, when out of his peculiar tomb   120
He comes again to Camelot. Time swings
A mighty scythe, and some day all your peace
Goes down before its edge like so much clover.
No, it is not for peace that Merlin comes,
Without a trumpet—and without a beard,   125
If what you say men say of him be true—
Nor yet for sudden war."

                Gawaine, for a moment,
Met then the ambiguous gaze of Dagonet,
And, making nothing of it, looked abroad
As if at something cheerful on all sides,   130
And back again to the fool's unasking eyes:
"Well, Dagonet, if Merlin would have peace,
Let Merlin stay away from Brittany,"
Said he, with admiration for the man
Whom Folly called a fool: "And we have known him;   135
We knew him once when he knew everything."

"He knew as much as God would let him know
Until he met the lady Vivian.
I tell you that, for the world knows all that;
Also it knows he told the King one day   140
That he was to be buried, and alive,
In Brittany; and that the King should see
The face of him no more. Then Merlin sailed
Away to Vivian in Broceliande,
Where now she crowns him and herself with flowers   145
And feeds him fruits and wines and many foods
Of many savors, and sweet ortolans.
Wise books of every lore of every land
Are there to fill his days, if he require them,
And there are players of all instruments—   150
Flutes, hautboys, drums, and viols; and she sings
To Merlin, till he trembles in her arms
And there forgets that any town alive
Had ever such a name as Camelot.
So Vivian holds him with her love, they say,   155
And he, who has no age, has not grown old.
I swear to nothing, but that's what they say.
That's being buried in Broceliande
For too much wisdom and clairvoyancy.
But you and all who live, Gawaine, have heard   160
This tale, or many like it, more than once;
And you must know that Love, when Love invites
Philosophy to play, plays high and wins,

Or low and loses. And you say to me,
'If Merlin would have peace, let Merlin stay   165
Away from Brittany.' Gawaine, you are young,
And Merlin's in his grave."

                    "Merlin said once
That I was young, and it's a joy for me
That I am here to listen while you say it.
Young or not young, if that be burial,   170
May I be buried long before I die.
I might be worse than young; I might be old."—
Dagonet answered, and without a smile:
"Somehow I fancy Merlin saying that;
A fancy—a mere fancy." Then he smiled: 175
"And such a doom as his may be for you,
Gawaine, should your untiring divination
Delve in the veiled eternal mysteries
Too far to be a pleasure for the Lord.
And when you stake your wisdom for a woman,   180
Compute the woman to be worth a grave,
As Merlin did, and say no more about it.
But Vivian, she played high. Oh, very high!
Flutes, hautboys, drums, and viols,—and her love.
Gawaine, farewell."

                    "Farewell, Sir Dagonet,   185
And may the devil take you presently."
He followed with a vexed and envious eye,
And with an arid laugh, Sir Dagonet's
Departure, till his gaunt obscurity
Was cloaked and lost amid the glimmering trees.   190
"Poor fool!" he murmured. "Or am I the fool?
With all my fast ascendency in arms,
That ominous clown is nearer to the King
Than I am—yet; and God knows what he knows,
And what his wits infer from what he sees   195
And feels and hears. I wonder what he knows
Of Lancelot, or what I might know now,
Could I have sunk myself to sound a fool
To springe a friend. . . . No, I like not this day.
There's a cloud coming over Camelot   200
Larger than any that is in the sky,—
Or Merlin would be still in Brittany,
With Vivian and the viols. It's all too strange."

And later, when descending to the city,
Through unavailing casements he could hear   205

The roaring of a mighty voice within,
Confirming fervidly his own conviction:
"It's all too strange, and half the world's half crazy!"
He scowled: "Well, I agree with Lamorak."
He frowned, and passed: "And I like not this day."   210

II

Sir Lamorak, the man of oak and iron,
Had with him now, as a care-laden guest,
Sir Bedivere, a man whom Arthur loved
As he had loved no man save Lancelot.
Like one whose late-flown shaft of argument   215
Had glanced and fallen afield innocuously,
He turned upon his host a sudden eye
That met from Lamorak's an even shaft
Of native and unused authority;
And each man held the other till at length   220
Each turned away, shutting his heavy jaws
Again together, prisoning thus two tongues
That might forget and might not be forgiven.
Then Bedivere, to find a plain way out,
Said, "Lamorak, let us drink to some one here,   225
And end this dryness. Who shall it be—the King,
The Queen, or Lancelot?"—"Merlin," Lamorak growled;
And then there were more wrinkles round his eyes
Than Bedivere had said were possible.
"There's no refusal in me now for that,"   230
The guest replied; "so, 'Merlin' let it be.
We've not yet seen him, but if he be here,
And even if he should not be here, say 'Merlin.'"
They drank to the unseen from two new tankards,
And fell straightway to sighing for the past,   235
And what was yet before them. Silence laid
A cogent finger on the lips of each
Impatient veteran, whose hard hands lay clenched
And restless on his midriff, until words
Were stronger than strong Lamorak:

                        "Bedivere,"   240
Began the solid host, "you may as well
Say now as at another time hereafter
That all your certainties have bruises on' em,
And all your pestilent asseverations
Will never make a man a salamander—   245
Who's born, as we are told, so fire won't bite him,—
Or a slippery queen a nun who counts and burns

Herself to nothing with her beads and candles.
There's nature, and what's in us, to be sifted
Before we know ourselves, or any man   250
Or woman that God suffers to be born.
That's how I speak; and while you strain your mazard,
Like Father Jove, big with a new Minerva,
We'll say, to pass the time, that I speak well.
God's fish! The King had eyes; and Lancelot   255
Won't ride home to his mother, for she's dead.
The story is that Merlin warned the King
Of what's come now to pass; and I believe it
And Arthur, he being Arthur and a king,
Has made a more pernicious mess than one,   260
We're told, for being so great and amorous:
It's that unwholesome and inclement cub
Young Modred I'd see first in hell before
I'd hang too high the Queen or Lancelot;
The King, if one may say it, set the pace,   265
And we've two strapping bastards here to prove it.
Young Borre, he's well enough; but as for Modred,
I squirm as often as I look at him.
And there again did Merlin warn the King,
The story goes abroad; and I believe it."   270

Sir Bedivere, as one who caught no more
Than what he would of Lamorak's outpouring,
Inclined his grizzled head and closed his eyes
Before he sighed and rubbed his beard and spoke:
"For all I know to make it otherwise,   275
The Queen may be a nun some day or other;
I'd pray to God for such a thing to be,
If prayer for that were not a mockery.
We're late now for much praying, Lamorak,
When you and I can feel upon our faces   280
A wind that has been blowing over ruins
That we had said were castles and high towers—
Till Merlin, or the spirit of him, came
As the dead come in dreams. I saw the King
This morning, and I saw his face. Therefore,   285
I tell you, if a state shall have a king,
The king must have the state, and be the state;
Or then shall we have neither king nor state,
But bones and ashes, and high towers all fallen:
And we shall have, where late there was a kingdom,   290
A dusty wreck of what was once a glory—
A wilderness whereon to crouch and mourn
And moralize, or else to build once more

For something better or for something worse.
Therefore again, I say that Lancelot   295
Has wrought a potent wrong upon the King,
And all who serve and recognize the King,
And all who follow him and all who love him.
Whatever the stormy faults he may have had,
To look on him today is to forget them;   300
And if it be too late for sorrow now
To save him—for it was a broken man
I saw this morning, and a broken king—
The God who sets a day for desolation
Will not forsake him in Avilion,   305
Or whatsoever shadowy land there be
Where peace awaits him on its healing shores."

Sir Lamorak, shifting in his oaken chair,
Growled like a dog and shook himself like one:
"For the stone-chested, helmet-cracking knight   310
That you are known to be from Lyonnesse
To northward, Bedivere, you fol-de-rol
When days are rancid, and you fiddle-faddle
More like a woman than a man with hands
Fit for the smiting of a crazy giant   315
With armor an inch thick, as we all know
You are, when you're not sermonizing at us.
As for the King, I say the King, no doubt,
Is angry, sorry, and all sorts of things,
For Lancelot, and for his easy Queen,   320
Whom he took knowing she'd thrown sparks already
On that same piece of tinder, Lancelot,
Who fetched her with him from Leodogran
Because the King—God save poor human reason!—
Would prove to Merlin, who knew everything   325
Worth knowing in those days, that he was wrong.
I'll drink now and be quiet,—but, by God,
I'll have to tell you, Brother Bedivere,
Once more, to make you listen properly,
That crowns and orders, and high palaces,   330
And all the manifold ingredients
Of this good solid kingdom, where we sit
And spit now at each other with our eyes,
Will not go rolling down to hell just yet
Because a pretty woman is a fool.   335
And here's Kay coming with his fiddle face
As long now as two fiddles. Sit ye down,
Sir Man, and tell us everything you know
Of Merlin—or his ghost without a beard.
What mostly is it?"

                    Sir Kay, the seneschal,   340
Sat wearily while he gazed upon the two:
"To you it mostly is, if I err not,
That what you hear of Merlin's coming back
Is nothing more or less than heavy truth.
But ask me nothing of the Queen, I say,   345
For I know nothing. All I know of her
Is what her eyes have told the silences
That now attend her; and that her estate
Is one for less complacent execration
Than quips and innuendoes of the city   350
Would augur for her sin—if there be sin—
Or for her name—if now she have a name.
And where, I say, is this to lead the King,
And after him, the kingdom and ourselves?
Here be we, three men of a certain strength   355
And some confessed intelligence, who know
That Merlin has come out of Brittany—
Out of his grave, as he would say it for us—
Because the King has now a desperation
More strong upon him than a woman's net   360
Was over Merlin—for now Merlin's here,
And two of us who knew him know how well
His wisdom, if he have it any longer,
Will by this hour have sounded and appraised
The grief and wrath and anguish of the King,   365
Requiring mercy and inspiring fear
Lest he forego the vigil now most urgent,
And leave unwatched a cranny where some worm
Or serpent may come in to speculate."

"I know your worm, and his worm's name is Modred—   370
Albeit the streets are not yet saying so,"
Said Lamorak, as he lowered his wrath and laughed
A sort of poisonous apology
To Kay: "And in the meantime, I'll be gyved!
Here's Bedivere a-wailing for the King,   375
And you, Kay, with a moist eye for the Queen.
I think I'll blow a horn for Lancelot;
For by my soul a man's in sorry case
When Guineveres are out with eyes to scorch him:
I'm not so ancient or so frozen certain   380
That I'd ride horses down to skeletons
If she were after me. Has Merlin seen him—
This Lancelot, this Queen-fed friend of ours?"

Kay answered sighing, with a lonely scowl:
"The picture that I conjure leaves him out;   385

The King and Merlin are this hour together,
And I can say no more; for I know nothing.
But how the King persuaded or beguiled
The stricken wizard from across the water
Outriddles my poor wits. It's all too strange."   390

"It's all too strange, and half the world's half crazy!"
Roared Lamorak, forgetting once again
The devastating carriage of his voice.
"Is the King sick?" he said, more quietly;
"Is he to let one damned scratch be enough   395
To paralyze the force that heretofore
Would operate a way through hell and iron,
And iron already slimy with his blood:
Is the King blind—with Modred watching him?
Does he forget the crown for Lancelot?   400
Does he forget that every woman mewing
Shall one day be a handful of small ashes?"

"You speak as one for whom the god of Love
Has yet a mighty trap in preparation.
We know you, Lamorak," said Bedivere: 405
"We know your for a short man, Lamorak,—
In deeds, if not in inches or in words;
But there are fens and heights and distances
That your capricious ranging has not yet
Essayed in this weird region of man's love.   410
Forgive me, Lamorak, but your words are words.
Your deeds are what they are; and ages hence
Will men remember your illustriousness,
If there be gratitude in history.
For me, I see the shadow of the end,   415
Wherein to serve King Arthur to the end,
And, if God have it so, to see the Grail
Before I die."

                But Lamorak shook his head:
"See what you will, or what you may. For me,
I see no other than a stinking mess—   420
With Modred stirring it, and Agravaine
Spattering Camelot with as much of it
As he can throw. The Devil got somehow
Into God's workshop once upon a time,
And out of the red clay that he found there   425
He made a shape like Modred, and another
As like as eyes are to this Agravaine.
'I never made 'em,' said the good Lord God,
'But let 'em go, and see what comes of 'em.'

And that's what we're to do. As for the Grail,   430
I've never worried it, and so the Grail
Has never worried me."

                    Kay sighed. "I see
With Bedivere the coming of the end,"
He murmured; "for the King I saw today
Was not, nor shall he ever be again,   435
The King we knew. I say the King is dead;
The man is living, but the King is dead.
The wheel is broken."

                    "Faugh!" said Lamorak;
"There are no dead kings yet in Camelot;
But there is Modred who is hatching ruin,—   440
And when it hatches I may not be here.
There's Gawaine too, and he does not forget
My father, who killed his. King Arthur's house
Has more divisions in it than I like
In houses; and if Modred's aim be good   445
For backs like mine, I'm not long for the scene."

III

King Arthur, as he paced a lonely floor
That rolled a muffled echo, as he fancied,
All through the palace and out through the world,
Might now have wondered hard, could he have heard   450
Sir Lamorak's apathetic disregard
Of what Fate's knocking made so manifest
And ominous to others near the King—
If any, indeed, were near him at this hour
Save Merlin, once the wisest of all men,   455
And weary Dagonet, whom he had made
A knight for love of him and his abused
Integrity. He might have wondered hard
And wondered much; and after wondering,
He might have summoned, with as little heart   460
As he had now for crowns, the fond, lost Merlin,
Whose Nemesis had made of him a slave,
A man of dalliance, and a sybarite.

"Men change in Brittany, Merlin," said the King;
And even his grief had strife to freeze again   465
A dreary smile for the transmuted seer
Now robed in heavy wealth of purple silk,
With frogs and foreign tassels. On his face,

Too smooth now for a wizard or a sage,
Lay written, for the King's remembering eyes,   470
A pathos of a lost authority
Long faded, and unconscionably gone;
And on the King's heart lay a sudden cold:
"I might as well have left him in his grave,
As he would say it, saying what was true,—   475
As death is true. This Merlin is not mine,
But Vivian's. My crown is less than hers,
And I am less than woman to this man."

Then Merlin, as one reading Arthur's words
On viewless tablets in the air before him: 480
"Now, Arthur, since you are a child of mine—
A foster-child, and that's a kind of child—
Be not from hearsay or despair too eager
To dash your meat with bitter seasoning,
So none that are more famished than yourself   485
Shall have what you refuse. For you are King,
And if you starve yourself, you starve the state;
And then by sundry looks and silences
Of those you loved, and by the lax regard
Of those you knew for fawning enemies,   490
You may learn soon that you are King no more,
But a slack, blasted, and sad-fronted man,
Made sadder with a crown. No other friend
Than I could say this to you, and say more;
And if you bid me say no more, so be it."   495

The King, who sat with folded arms, now bowed
His head and felt, unfought and all aflame
Like immanent hell-fire, the wretchedness
That only those who are to lead may feel—
And only they when they are maimed and worn   500
Too sore to covet without shuddering
The fixed impending eminence where death
Itself were victory, could they but lead
Unbitten by the serpents they had fed.
Turning, he spoke: "Merlin, you say the truth: 505
There is no man who could say more to me
Today, or say so much to me, and live.
But you are Merlin still, or part of him;
I did you wrong when I thought otherwise,
And I am sorry now. Say what you will.   510
We are alone, and I shall be alone
As long as Time shall hide a reason here
For me to stay in this infested world

Where I have sinned and erred and heeded not
Your counsel; and where you yourself—God save us!—   515
Have gone down smiling to the smaller life
That you and your incongruous laughter called
Your living grave. God save us all, Merlin,
When you, the seer, the founder, and the prophet,
May throw the gold of your immortal treasure   520
Back to the God that gave it, and then laugh
Because a woman has you in her arms. . . .
Why do you sting me now with a small hive
Of words that are all poison? I do not ask
Much honey; but why poison me for nothing,   525
And with a venom that I know already
As I know crowns and wars? Why tell a king—
A poor, foiled, flouted, miserable king—
That if he lets rats eat his fingers off
He'll have no fingers to fight battles with?   530
I know as much as that, for I am still
A king—who thought himself a little less
Than God; a king who built him palaces
On sand and mud, and hears them crumbling now,
And sees them tottering, as he knew they must.   535
Your are the man who made me to be King—
Therefore, say anything."

           Merlin, stricken deep
With pity that was old, being born of old
Foreshadowings, made answer to the King:
"This coil of Lancelot and Guinevere   540
Is not for any mortal to undo,
Or to deny, or to make otherwise;
But your most violent years are on their way
To days, and to a sounding of loud hours
That are to strike for war. Let not the time   545
Between this hour and then be lost in fears,
Or told in obscurations and vain faith
In what has been your long security;
For should your force be slower then than hate,
And your regret be sharper than your sight,   550
And your remorse fall heavier than your sword,—
Then say farewell to Camelot, and the crown.
But say not you have lost, or failed in aught
Your golden horoscope of imperfection
Has held in starry words that I have read.   555
I see no farther now than I saw then,
For no man shall be given of everything
Together in one life; yet I may say

The time is imminent when he shall come
For whom I founded the Siege Perilous;   560
And he shall be too much a living part
Of what he brings, and what he burns away in,
To be for long a vexed inhabitant
Of this mad realm of stains and lower trials.
And here the ways of God again are mixed: 565
For this new knight who is to find the Grail
For you, and for the least who pray for you
In such lost coombs and hollows of the world
As you have never entered, is to be
The son of him you trusted—Lancelot,   570
Of all who ever jeopardized a throne
Sure the most evil-fated, saving one,
Your son, begotten, though you knew not then
Your leman was your sister, of Morgause;
For it is Modred now, not Lancelot,   575
Whose native hate plans your annihilation—
Though he may smile till he be sick, and swear
Allegiance to an unforgiven father
Until at last he shake an empty tongue
Talked out with too much lying—though his lies   580
Will have a truth to steer them. Trust him not,
For unto you the father, he the son
Is like enough to be the last of terrors—
If in a field of time that looms to you
Far larger than it is you fail to plant   585
And harvest the old seeds of what I say,
And so be nourished and adept again
For what may come to be. But Lancelot
Will have you first; and you need starve no more
For the Queen's love, the love that never was.   590
Your Queen is now your Kingdom, and hereafter
Let no man take it from you, or you die.
Let no man take it from you for a day;
For days are long when we are far from what
We love, and mischief's other name is distance.   595
Let that be all, for I can say no more;
Not even to Blaise the Hermit, were he living,
Could I say more than I have given you now
To hear; and he alone was my confessor."

The King arose and paced the floor again.   600
"I get gray comfort of dark words," he said;
"But tell me not that you can say no more:
You can, for I can fear you saying it.
Yet I'll not ask for more. I have enough—

Until my new knight comes to prove and find   605
The promise and the glory of the Grail,
Though I shall see no Grail. For I have built
On sand and mud, and I shall see no Grail."—
"Nor I," said Merlin. "Once I dreamed of it,
But I was buried. I shall see no Grail,   610
Nor would I have it otherwise. I saw
Too much, and that was never good for man.
The man who goes alone too far goes mad—
In one way or another. God knew best,
And he knows what is coming yet for me.   615
I do not ask. Like you, I have enough."

That night King Arthur's apprehension found
In Merlin an obscure and restive guest,
Whose only thought was on the hour of dawn,
When he should see the last of Camelot   620
And ride again for Brittany; and what words
Were said before the King was left alone
Were only darker for reiteration.
They parted, all provision made secure
For Merlin's early convoy to the coast,   625
And Arthur tramped the past. The loneliness
Of kings, around him like the unseen dead,
Lay everywhere; and he was loath to move,
As if in fear to meet with his cold hand
The touch of something colder. Then a whim,   630
Begotten of intolerable doubt,
Seized him and stung him until he was asking
If any longer lived among his knights
A man to trust as once he trusted all,
And Lancelot more than all. "And it is he   635
Who is to have me first," so Merlin says,—
"As if he had me not in hell already.
Lancelot! Lancelot!" He cursed the tears
That cooled his misery, and then he asked
Himself again if he had one to trust   640
Among his knights, till even Bedivere,
Tor, Bors, and Percival, rough Lamorak,
Griflet, and Gareth, and gay Gawaine, all
Were dubious knaves,—or they were like to be,
For cause to make them so; and he had made   645
Himself to be the cause. "God set me right,
Before this folly carry me on farther,"
He murmured; and he smiled unhappily,
Though fondly, as he thought: "Yes, there is one
Whom I may trust with even my soul's last shred;   650

And Dagonet will sing for me tonight
An old song, not too merry or too sad."

When Dagonet, having entered, stood before
The King as one affrighted, the King smiled:
"You think because I call for you so late   655
That I am angry, Dagonet? Why so?
Have you been saying what I say to you,
And telling men that you brought Merlin here?
No? So I fancied; and if you report
No syllable of anything I speak,   660
You will have no regrets, and I no anger.
What word of Merlin was abroad today?"

"Today have I heard no man save Gawaine,
And to him I said only what all men
Are saying to their neighbors. They believe   665
That you have Merlin here, and that his coming
Denotes no good. Gawaine was curious,
But ever mindful of your majesty.
He pressed me not, and we made light of it."

"Gawaine, I fear, makes light of everything,"   670
The King said, looking down. "Sometimes I wish
I had a full Round Table of Gawaines.
But that's a freak of midnight,—never mind it.
Sing me a song—one of those endless things
That Merlin liked of old, when men were younger   675
And there were more stars twinkling in the sky.
I see no stars that are alive tonight,
And I am not the king of sleep. So then,
Sing me an old song."

                    Dagonet's quick eye
Caught sorrow in the King's; and he knew more,   680
In a fool's way, than even the King himself
Of what was hovering over Camelot.
"O King," he said, "I cannot sing tonight.
If you command me I shall try to sing,
But I shall fail; for there are no songs now   685
In my old throat, or even in these poor strings
That I can hardly follow with my fingers.
Forgive me—kill me—but I cannot sing."
Dagonet fell down then on both his knees
And shook there while he clutched the King's cold hand   690
And wept for what he knew.

                              "There, Dagonet;
I shall not kill my knight, or make him sing.
No more; get up, and get you off to bed.
There'll be another time for you to sing,
So get you to your covers and sleep well."   695
Alone again, the King said, bitterly:
"Yes, I have one friend left, and they who know
As much of him as of themselves believe
That he's a fool. Poor Dagonet's a fool.
And if he be a fool, what else am I   700
Than one fool more to make the world complete?
'The love that never was!' . . . Fool, fool, fool, fool!"

The King was long awake. No covenant
With peace was his tonight; and he knew sleep
As he knew the cold eyes of Guinevere   705
That yesterday had stabbed him, having first
On Lancelot's name struck fire, and left him then
As now they left him—with a wounded heart,
A wounded pride, and a sickening pang worse yet
Of lost possession. He thought wearily   710
Of watchers by the dead, late wayfarers,
Rough-handed mariners on ships at sea,
Lone-yawning sentries, wastrels, and all others
Who might be saying somewhere to themselves,
"The King is now asleep in Camelot;   715
God save the King."—"God save the King, indeed,
If there be now a king to save," he said.
Then he saw giants rising in the dark,
Born horribly of memories and new fears
That in the gray-lit irony of dawn   720
Were partly to fade out and be forgotten;
And then there might be sleep, and for a time
There might again be peace. His head was hot
And throbbing; but the rest of him was cold,
As he lay staring hard where nothing stood,   725
And hearing what was not, even while he saw
And heard, like dust and thunder far away,
The coming confirmation of the words
Of him who saw so much and feared so little
Of all that was to be. No spoken doom   730
That ever chilled the last night of a felon
Prepared a dragging anguish more profound
And absolute than Arthur, in these hours,
Made out of darkness and of Merlin's words;
No tide that ever crashed on Lyonnesse   735
Drove echoes inland that were lonelier

For widowed ears among the fisher-folk,
Than for the King were memories tonight
Of old illusions that were dead for ever.

IV
The tortured King—seeing Merlin wholly meshed   740
In his defection, even to indifference,
And all the while attended and exalted
By some unfathomable obscurity
Of divination, where the Grail, unseen,
Broke yet the darkness where a king saw nothing—   745
Feared now the lady Vivian more than Fate;
For now he knew that Modred, Lancelot,
The Queen, the King, the Kingdom, and the World,
Were less to Merlin, who had made him King,
Than one small woman in Broceliande.   750
Whereas the lady Vivian, seeing Merlin
Acclaimed and tempted and allured again
To service in his old magnificence,
Feared now King Arthur more than storms and robbers;
For Merlin, though he knew himself immune   755
To no least whispered little wish of hers
That might afflict his ear with ecstasy,
Had yet sufficient of his old command
Of all around him to invest an eye
With quiet lightning, and a spoken word   760
With easy thunder, so accomplishing
A profit and a pastime for himself—
And for the lady Vivian, when her guile
Outlived at intervals her graciousness;
And this equipment of uncertainty,   765
Which now had gone away with him to Britain
With Dagonet, so plagued her memory
That soon a phantom brood of goblin doubts
Inhabited his absence, which had else
Been empty waiting and a few brave fears,   770
And a few more, she knew, that were not brave,
Or long to be disowned, or manageable.
She thought of him as he had looked at her
When first he had acquainted her alarm
At sight of the King's letter with its import;   775
And she remembered now his very words:
"The King believes today as in his boyhood
That I am Fate," he said; and when they parted
She had not even asked him not to go;
She might as well, she thought, have bid the wind   780

Throw no more clouds across a lonely sky
Between her and the moon,—so great he seemed
In his oppressed solemnity, and she,
In her excess of wrong imagining,
So trivial in an hour, and, after all   785
A creature of a smaller consequence
Than kings to Merlin, who made kings and kingdoms
And had them as a father; and so she feared
King Arthur more than robbers while she waited
For Merlin's promise to fulfil itself,   790
And for the rest that was to follow after:
"He said he would come back, and so he will.
He will because he must, and he is Merlin,
The master of the world—or so he was;
And he is coming back again to me   795
Because he must and I am Vivian.
It's all as easy as two added numbers:
Some day I'll hear him ringing at the gate,
As he rang on that morning in the spring,
Ten years ago; and I shall have him then   800
For ever. He shall never go away
Though kings come walking on their hands and knees
To take him on their backs." When Merlin came,
She told him that, and laughed; and he said strangely:
"Be glad or sorry, but no kings are coming.   805
Not Arthur, surely; for now Arthur knows
That I am less than Fate."

                                    Ten years ago
The King had heard, with unbelieving ears
At first, what Merlin said would be the last
Reiteration of his going down   810
To find a living grave in Brittany:
"Buried alive I told you I should be,
By love made little and by woman shorn,
Like Samson, of my glory; and the time
Is now at hand. I follow in the morning   815
Where I am led. I see behind me now
The last of crossways, and I see before me
A straight and final highway to the end
Of all my divination. You are King,
And in your kingdom I am what I was.   820
Wherever I have warned you, see as far
As I have seen; for I have shown the worst
There is to see. Require no more of me,
For I can be no more than what I was."
So, on the morrow, the King said farewell;   825

And he was never more to Merlin's eye
The King than at that hour; for Merlin knew
How much was going out of Arthur's life
With him, as he went southward to the sea.

Over the waves and into Brittany   830
Went Merlin, to Broceliande. Gay birds
Were singing high to greet him all along
A broad and sanded woodland avenue
That led him on forever, so he thought,
Until at last there was an end of it;   835
And at the end there was a gate of iron,
Wrought heavily and invidiously barred.
He pulled a cord that rang somewhere a bell
Of many echoes, and sat down to rest,
Outside the keeper's house, upon a bench   840
Of carven stone that might for centuries
Have waited there in silence to receive him.
The birds were singing still; leaves flashed and swung
Before him in the sunlight; a soft breeze
Made intermittent whisperings around him   845
Of love and fate and danger, and faint waves
Of many sweetly-stinging fragile odors
Broke lightly as they touched him; cherry-boughs
Above him snowed white petals down upon him,
And under their slow falling Merlin smiled   850
Contentedly, as one who contemplates
No longer fear, confusion, or regret,
May smile at ruin or at revelation.

A stately fellow with a forest air
Now hailed him from within, with searching words   855
And curious looks, till Merlin's glowing eye
Transfixed him and he flinched: "My compliments
And homage to the lady Vivian.
Say Merlin from King Arthur's Court is here,
A pilgrim and a stranger in appearance,   860
Though in effect her friend and humble servant.
Convey to her my speech as I have said it,
Without abbreviation or delay,
And so deserve my gratitude forever."
"But Merlin?" the man stammered; "Merlin? Merlin?"—   865
"One Merlin is enough. I know no other.
Now go you to the lady Vivian
And bring to me her word, for I am weary."
Still smiling at the cherry-blossoms falling
Down on him and around him in the sunlight,   870

He waited, never moving, never glancing
This way or that, until his messenger
Came jingling into vision, weighed with keys,
And inly shaken with much wondering
At this great wizard's coming unannounced   875
And unattended. When the way was open
The stately messenger, now bowing low
In reverence and awe, bade Merlin enter;
And Merlin, having entered, heard the gate
Clang back behind him; and he swore no gate   880
Like that had ever clanged in Camelot,
Or any other place if not in hell.
"I may be dead; and this good fellow here,
With all his keys," he thought, "may be the Devil,—
Though I were loath to say so, for the keys   885
Would make him rather more akin to Peter;
And that's fair reasoning for this fair weather."

"The lady Vivian says you are most welcome,"
Said now the stately-favored servitor,
"And are to follow me. She said, 'Say Merlin—   890
A pilgrim and a stranger in appearance,
Though in effect my friend and humble servant—
Is welcome for himself, and for the sound
Of his great name that echoes everywhere.'"—
"I like you and I like your memory,"   895
Said Merlin, curiously, "but not your gate.
Why forge for this elysian wilderness
A thing so vicious with unholy noise?"—
"There's a way out of every wilderness
For those who dare or care enough to find it,"   900
The guide said: and they moved along together,
Down shaded ways, through open ways with hedgerows,
And into shade again more deep than ever,
But edged anon with rays of broken sunshine
In which a fountain, raining crystal music,   905
Made faery magic of it through green leafage,
Till Merlin's eyes were dim with preparation
For sight now of the lady Vivian.
He saw at first a bit of living green
That might have been a part of all the green   910
Around the tinkling fountain where she gazed
Upon the circling pool as if her thoughts
Were not so much on Merlin—whose advance
Betrayed through his enormity of hair
The cheeks and eyes of youth—as on the fishes.   915
But soon she turned and found him, now alone,

And held him while her beauty and her grace
Made passing trash of empires, and his eyes
Told hers of what a splendid emptiness
Her tedious world had been without him in it   920
Whose love and service were to be her school,
Her triumph, and her history: "This is Merlin,"
She thought; "and I shall dream of him no more.
And he has come, he thinks, to frighten me
With beards and robes and his immortal fame;   925
Or is it I who think so? I know not.
I'm frightened, sure enough, but if I show it,
I'll be no more the Vivian for whose love
He tossed away his glory, or the Vivian
Who saw no man alive to make her love him   930
Till she saw Merlin once in Camelot,
And seeing him, saw no other. In an age
That has no plan for me that I can read
Without him, shall he tell me what I am,
And why I am, I wonder?" While she thought,   935
And feared the man whom her perverse negation
Must overcome somehow to soothe her fancy,
She smiled and welcomed him; and so they stood,
Each finding in the other's eyes a gleam
Of what eternity had hidden there.   940

"Are you always all in green, as you are now?"
Said Merlin, more employed with her complexion,
Where blood and olive made wild harmony
With eyes and wayward hair that were too dark
For peace if they were not subordinated;   945
"If so you are, then so you make yourself
A danger in a world of many dangers.
If I were young, God knows if I were safe
Concerning you in green, like a slim cedar,
As you are now, to say my life was mine: 950
Were you to say to me that I should end it,
Longevity for me were jeopardized.
Have you your green on always and all over?"

"Come here, and I will tell you about that,"
Said Vivian, leading Merlin with a laugh   955
To an arbored seat where they made opposites:
"If you are Merlin—and I know you are,
For I remember you in Camelot,—
You know that I am Vivian, as I am;
And if I go in green, why, let me go so,   960
And say at once why you have come to me

Cloaked over like a monk, and with a beard
As long as Jeremiah's. I don't like it.
I'll never like a man with hair like that
While I can feed a carp with little frogs.   965
I'm rather sure to hate you if you keep it,
And when I hate a man I poison him."

"You've never fed a carp with little frogs,"
Said Merlin; "I can see it in your eyes."—
"I might then, if I haven't," said the lady;   970
"For I'm a savage, and I love no man
As I have seen him yet. I'm here alone,
With some three hundred others, all of whom
Are ready, I dare say, to die for me;
I'm cruel and I'm cold, and I like snakes;   975
And some have said my mother was a fairy,
Though I believe it not."

                            "Why not believe it?"
Said Merlin; "I believe it. I believe
Also that you divine, as I had wished,
In my surviving ornament of office   980
A needless imposition on your wits,
If not yet on the scope of your regard.
Even so, you cannot say how old I am,
Or yet how young. I'm willing cheerfully
To fight, left-handed, Hell's three headed hound   985
If you but whistle him up from where he lives;
I'm cheerful and I'm fierce, and I've made kings;
And some have said my father was the Devil,
Though I believe it not. Whatever I am,
I have not lived in Time until to-day."   990
A moment's worth of wisdom there escaped him,
But Vivian seized it, and it was not lost.

Embroidering doom with many levities,
Till now the fountain's crystal silver, fading
Became a splash and a mere chilliness,   995
They mocked their fate with easy pleasantries
That were too false and small to be forgotten,
And with ingenious insincerities
That had no repetition or revival.
At last the lady Vivian arose,   1000
And with a crying of how late it was
Took Merlin's hand and led him like a child
Along a dusky way between tall cones
Of tight green cedars: "Am I like one of these?

You said I was, though I deny it wholly."—   1005
"Very," said Merlin, to his bearded lips
Uplifting her small fingers.—"O, that hair!"
She moaned, as if in sorrow: "Must it be?
Must every prophet and important wizard
Be clouded so that nothing but his nose   1010
And eyes, and intimations of his ears,
Are there to make us know him when we see him?
Praise heaven I'm not a prophet! Are you glad?"—

He did not say that he was glad or sorry;
For suddenly came flashing into vision   1015
A thing that was a manor and a castle,
With walls and roofs that had a flaming sky
Behind them, like a sky that he remembered,
And one that had from his rock-sheltered haunt
Above the roofs of his forsaken city   1020
Made flame as if all Camelot were on fire.
The glow brought with it a brief memory
Of Arthur as he left him, and the pain
That fought in Arthur's eyes for losing him,
And must have overflowed when he had vanished.   1025
But now the eyes that looked hard into his
Were Vivian's, not the King's; and he could see,
Or so he thought, a shade of sorrow in them.
She took his two hands: "You are sad," she said.—
He smiled: "Your western lights bring memories   1030
Of Camelot. We all have memories—
Prophets, and women who are like slim cedars;
But you are wrong to say that I am sad."—
"Would you go back to Camelot?" she asked,
Her fingers tightening. Merlin shook his head.   1035
"Then listen while I tell you that I'm glad,"
She purred, as if assured that he would listen:
"At your first warning, much too long ago,
Of this quaint pilgrimage of yours to see
'The fairest and most orgulous of ladies'—   1040
No language for a prophet, I am sure—
Said I, 'When this great Merlin comes to me,
My task and avocation for some time
Will be to make him willing, if I can,
To teach and feed me with an ounce of wisdom.'   1045
For I have eaten to an empty shell,
After a weary feast of observation
Among the glories of a tinsel world
That had for me no glory till you came,
A life that is no life. Would you go back   1050

To Camelot?"—Merlin shook his head again,
And the two smiled together in the sunset.

They moved along in silence to the door,
Where Merlin said: "Of your three hundred here
There is but one I know, and him I favor;   1055
I mean the stately one who shakes the keys
Of that most evil sounding gate of yours,
Which has a clang as if it shut forever."—
"If there be need, I'll shut the gate myself,"
She said. "And you like Blaise? Then you shall have him.   1060
He was not born to serve, but serve he must,
It seems, and be enamoured of my shadow.
He cherishes the taint of some high folly
That haunts him with a name he cannot know,
And I could fear his wits are paying for it.   1065
Forgive his tongue, and humor it a little."—
"I knew another one whose name was Blaise,"
He said; and she said lightly, "Well, what of it?"—
"And he was nigh the learnedest of hermits;
His home was far away form everywhere,   1070
And he was all alone there when he died."—
"Now be a pleasant Merlin," Vivian said,
Patting his arm, "and have no more of that;
For I'll not hear of dead men far away,
Or dead men anywhere this afternoon.   1075
There'll be a trifle in the way of supper
This evening, but the dead shall not have any.
Blaise and this man will tell you all there is
For you to know. Then you'll know everything."
She laughed, and vanished like a humming-bird.   1080

V

The sun went down, and the dark after it
Starred Merlin's new abode with many a sconced
And many a moving candle, in whose light
The prisoned wizard, mirrored in amazement,
Saw fronting him a stranger, falcon-eyed,   1085
Firm-featured, of a negligible age,
And fair enough to look upon, he fancied,
Though not a warrior born, nor more a courtier.
A native humor resting in his long
And solemn jaws now stirred, and Merlin smiled   1090
To see himself in purple, touched with gold,
And fledged with snowy lace.—The careful Blaise,
Having drawn some time before from Merlin's wallet

The sable raiment of a royal scholar,
Had eyed it with a long mistrust and said: 1095
"The lady Vivian would be vexed, I fear,
To meet you vested in these learned weeds
Of gravity and death; for she abhors
Mortality in all its hues and emblems—
Black wear, long argument, and all the cold   1100
And solemn things that appertain to graves."—
And Merlin, listening, to himself had said,
"This fellow has a freedom, yet I like him;"
And then aloud: "I trust you. Deck me out,
However, with a temperate regard   1105
For what your candid eye may find in me
Of inward coloring. Let them reap my beard,
Moreover, with a sort of reverence,
For I shall never look on it again.
And though your lady frown her face away   1110
To think of me in black, for God's indulgence,
Array me not in scarlet or in yellow."—
And so it came to pass that Merlin sat
At ease in purple, even though his chin
Reproached him as he pinched it, and seemed yet   1115
A little fearful of its nakedness.
He might have sat and scanned himself for ever
Had not the careful Blaise, regarding him,
Remarked again that in his proper judgment,
And on the valid word of his attendants,   1120
No more was to be done. "Then do no more,"
Said Merlin, with a last look at his chin;
"Never do more when there's no more to do,
And you may shun thereby the bitter taste
Of many disillusions and regrets.   1125
God's pity on us that our words have wings
And leave our deeds to crawl so far below them;
For we have all two heights, we men who dream,
Whether we lead or follow, rule or serve."—
"God's pity on us anyhow," Blaise answered,   1130
"Or most of us. Meanwhile, I have to say,
As long as you are here, and I'm alive,
Your summons will assure the loyalty
Of all my diligence and expedition.
The gong that you hear singing in the distance   1135
Was rung for your attention and your presence."—
"I wonder at this fellow, yet I like him,"
Said Merlin; and he rose to follow him.

The lady Vivian in a fragile sheath
Of crimson, dimmed and veiled ineffably   1140

By the flame-shaken gloom wherein she sat,
And twinkled if she moved, heard Merlin coming,
And smiled as if to make herself believe
He joy was all a triumph; yet her blood
Confessed a tingling of more wonderment   1145
Than all her five and twenty worldly years
Of waiting for this triumph could remember;
And when she knew and felt the slower tread
Of his unseen advance among the shadows
To the small haven of uncertain light   1150
That held her in it as a torch-lit shoal
Might hold a smooth red fish, her listening skin
Responded with a creeping underneath it,
And a crinkling that was incident alike
To darkness, love, and mice. When he was there,   1155
She looked up at him in a whirl of mirth
And wonder, as in childhood she had gazed
Wide-eyed on royal mountebanks who made
So brief a shift of the impossible
That kings and queens would laugh and shake themselves;   1160
Then rising slowly on her little feet,
Like a slim creature lifted, she thrust out
Her two small hands as if to push him back—
Whereon he seized them. "Go away," she said;
"I never saw you in my life before."—   1165
"You say the truth," he answered; "when I met
Myself an hour ago, my words were yours.
God made the man you see for you to like,
If possible. If otherwise, turn down
These two prodigious and remorseless thumbs   1170
And leave your lions to annihilate him."—

"I have no other lion than yourself,"
She said: "and since you cannot eat yourself,
Pray do a lonely woman, who is, you say,
More like a tree than any other thing   1175
In your discrimination, the large honor
Of sharing with her a small kind of supper."—
"Yes, you are like a tree,—or like a flower;
More like a flower to-night." He bowed his head
And kissed the ten small fingers he was holding,   1180
As calmly as if each had been a son;
Although his heart was leaping and his eyes
Had sight for nothing save a swimming crimson
Between two glimmering arms. "More like a flower
To-night," he said, as now he scanned again   1185
The immemorial meaning of her face

And drew it nearer to his eyes. It seemed
A flower of wonder with a crimson stem
Came leaning slowly and regretfully
To meet his will—a flower of change and peril　　　　1190
That had a clinging blossom of warm olive
Half stifled with a tyranny of black,
And held the wayward fragrance of a rose
Made woman by delirious alchemy.
She raised her face and yoked his willing neck　　　　1195
With half her weight; and with hot lips that left
The world with only one philosophy
For Merlin or for Anaxagoras,
Called his to meet them and in one long hush
Of capture to surrender and make hers　　　　1200
The last of anything that might remain
Of what was now their beardless wizardry.
Then slowly she began to push herself
Away, and slowly Merlin let her go
As far from him as his outreaching hands　　　　1205
Could hold her fingers while his eyes had all
The beauty of the woodland and the world
Before him in the firelight, like a nymph
Of cities, or a queen a little weary
Of inland stillness and immortal trees.　　　　1210
"Are you to let me go again sometime,"
She said,—"before I starve to death, I wonder?
If not, I'll have to bite the lion's paws,
And make him roar. He cannot shake his mane,
For now the lion has no mane to shake;　　　　1215
The lion hardly knows himself without it,
And thinks he has no face, but there's a lady
Who says he had no face until he lost it.
So there we are. And there's a flute somewhere,
Playing a strange old tune. You know the words:　　　　1220
'The Lion and the Lady are both hungry.'"

Fatigue and hunger—tempered leisurely
With food that some devout magician's oven
Might after many failures have delivered,
And wine that had for decades in the dark　　　　1225
Of Merlin's grave been slowly quickening,
And with half-heard, dream-weaving interludes
Of distant flutes and viols, made more distant
By far, nostalgic hautboys blown from nowhere,—
Were tempered not so leisurely, may be,　　　　1230
With Vivian's inextinguishable eyes
Between two shining silver candlesticks

That lifted each a trembling flame to make
The rest of her a dusky loveliness
Against a bank of shadow. Merlin made,   1235
As well as he was able while he ate,
A fair division of the fealty due
To food and beauty, albeit more times than one
Was he at odds with his urbanity
In honoring too long the grosser viand.   1240
"The best invention in Broceliande
Has not been over-taxed in vain, I see,"
She told him, with her chin propped on her fingers
And her eyes flashing blindness into his:
"I put myself out cruelly to please you,   1245
And you, for that, forget almost at once
The name and image of me altogether.
You needn't, for when all is analyzed,
It's only a bird-pie that you are eating."

"I know not what you call it," Merlin said;   1250
"Nor more do I forget your name and image,
Though I do eat; and if I did not eat,
Your sending out of ships and caravans
To get whatever 'tis that's in this thing
Would be a sorrow for you all your days;   1255
And my great love, which you have seen by now,
Might look to you a lie; and like as not
You'd actuate some sinewed mercenary
To carry me away to God knows where
And seal me in a fearsome hole to starve,   1260
Because I made of this insidious picking
An idle circumstance. My dear fair lady—
And there is not another under heaven
So fair as you are as I see you now—
I cannot look at you too much and eat;   1265
And I must eat, or be untimely ashes,
Whereon the light of your celestial gaze
Would fall, I fear me, for no longer time
Than on the solemn dust of Jeremiah—
Whose beard you likened once, in heathen jest,   1270
To mine that now is no man's."

                                 "Are you sorry?"
Said Vivian, filling Merlin's empty goblet;
"If you are sorry for the loss of it,
Drink more of this and you may tell me lies
Enough to make me sure that you are glad;   1275
But if your love is what you say it is,

Be never sorry that my love took off
That horrid hair to make your face at last
A human fact. Since I have had your name
To dream of and say over to myself,   1280
The visitations of that awful beard
Have been a terror for my nights and days—
For twenty years. I've seen it like an ocean,
Blown seven ways at once and wrecking ships,
With men and women screaming for their lives;   1285
I've seen it woven into shining ladders
That ran up out of sight and so to heaven,
All covered with white ghosts with hanging robes
Like folded wings,—and there were millions of them,
Climbing , climbing, climbing, all the time;   1290
And all the time that I was watching them
I thought how far above me Merlin was,
And wondered always what his face was like.
But even then, as a child, I knew the day
Would come some time when I should see his face   1295
And hear his voice, and have him in my house
Till he should care no more to stay in it,
And go away to found another kingdom."—
"Not that," he said; and, sighing, drank more wine;
"One kingdom for one Merlin is enough."—   1300
"One Merlin for one Vivian is enough,"
She said. "If you care much, remember that;
But the Lord knows how many Vivians
One Merlin's entertaining eye might favor,
Indifferently well and all at once,   1305
If they were all at hand. Praise heaven they're not."

"If they were in the world—praise heaven they're not—
And if one Merlin's entertaining eye
Saw two of them, there might be left him then
The sight of no eye to see anything—   1310
Not even the Vivian who is everything,
She being Beauty, Beauty being She,
She being Vivian, and so on for ever."—
"I'm glad you don't see two of me," she said;
"For there's a whole world yet for you to eat   1315
And drink and say to me before I know
The sort of creature that you see in me.
I'm withering for a little more attention,
But, being woman, I can wait. These cups
That you see coming are for the last there is   1320
Of what my father gave to kings alone,
And far from always. You are more than kings

To me; therefore I give it all to you,
Imploring you to spare no more of it
Than a small cockle-shell would hold for me   1325
To pledge your love and mine in. Take the rest,
That I may see tonight the end of it.
I'll have no living remnant of the dead
Annoying me until it fades and sours
Of too long cherishing; for Time enjoys   1330
The look that's on our faces when we scowl
On unexpected ruins, and thrift itself
May be a sort of slow unwholesome fire
That eats away to dust the life that feeds it.
You smile, I see, but I said what I said.   1335
One hardly has to live a thousand years
To contemplate a lost economy;
So let us drink it while it's yet alive
And you and I are not untimely ashes.
My last words are your own, and I don't like 'em."—   1340
A sudden laughter scattered from her eyes
A threatening wisdom. He smiled and let her laugh,
Then looked into the dark where there was nothing:
"There's more in this than I have seen," he thought,
"Though I shall see it."—"Drink," she said again;   1345
"There's only this much in the world of it,
And I am near to giving all to you
Because you are so great and I so little."

With a long-kindling gaze that caught from hers
A laughing flame, and with a hand that shook   1350
Like Arthur's kingdom, Merlin slowly raised
A golden cup that for a golden moment
Was twinned in air with hers; and Vivian,
Who smiled at him across their gleaming rims,
From eyes that made a fuel of the night   1355
Surrounding her, shot glory over gold
At Merlin, while their cups touched and his trembled.
He drank, not knowing what, nor caring much
For kings who might have cared less for themselves,
He thought, had all the darkness and wild light   1360
That fell together to make Vivian
Been there before them then to flower anew
Through sheathing crimson into candle-light
With each new leer of their loose, liquorish eyes.
Again he drank, and he cursed every king   1365
Who might have touched her even in her cradle;
For what were kings to such as he, who made them
And saw them totter—for the world to see,

And heed, if the world would? He drank again
And yet again—to make himself assured   1370
No manner of king should have the last of it—
The cup that Vivian filled unfailingly
Until she poured for nothing. "At the end
Of this incomparable flowing gold,"
She prattled on to Merlin, who observed   1375
Her solemnly, "I fear there may be specks."—
He sighed aloud, whereat she laughed at him
And pushed the golden cup a little nearer.
He scanned it with a sad anxiety,
And then her face likewise, and shook his head   1380
As if at her concern for such a matter:
"Specks? What are specks? Are you afraid of them?"
He murmured slowly, with a drowsy tongue;
"There are specks everywhere. I fear them not.
If I were king in Camelot, I might   1385
Fear more than specks. But now I fear them not.
You are too strange a lady to fear specks."

He stared a long time at the cup of gold
Before him but he drank no more. There came
Between him and the world a crumbling sky   1390
Of black and crimson, with a crimson cloud
That held a far off town of many towers.
All swayed and shaken, till at last they fell,
And there was nothing but a crimson cloud
That crumbled into nothing, like the sky   1395
That vanished with it, carrying away
The world, the woman, and all memory of them,
Until a slow light of another sky
Made gray an open casement, showing him
Faint shapes of an exotic furniture   1400
That glimmered with a dim magnificence,
And letting in the sound of many birds
That were, as he lay there remembering,
The only occupation of his ears
Until it seemed they shared a fainter sound,   1405
As if a sleeping child with a black head
Beside him drew the breath of innocence.

One shining afternoon around the fountain,
As on the shining day of his arrival,
The sunlight was alive with flying silver   1410
That had for Merlin a more dazzling flash
Than jewels rained in dreams, and a richer sound
Than harps, and all the morning stars together,—

When jewels and harps and stars and everything
That flashed and sang and was not Vivian,   1415
Seemed less than echoes of her least of words—
For she was coming. Suddenly, somewhere
Behind him, she was coming; that was all
He knew until she came and took his hand
And held it while she talked about the fishes.   1420
When she looked up he thought a softer light
Was in her eyes than once he had found there;
And had there been left yet for dusky women
A beauty that was heretofore not hers,
He told himself he must have seen it then   1425
Before him in the face at which he smiled
And trembled. "Many men have called me wise,"
He said, "but you are wiser than all wisdom
If you know what you are."—"I don't," she said;
"I know that you and I are here together;   1430
I know that I have known for twenty years
That life would be almost a constant yawning
Until you came; and now that you are here,
I know that you are not to go away
Until you tell me that I'm hideous;   1435
I know that I like fishes, ferns, and snakes,—
Maybe because I liked them when the world
Was young and you and I were salamanders;
I know, too, a cool place not far from here,
Where there are ferns that are like marching men   1440
Who never march away. Come now and see them,
And do as they do—never march away.
When they are gone, some others, crisp and green,
Will have their place, but never march away."—
He smoothed her silky fingers, one by one: 1445
"Some other Merlin, also, do you think,
Will have his place—and never march away?"—
Then Vivian laid a finger on his lips
And shook her head at him before she laughed:
"There is no other Merlin than yourself,   1450
And you are never going to be old."

Oblivious of a world that made of him
A jest, a legend, and a long regret,
And with a more commanding wizardry
Than his to rule a kingdom where the king   1455
Was Love and the queen Vivian, Merlin found
His queen without the blemish of a word
That was more rough than honey from her lips,
Or the first adumbration of a frown

To cloud the night-wild fire that in her eyes   1460
Had yet a smoky friendliness of home,
And a foreknowing care for mighty trifles.
"There are miles and miles for you to wander in,"
She told him once: "Your prison yard is large,
And I would rather take my two ears off   1465
And feed them to the fishes in the fountain
Than buzz like an incorrigible bee
For always around yours, and have you hate
The sound of me; for some day then, for certain,
Your philosophic rage would see in me   1470
A bee in earnest, and your hand would smite
My life away. And what would you do then?
I know: for years and years you'd sit alone
Upon my grave, and be the grieving image
Of lean remorse, and suffer miserably;   1475
And often, all day long, you'd only shake
Your celebrated head and all it holds,
Or beat it with your fist the while you groaned
Aloud and went on saying to yourself:
'Never should I have killed her, or believed   1480
She was a bee that buzzed herself to death,
First having made me crazy, had there been
Judicious distance and wise absences
To keep the two of us inquisitive.'"—
"I fear you bow your unoffending head   1485
Before a load that should be mine," said he;
"If so, you led me on by listening.
You should have shrieked and jumped, and then fled yelling;
That's the best way when a man talks too long.
God's pity on me if I love your feet   1490
More now than I could ever love the face
Of any one of all those Vivians
You summoned out of nothing on the night
When I saw towers. I'll wander and amend."—
At that she flung the noose of her soft arms   1495
Around his neck and kissed him instantly:
"You are the wisest man that ever was,
And I've a prayer to make: May all you say
To Vivian be a part of what you knew
Before the curse of her unquiet head   1500
Was on your shoulder, as you have it now,
To punish you for knowing beyond knowledge.
You are the only one who sees enough
To make me see how far away I am
From all that I have seen and have not been;   1505
You are only thing there is alive

Between me as I am and as I was
When Merlin was a dream. You are to listen
When I say now to you that I'm alone.
Like you, I saw too much; and unlike you   1510
I made no kingdom out of what I saw—
Or none save this one there that you must rule,
Believing you are ruled. I see too far
To rule myself. Time's way with you and me
Is our way, in that we are out of Time   1515
And out of tune with Time. We have this place,
And you must hold us in it or we die.
Look at me now and say if what I say
Be folly or not; for my unquiet head
Is no conceit of mine. I had it first   1520
When I was born; and I shall have it with me
Till my unquiet soul is on its way
To be, I hope, where souls are quieter.
So let the first and last activity
Of what you say so often is your love   1525
Be always to remember that our lyres
Are not strung for Today. On you it falls
To keep them in accord here with each other,
For you have wisdom; I have only sight
For distant things—and you. And you are Merlin.   1530
Poor wizard! Vivian is your punishment
For making kings of men who are not kings;
And you are mine, by the same reasoning,
For living out of Time and out of tune
With anything but you. No other man   1535
Could make me say so much of what I know
As I say now to you. And you are Merlin!"

She looked up at him till his way was lost
Again in the familiar wilderness
Of night that love made for him in her eyes,   1540
And there he wandered as he said he would;
He wandered also in his prison-yard,
And, when he found her coming after him,
Beguiled her with her own admonishing
And frowned upon her with a fierce reproof   1545
That many a time in the old world outside
Had set the mark of silence on strong men—
Whereat she laughed, not always wholly sure,
Nor always wholly glad, that he who played
So lightly was the wizard of her dreams: 1550
"No matter—if only Merlin keep the world
Away," she thought. "Our lyres have many strings,
But he must know them all, for he is Merlin."

And so for years, till ten of them were gone,—
Ten years, ten seasons, or ten flying ages—   1555
Fate made Broceliande a paradise,
By none invaded, until Dagonet,
Like a discordant, awkward bird of doom,
Flew in with Arthur's message. For the King,
In sorrow cleaving to simplicity,   1560
And having in his love a quick remembrance
Of Merlin's old affection for the fellow,
Had for this vain, reluctant enterprise
Appointed him—the knight who made men laugh,
And was a fool because he played the fool.   1565

"The King believes today, as in his boyhood,
That I am Fate; and I can do no more
Than show again what in his heart he knows,"
Said Merlin to himself and Vivian:
"This time I go because I made him King,   1570
Thereby to be a mirror for the world;
This time I go, but never after this,
For I can be no more than what I was,
And I can do no more than I have done."
He took her slowly in his arms and felt   1575
Her body throbbing like a bird against him:
"This time I go; I go because I must."

And in the morning, when he rode away
With Dagonet and Blaise through the same gate
That once had clanged as if to shut for ever,   1580
She had not even asked him not to go;
For it was then that in his lonely gaze
Of helpless love and sad authority
She found the gleam of his imprisoned power
That Fate withheld; and, pitying herself,   1585
She pitied the fond Merlin she had changed,
And saw the Merlin who had changed the world.

VI
"No kings are coming on their hands and knees,
Nor yet on horses or in chariots,
To carry me away from you again,"   1590
Said Merlin, winding around Vivian's ear
A shred of her black hair. "King Arthur knows
That I have done with kings, and that I speak
No more their crafty language. Once I knew it,
But now the only language I have left   1595

Is one that I must never let you hear
Too long, or know too well. When towering deeds
Once done shall only out of dust and words
Be done again, the doer may then be wary
Lest in the complement of his new fabric   1600
There be more words than dust."

                 "Why tell me so?"
Said Vivian; and a singular thin laugh
Came after her thin question. "Do you think
That I'm so far away from history
That I require, even of the wisest man   1605
Who ever said the wrong thing to a woman,
So large a light on what I know already—
When all I seek is here before me now
In your new eyes that you have brought for me
From Camelot? The eyes you took away   1610
Were sad and old; and I could see in them
A Merlin who remembered all the kings
He ever saw, and wished himself, almost,
Away from Vivian, to make other kings,
And shake the world again in the old manner.   1615
I saw myself no bigger than a beetle
For several days, and wondered if your love
Were large enough to make me any larger
When you came back. Am I a beetle still?"
She stood up on her toes and held her cheek   1620
For some time against his, and let him go.

"I fear the time has come for me to wander
A little in my prison-yard," he said.—
"No, tell me everything that you have seen
And heard and done, and seen done, and heard done,   1625
Since you deserted me. And tell me first
What the King thinks of me."—"The King believes
That you are almost what you are," he told her:
"The beauty of all ages that are vanished,
Reborn to be the wonder of one woman."—   1630
"I knew he hated me. What else of him?"—
"And all that I have seen and heard and done,
Which is not much, would make a weary telling;
And all your part of it would be to sleep,
And dream that Merlin had his beard again."—   1635
"Then tell me more about your good fool knight,
Sir Dagonet. If Blaise were not half-mad
Already with his pondering on the name
And shield of his unshielding nameless father,

I'd make a fool of him. I'd call him Ajax;   1640
I'd have him shake his fist at thunder-storms,
And dance a jig as long as there was lightning,
And so till I forgot myself entirely.
Not even your love may do so much as that."—
"Thunder and lightning are no friends of mine,"   1645
Said Merlin slowly, "more than they are yours;
They bring me nearer to the elements
From which I came than I care now to be."—
"You owe a service to those elements;
For by their service you outwitted age   1650
And made the world a kingdom of your will."—
He touched her hand, smiling: "Whatever service
Of mine awaits them will not be forgotten,"
He said: and the smile faded on his face.—
"Now of all graceless and ungrateful wizards—"   1655
But there she ceased, for she found in his eyes
The first of a new fear. "The wrong word rules
Today," she said; "and we'll have no more journeys."

Although he wandered rather more than ever
Since he had come again to Brittany   1660
From Camelot, Merlin found eternally
Before him a new loneliness that made
Of garden, park, and woodland, all alike,
A desolation and a changelessness
Defying reason, without Vivian   1665
Beside him, like a child with a black head,
Or moving on before him, or somewhere
So near him that, although he saw it not
With eyes, he felt the picture of her beauty
And shivered at the nearness of her being.   1670
Without her now there was no past or future,
And a vague, soul-consuming premonition
He found the only tenant of the present;
He wondered, when she was away from him,
If his avenging injured intellect   1675
Might shine with Arthur's kingdom a twin mirror,
Fate's plaything, for new ages without eyes
To see therein themselves and their declension.
Love made his hours a martyrdom without her;
The world was like an empty house without her,   1680
Where Merlin was a prisoner of love
Confined within himself by too much freedom,
Repeating an unending exploration
Of many solitary silent rooms,
And only in a way remembering now   1685

That once their very solitude and silence
Had by the magic of expectancy
Made sure what now he doubted—though his doubts,
Day after day, were founded on a shadow.

For now to Merlin, in his paradise,   1690
Had come an unseen angel with a sword
Unseen, the touch of which was a long fear
For longer sorrow that had never come,
Yet might if he compelled it. He discovered,
One golden day in autumn as he wandered,   1695
That he had made the radiance of two years
A misty twilight when he might as well
Have had no mist between him and the sun,
The sun being Vivian. On his coming then
To find her all in green against a wall   1700
Of green and yellow leaves, and crumbling bread
For birds around the fountain while she sang
And the birds ate the bread, he told himself
That everything today was as it was
At first, and for a minute he believed it.   1705
"I'd have you always all in green out here,"
He said, "if I had much to say about it."—
She clapped her crumbs away and laughed at him:
"I've covered up my bones with every color
That I can carry on them without screaming,   1710
And you have liked them all—or made me think so."—
"I must have liked them if you thought I did,"
He answered, sighing; "but the sight of you
Today as on the day I saw you first,
All green, all wonderful" . . . He tore a leaf   1715
To pieces with a melancholy care
That made her smile.—"Why pause at 'wonderful'?
You've hardly been yourself since you came back
From Camelot, where that unpleasant King
Said things that you have never said to me."—   1720
He looked upon her with a worn reproach:
"The King said nothing that I keep from you."—
"What is it then?" she asked, imploringly;
"You man of moods and miracles, what is it?"—
He shook his head and tore another leaf: 1725
"There is no need of asking what it is;
Whatever you or I may choose to name it,
The name of it is Fate, who played with me
And gave me eyes to read of the unwritten
More lines than I have read. I see no more   1730
Today than yesterday, but I remember.

My ways are not the ways of other men;
My memories go forward. It was you
Who said that we were not in tune with Time;
It was not I who said it."— "But you knew it;   1735
What matter then who said it?"—"It was you
Who said that Merlin was your punishment
For being in tune with him and not with Time—
With Time or with the world; and it was you
Who said you were alone, even here with Merlin;   1740
It was not I who said it. It is I
Who tell you now my inmost thoughts." He laughed
As if at hidden pain around his heart,
But there was not much laughing in his eyes.
They walked, and for a season they were silent: 1745
"I shall know what you mean by that," she said,
"When you have told me. Here's an oak you like,
And here's a place that fits me wondrous well
To sit in. You sit there. I've seen you there
Before; and I have spoiled your noble thoughts   1750
By walking all my fingers up and down
Your countenance, as if they were the feet
Of a small animal with no great claws.
Tell me a story now about the world,
And the men in it, what they do in it,   1755
And why it is they do it all so badly."—
"I've told you every story that I know,
Almost," he said.—"O, don't begin like that."—
"Well, once upon a time there was a King."—
"That has a more commendable address;   1760
Go on, and tell me all about the King;
I'll bet the King had warts or carbuncles,
Or something wrong in his divine insides,
To make him wish that Adam had died young."

Merlin observed her slowly with a frown   1765
Of saddened wonder. She laughed rather lightly.
And at his heart he felt again the sword
Whose touch was a long fear for longer sorrow.
"Well, once upon a time there was a king,"
He said again, but now in a dry voice   1770
That wavered and betrayed a venturing.
He paused, and would have hesitated longer,
But something in him that was not himself
Compelled an utterance that his tongue obeyed,
As an unwilling child obeys a father   1775
Who might be richer for obedience
If he obeyed the child: "There was a king

Who would have made his reign a monument
For kings and peoples of the waiting ages
To reverence and remember, and to this end   1780
He coveted and won, with no ado
To make a story of, a neighbor queen
Who limed him with her smile and had of him,
In token of their sin, what he found soon
To be a sort of mongrel son and nephew—   1785
And a most precious reptile in addition—
To ornament his court and carry arms,
And latterly to be the darker half
Of ruin. Also the king, who made of love
More than he made of life and death together,   1790
Forgot the world and his example in it
For yet another woman—one of many—
And this one he made Queen, albeit he knew
That her unsworn allegiance to the knight
That he had loved the best of all his order   1795
Must one day bring along the coming end
Of love and honor and of everything;
And with a kingdom builded on two pits
Of living sin,—so founded by the will
Of one wise counsellor who loved the king,   1800
And loved the world and therefore made him king
To be a mirror for it,—the king reigned well
For certain years, awaiting a sure doom;
For certain years he waved across the world
A royal banner with a Dragon on it;   1805
And men of every land fell worshipping
The Dragon as it were the living God,
And not the living sin."

                              She rose at that,
And after a calm yawn, she looked at Merlin:
"Why all this new insistence upon sin?"   1810
She said; "I wonder if I understand
This king of yours, with all his pits and dragons;
I know I do not like him." A thinner light
Was in her eyes than he had found in them
Since he became the willing prisoner   1815
That she had made of him; and on her mouth
Lay now a colder line of irony
Than all his fears or nightmares could have drawn
Before today: "What reason do you know
For me to listen to this king of yours?   1820
What reading has a man of woman's days,
Even though the man be Merlin and a prophet?"

"I know no call for you to love the king,"
Said Merlin, driven ruinously along
By the vindictive urging of his fate;   1825
"I know no call for you to love the king,
Although you serve him, knowing not yet the king
You serve. There is no man, or any woman,
For whom the story of the living king
Is not the story of the living sin.   1830
I thought my story was the common one,
For common recognition and regard."

"Then let us have no more of it," she said;
"For we are not so common, I believe,
That we need kings and pits and flags and dragons   1835
To make us know that we have let the world
Go by us. Have you missed the world so much
That you must have it in with all its clots
And wounds and bristles on to make us happy—
Like Blaise, with shouts and horns and seven men   1840
Triumphant with a most unlovely boar?
Is there no other story in the world
Than this one of a man that you made king
To be a moral for the speckled ages?
You said once long ago, if you remember,   1845
'You are too strange a lady to fear specks';
And it was you, you said, who feared them not.
Why do you look at me as at a snake
All coiled to spring at you and strike you dead?
I am not going to spring at you, or bite you;   1850
I'm going home. And you, if you are kind,
Will have no fear to wander for an hour.
I'm sure the time has come for you to wander;
And there may come a time for you to say
What most you think it is that we need here   1855
To make of this Broceliande a refuge
Where two disheartened sinners may forget
A world that has today no place for them."

A melancholy wave of revelation
Broke over Merlin like a rising sea,   1860
Long viewed unwillingly and long denied.
He saw what he had seen, but would not feel,
Till now the bitterness of what he felt
Was in his throat, and all the coldness of it
Was on him and around him like a flood   1865
Of lonelier memories than he had said
Were memories, although he knew them now

For what they were—for what his eyes had seen,
For what his ears had heard and what his heart
Had felt, with him not knowing what it felt.   1870
But now he knew that his cold angel's name
Was Change, and that a mightier will than his
Or Vivian's had ordained that he be there.
To Vivian he could not say anything
But words that had no more of hope in them   1875
Than anguish had of peace: "I meant the world . . .
I meant the world," he groaned; "not you—not me."

Again the frozen line of irony
Was on her mouth. He looked up once at it.
And then away—too fearful of her eyes   1880
To see what he could hear now in her laugh
That melted slowly into what she said,
Like snow in icy water: "This world of yours
Will surely be the end of us. And why not?
I'm overmuch afraid we're part of it,—   1885
Or why do we build walls up all around us,
With gates of iron that make us think the day
Of judgment's coming when they clang behind us?
And yet you tell me that you fear no specks!
With you I never cared for them enough   1890
To think of them. I was too strange a lady.
And your return is now a speckled king
And something that you call a living sin—
That's like an uninvited poor relation
Who comes without a welcome, rather late,   1895
And on a foundered horse."

                              "Specks? What are specks?"
He gazed at her in a forlorn wonderment
That made her say: "You said, 'I fear them not.'
'If I were king in Camelot,' you said,
'I might fear more than specks.' Have you forgotten?   1900
Don't tell me, Merlin, you are growing old.
Why don't you make somehow a queen of me,
And give me half the world? I'd wager thrushes
That I should reign, with you to turn the wheel,
As well as any king that ever was.   1905
The curse on me is that I cannot serve
A ruler who forgets that he is king."

In his bewildered misery Merlin then
Stared hard at Vivian's face, more like a slave
Who sought for common mercy than like Merlin: 1910

"You speak a language that was never mine,
Or I have lost my wits. Why do you seize
The flimsiest of opportunities
To make of what I said another thing
Than love or reason could have let me say,   1915
Or let me fancy? Why do you keep the truth
So far away from me, when all your gates
Will open at your word and let me go
To some place where no fear or weariness
Of yours need ever dwell? Why does a woman,   1920
Made otherwise a miracle of love
And loveliness, and of immortal beauty,
Tear one word by the roots out of a thousand,
And worry it, and torture it, and shake it.
Like a small dog that has a rag to play with?   1925
What coil of an ingenious destiny
Is this that makes of what I never meant
A meaning as remote as hell from heaven?"

"I don't know," Vivian said reluctantly,
And half as if in pain; "I'm going home.   1930
I'm going home and leave you here to wander,
Pray take your kings and sins away somewhere
And bury them, and bury the Queen in also.
I know this king; he lives in Camelot,
And I shall never like him. There are specks   1935
Almost all over him. Long live the king,
But not the king who lives in Camelot,
With Modred, Lancelot, and Guinevere—
And all four speckled like a merry nest
Of addled eggs together. You made him King   1940
Because you loved the world and saw in him
From infancy a mirror for the millions.
The world will see itself in him, and then
The world will say its prayers and wash its face,
And build for some new king a new foundation   1945
Long live the King! . . . But now I apprehend
A time for me to shudder and grow old
And garrulous—and so become a fright
For Blaise to take out walking in warm weather—
Should I give way to long considering   1950
Of worlds you may have lost while prisoned here
With me and my light mind. I contemplate
Another name for this forbidden place,
And one more fitting. Tell me, if you find it,
Some fitter name than Eden. We have had   1955
A man and woman in it for some time,

And now, it seems, we have a Tree of Knowledge."
She looked up at the branches overhead
And shrugged her shoulders. Then she went away;
And what was left of Merlin's happiness,   1960
Like a disloyal phantom, followed her.

He felt the sword of his cold angel thrust
And twisted in his heart, as if the end
Were coming next, but the cold angel passed
Invisibly and left him desolate,   1965
With misty brow and eyes. "The man who sees
May see too far, and he may see too late
The path he takes unseen," he told himself
When he found thought again. "The man who sees
May go on seeing till the immortal flame   1970
That lights and lures him folds him in its heart,
And leaves of what there was of him to die
An item of inhospitable dust
That love and hate alike must hide away;
Or there may still be charted for his feet   1975
A dimmer faring, where the touch of time
Were like the passing of a twilight moth
From flower to flower into oblivion,
If there were not somewhere a barren end
Of moths and flowers, and glimmering far away   1980
Beyond a desert where the flowerless days
Are told in slow defeats and agonies,
The guiding of a nameless light that once
Had made him see too much—and has by now
Revealed in death, to the undying child   1985
Of Lancelot, the Grail. For this pure light
Has many rays to throw, for many men
To follow; and the wise are not all pure,
Nor are the pure all wise who follow it.
There are more rays than men. But let the man   1990
Who saw too much, and was to drive himself
From paradise, play too lightly or too long
Among the moths and flowers, he finds at last
There is a dim way out; and he shall grope
Where pleasant shadows lead him to the plain   1995
That has no shadow save his own behind him.
And there, with no complaint, nor much regret,
Shall he plod on, with death between him now
And the far light that guides him, till he falls
And has an empty thought of empty rest;   2000
Then Fate will put a mattock in his hands
And lash him while he digs himself the grave

That is to be the pallet and the shroud
Of his poor blundering bones. The man who saw
Too much must have an eye to see at last   2005
Where Fate has marked the clay; and he shall delve,
Although his hand may slacken, and his knees
May rock without a method as he toils;
For there's a delving that is to be done—
If not for God, for man. I see the light,   2010
But I shall fall before I come to it;
For I am old. I was young yesterday.
Time's hand that I have held away so long
Grips hard now on my shoulder. Time has won.
Tomorrow I shall say to Vivian   2015
That I am old and gaunt and garrulous,
And tell her one more story: I am old."

There were long hours for Merlin after that,
And much long wandering in his prison-yard,
Where now the progress of each heavy step   2020
Confirmed a stillness of impending change
And imminent farewell. To Vivian's ear
There came for many days no other story
Than Merlin's iteration of his love
And his departure from Broceliande,   2025
Where Merlin still remained. In Vivian's eye,
There was a quiet kindness, and at times
A smoky flash of incredulity
That faded into pain. Was this the Merlin—
This incarnation of idolatry   2030
And all but supplicating deference—
This bowed and reverential contradiction
Of all her dreams and her realities—
Was this the Merlin who for years and years
Before she found him had so made her love him   2035
That kings and princes, thrones and diadems,
And honorable men who drowned themselves
For love, were less to her than melon-shells?
Was this the Merlin whom her fate had sent
One spring day to come ringing at her gate,   2040
Bewildering her love with happy terror
That later was to be all happiness?
Was this the Merlin who had made the world
Half over, and then left it with a laugh
To be the youngest, oldest, weirdest, gayest,   2045
And wisest, and sometimes the foolishest
Of all the men of her consideration?
Was this the man who had made other men

As ordinary as arithmetic?
Was this man Merlin who came now so slowly   2050
Towards the fountain where she stood again
In shimmering green? Trembling, he took her hands
And pressed them fondly, one upon the other,
Between his:

          "I was wrong that other day,
For I have one more story. I am old."   2055
He waited like one hungry for the word
Not said; and she found in his eyes a light
As patient as a candle in a window
That looks upon the sea and is a mark
For ships that have gone down. "Tomorrow," he said,   2060
"Tomorrow I shall go away again
To Camelot; and I shall see the King
Once more; and I may come to you again
Once more; and I shall go away again
For ever. There is now no more than that   2065
For me to do; and I shall do no more.
I saw too much when I saw Camelot;
And I saw farther backward into Time,
And forward, than a man may see and live,
When I made Arthur king. I saw too far,   2070
But not so far as this. Fate played with me
As I have played with Time; and Time, like me,
Being less than Fate, will have on me his vengeance.
On Fate there is no vengeance, even for God."
He drew her slowly into his embrace   2075
And held her there, but when he kissed her lips
They were as cold as leaves and had no answer;
For Time had given him then, to prove his words,
A frozen moment of a woman's life.

When Merlin the next morning came again   2080
In the same pilgrim robe that he had worn
While he sat waiting where the cherry-blossoms
Outside the gate fell on him and around him
Grief came to Vivian at the sight of him;
And like a flash of a swift ugly knife,   2085
A blinding fear came with it. "Are you going?"
She said, more with her lips than with her voice;
And he said, "I am going. Blaise and I
Are going down together to the shore,
And Blaise is coming back. For this one day   2090
Be good enough to spare him, for I like him.
I tell you now, as once I told the King,

That I can be no more than what I was,
And I can say no more than I have said.
Sometimes you told me that I spoke too long   2095
And sent me off to wander. That was good.
I go now for another wandering,
And I pray God that all be well with you."

For long there was a whining in her ears
Of distant wheels departing. When it ceased,   2100
She closed the gate again so quietly
That Merlin could have heard no sound of it.

VII

By Merlin's Rock, where Dagonet the fool
Was given through many a dying afternoon
To sit and meditate on human ways   2105
And ways divine, Gawaine and Bedivere
Stood silent, gazing down on Camelot.
The two had risen and were going home:
"It hits more sore, Gawaine," said Bedivere,
"To think on all the tumult and affliction   2110
Down there, and all the noise and preparation
That hums of coming death, and, if my fears
Be born of reason, of what's more than death.
Wherefore, I say to you again, Gawaine,—
To you—that this late hour is not too late   2115
For you to change yourself and change the King:
For though the King may love me with a love
More tried, and older, and more sure, may be,
Than for another, for such a time as this
The friend who turns him to the world again   2120
Shall have a tongue more gracious and an eye
More shrewd than mine. For such a time as this
The King must have a glamour to persuade him."

"The King shall have a glamour, and anon,"
Gawaine said, and he shot death from his eyes;   2125
"If you were King, as Arthur is—or was—
And Lancelot had carried off your Queen,
And killed a score or so of your best knights—
Not mentioning my two brothers, whom he slew
Unarmored and unarmed—God save your wits!   2130
Two stewards with skewers could have done as much,
And you and I might now be rotting for it."

"But Lancelot's men were crowded,—they were crushed;
And there was nothing for them but to strike

Or die, not seeing where they struck. Think you   2135
They would have slain Gareth and Gaheris,
And Tor, and all those other friends of theirs?
God's mercy for the world he made, I say,
And for the blood that writes the story of it.
Gareth and Gaheris, Tor and Lamorak,—   2140
All dead, with all the others that are dead!
These years have made me turn to Lamorak
For counsel—and now Lamorak is dead."
"Why do you fling those two names in my face?
'Twas Modred made an end of Lamorak,   2145
Not I; and Lancelot now has done for Tor.
I'll urge no king on after Lancelot
For such a two as Tor and Lamorak:
Their father killed my father, and their friend
Was Lancelot, not I. I'll own my fault—   2150
I'm living; and while I've a tongue can talk,
I'll say this to the King: 'Burn Lancelot
By inches till he give you back the Queen;
Then hang him—drown him—or do anything
To rid the world of him.' He killed my brothers,   2155
And he was once my friend. Now damn the soul
Of him who killed my brothers! There you have me."

"You are a strong man, Gawaine, and your strength
Goes ill where foes are. You may cleave their limbs
And heads off, but you cannot damn their souls;   2160
What you may do now is to save their souls,
And bodies too, and like enough you own.
Remember that King Arthur is a king,
And where there is a king there is a kingdom.
Is not the kingdom any more to you   2165
Than one brief enemy? Would you see it fall
And the King with it, for one mortal hate
That burns out reason? Gawaine, you are king
Today. Another day may see no king
But Havoc, if you have no other word   2170
For Arthur now than hate for Lancelot.
Is not the world as large as Lancelot?
Is Lancelot, because one woman's eyes
Are brighter when they look on him, to sluice
The world with angry blood? Poor flesh! Poor flesh!   2175
And you, Gawaine,—are you so gaffed with hate
You cannot leave it and so plunge away
To stiller places and there see, for once,
What hangs on this pernicious expedition
The King in his insane forgetfulness   2180

Would undertake—with you to drum him on?
Are you as mad as he and Lancelot
Made ravening into one man twice as mad
As either? Is the kingdom of the world.
Now rocking, to go down in sound and blood   2185
And ashes and sick ruin, and for the sake
Of three men and a woman? If it be so,
God's mercy for the world he made, I say,—
And say again to Dagonet. Sir Fool,
Your throne is empty, and you may as well   2190
Sit on it and be ruler of the world
From now till supper-time."

                    Sir Dagonet,
Appearing, made reply to Bedivere's
Dry welcome with a famished look of pain,
On which he built a smile: "If I were King,   2195
You, Bedivere, should be my counsellor;
And we should have no more wars over women.
I'll sit me down and meditate on that."
Gawaine, for all his anger, laughed a little,
And clapped the fool's lean shoulder; for he loved him   2200
And was with Arthur when he made him knight.
Then Dagonet said on to Bedivere,
As if his tongue would make a jest of sorrow:
"Sometime I'll tell you what I might have done
Had I been Lancelot and you King Arthur—   2205
Each having in himself the vicious essence
That now lives in the other and makes war.
When all men are like you and me, my lord,
When all are rational or rickety,
There may be no more war. But what's here now?   2210
Lancelot loves the Queen, and he makes war
Of love; the King, being bitten to the soul
By love and hate that work in him together,
Makes war of madness; Gawaine hates Lancelot,
And he, to be in tune, makes war of hate;   2215
Modred hates everything, yet he can see
With one damned illegitimate small eye
His father's crown, and with another like it
He sees the beauty of the Queen herself;
He needs the two for his ambitious pleasure,   2220
And therefore he makes war of his ambition;
And somewhere in the middle of all this
There's a squeezed world that elbows for attention.
Poor Merlin, buried in Broceliande!
He must have had an academic eye   2225

For woman when he founded Arthur's kingdom,
And in Broceliande he may be sorry.
Flutes, hautboys, drums, and viols. God be with him!
I'm glad they tell me there's another world,
For this one's a disease without a doctor."   2230

"No, not so bad as that," said Bedivere;
"The doctor, like ourselves, may now be learning;
And Merlin may have gauged his enterprise
Whatever the cost he may have paid for knowing.
We pass, but many are to follow us,   2235
And what they build may stay; though I believe
Another age will have another Merlin,
Another Camelot, and another King.
Sir Dagonet, farewell."

                    "Farewell, Sir Knight,
And you, Sir Knight: Gawaine, you have the world   2240
Now in your fingers—an uncommon toy,
Albeit a small persuasion in the balance
With one man's hate. I'm glad you're not a fool,
For then you might be rickety, as I am,
And rational as Bedivere. Farewell.   2245
I'll sit here and be king. God save the King!"

But Gawaine scowled and frowned and answered nothing
As he went slowly down with Bedivere
To Camelot, where Arthur's army waited
The King's word for the melancholy march   2250
To Joyous Gard, where Lancelot hid the Queen
And armed his host, and there was now no joy,
As there was now no joy for Dagonet
While he sat brooding, with his wan cheek-bones
Hooked with his bony fingers: "Go, Gawaine,"   2255
He mumbled: "Go your way, and drag the world
Along down with you. What's a world or so
To you if you can hide an ell of iron
Somewhere in Lancelot, and hear him wheeze
And sputter once or twice before he goes   2260
Wherever the Queen sends him? There's a man
Who should have been a king, and would have been,
Had he been born so. So should I have been
A king, had I been born so, fool or no:
King Dagonet, or Dagonet the King;   2265
King-Fool, Fool-King; 'twere not impossible.
I'll meditate on that and pray for Arthur,
Who made me all I am, except a fool.

Now he goes mad for love, as I might go
Had I been born a king and not a fool   2270
Today I think I'd rather be a fool;
Today the world is less than one scared woman—
Wherefore a field of waving men may soon
Be shorn by Time's indifferent scythe, because
The King is mad. The seeds of history   2275
Are small, but given a few gouts of warm blood
For quickening, they sprout out wondrously
And have a leaping growth whereof no man
May shun such harvesting of change or death,
Of life, as may fall on him to be borne.   2280
When I am still alive and rickety,
And Bedivere's alive and rational—
If he come out of this, and there's a doubt,—
The King, Gawaine, Modred, and Lancelot
May all be lying underneath a weight   2285
Of bloody sheaves too heavy for their shoulders
All spent, and all dishonored, and all dead;
And if it come to be that this be so,
And it be true that Merlin saw the truth,
Such harvest were the best. Your fool sees not   2290
So far as Merlin sees: yet if he saw
The truth—why then, such harvest were the best
I'll pray for Arthur; I can do no more."

"Why not for Merlin? Or do you count him,
Is this extreme, so foreign to salvation   2295
That prayer would be a stranger to his name?"

Poor Dagonet, with terror shaking him,
Stood up and saw before him an old face
Made older with an inch of silver beard,
And faded eyes more eloquent of pain   2300
And ruin than all the faded eyes of age
Till now had ever been, although in them
There was a mystic and intrinsic peace
Of one who sees where men of nearer sight
See nothing. On their way to Camelot,   2305
Gawaine and Bedivere had passed him by,
With lax attention for the pilgrim cloak
They passed, and what it hid: yet Merlin saw
Their faces, and he saw the tale was true
That he had lately drawn from solemn strangers.   2310

"Well, Dagonet, and by your leave," he said,
"I'll rest my lonely relics for a while

On this rock that was mine and now is yours.
I favor the succession; for you know
Far more than many doctors, though your doubt   2315
Is your peculiar poison. I foresaw
Long since, and I have latterly been told
What moves in this commotion down below
To show men what it means. It means the end—
If men whose tongues had less to say to me   2320
Than had their shoulders are adept enough
To know; and you may pray for me or not,
Sir Friend, Sir Dagonet."

                         "Sir fool, you mean,"
Dagonet said, and gazed on Merlin sadly:
"I'll never pray again for anything,   2325
And last of all for this that you behold—
The smouldering faggot of unlovely bones
That God has given to me to call Myself.
When Merlin comes to Dagonet for prayer,
It is indeed the end."

                         "And in the end   2330
Are more beginnings, Dagonet, than men
Shall name or know today. It was the end
Of Arthur's insubstantial majesty
When to him and his knights the Grail foreshowed
The quest of life that was to be the death   2335
Of many, and the slow discouraging
Of many more. Or do I err in this?"
"No," Dagonet replied; "there was a Light;
And Galahad, in the Siege Perilous,
Alone of all on whom it fell, was calm;   2340
There was a Light wherein men saw themselves
In one another as they might become—
Or so they dreamed. There was a long to-do,
And Gawaine, of all forlorn ineligibles,
Rose up the first, and cried more lustily   2345
Than any after him that he should find
The Grail, or die for it,—though he did neither;
For he came back as living and as fit
For new and old iniquity as ever.
Then Lancelot came back, and Bors came back,—   2350
Like men who had seen more than men should see,
And still come back. They told of Percival
Who saw too much to make of this worn life
A long necessity, and of Galahad,
Who died and is alive. They all saw Something.   2355

God knows the meaning or the end of it,
But they saw Something. And if I've an eye,
Small joy has the Queen been to Lancelot
Since he came back from seeing what he saw;
For though his passion hold him like hot claws,　　　2360
He's neither in the world nor out of it.
Gawaine is king, though Arthur wears the crown;
And Gawaine's hate for Lancelot is the sword
That hangs by one of Merlin's fragile hairs
Above the world. Were you to see the King,　　　2365
The frenzy that has overthrown his wisdom,
Instead of him and his upheaving empire,
Might have an end."

　　　　　　　　"I came to see the King,"
Said Merlin, like a man who labors hard
And long with an importunate confession.　　　2370
"No, Dagonet, you cannot tell me why,
Although your tongue is eager with wild hope
To tell me more than I may tell myself
About myself. All this that was to be
Might show to man how vain it were to wreck　　　2375
The world for self if it were all in vain.
When I began with Arthur I could see
In each bewildered man who dots the earth
A moment with his days a groping thought
Of an eternal will, strangely endowed　　　2380
With merciful illusions whereby self
Becomes the will itself and each man swells
In fond accordance with his agency.
Now Arthur, Modred, Lancelot, and Gawaine
Are swollen thoughts of this eternal will　　　2385
Which have no other way to find the way
That leads them on to their inheritance
Than by the time-infuriating flame
Of a wrecked empire, lighted by the torch
Of woman, who, together with the light　　　2390
That Galahad found, is yet to light the world."

A wan smile crept across the weary face
Of Dagonet the fool: "If you knew that
Before your burial in Broceliande,
No wonder your eternal will accords　　　2395
With all your dreams of what the world requires.
My master, I may say this unto you
Because I am a fool, and fear no man;
My fear is that I've been a groping thought

That never swelled enough. You say the torch   2400
Of woman and the light that Galahad found
Are some day to illuminate the world?
I'll meditate on that. The world is done
For me; and I have been, to make men laugh,
A lean thing of no shape and many capers.   2405
I made them laugh, and I could laugh anon
Myself to see them killing one another
Because a woman with corn-colored hair
Has pranked a man with horns. 'Twas but a flash
Of chance, and Lancelot, the other day   2410
That saved this pleasing sinner from the fire
That she may spread for thousands. Were she now
The cinder the King willed, or were you now
To see the King, the fire might yet go out;
But the eternal will says otherwise.   2415
So be it; I'll assemble certain gold
That I may say is mine and get myself
Away from this accurst unhappy court,
And in some quiet place where shepherd clowns
And cowherds may have more respondent ears   2420
Than kings and kingdom-builders, I shall troll
Old men to easy graves and be a child
Again among the children of the earth.
I'll have no more kings, even though I loved
King Arthur, who is mad, as I could love   2425
No other man save Merlin, who is dead."

"Not wholly dead, but old. Merlin is old."
The wizard shivered as he spoke, and stared
Away into the sunset where he saw
Once more, as through a cracked and cloudy glass,   2430
A crumbling sky that held a crimson cloud
Wherein there was a town of many towers
All swayed and shaken, in a woman's hand
This time, till out of it there spilled and flashed
And tumbled, like loose jewels, town, towers, and walls,   2435
And there was nothing but a crumbling sky
That made anon of black and red and ruin
A wild and final rain on Camelot.
He bowed, and pressed his eyes: "Now by my soul,
I have seen this before—all black and red—   2440
Like that—like that—like Vivian—black and red;
Like Vivian, when her eyes looked into mine
Across the cups of gold. A flute was playing—
Then all was black and red."

Another smile
Crept over the wan face of Dagonet,   2445
Who shivered in his turn. "The torch of woman,"
He muttered, "and the light that Galahad found,
Will some day save us all, as they saved Merlin.
Forgive my shivering wits, but I am cold,
And it will soon be dark. Will you do down   2450
With me to see the King, or will you not?
If not, I go tomorrow to the shepherds.
The world is mad, and I'm a groping thought
Of your eternal will; the world and I
Are strangers, and I'll have no more of it—   2455
Except you go with me to see the King."

"No, Dagonet, you cannot leave me now,"
Said Merlin, sadly. "You and I are old;
And, as you say, we fear no man. God knows
I would not have the love that once you had   2460
For me be fear of me, for I am past
All fearing now. But Fate may send a fly
Sometimes, and he may sting us to the grave,
So driven to test our faith in what we see.
Are you, now I am coming to an end,   2465
As Arthur's days are coming to an end,
To sting me like a fly? I do not ask
Of you to say that you see what I see,
Where you see nothing; nor do I require
Of any man more vision than is his;   2470
Yet I could wish for you a larger part
For your last entrance here than this you play
Tonight of a sad insect stinging Merlin.
The more you sting, the more he pities you;
And you were never overfond of pity.   2475
Had you been so, I doubt if Arthur's love,
Or Gawaine's, would have made of you a knight.
No, Dagonet, you cannot leave me now,
Nor would you if you could. You call yourself
A fool, because the world and you are strangers.   2480
You are a proud man, Dagonet; you have suffered
What I alone have seen. You are no fool;
And surely you are not a fly to sting
My love to last regret. Believe or not
What I have seen, or what I say to you,   2585
But say no more to me that I am dead
Because the King is mad, and you are old,
And I am older. In Broceliande
Time overtook me as I knew he must;

And I, with a fond overplus of words,   2490
Had warned the lady Vivian already,
Before these wrinkles and this hesitancy
Inhibiting my joints oppressed her sight
With age and dissolution. She said once
That she was cold and cruel; but she meant   2495
That she was warm and kind, and over-wise
For woman in a world where men see not
Beyond themselves. She saw beyond them all,
As I did; and she waited, as I did,
The coming of a day when cherry-blossoms   2500
Were to fall down all over me like snow
In springtime. I was far from Camelot
That afternoon; and I am farther now
From her. I see no more for me to do
Than to leave her and Arthur and the world   2505
Behind me, and to pray that all be well
With Vivian, whose unquiet heart is hungry
For what is not, and what shall never be
Without her, in a world that men are making,
Knowing not how, nor caring yet to know   2510
How slowly and how grievously they do it,—
Though Vivian, in her golden shell of exile,
Knows now and cares, not knowing that she cares,
Nor caring that she knows. In time to be,
The like of her shall have another name   2515
Than Vivian, and her laugh shall be a fire,
Not shining only to consume itself
With what it burns. She knows not yet the name
Of what she is, for now there is no name;
Some day there shall be. Time has many names,   2520
Unwritten yet, for what we say is old
Because we are so young that it seems old.
And this is all a part of what I saw
Before you saw King Arthur. When we parted.
I told her I should see the King again,   2525
And, having seen him, might go back again
To see her face once more. But I shall see
No more the lady Vivian. Let her love
What man she may, no other love than mine
Shall be an index of her memories.   2530
I fear no man who may come after me,
And I see none. I see her, still in green,
Beside the fountain. I shall not go back.
We pay for going back; and all we get
Is one more needless ounce of weary wisdom   2535
To bring away with us. If I come not,

The lady Vivian will remember me,
And say: 'I knew him when his heart was young,
Though I have lost him now. Time called him home,
And that was as it was; for much is lost   2540
Between Broceliande and Camelot.'"

He stared away into the west again,
Where now no crimson cloud or phantom town
Deceived his eyes. Above a living town
There were gray clouds and ultimate suspense,   2545
And a cold wind was coming. Dagonet,
Now crouched at Merlin's feet in his dejection,
Saw multiplying lights far down below,
Where lay the fevered streets. At length he felt
On his lean shoulder Merlin's tragic hand   2550
And trembled, knowing that a few more days
Would see the last of Arthur and the first
Of Modred, whose dark patience had attained
To one precarious half of what he sought:
"And even the Queen herself may fall to him,"   2555
Dagonet murmured.—"The Queen fall to Modred?
Is that your only fear tonight?" said Merlin;
"She may, but not for long."—"No, not my fear;
For I fear nothing. But I wish no fate
Like that for any woman the King loves,   2560
Although she be the scourge and the end of him
That you saw coming, as I see it now."
Dagonet shook, but he would have no tears,
He swore, for any king, queen, knave, or wizard—
Albeit he was a stranger among those   2565
Who laughed at him because he was a fool.
"You said the truth, I cannot leave you now,"
He stammered, and was angry for the tears
That mocked his will and choked him.

                                        Merlin smiled,
Faintly, and for the moment: "Dagonet,   2570
I need your word as one of Arthur's knights
That you will go on with me to the end
Of my short way, and say unto no man
Or woman that you found or saw me here.
No good would follow, for a doubt would live   2575
Unstifled of my loyalty to him
Whose deeds are wrought for those who are to come;
And many who see not what I have seen,
Or what you see tonight, would prattle on
For ever, and their children after them,   2580

Of what might once have been had I gone down
With you to Camelot to see the King.
I came to see the King,—but why see kings?
All this that was to be is what I saw
Before there was an Arthur to be king,   2585
And so to be a mirror wherein men
May see themselves, and pause. If they see not,
Or if they do see and they ponder not,—
I saw; but I was neither Fate nor God.
I saw too much; and this would be the end,   2590
Were there to be an end. I saw myself—
A sight no other man has ever seen;
And through the dark that lay beyond myself
I saw two fires that are to light the world."

On Dagonet the silent hand of Merlin   2595
Weighed now as living iron that held him down
With a primeval power. Doubt, wonderment,
Impatience, and a self-accusing sorrow
Born of an ancient love, possessed and held him
Until his love was more than he could name,   2600
And he was Merlin's fool, not Arthur's now:
"Say what you will, I say that I'm the fool
Of Merlin, King of Nowhere; which is Here.
With you for king and me for court, what else
Have we to sigh for but a place to sleep?   2605
I know a tavern that will take us in;
And on the morrow I shall follow you
Until I die for you. And when I die . . ."—
"Well, Dagonet, the King is listening."—
And Dagonet answered, hearing in the words   2610
Of Merlin a grave humor and a sound
Of graver pity, "I shall die a fool."
He heard what might have been a father's laugh,
Faintly behind him; and the living weight
Of Merlin's hand was lifted. They arose,   2615
And, saying nothing, found a groping way
Down through the gloom together. Fiercer now,
The wind was like a flying animal
That beat the two of them incessantly
With icy wings, and bit them as they went.   2620
The rock above them was an empty place
Where neither seer nor fool should view again
The stricken city. Colder blew the wind
Across the world, and on it heavier lay
The shadow and the burden of the night;   2625
And there was darkness over Camelot.

chapter 12

TERENCE HANBURY WHITE:
THE ONCE AND FUTURE KING

U N D E R   T H E   canonical influence of Tennyson and the cataclysmic events of the Great War, which paradoxically made the *Idylls*'s vision seem at once prophetic and no longer relevant to modern experience, it was not until the eve of the century's second great war that another British writer redefined the Arthurian legend. That writer was Terence Hanbury White (1906–1964), an iconoclastic man who has sometimes been compared to Ernest Hemingway for his looks and his fascination with war and sport. White felt compelled to investigate many skills and ideas; he was handsome, talented, and neurotic.

In a letter of January 1938 to his former Cambridge tutor and life-long friend L.J. Potts he recalls with typical humor that he once wrote a thesis on *Le Morte Darthur* and describes a new project: "Naturally I did not read Malory when writing the thesis on him, but one night last autumn I got desperate among my books and picked him up in lack of anything else. . . . Anyway, I somehow started writing a book. It is not a satire. Indeed, I am afraid it is rather warm-hearted—mainly about birds and beasts. It seems impossible to determine whether it is for grown-ups or children. It is more or less a kind of wish-fulfilment of the things I should like to have happened to me when I was a boy" (Warner, p. 98).

That book was *The Sword in the Stone*, which made White financially independent and led to four more novels on the Arthurian legend, one of them unpublished until 1977. While its lighthearted and episodic revision of the legend gradually and purposefully darkened through the later books, this novel became an instantaneous success, even inspiring the Disney studio to buy movie rights and eventually produce a full-length animated movie in 1965. White portrayed many elements of himself in the young Arthur, who is named Wart, and especially in Merlyn (like Tennyson, the author fancied himself as a wizard and grew a full, "Merlynesque" beard). The delightful adventures of Wart's childhood compensated partially for White's own unhappy youth. He had been born in Bombay, India, where his father was a district superintendent of police, but spent most of his early life in England. His parents separated in 1915, and his mother's demands apparently so suffocated him that for the rest of his life his relationships with women were strained. He took revenge on her in the self-centered and spiderish Morgause of *The Witch in the Wood*, and never married.

After attending Cheltenham Military College, White entered Cambridge. He overcame a serious bout with tuberculosis, began his creative writing (encouraged by Potts), and graduated in 1929, the year his first book appeared, *Loved Helen and Other Poems*. Between 1930 and 1936 he held teaching positions at two schools, and was temporarily blinded in an automobile accident. When *The Sword in the Stone* was published, he moved to Ireland, where he lived for six years before returning to England and finally settling on the channel island of Alderney to escape double taxation of his royalties by both Britain and the United States. For most of this time White found companionship less often with other people than with his pets (many of whom, such as the hawks Gos and Cully, his Irish setter Brownie, and owl Archimedes, were included in his Arthurian books). He struggled against his acknowledged homosexuality and, in his later years, heart trouble as well. It was not entirely a happy life.

If Wart represents the wish-fulfillment of White's youth, Merlyn epitomizes much of White's hard-earned wisdom about life. Like White, Merlyn knows that twentieth-century existence—in fact, existence in any century—is tragic, and in a compensatory stroke of genius his author has him live backwards, so that "he knows what is going to happen, but not what *has* happened" (*Letters*, p. 128). This may be physically impossible, but it accounts for the wizard's prophetic insight, provides marvelous opportunities for comic anachronisms, and explains why Merlyn cannot always perceive the causes of disaster and thus prevent it from occurring. One telling instance of the limitation placed upon his knowledge by living backwards is his inability to "remember" that he has not told Arthur who Morgause is until she has seduced the young king. White also gave the wizard many of his own mercurial and eccentric characteristics—particularly in two areas.

The first is his love of learning and doing new things. The most quoted speech in *The Once and Future King*, the omnibus revision of his Arthurian novels, is Merlyn on the importance of education: "The best thing for being sad," he tells Wart, "is to learn something. That is the only thing that never fails. You may grow old and trembling in your anatomics, you may lie awake at night listening to the disorder of your veins, you may miss your only love, you may see the world about you devastated by evil lunatics, or know your honor trampled in the sewers of baser minds. There is only one thing for it then—to learn" (p. 185). Learning, however, is not enough to save the world—only to help us understand it and realize our own potential as much as possible in spite of worldly snares and limitations. However, as Merlyn remembers in *The Book of Merlyn*, Don Quixote went mad from too much learning; it cannot replace people's physical and temporal environment. The main purpose of learning, apart from individual solace and self-improvement, is to increase the "stock of ideas" so that humanity may someday find a way to progress (*Merlyn*, p. 11; Kellman, pp. 133–134). Learning offers more of a hope than an answer; instead of helping Arthur to forestall his tragedy, it prepares him to comprehend and, finally, to accept it.

The other area is White's fervent pacifism. Like Twain, White can leap astride a soapbox in his fiction and brilliantly satirize "the damned human race," but his main concern is humankind's inexplicable capacity for cruelty and violence. War is only the most obvious expression of inhumanity; White theorized first that it arose from our territorial instincts, then that it came from economic motives, and finally that it was simply innate. John Crane observes that in *The Once and Future King,* "Arthur discovers this truth more and more as he attempts to channel the Might available to him and the men of his Round Table toward some constructive end, only to have petty selfishnesses, his own and that of others, continually channel it back to the cursed philosophy of Might is Right" (p. 81). While *The Book of Merlyn* hammers this theme most persistently, the selections included here also show White's love of learning and concern about the human instinct for violent self-aggrandizement. The early parts of *The Once and Future King* establish these issues, even though they are usually thought of as fanciful and lighthearted, and clearly take greater liberties with Arthurian legend than the later sections. In revising his earlier books into the omnibus novel, White emphasized his concerns more by omitting the less relevant episodes than by thoroughly rewriting the ones that remained.

The Once and Future King has been the most popular version of the Arthurian legend in this century. In addition to the Disney film, it became the basis for the musical *Camelot* (Lerner and Loewe paid White $400,000 for the rights); although both treatments trivialized White's work, they vastly enlarged the audience for it. Structurally, the four-part work is superior to the earlier books; modulating gradually from comedy to tragedy, it superbly illustrates Northrop Frye's anatomy of romance into four phases of spring or birth, summer or triumph, autumn or decay, and winter or death and dissolution. As a primarily comic figure, Merlyn is present only for the first two phases; then, "sleek and snowy and shining," he is laid to rest by his uncaring Nimue. Like White's description of Merlyn's treehouse and reconception of Arthur's childhood, his presentation of Arthur's world is a glorious hodgepodge of influences. It is similar to *The Faerie Queene* in creating an alternative world, called Gramarye (a Middle English word meaning "magic"). It is like Twain's Camelot in combining historical anachronisms with the Middle Ages; even including Malory as a young page before the final battle on Salisbury plain. It is comic and tragic, medieval, Victorian, and modern all at once. As White himself attempts to describe it to a friend, "I am putting myself as far as possible in Malory's mind which was a dreamer's and bundling everything together in the way I think he bundled it. . . . I am trying to write of *an imaginary world which was imagined in the 15th century.* . . . (Malory has just told me that I am welcome to speak for him). . . and he says to tell you that I am after the spirit of Morte d'Arthur seen through the eyes of 1939" (Warner, pp. 133–34). White's "backsight," then, is like his wizard's. Martin Kellman elucidates, "For Merlyn, as for White and his novel, all of history exists synchronically, at once, rather than as a procession to some great goal. . ." (p. 90). This is why neither Merlyn nor Arthur has a successful solution for the equation Might makes Right. Knowledge of neither the past nor the future seems to offer a solution to problems as they happen; we are doomed to "repeat" historical cycles in the eternal present.

Bibliographic note: The publishing history of White's Arthurian works is complicated. First to appear was *The Sword in the Stone* (1938); next *The Witch in the Wood* (1939), which was later retitled *The Queen of Air and Darkness*; then *The Ill-Made Knight* (1940). *The Candle in the Wind* was written in 1940, but not published until it appeared as the conclusion of White's revision of all four novels, *The Once and Future King* (1958). These books were published in London by Collins, and in New York by G.P. Putnam's Sons. In 1941 White also wrote a fifth volume, in which Merlyn appears to Arthur upon the eve of the final battle and reeducates him with the help of several animals that appeared in the first book. Two episodes in which Arthur becomes an ant and a goose focus upon the thematic contrast between totalitarianism and utopian pacifism, and were incorporated in the first part of *The Once and Future King*. The entire book was not published until 1977 as *The Book of Merlyn* (Austin: University of Texas Press). Since it is considerably preachier than the first four, its excision can be counted as artistically fortunate.

The selections I have chosen come from the first edition of *The Sword in the Stone* and from *The Once and Future King*. The first three are from the Sword in the Stone section of *The Once and Future King*, Chapters 3 and 4, where Wart first meets Merlyn and brings him home to become his tutor, and Chapter 5, where the wizard inaugurates Wart's training by turning both of them into fish in the castle moat. Next are two self-contained episodes printed only in the earlier *Sword in the Stone*: from Chapter 6, where Merlyn rescues Wart from Madame Mim by magical combat, and from Chapter 19, where White makes his nod to Merlin's fountain Galabes, first named in Layamon's *Brut* (c. 1200), by taking Wart and the wizard to the castle of the giant Galapas, where they find King Pellinore held prisoner and attempt to rescue him. The last selections are from the Queen of Air and Darkness section of *The Once and Future King:* Chapter 2, where Merlyn deflates Arthur's thoughtless love of warfare after the young king has won an early victory against Lot, and Chapter 10, before the final battle with Lot, where Merlyn tries to explain why he must succumb to Nimue. Essential sources of information about T.H. White and *The Once and Future King* are Sylvia Townsend Warner's *T.H. White: A Biography* (London: Jonathan Cape and Chatto & Windus, 1967; New York: Viking, 1968); *Letters to a Friend: The Correspondence Between T.H. White and L.J. Potts*, ed. François Gallix (New York: Putnam, 1982); John K. Crane's *T.H. White*, Twayne's English Authors Series 172 (Boston: Twayne, 1974); and most recently Martin Kellman's *T.H. White and the Matter of Britain: A Literary Overview* (Lewiston, N.Y.: Edwin Mellen, 1988).

The Once and Future King

The Wart Meets Merlin

[*Searching for an escaped hawk named Cully, the Wart enters the forest surrounding Sir Ector's castle. There he encounters several adventures; then, hearing a strange noise, he walks toward it.*]

There was a clearing in the forest, and in this clearing there was a snug cottage built of stone. It was a cottage, although the Wart could not notice this at the time, which was divided into two bits. The main bit was the hall or every-purpose room, which was high because it extended from floor to roof, and this room had a fire on the floor whose smoke came out eventually from a hole in the thatch of the roof. The other half of the cottage was divided into two rooms by a horizontal floor which made the top half into a bedroom and study, while the bottom half served for a larder, storeroom, stable and barn. A white donkey lived in this downstairs room, and a ladder led to the one upstairs.

There was a well in front of the cottage, and the metallic noise which the Wart had heard was caused by a very old gentleman who was drawing water out of it by means of a handle and chain.

Clank, clank, clank, went the chain, until the bucket hit the lip of the well, and "Drat the whole thing!" said the old gentleman. "You would think that after all these years of study you could do better for yourself than a by-our-lady well with a by-our-lady bucket, whatever the by-our-lady cost.

"By this and by that," added the old gentleman, heaving his bucket out of the well with a malevolent glance, "why can't they get us the electric light and company's water?"

He was dressed in a flowing gown with fur tippets which had the signs of the zodiac embroidered over it, with various cabalistic signs, such as triangles with eyes in them, queer crosses, leaves of trees, bones of birds and animals, and a planetarium whose stars shone like bits of looking-glass with the sun on them. He had a pointed hat like a dunce's cap, or like the headgear worn by ladies of that time, except that the ladies were accustomed to have a bit of veil floating from the top of it. He also had a wand of lignum vitae, which he had laid down in the grass beside him, and a pair of horn-rimmed spectacles like those of King Pellinore. They were unusual spectacles, being without ear pieces, but shaped rather like scissors or like the antennae of the tarantula wasp.

"Excuse me, sir," said the Wart, "but can you tell me the way to Sir Ector's castle, if you don't mind?"

The aged gentleman put down his bucket and looked at him.

"Your name would be the Wart."

"Yes, sir, please, sir."

"My name," said the old man, "is Merlyn."

"How do you do?"

"How do."

When these formalities had been concluded, the Wart had leisure to look at him more closely. The magician was staring at him with a kind of unwinking and benevolent curiosity which made him feel that it would not be at all rude to stare back, no ruder than it would be to stare at one of his guardian's cows who happened to be thinking about his personality as she leaned her head over a gate.

Merlyn had a long white beard and long white moustaches which hung down on either side of it. Close inspection showed that he was far from clean. It was not that he had dirty fingernails, or anything like that, but some large bird seemed to have been nesting in his hair. The Wart was familiar with the nests of Spar-hawk and Gos, the crazy conglomerations of sticks and oddments which had been taken over from squirrels or crows, and he knew how the twigs and the tree foot were splashed with white mutes, old bones, muddy feathers and castings. This was the impression which he got from Merlyn. The old man was streaked with droppings over his shoulders, among the stars and triangles of his gown, and a large spider was slowly lowering itself from the tip of his hat, as he gazed and slowly blinked at the little boy in front of him. He had a worried expression, as though he were trying to remember some name which began with Chol but which was pronounced in quite a different way, possibly Menzies or was it Dalziel? His mild blue eyes, very big and round under the tarantula spectacles, gradually filmed and clouded over as he gazed at the boy, and then he turned his head away with a resigned expression, as though it was all too much for him after all.

"Do you like peaches?"

"Very much indeed," said the Wart, and his mouth began to water so that it was full of sweet, soft liquid.

"They are scarcely in season," said the old man reprovingly, and he walked off in the direction of the cottage.

The Wart followed after, since this was the simplest thing to do, and offered to carry the bucket (which seemed to please Merlyn, who gave it to him) and waited while he counted the keys—while he muttered and mislaid them and dropped them in the grass. Finally, when they had got their way into the black and white home with as much trouble as if they were burgling it, he climbed up the ladder after his host and found himself in the upstairs room.

It was the most marvellous room that he had ever been in.

There was a real corkindrill hanging from the rafters, very life-like and horrible with glass eyes and scaly tail stretched out behind it. When its master came into the room it winked one eye in salutation, although it was stuffed. There were thousands of brown books in leather bindings, some chained to the book-shelves and others propped against each other as if they had had too much to drink and did not really trust themselves. These gave out a smell of must and solid brownness which was most secure. Then there were stuffed birds, popinjays, and maggot-pies and king-fishers, and peacocks with all their feathers but two, and tiny birds like beetles, and a reputed phoenix which smelt of incense and cinnamon. It could not have been a real phoenix, because there is only one of these at a time. Over by the mantelpiece there was a fox's mask, with GRAFTON, BUCKINGHAM TO DAVENTRY, 2 HRS 20 MINS written under it, and also a forty-pound salmon with AWE, 43 MIN., BULLDOG written under it, and a very lifelike basilisk with CROWHURST OTTER HOUNDS in Roman print. There were several boars' tusks and the claws of tigers and libbards mounted in symmetrical patterns, and a big head of Ovis Poli, six live grass snakes in a kind of aquarium, some nests of the solitary wasp nicely set up in a glass cylinder, an ordinary beehive whose inhabitants went in and out of the window unmolested, two young hedgehogs in cotton wool, a pair of badgers which immediately began to cry Yik-Yik-Yik-Yik in loud voices as soon as the magician appeared, twenty boxes which contained stick caterpillars and sixths of the puss-moth, and even an oleander that was worth sixpence—all feeding on the appropriate leaves—a guncase with all sorts of weapons which would not be invented for half a thousand years, a rod-box ditto, a chest of drawers full of salmon flies which had been tied by Merlyn himself, another chest whose drawers were labelled Mandragora, Mandrake, Old Man's Beard, etc., a bunch of turkey feathers and goose-quills for making pens, an astrolabe, twelve pairs of boots, a dozen purse-nets, three dozen rabbit wires, twelve corkscrews, some ants' nests between two glass plates, ink-bottles of every possible colour from red to violet, darning-needles, a gold medal for being the best scholar at Winchester, four or five recorders, a nest of field mice all alive-o, two skulls, plenty of cut glass, Venetian glass, Bristol glass and a bottle of Mastic varnish, some satsuma china and some cloisonné, the fourteenth edition of the Encyclopaedia Britannica (marred as it was by the sensationalism of the popular plates), two paint-boxes (one oil, one watercolour), three globes of the known geographical world, a few fossils, the stuffed head of a cameleopard, six pismires, some glass retorts with cauldrons, bunsen burners, etc., and a complete set of cigarette cards depicting wild fowl by Peter Scott.

Merlyn took off his pointed hat when he came into this chamber, because it was too high for the roof, and immediately there was a scamper in one of the dark corners and a flap of soft wings, and a tawny owl was sitting on the black skull-cap which protected the top of his head.

"Oh, what a lovely owl!" cried the Wart.

But when he went up to it and held out his hand, the owl grew half as tall again, stood up as stiff as a poker, closed its eyes so that there was only the smallest slit to peep through—as you are in the habit of doing when told to shut your eyes at hide-and-seek—and said in a doubtful voice:

"There is no owl."

Then it shut its eyes entirely and looked the other way.

"It is only a boy," said Merlyn.

"There is no boy," said the owl hopefully, without turning round.

The Wart was so startled by finding that the owl could talk that he forgot his manners and came closer still. At this the bird became so nervous that it made a mess on Merlyn's head—the whole room was quite white with droppings—and flew off to perch on the farthest tip of the corkindrill's tail, out of reach.

"We see so little company," explained the magician, wiping his head with half a worn-out pair of pyjamas which he kept for that purpose, "that Archimedes is a little shy of strangers. Come, Archimedes, I want you to meet a friend of mine called Wart."

Here he held out his hand to the owl, who came waddling like a goose along the corkindrill's back—he waddled with this rolling gait so as to keep his tail from being damaged—and hopped down to Merlyn's finger with every sign of reluctance.

"Hold out your finger and put it behind his legs. No, lift it up under his train."

When the Wart had done this, Merlyn moved the owl gently backward, so that the boy's finger pressed against its legs from behind, and it either had to step back on the finger or get pushed off its balance altogether. It stepped back. The Wart stood there delighted, while the furry feet held tight on his finger and the sharp claws prickled his skin.

"Say how d'you do properly," said Merlyn.

"I will not," said Archimedes, looking the other way and holding tight.

"Oh, he *is* lovely," said the Wart again. "Have you had him long?"

"Archimedes has stayed with me since he was small, indeed since he had a tiny head like a chicken's."

"I wish he would talk to me."

"Perhaps if you were to give him this mouse here, politely, he might learn to know you better."

Merlyn took a dead mouse out of his skull-cap—"I always keep them there, and worms too, for fishing. I find it most convenient"—and handed it to the Wart, who held it out rather gingerly toward Archimedes. The nutty curved beak looked as if it were capable of doing damage, but Archimedes looked closely at the mouse, blinked at the Wart, moved nearer on the finger, closed his eyes and leaned forward. He stood there with closed eyes and an expression of rapture on his face, as if he were saying Grace, and then, with the absurdest sideways nibble, took the morsel so gently that he would not have broken a soap bubble. He remained leaning forward with closed eyes, with the mouse suspended from his beak, as if he were not sure what to do with it. Then he lifted his right foot—he was right-handed, though people say only men are—and took hold of the mouse. He held it up like a boy holding a stick or rock or a constable with his truncheon, looked at it, nibbled its tail. He turned it round so that it was head first, for the Wart had offered it the wrong way round, and gave one gulp. He looked round at the company with the tail hanging out of the corner of his mouth—as much as to say, "I wish you would not all stare at me so"—turned his head away, politely swallowed the tail, scratched his sailor's beard with his left toe, and began to ruffle out his feathers.

"Let him alone," said Merlyn. "Perhaps he does not want to be friends with you until he knows what you are like. With owls, it is never easy-come and easy-go."

"Perhaps he will sit on my shoulder," said the Wart, and with that he instinctively lowered his hand, so that the owl, who liked to be as high as possible, ran up the slope and stood shyly beside his ear.

"Now breakfast," said Merlyn.

The Wart saw that the most perfect breakfast was laid out neatly for two, on a table before the window. There were peaches. There were also melons, strawberries and cream, rusks, brown trout piping hot, grilled perch which were much nicer, chicken devilled enough to burn one's mouth out, kidneys and mushrooms on toast, fricassee, curry, and a choice of boiling coffee or best chocolate made with cream in large cups.

"Have some mustard," said the magician, when they had got to the kidneys.

The mustard-pot got up and walked over to his plate on thin silver legs that waddled like the owl's. Then it uncurled its handles and one handle lifted its lid with exaggerated courtesy while the other helped him to a generous spoonful.

"Oh, I love the mustard-pot!" cried the Wart. "Wherever did you get it?"

At this the pot beamed all over its face and began to strut a bit, but Merlyn rapped it on the head with a teaspoon, so that it sat down and shut up at once.

"It is not a bad pot," he said grudgingly. "Only it is inclined to give itself airs."

The Wart was so much impressed by the kindness of the old man, and particularly by the lovely things which he possessed, that he hardly liked to ask him personal questions. It seemed politer to sit still and to speak when he was spoken to. But Merlyn did not speak much, and when he did speak it was never in questions, so that the Wart had little opportunity for conversation. At last his curiosity got the better of him, and he asked something which had been puzzling him for some time.

"Would you mind if I ask you a question?"

"It is what I am for."

"How did you know to set breakfast for two?"

The old gentleman leaned back in his chair and lighted an enormous meerschaum pipe—Good gracious, he breathes fire, thought the Wart, who had never heard of tobacco—before he was ready to reply. Then he looked puzzled, took off his skullcap—three mice fell out—and scratched in the middle of his bald head.

"Have you ever tried to draw in a looking-glass?" he asked.

"I don't think I have."

"Looking-glass," said Merlyn, holding out his hand. Immediately there was a tiny lady's vanity-glass in his hand.

"Not that kind, you fool," he said angrily. "I want one big enough to shave in."

The vanity-glass vanished, and in its place there was a shaving mirror about a foot square. He then demanded pencil and paper in quick succession; got an unsharpened pencil and the *Morning Post*; sent them back; got a fountain pen with no ink in it and six reams of brown paper suitable for parcels; sent them back; flew into a passion in which he said by-our-lady quite often, and ended up with a carbon pencil and some cigarette papers which he said would have to do.

He put one of the papers in front of the glass and made five dots.

"Now," he said, "I want you to join those five dots up to make a W, looking only in the glass."

The Wart took the pen and tried to do as he was bid.

"Well, it is not bad," said the magician doubtfully, "and in a way it does look a bit like an M."

Then he fell into a reverie, stroking his beard, breathing fire, and staring at the paper.

"About the breakfast?"

"Ah, yes. How did I know to set breakfast for two? That was why I showed you the looking-glass. Now ordinary people are born forwards in Time, if you understand what I mean, and nearly everything in the world goes forward too. This makes it quite easy for the ordinary people to live, just as it would be easy to join those five dots into a W if you were allowed to look at them forwards, instead of backwards and inside out. But I unfortunately was born at the wrong end of time, and I have to live backwards from in front, while surrounded by a lot of people living forwards from behind. Some people call it having second sight."

He stopped talking and looked at the Wart in an anxious way.

"Have I told you this before?"

"No, we only met about half an hour ago."

"So little time to pass?" said Merlyn, and a big tear ran down to the end of his nose. He wiped if off with his pyjamas and added anxiously, "Am I going to tell it you again?"

"I do not know," said the Wart, "unless you have not finished telling me yet."

"You see, one gets confused with Time, when it is like that. All one's tenses get muddled, for one thing. If you know what is *going* to happen to people, and not what *has* happened to them, it makes it difficult to prevent it happening, if you don't want it to have happened, if you see what I mean? Like drawing in a mirror."

The Wart did not quite see, but was just going to say that he was sorry for Merlyn if these things made him unhappy, when he felt a curious sensation at his ear. "Don't jump," said the old man, just as he was going to do so, and the Wart sat still. Archimedes, who had been standing forgotten on his shoulder all this time, was gently touching himself against him. His beak was right against the lobe of the ear, which its bristles made to tickle, and suddenly a soft hoarse voice whispered, "How d'you do," so that it sounded right inside his head.

"Oh, owl!" cried the Wart, forgetting about Merlyn's troubles instantly. "Look, he has decided to talk to me!"

The Wart gently leaned his head against the smooth feathers, and the tawny owl, taking the rim of his ear in its beak, quickly nibbled right round it with the smallest nibbles.

"I shall call him Archie!"

"I trust you will do nothing of the sort," exclaimed Merlyn instantly, in a stern and angry voice, and the owl withdrew to the farthest corner of his shoulder.

"Is it wrong?"

"You might as well call me Wol, or Olly," said the owl sourly, "and have done with it.

"Or Bubbles," it added in a bitter voice.

Merlyn took the Wart's hand and said kindly, "You are young, and do not understand these things. But you will learn that owls are the most courteous, single-hearted and faithful creatures living. You must never be familiar, rude or vulgar with them, or make them look ridiculous. Their mother is Athene, the goddess of wisdom, and, although they are often ready to play the buffoon to amuse you, such conduct is the prerogative of the truly wise. No owl can possibly be called Archie."

"I am sorry, owl," said the Wart.

"And I am sorry, boy," said the owl. "I can see that you spoke in ignorance, and I bitterly regret that I should have been so petty as to take offence where none was intended."

The owl really did regret it, and looked so remorseful that Merlyn had to put on a cheerful manner and change the conversation.

"Well," said he, "now that we have finished breakfast, I think it is high time that we should all three find our way back to Sir Ector.

"Excuse me a moment," he added as an afterthought, and, turning round to the breakfast things, he pointed a knobbly finger at them and said in a stern voice, "Wash up."

At this all the china and cutlery scrambled down off the table, the cloth emptied the crumbs out of the window, and the napkins folded themselves up. All ran off down the ladder, to where Merlyn had left the bucket, and there was such a noise and yelling as if a lot of children had been let out of school. Merlyn went to the door and shouted, "Mind, nobody is to get broken." But his voice was entirely drowned in shrill squeals, splashes, and cries of "My, it is cold," "I shan't stay in long," "Look out, you'll break me," or "Come on, let's duck the teapot."

"Are you really coming all the way home with me?" asked the Wart, who could hardly believe the good news.

"Why not? How else can I be your tutor?"

At this the Wart's eyes grew rounder and rounder, until they were about as big as the owl's who was sitting on his shoulder, and his face got redder and redder, and a breath seemed to gather itself beneath his heart.

"My!" exclaimed the Wart, while his eyes sparked with excitement at the discovery. "I must have been on a Quest!"

The Wart started talking before he was half-way over the drawbridge. "Look who I have brought," he said. "Look! I have been on a Quest! I was shot at with three arrows. They had black and yellow stripes. The owl is called Archimedes. I saw King Pellinore. This is my tutor, Merlyn. I went on a Quest for him. He was after the Questing Beast. I mean King Pellinore. It was terrible in the forest. Merlyn made the plates wash up. Hallo, Hob. Look, we have got Cully."

Hob just looked at the Wart, but so proudly that the Wart went quite red. It was such a pleasure to be back home again with all his friends, and everything achieved.

Hob said gruffly, "Ah, master, us shall make an austringer of 'ee yet."

He came for Cully, as if he could not keep his hands off him longer, but he patted the Wart too, fondling them both because he was not sure which he was gladder to see back. He took Cully on his own fist, reassuming him like a lame man putting on his accustomed wooden leg, after it had been lost.

"Merlyn caught him," said the Wart. "He sent Archimedes to look for him on the way home. Then Archimedes told us that he had been and killed a pigeon and was eating it. We went and frightened him off. After that, Merlyn stuck six of the tail feathers round the pigeon in a circle, and made a loop in a long piece of string to go round the feathers. He tied one end to a stick in the ground, and we went away behind a bush with the other end. He said he would not use magic. He said you could not use magic in Great Arts, just as it would be unfair to make a great statue by magic. You have to cut it out with a chisel, you see. Then Cully came down to finish the pigeon, and we pulled the string, and the loop slipped over the feathers and caught him round the legs. He was angry! But we gave him the pigeon."

Hob made a duty to Merlyn, who returned it courteously. They looked upon one another with grave affection, knowing each other to be masters of the same trade. When they could be alone together they would talk about falconry, although Hob was naturally a silent man. Meanwhile they must wait their time.

"Oh, Kay," cried the Wart, as the latter appeared with their nurse and other delighted welcomers. "Look, I have got a magician for our tutor. He has a mustard-pot that walks."

"I am glad you are back, " said Kay.

"Alas, where did you sleep, Master Art?" exclaimed the nurse. "Look at your clean jerkin all muddied and torn. Such a turn as you gave us, I really don't know. But look at your poor hair with all them twigs in it. Oh, my own random, wicked little lamb."

Sir Ector came bustling out with his greaves on back to front, and kissed the Wart on both cheeks. "Well, well, well," he exclaimed moistly. "Here we are again, hey? What the devil have we been doin', hey? Settin' the whole household upside down."

But inside himself he was proud of the Wart for staying out after a hawk, and prouder still to see that he had got it, for all the while Hob held the bird in the air for everybody to see.

"Oh, sir," said the Wart, "I have been on that quest you said for a tutor, and I have found him. Please, he is this gentleman here, and he is called Merlyn. He has got some badgers and hedgehogs and mice and ants and things on this white donkey here, because we could not leave them behind to starve. He is a great magician, and can make things come out of the air."

"Ah, a magician," said Sir Ector, putting on his glasses and looking closely at Merlyn. "White magic, I hope?"

"Assuredly," said Merlyn, who stood patiently among the throng with his arms folded in his necromantic gown, while Archimedes sat very stiff and elongated on the top of his head.

"Ought to have some testimonials," said Sir Ector doubtfully. "It's usual."

"Testimonials," said Merlyn, holding out his hand.

Instantly there were some heavy tablets in it, signed by Aristotle, a parchment signed by Hecate, and some typewritten duplicates signed by the Master of Trinity, who could not remember having met him. All these gave Merlyn an excellent character.

"He had 'em up his sleeve," said Sir Ector wisely. "Can you do anything else?"

"Tree," said Merlyn. At once there was an enormous mulberry growing in the middle of the courtyard, with its luscious blue fruits ready to patter down. This was all the more remarkable, since mulberries only became popular in the days of Cromwell.

"They do it with mirrors," said Sir Ector.

"Snow," said Merlyn. "And an umbrella," he added hastily.

Before they could turn round, the copper sky of summer had assumed a cold and lowering bronze, while the biggest white flakes that ever were seen were floating about them and settling on the battlements. An inch of snow had fallen before they could speak, and all were trembling with the wintry blast. Sir Ector's nose was blue, and had an icicle hanging from the end of it, while all except Merlyn had a ledge of snow upon their shoulders. Merlyn stood in the middle, holding his umbrella high because of the owl.

"It's done by hypnotism," said Sir Ector, with chattering teeth. "Like those wallahs from the Indies.

"But that'll do," he added hastily, "that'll do very well. I'm sure you'll make an excellent tutor for teachin' these boys."

The snow stopped immediately and the sun came out—"Enough to give a body a pewmonia," said the nurse, "or to frighten the elastic commissioners"—while Merlyn folded up his umbrella and handed it back to the air, which received it.

"Imagine the boy doin' a quest like that by himself," exclaimed Sir Ector. "Well, well, well! Wonders never cease."

"I do not think much of it as a quest," said Kay. "He only went after the hawk, after all."

"And got the hawk, Master Kay," said Hob reprovingly.

"Oh, well," said Kay, "I bet the old man caught it for him."

"Kay," said Merlyn, suddenly terrible, "thou wast ever a proud and ill-tongued speaker, and a misfortunate one. Thy sorrow will come from thine own mouth."

At this everybody felt uncomfortable, and Kay, instead of flying into his usual passion, hung his head. He was not at all an unpleasant person really, but clever, quick, proud, passionate and ambitious. He was one of those people who would be neither a follower nor a leader, but only an aspiring heart, impatient in the failing body which imprisoned it. Merlyn repented of his rudeness at once. He made a little silver hunting-knife come out of the air, which he gave him to put things right. The knob of the handle was made of the skull of a stoat, oiled and polished like ivory, and Kay loved it.

The Castle Moat

"Shall we go out?" asked Merlyn. "I think it is about time we began lessons."

The Wart's heart sank at this. His tutor had been there a month, and it was now August, but they had done no lessons so far. Now he suddenly remembered that this was what Merlyn was for, and he thought with dread of Summulae Logicales and the filthy astrolabe. He knew that it had to be borne, however, and got up obediently enough, after giving Cavall a last reluctant pat. He thought that it might not be so bad with Merlyn, who might be able to make even the old Organon interesting, particularly if he would do some magic.

They went into the courtyard, into a sun so burning that the heat of hay-making seemed to have been nothing. It was baking. The thunder-clouds which usually go with hot weather were there, high columns of cumulus with glaring edges, but there was not going to be any thunder. It was too hot even for that. "If only," thought the Wart, "I did not have to go into a stuffy classroom, but could take off my clothes and swim in the moat."

They crossed the courtyard, having almost to take deep breaths before they darted across it, as if they were going quickly through an oven. The shade of the gatehouse was cool, but the barbican, with its close walls, was hottest of all. In one last dash across the desert they had reached the drawbridge—could Merlyn have guessed what he was thinking?—and were staring down into the moat.

It was the season of water-lilies. If Sir Ector had not kept one section free of them for the boys' bathing, all the water would have been covered. As it was, about twenty yards on each side of the bridge were cut each year, and one could dive in from the bridge itself. The moat was deep. It was used as a stew, so that the inhabitants of the castle could have fish on Fridays, and for this reason the architects had been careful not to let the drains and sewers run into it. It was stocked with fish every year.

"I wish I was a fish," said the Wart.

"What sort of fish?"

It was almost too hot to think about this, but the Wart stared down into the cool amber depths where a school of small perch were aimlessly hanging about.

"I think I should like to be a perch," he said. "They are braver than the silly roach, and not quite so slaughterous as the pike are."

Merlyn took off his hat, raised his staff of lignum vitae politely in the air, and said slowly, "Snylrem stnemilpmoc ot enutpen dna lliw eh yldnik tpecca siht yob sa a hsif?"

Immediately there was a loud blowing of sea-shells, conches and so forth, and a stout, jolly-looking gentleman appeared seated on a well-blown-up cloud above the battlements. He had an anchor tattooed on his stomach and a handsome mermaid with Mabel written under her on his chest. He ejected a quid of tobacco, nodded affably to Merlyn and pointed his trident at the Wart. The Wart found he had no clothes on. He found that he had tumbled off the drawbridge, landing with a smack on his side in the water. He found that the moat and the bridge had grown hundreds of times bigger. He knew that he was turning into a fish.

"Oh, Merlyn," he cried, "please come too."

"For this once," said a large and solemn tench beside his ear, "I will come. But in future you will have to go by yourself. Education is experience, and the essence of experience is self-reliance."

The Wart found it difficult to be a new kind of creature. It was no good trying to swim like a human being, for it made him go corkscrew and much too slowly. He did not know how to swim like a fish.

"Not like that," said the tench in ponderous tones. "Put your chin on your left shoulder and do jack-knives. Never mind about the fins to begin with."

The Wart's legs had fused together into his backbone and his feet and toes had become a tail fin. His arms had become two more fins—of a delicate pink—and he had sprouted some more somewhere about his stomach. His head faced over his shoulder, so that when he bent in the middle his toes were moving toward his ear instead of toward his forehead. He was a beautiful olive-green, with rather scratchy plate-armour all over him, and dark bands down his sides. He was not sure which were his sides and which were his back and front, but what now appeared to be his belly had an attractive whitish colour, while his back was armed with a splendid great fin that could be erected for war and had spikes in it. He did jack-knives as the tench directed and found that he was swimming vertically downward into the mud.

"Use your feet to turn to left or right," said the tench, "and spread those fins on your tummy to keep level. You are living in two planes now, not one."

The Wart found that he could keep more or less level by altering the inclination of his arm fins and the ones on his stomach. He swam feebly off, enjoying himself very much.

"Come back," said the tench. "You must learn to swim before you can dart."

The Wart returned to his tutor in a series of zig-zags and remarked, "I do not seem to keep quite straight."

"The trouble with you is that you do not swim from the shoulder. You swim as if you were a boy, bending at the hips. Try doing your jack-knives right from the neck downward, and move your body exactly the same amount to the right as you are going to move it to the left. Put your back into it."

Wart gave two terrific kicks and vanished altogether in a clump of mare's tail several yards away.

"That's better," said the tench, now out of sight in the murky olive water, and the Wart backed himself out of his tangle with infinite trouble, by wriggling his arm fins. He undulated back toward the voice in one terrific shove, to show off.

"Good," said the tench, as they collided end to end. "But direction is the better part of valour.

"Try if you can do this one," it added.

Without apparent exertion of any kind it swam off backward under a water-lily. Without apparent exertion—but the Wart, who was an enterprising learner, had been watching the slightest movement of its fins. He moved his own fins anti-clockwise, gave the tip of his tail a cunning flick, and was lying alongside the tench.

"Splendid," said Merlyn. "Let us go for a little swim."

The Wart was on an even keel now, and reasonably able to move about. He had leisure to look at the extraordinary universe into which the tattooed gentleman's trident had plunged him. It was different from the universe to which he had been accustomed. For one thing, the heaven or sky above him was now a perfect circle. The horizon had closed to this. In order to imagine yourself into the Wart's position, you would have to picture a round horizon, a few inches about your head, instead of the flat horizon which you usually see. Under this horizon of air you would have to imagine another horizon of under water, spherical and practically upside down—for the surface of the water acted partly as a mirror to what was below it. It is difficult to imagine. What makes it a great deal more difficult to imagine is that everything which human beings would consider to be above the water level was fringed with all the colours of the spectrum. For instance, if you had happened to be fishing for the Wart, he would have seen you, at the rim of the tea saucer which was the upper air to him, not as one person waving a fishing-rod, but as seven people, whose outlines were red, orange, yellow, green, blue, indigo and violet, all waving the same rod whose colours were as varied. In fact, you would have been a rainbow man to him, a beacon of flashing and radiating colours, which ran into one another and had rays all about. You would have burned upon the water like Cleopatra in the poem.

The next most lovely thing was that the Wart had no weight. He was not earth-bound any more and did not have to plod along on a flat surface, pressed down by gravity and the weight of the atmosphere. He could do what men have always wanted to do, that is, fly. There is practically no difference between flying in the water and flying in the air. The best of it was that he did not have to fly in a machine, by pulling levers and sitting still, but could do it with his own body. It was like the dreams people have.

Just as they were going to swim off on their tour of inspection, a timid young roach appeared from between two waving bottle bushes of mare's tail and hung about, looking pale with agitation. It looked at them with big, apprehensive eyes and evidently wanted something, but could not make up its mind.

"Approach," said Merlyn gravely.

At this the roach rushed up like a hen, burst into tears, and began stammering its message.

"If you p-p-p-please, doctor," stammered the poor creature, gabbling so that they could scarcely understand what it said, "we have such a d-dretful case of s-s-s-something or other in our family, and we w-w-w-wondered if you could s-s-s-spare the time? It's our d-d-d-dear Mamma, who w-w-w-will swim a-a-all the time upside d-d-d-down, and she d-d-d-does look so horrible and s-s-s-speaks so strange, that we r-r-r-really thought she ought to have a d-d-d-doctor, if it w-w-w-wouldn't be too much? C-C-C-Clara says to say so, Sir, if you s-s-s-see w-w-w-what I m-m-m-mean?"

Here the poor roach began fizzing so much, what with its stammer and its tearful disposition, that it became quite inarticulate and could only stare at Merlyn with mournful eyes.

"Never mind, my little man," said Merlyn. "There, there, lead me to you dear Mamma, and we shall see what we can do."

They all three swam off into the murk under the drawbridge, upon their errand of mercy.

"Neurotic, these roach," whispered Merlyn, behind his fin. "It is probably a case of nervous hysteria, a matter for the psychologist rather than the physician."

The roach's Mamma was lying on her back as he had described. She was squinting, had folded her fins on her chest, and very now and then she blew a bubble. All her children were gathered round her in a circle, and every time she blew they nudged each other and gasped. She had a seraphic smile on her face.

"Well, well, well," said Merlyn, putting on his best bed-side manner, "and how is Mrs. Roach today?"

He patted the young roaches on the head and advanced with stately motions toward his patient. It should perhaps be mentioned that Merlyn was a ponderous, deep-beamed fish of about five pounds, leather coloured, with small scales, adipose in his fins, rather slimy, and having a bright marigold eye—a respectable figure.

Mrs. Roach held out a languid fin, sighed emphatically and said, "Ah doctor, so you've come at last?"

"Hum," said the physician, in his deepest tone.

Then he told everybody to close their eyes—the Wart peeped—and began to swim round the invalid in a slow and stately dance. As he danced he sang. His song was this:

Therapeutic,
Elephantic,
Diagnosis,
Boom!
Pancreatic,
Microstatic,
Anti-toxic,

Doom!
With a normal catabolism,
Gabbleism and babbleism,
Snip, Snap, Snorum,
Cut out his abdonorum.
Dyspepsia,
Anaemia,
Toxaemia.
One, two, three,
And out goes He,
With a fol-de-rol-derido for the Five Guinea Fee.

At the end of the song he was swimming round his patient so close that he actually touched her, stroking his brown smooth-scaled flanks against her more rattly pale ones. Perhaps he was healing her with his slime—for all the fishes are said to go to The Tench for medicine—or perhaps lob-worm, it was by touch or massage or hypnotism. In any case, Mrs. Roach suddenly stopped squinting, turned the right way up, and said, "Oh, doctor, dear doctor, I feel I could eat a little lob-worm now."

"No lob-worm," said Merlyn, "not for two days. I shall give you prescription for a strong broth of algae every two hours, Mrs. Roach. We must build up your strength, you know. After all, Rome was not built in a day."

Then he patted all the little roaches once more, told them to grow up into brave little fish, and swam off with an air of importance into the gloom. As he swam, he puffed his mouth in and out.

"What did you mean by that about Rome?" asked the Wart, when they were out of earshot.

"Heaven knows."

They swam along, Merlyn occasionally advising him to put his back into it when he forgot, and the strange under-water world began to dawn about them, deliciously cool after the heat of the upper air. The great forests of weed were delicately traced, and in them there hung motionless many schools of sticklebacks learning to do their physical exercises in strict unison. On the word One they all lay still; at Two they faced about; at Three they all shot together into a cone, whose apex was a bit of something to eat. Water snails slowly ambled about on the stems of the lilies or under their leaves, while fresh-water mussels lay on the bottom doing nothing in particular. Their flesh was salmon pink, like a very good strawberry cream ice. The small congregations of perch—it was a strange thing, but all the bigger fish seemed to have hidden themselves—had delicate circulations, so that they blushed or grew pale as easily as a lady in a Victorian novel. Only their blush was a deep olive colour, and it was the blush of rage. Whenever Merlyn and his companion swam past them, they raised their spiky dorsal fins in menace, and only lowered them when they saw that Merlyn was a tench. The black bars on their sides made them look as if they had been grilled, and these also could become darker or lighter. Once the two travellers passed under a swan. The white creature floated above like a Zeppelin, all indistinct except what was under the water. The latter part was quite clear and showed that the swan was floating slightly on one side with one leg cocked over its back.

"Look," said the Wart, "it is the poor swan with the deformed leg. It can only paddle with one leg, and the other side of it is hunched."

"Nonsense," said the swan snappily, putting its head into the water and giving them a frown with its black nares. "Swans like to rest in this position, and you can keep your fishy sympathy to yourself, so there." It continued to glare at them from up above, like a white snake suddenly let down through the ceiling, until they were out of sight.

"You swim along," said the tench, "as if there was nothing to be afraid of in the world. Don't you see that this place is exactly like the forest which you had to come through to find me?"

"Is it?"

"Look over there."

The Wart looked, and at first saw nothing. Then he saw a small translucent shape hanging motionless near the surface. It was just outside the shadow of a water-lily and was evidently enjoying the sun. It was a baby pike, absolutely rigid and probably asleep, and it looked like a pipe stem or a sea-horse stretched out flat. It would be a brigand when it grew up.

"I am taking you to see one of those," said the tench, "the Emperor of these purlieus. As a doctor I have immunity, and I dare say he will respect you as my companion as well—but you had better keep your tail bent in case he is feeling tyrannical."

"Is he the King of the Moat?"

"He is. Old Jack they call him, and some call him Black Peter, but for the most part they do not mention him by name at all. They just call him Mr. P. You will see what it is to be a king."

The Wart began to hang behind his conductor a little, and perhaps it was as well that he did, for they were almost on top of their destination before he noticed it. When he did see the old despot he started back in horror, for Mr. P. was four feet long, his weight incalculable. The great body, shadowy and almost invisible among the stems, ended in a face which had been ravaged by all the passions of an absolute monarch—by cruelty, sorrow, age, pride, selfishness, loneliness, and thoughts too strong for individual brains. There he hung or hoved, his vast ironic mouth permanently drawn downward in a kind of melancholy, his lean clean-shaven chops giving him an American expression, like that of Uncle Sam. He was remorseless, disillusioned, logical, predatory, fierce, pitiless—but his great jewel of an eye was that of a stricken deer, large, fearful, sensitive and full of griefs. He made no movement, but looked upon them with his bitter eye.

The Wart thought to himself that he did not care for Mr. P.

"Lord," said Merlyn, not paying attention to his nervousness, "I have brought a young professor who would learn to profess."

"To profess what?" asked the King of the Moat slowly, hardly opening his jaws and speaking through his nose.

"Power," said the tench.

"Let him speak for himself."

"Please," said the Wart, "I don't know what I ought to ask."

"There is nothing," said the monarch, "except the power which you pretend to seek: power to grind and power to digest, power to seek and power to find, power to await and power to claim, all power and pitilessness springing from the nape of the neck."

"Thank you."

"Love is a trick played on us by the forces of evolution. Pleasure is the bait laid down by the same. There is only power. Power is of the individual mind, but the mind's power is not enough. Power of the body decides everything in the end, and only Might is Right.

"Now I think it is time that you should go away, young master, for I find this conversation uninteresting and exhausting. I think you ought to go away really almost at once, in case my disillusioned mouth should suddenly determine to introduce you to my great gills, which have teeth in them also. Yes, I really think you might be wise to go away this moment. Indeed, I think you ought to put your back into it. And so, a long farewell to all my greatness."

The Wart had found himself almost hypnotized by the big words, and hardly noticed that the tight mouth was coming closer and closer to him. It came imperceptibly, as the lecture distracted his attention, and suddenly it was looming within an inch of his nose. One the last sentence it opened, horrible and vast, the skin stretching ravenously from bone to bone and tooth to tooth. Inside there seemed to be nothing but teeth, sharp teeth like thorns in rows and ridges everywhere, like the nails in labourers' boots, and it was only at the last second that he was able to regain his own will, to pull himself together, to recollect his instructions and to escape. All those teeth clashed behind him at the tip of his tail, as he gave the heartiest jack-knife he had ever given.

In a second he was on dry land once again, standing beside Merlyn on the piping drawbridge, panting in his stuffy clothes.

Madam Mim

[On another jaunt into the forest Wart is captured by the witch Mim. With her familiars, the crow Greediguts and cat Hecate looking on avidly, she prepares to roast him.]

"Murderess," cried the Wart. "You will rue this ere the night is out."

"Cubling," said the witch. "It's a shame to kill him, that it is. Look how his little downy hair stares in the lamplight, and how his poor eyes pop out of his head. Greediguts will be sorry to miss those eyes, so she will. Sometimes one could almost be a vegetarian, when one has to do a deed like this."

The witch laid Wart over her lap, with his head between her knees, and carefully began to take his clothes off with a practiced hand. He kicked and squirmed as much as he could, reckoning that every hindrance would put off the time when he would be actually knocked on the head, and thus increase the time in which the black goat could bring Merlyn to his rescue. During this time the witch sang her plucking song, of:

> Pull the feather with the skin,
> Not against the grain-o.
> Pluck the soft ones out from in,
> The great with might and main-o.
> Even if he wriggles,
> Never heed his squiggles,
> For mercifully little boys are quite immune to pain-o.

She varied this song with the other kitchen song of the happy cook:

> Soft skin for crackling,
> Oh, my lovely duckling,
> The skewers go here,
> And the string goes there
> And such is my scrumptious suckling.

"You will be sorry for this," cried the Wart, "even if you live to be a thousand."

"He has spoken enough," said Madame Mim. "It is time that we knocked him on the napper."

> Hold him by the legs, and
> When up goes his head,
> Clip him with the palm-edge, and
> Then he is dead.

The dreadful witch now lifted the Wart into the air and prepared to have her will of him; but at that very moment there was a fizzle of summer lightning without any crash and in the nick of time Merlyn was standing on the threshold.

"Ha!" said Merlyn. "Now we shall see what a double-first at Dom-Daniel avails against the private education of my master Bleise."

Madame Mim put the Wart down without looking at him, rose from her chair, and drew herself to her full magnificent height. Her glorious hair began to crackle, and sparks shot out of her flashing eyes. She and Merlyn stood facing each other a full sixty seconds, without a word spoken, and then Madame Mim swept a royal curtsey and Merlyn bowed a frigid bow. He stood aside to let her go first out of the doorway and then followed her into the garden.

It ought perhaps to be explained, before we go any further, that in those far-off days, when there was actually a college for Witches and Warlocks under the sea at Dom-Daniel and when all wizards were either black or white, there was a good deal of ill-feeling between the different creeds. Quarrels between white and black were settled ceremonially, by means of duels. A wizard's duel was run like this. The two principals would stand opposite each other in some large space free from obstructions, and await the signal to begin. When the signal was given they were at liberty to turn themselves into things. It was rather like the game that can be played by two people with their fists. They say One, Two, Three, and at Three they either stick out two fingers for scissors, or the flat palm for paper, or the clenched fist for stone. If your hand becomes paper when your opponent's become scissors, then he cuts you and wins: but if yours has turned into stone, his scissors are blunted, and the win is yours. The object of the wizard in the duel was to turn himself into some kind of animal, vegetable or mineral which would destroy the particular animal, vegetable or mineral which had been selected by his opponent. Sometimes it went on for hours.

Merlyn had Archimedes for his second, Madame Mim had the gore-crow for hers, while Hecate, who always had to be present at these affairs in order to keep them regular, sat on the top of a step-ladder in the middle, to umpire. She was a cold, shining, muscular lady, the color of moonlight. Merlyn and Madame Mim rolled up their sleeves, gave their surcoats to Hecate to hold, and the latter put on a celluloid eye-shade to watch the battle.

At the first gong Madame Mim immediately turned herself into a dragon. It was the accepted opening move and Merlyn ought to have replied by being a thunderstorm or something like that. Instead, he caused a great deal of preliminary confusion by becoming a field mouse, which was quite invisible in the grass, and nibbled Madame Mim's tail, as she stared about in all directions, for about five minutes before she noticed him. But when she did notice the nibbling, she was a furious cat in two flicks.

Wart held his breath to see what the mouse would become next—he thought perhaps a tiger which could kill the cat—but Merlyn merely became another cat. He stood opposite her and made faces. This most irregular procedure put Madame Mim quite out of her stride, and it took her more than a minute to regain her bearings and become a dog. Even as she became it, Merlyn was another dog standing opposite her, of the same sort.

"Oh, well played, sir!" cried the Wart, beginning to see the plan.

Madame Mim was furious. She felt herself out of her depth against these unusual stone-walling tactics and experienced an internal struggle not to lose her temper. She knew that if she did lose it she would lose her judgment, and the battle as well. She did some quick thinking. If whenever she turned herself into a menacing animal, Merlyn was merely going to turn into the same kind, the thing would become either a mere dog-fight or stalemate. She had better alter her own tactics and give Merlyn a surprise.

At this moment the gong went for the end of the first round. The combatants retired into their respective corners and their seconds cooled them by flapping their wings, while Archimedes gave Merlyn a little massage by nibbling with his beak.

"Second round," commanded Hecate. "Seconds out of the ring. . . .

Time!"

Clang went the gong, and the two desperate wizards stood face to face. Madam Mim had gone on plotting during her rest. She had decided to try a new tack by leaving the offensive to Merlyn, beginning by assuming a defensive shape herself. She turned into a spreading oak.

Merlyn stood baffled under the oak for a few seconds. Then he most cheekily—and, as it turned out, rashly—became a powdery little blue-tit, which flew up and sat perkily on Madame Mim's branches. You could see the oak boiling with indignation for a moment; but then its rage became icy cold, and the poor little blue-tit was sitting, not on an oak, but on a snake. The snake's mouth was open, and the bird was actually perching on its jaws. As the jaws clashed together, but only in the nick of time, the bird whizzed off as a gnat into the safe air. Madame Mim had got it on the run, however, and the speed of the contest now became bewildering. The quicker the attacker could assume a form, the less time the fugitive had to think of a form which would elude it, and now the changes were as quick as thought. The gnat was scarcely in the air when the snake had turned into a toad whose curious tongue, rooted at the front instead of the back of the jaw, was already unrolling in the flick which would snap it in. The gnat, flustered by the sore pursuit, was bounced into an offensive role, and the hard-pressed Merlyn now stood before the toad in the shape of a mollern which could attack it. But Madame Mim was in her element. The game was going according to the normal rules now, and in less than an eye's blink the toad had turned into a peregrine falcon which was diving at two hundred and fifty miles an hour upon the heron's back. Poor Merlyn, beginning to lose his nerve, turned wildly into an elephant—this move usually won a little breathing space—but Madame Mim, relentless, changed from the falcon into an aullay on the instant. An aullay was as much bigger than an elephant as an elephant is larger than a sheep. It was a sort of horse with an elephant's trunk. Madame Mim raised this trunk in the air, gave a shriek like a railway engine, and rushed upon her panting foe. In a flick Merlyn had disappeared.

"One," said Hecate. "Two. Three. Four. Five. Six. Seven. Eight. Nine—"

But before the fatal Ten which would have counted him out, Merlyn reappeared in a bed of nettles, mopping his brow. He had been standing among them as a nettle.

The aullay saw no reason to change its shape. It rushed upon the man before it with another piercing scream. Merlyn vanished again just as the thrashing trunk descended, and all stood still a moment, looking about them, wondering where he would step out next.

"One," began Hecate again, but even as she proceeded with her counting, strange things began to happen. The aullay got hiccoughs, turned red, swelled visibly, began whooping, came out in spots, staggered three times, rolled its eyes, fell rumbling to the ground. It groaned, kicked and said Farewell. The Wart cheered, Archimedes hooted till he cried, the gore-crow fell down dead, and Hecate, on the top of her ladder, clapped so much that she nearly tumbled off. It was a master stroke.

The ingenious magician had turned himself successively into the microbes, not yet discovered, of hiccoughs, scarlet fever, mumps, whooping cough, measles and heat spots, and from a complication of all these complaints the infamous Madame Mim had immediately expired.

Galapas

It was a fine summer night, the last night which would give any excuse for fires, and Reverend Sidebottom was reading out his tale. Wart lay snoozing among the lean ribs of the gaze-hounds; Sir Ector sipped his wine with his eyes brooding on the logs which lit the evening; Kay played chess with himself rather badly; and Merlyn, with his long beard saffron in the firelight, sat cross-legged knitting, beside the Wart.

"There was once discovered at Rome," read Reverend Sidebottom through his nose, *"an uncorrupted body, taller than the wall of the city, on which the following words were inscribed—'Pallas, the son of Evander, whom the lance of a crooked soldier slew, is interred here.' A candle burned at his head which neither water nor wind could extinguish, until air was admitted through a hole made with the point of a needle beneath the flame. The wound of which this giant had died was four feet and a half long. Having been killed after the overthrow of Troy, he remained in his tomb two thousand two hundred and forty years."*

"Have you ever seen a giant?" asked Merlyn softly, so as not to interrupt the reading. "No, I remember you haven't. Just catch hold of my hand a moment, and shut your eyes."

The vicar was droning on about the gigantic son of Evander, Sir Ector was staring into the fire, and Kay was making a slight click as he moved one of the chessmen, but the Wart and Merlyn were immediately standing hand in hand in an unknown forest.

"This is the Forest of the Burbly Water," said Merlyn, "and we are going to visit the giant Galapas. Now listen. You are invisible at the moment, because you are holding my hand. I am able to keep myself invisible by an exercise of will-power—an exceedingly exhausting job it is—and I can keep you invisible so long as you hold on to me. It takes twice as much will-power, but there. If, however, you let go of me even for a moment, during that moment you will become visible, and, if you do it in the presence of Galapas, he will munch you up in two bites. So hold on."

"Very well," said the Wart.

"Don't say 'Very well.' It isn't very well at all. On the contrary, it is very ill indeed. And another thing. The whole of this beastly wood is dotted with pitfalls and I shall be grateful if you will look where you are going."

"What sort of pitfalls?"

"He digs a lot of pits about ten feet deep, with smooth clay walls, and covers them over with dead branches, pine needles and such-like. Then, if people walk about, they tumble into them, and he goes round with his bow every morning to finish them off. When he has shot them dead, he climbs in and collects them for dinner. He can hoist himself out of a ten-foot pit quite easily."

"Very well," said the Wart again, and corrected himself to, "I will be careful."

Being invisible is not so pleasant as it sounds. After a few minutes of it you forget where you last left your hands and legs—or at least you can only guess to within three or four inches—and the result is that it is by no means easy to make your way through a brambly wood. You can see the brambles all right, but where exactly you are in relation to them becomes more confusing. The only guide to your legs, for the feeling in them soon becomes complicated, is by looking for your footprints—these you can see in the neatly flattened grass below you—and, as for your arms and hands, it becomes hopeless unless you concentrate your mind to remember where you put them last. You can generally tell where your body is, either by the unnatural bend of a thorn branch, or by the pain of one of its thorns, or by the strange feeling of *centralness* which all human beings have, because we keep our souls in the region of our liver.

"Hold on," said Merlyn, "and for glory's sake don't trip up."

They proceeded to tread their tipsy way through the forest, staring carefully at the earth in front of them in case it should give way, and stopping very often when an extra large bramble fastened itself in their flesh. When Merlyn was stuck with a bramble, he swore, and when he swore he lost some of his concentration and they both became dimly visible, like autumn mist. The rabbits upwind of them stood on their hind legs at this, and exclaimed, "Good gracious!"

"What are we going to do?" asked the Wart.

"Well," said Merlyn, "here we are at the Burbly Water. You can see the giant's castle on the opposite bank, and we shall have to swim across. It may be difficult to walk when you are invisible, but to swim is perfectly impossible, even with years of practice. You are always getting your nose under water. So I shall have to let go of you until we have swum across in our own time. Don't forget to meet me quickly on the other bank."

The Wart went down into the warm starlit water, which ran musically like a real salmon stream, and struck out for the other side. He swam fast, across and down river, with a kind of natural dog-stroke, and he had to go about a quarter of a mile below his landing-place along the bank before Merlyn also came out to meet him, dripping. Merlyn swam the breast-stroke, very slowly and with great precision, watching ahead of him over the bow wave of his beard, with that faintly anxious expression of a faithful retriever.

"Now," said Merlyn, "catch hold again, and we will see what Galapas is about."

They walked invisible across the sward, where many unhappy-looking gardeners with iron collars round their necks were mowing, weeding and sweeping by torchlight, although it was so late, in what had begun to be a garden. They were slaves.

"Talk in whispers," said Merlyn, "if you have to talk."

There was a brick wall in front of them, with fruit trees nailed along it, and this they were forced to climb. They did so by the usual methods of bending over, climbing on each other's backs, giving a hand up from on top, and so forth, but every time that the Wart was compelled to let go of his magician for a moment he became visible. It was like an early cinematograph flickering very badly, or one of those magic lanterns where you put in slide after slide. A slave gardener, looking at that part of the wall, sadly tapped himself on the head and went away into a shrubbery to be sick.

"Hush," whispered Merlyn from the top of the wall, and they looked down upon the giant in person, as he took his evening ease by candlelight upon the bowling green.

"But he's not big at all," whispered the Wart disappointedly.

"He is ten feet high," hissed Merlyn, "and that is *extremely* big for a giant. I chose the best one I knew. Even Goliath was only six cubits and a span—or nine feet four inches. If you don't like him you can go home."

"I'm sorry. I didn't mean to be ungrateful, Merlyn, only I thought they were sixty feet long and that sort of thing."

"Sixty feet," sniffed the necromancer.

The giant had heard something at the top of the wall, and looked up towards them, remarking in a rumbling tone, "How the bats squeak at night!" Then he poured himself out another hornful of madeira and tossed it off in one draught.

Merlyn lowered his voice and explained. "People find the teeth and bones of creatures like your friend Atlantosaurus, and then they tell stories about human giants. One of them found a tooth weighing two hundred ounces. It's dragons, not giants, that grow really big."

"But can't humans grow big too?"

"I don't understand it myself, but it is something about the composition of their bones. If a human was to grow sixty feet high, he would simply snap his bones with the weight of their own gravity. The biggest real giant was Eleazer, and he was only ten feet and a half."

"Well," said the Wart, "I must say it is rather a disappointment."

"I don't mean being brought to see him," he added hastily, "but that they don't grow like I thought. Still, I suppose ten feet is quite big when you come to think of it."

"It is twice as high as you are," said Merlyn. "You would just come up to his navel, and he could pitch you up to a corn rick about as high as you can throw a sheaf."

They had become interested in this discussion, so that they got less and less careful of their voices, and now the giant rose up out of his easy-chair. He came towards them with a three-gallon bottle of wine in his hand, and stared earnestly at the wall on which they were sitting. Then he threw the bottle at the wall rather to their left, said in an angry voice, "Beastly screech owls!" and proceeded to stump off into the castle.

"Follow him," cried Merlyn quickly.

They scrambled down off the wall, joined hands, and hurried after the giant by the garden door.

In the beginning the downstair parts were reasonably civilized, with green baize doors behind which butlers and footmen—though with iron collars round their necks—were polishing silver and finishing off the decanters. Later on there were strong-rooms with ancient safes in them, that contained the various gold cups, épergnes and other trophies won at jousts and horse-races by the giant. Next there were dismal cellars with cobwebs over the wine bins, and dreary-looking rats peeping thoughtfully at the bodiless footprints in the dust, and several corpses of human beings hanging up in the game cupboards until they should be ready to eat. It was like the place for adults only in the Chamber of Horrors at Madame Tussaud's.

At the very bottom of the castle they came upon the dungeons. Here the chalky walls dripped with greasy moisture, and there were pathetic messages and graffiti scratched upon the stone. "Pray for poor Priscilla," said one, and another said, "Oh, if I had only paid for my dog license honestly, I should never have come to this pass." There was a picture of a man hanging from a gallows, with arms and legs sticking out like those of a Guy Fawkes in all directions, and another of a demon with horns. A fifth carving said, "Midnight Sun for the two-thirty," while a sixth said, "Oh, yeah?" and a seventh exclaimed, "Alas, that I should have forgotten to feed my poor canary: now I am in the same dread doom." A message which had been scratched out said, "Beastly old Galapas loves Madame Mim, the dirty hound," and somebody else had written, "Repent and be saved for the Kingdom of Hell is at hand." There were kisses, dates, pious ejaculations, mottoes such as "Waste not, want not," and "Good night, ladies," also hearts with arrows in them, skulls and crossbones, pictures of pigs drawn with the eyes shut, and pathetic messages such as, "Don't forget to take the potatoes off at half-past twelve," "The key is under the geranium," "Revenge me on stinking Galapas, by whom I am foully slain," or merely "Mazawatee Mead for Night Starvation." It was a grimly place.

"Ha!" cried Galapas, stopping outside one of his cells. "Are you going to give me back my patent unbreakable helm, or make me another one?"

"It's not your helm," answered a feeble voice. "I invented it, and I patented it, and you can go sing for another one, you beast."

"No dinner tomorrow," said Galapas cruelly, and went on to the next cell.

"What about that publicity?" asked the giant. "Are you going to say that the Queen of Sheba made an unprovoked attack upon me and that I took her country in self-defense?"

"No, I'm not," said the journalist in the cell.

"Rubber truncheons for you," said Galapas, "in the morning."

"Where have you hidden my elastic stays?" thundered the giant at the third cell.

"I shan't tell you," said the cell.

"If you don't tell me," said Galapas, "I shall have your feet burnt."

"You can do what you like."

"Oh, come on," pleaded the giant. "My stomach hangs down without them. If you will tell me where you put them I will make you a general, and you shall go hunting in Poland in a fur cap. Or you can have a pet lion, or a comic beard, and you can fly to America with an Armada. Would you like to marry any of my daughters?"

"I think all your propositions are foul," said the cell. "You had better have a public trial of me for propaganda."

"You are just a mean, horrible bully," said the giant, and went on to the next cell.

"Now then," said Galapas. "What about that ransom, you dirty English pig?"

"I'm not a pig," said the cell, "and I'm not dirty, or I wasn't until I fell into that beastly pit. Now I've got pine needles all down my back. What have you done with my tooth-brush, you giant, and where have you put my poor little brachet, what?"

"Never mind your brachet and your tooth-brush," shouted Galapas, "what about that ransom, you idiot, or are you too steeped in British sottishness to understand anything at all?"

"I want to brush my teeth," answered King Pellinore obstinately. "They feel funny, if you understand what I mean, and it makes me feel not very well."

"Uomo bestiale," cried the giant. "Have you no finer feelings?"

"No," said King Pellinore, "I don't think I have. I want to brush my teeth, and I am getting cramp through sitting all the time on this bench, or whatever you call it."

"Unbelievable sot," screamed the master of the castle. "Where is your soul, you shop-keeper? Do you think of nothing but your teeth?"

"I think of lots of things, old boy," said King Pellinore. "I think how nice it would be to have a poached egg, what?"

"Well, you shan't have a poached egg, you shall just stay there until you pay my ransom. How do you suppose I am to run my business if I don't have my ransoms? What about my concentration camps, and my thousand-dollar wreaths at funerals? Do you suppose that all this is run on nothing? Why, I had to send a wreath for King Gwythno Garanhir which consisted of a Welsh Harp forty feet long, made entirely out of orchids. It said, 'Melodious Angels Sing Thee to Thy Rest.'"

"I think that was a very good wreath," said King Pellinore admiringly. "But couldn't I have my tooth-brush, what? Dash it all, really, it isn't much compared with a wreath like that. Or is it?"

"Imbecile," exclaimed the giant, and moved on to the next cell.

"We shall have to rescue him," whispered the Wart. "It is poor old King Pellinore, and he must have fallen into one of those traps you were telling me about, while he was after the Questing Beast."

"Let him stay," said Merlyn. "A chap who doesn't know enough to keep himself out of the clutches of one of these giants isn't worth troubling about."

"Perhaps he was thinking of something else," whispered the Wart.

"Well, he shouldn't have been," hissed the magician. "Giants like this do absolutely no harm in the long run, and you can keep them quite quiet by the smallest considerations, such as giving them back their stays. Anybody knows that. If he has got himself into trouble with Galapas, let him stay in it. Let him pay the ransom."

"I know for a fact," said the Wart, "that he hasn't got the money. He can't even afford to buy himself a feather bed."

"Then he should be polite," said Merlyn doubtfully.

"He is trying to be," said the Wart. "He doesn't understand very much. Oh, please, King Pellinore is a friend of mine and I don't like to see him in these forbidding cells without a single helper."

"Whatever can we do?" cried Merlyn angrily. "The cells are firmly locked."

There was really nothing to do, but the magician's louder cry had altered matters into a crisis. Forgetting to be silent as well as invisible, Merlyn had spoken too loudly for the safety of his expedition.

"Who's there?" shrieked Galapas, wheeling round at the fifth cell.

"It's nothing," cried Merlyn, "Only a mouse."

The giant Galapas whipped out his mighty sword, and stared backwards down the narrow passage with his torch held high above his head. "Nonsense," he pronounced. "Mouses don't talk in human speech."

"Eek," said Merlyn, hoping that this would do.

"You can't fool me," said Galapas, "Now I shall come for you with my shining blade, and I shall see what you are, by yea or by nay."

He came down towards them, holding the blue glittering edge in front of him, and his fat eyes were brutal and piggish in the torchlight. You can imagine that it was not very pleasant having a person who weighed five hundred pounds looking for you in a narrow passage, with a sword as long as yourself, in the hopes of sticking it into your liver.

"Don't be silly," said Merlyn. "It is only a mouse, or two mice. You ought to know better."

"It is an invisible magician," said Galapas. "And as for invisible magicians, I slit them up, see? I shed their bowels upon the earth, see? I rip them and tear them, see, so that their invisible guts fall out upon the earth. Now, where are you, magician, so that I may slice and zip?"

"We are behind you," said Merlyn anxiously. "Look, in that further corner behind your back."

"Yes," said Galapas grimly, "except for your voice."

"Hold on," cried Merlyn, but the Wart in the confusion had slipped his hand.

"A visible magician," remarked the giant, "this time. But only a small one. We shall see whether the sword goes in with a slide."

"Catch hold, you idiot," cried Merlyn frantically, and with several fumblings they were hand in hand.

"Gone again," said Galapas, and swiped with his sword towards where they had been. It struck blue sparks from the stones.

Merlyn put his invisible mouth right up to the Wart's invisible ear, and whispered, "Lie flat in the passage. We will press ourselves one to each side, and hope that he will go beyond us."

This worked; but the Wart, in wriggling along the floor, lost contact with his protector once again. He groped everywhere but could not find him, and of course he was now visible again, like any other person.

"Ha!" cried Galapas. "The same small one, equally visible."

He made a swipe into the darkness, but Merlyn had snatched his pupil's hand again, and just dragged him out of danger.

"Mysterious chaps," said the giant. "The best thing would be to go snip-snap along the floor.

"That's the way they cut up spinach, you know," added the giant, "or anything you have to chip small."

Merlin and the Wart crouched hand in hand at the furthest corner of the corridor, while the horrible giant Galapas slowly minced his way towards them, laughing from the bottom of his thunderous belly, and not sparing a single inch of the ground. Click, click, went his razor sword upon the brutal stones, and there seemed to be no hope of rescue. He was behind them now and had cut them off.

"Good-by," whispered the Wart. "It was worth it."

"Good-by," said Merlin. "I don't think it was at all."

"You may well say Good-by," sneered the giant, "for soon this choppy blade will rip you."

"My dear friends," shouted King Pellinore out of his cell, "don't you say Good-by at all. I think I can hear something coming, and while there is life there is hope."

"Yah," cried the imprisoned inventor, also coming to their help. He feebly rattled the bars of his cell. "You leave those persons alone, you grincing giant, or I won't make you an unbreakable helmet, ever."

"What about your stays?" exclaimed the next cell fiercely, to distract his attention. "Fatty!"

"I am not fat," shouted Galapas, stopping half-way down the passage.

"Yes, you are," replied the cell. Fatty!"

"Fatty!" shouted all the prisoners together. "Fat old Galapas.

"Fat old Galapas cried for his mummy.

"He couldn't find his stays and down fell his tummy!"

"All right," said the giant, looking perfectly blue in the face. "All right, my beauties. I'll just finish these two off and then it will be truncheons for supper."

"Truncheons yourself," they answered. "You leave those two alone."

"Truncheons," was all the giant said. "Truncheons and a few little thumbscrews to finish up with. Now then, where are we?"

There was a distant noise, a kind of barking; and King Pellinore, who had been listening at his barred window while this was going on, began to jump and hop.

"It's it!" he shouted in high delight. "It's it."

"What's it?" they asked him.

"It!" explained the King. "It, itself."

While he was explaining, the noise had come nearer and now was clamoring just outside the dungeon door, behind the giant. It was a pack of hounds.

"Wouff!" cried the door, while the giant and all his victims stood transfixed.

"Wouff!" cried the door again, and the hinges creaked.

"Wouff!" cried the door for the third time, and the hinges broke.

"Wow!" cried the giant Galapas, as the door crashed to the stone flags with a tremendous slap, and the Beast Glatisant bounded into the corridor.

"Let go of me, you awful animal," cried the giant, as the Questing Beast fixed its teeth into the seat of his pants.

"Help! Help!" squealed the giant, as the monster ran him out of the broken door.

"Good old Beast!" yelled King Pellinore, from behind his bars. "Look at that, I ask you! Good old Beast. Leu, leu, leu, leu! Fetch him along then, old lady: bring him on, then, bring him on. Good old girl, bring him on: bring him on, then, bring him on."

"Dead, dead," added King Pellinore rather prematurely. "Bring him on dead, then: bring him on dead. There you are then, good old girl. Hie lost! Hie lost! Leu, leu, leu, leu! What do you know about that, for a retriever entirely self-trained?"

"Hourouff," barked the Questing Beast in the far distance. "Hourouff, hourouff." And they could just hear the giant Galapas running round and round the circular stairs, towards the highest turret in his castle.

Merlyn and the Wart hurriedly opened all the cell doors with the keys which the giant had dropped—though the Beast would no doubt have been able to break them down even if he had not—and the pathetic prisoners came out blinking into the torchlight. They were thin and bleached like mushrooms, but their spirits were not broken.

"Well," they said. "Isn't this a bit of all right?"

"No more thumbscrews for supper."

"No more dungeons, no more stench," sang the inventor. "No more sitting on this hard bench."

"I wonder where he can have put my tooth-brush?"

"That's a splendid animal of yours, Pellinore. We owe her all our lives."

"Three cheers for Glatisant!"

"And the brachet must be somewhere about."

"Oh, come along, my dear fellow. You can clean your teeth some other time, with a stick or something, when we get out. The thing to do is to set free all the slaves and to run away before the Beast lets him out of the Tower."

"As far as that goes, we can pinch the épergnes on the way out."

"Lordy, I shan't be sorry to see a nice fire again. That place fair gave me the rheumatics."

"Let's burn all his truncheons, and write what we think of him on the walls."

"Good old Glatisant!"

"Three cheers for Pellinore!"

"Three cheers for everybody else!"

"Huzza! Huzza! Huzza!"

Merlyn and the Wart slipped away invisibly from the rejoicings. They left the slaves thronging out of the Castle while King Pellinore carefully unlocked the iron rings from their necks with a few appropriate words, as if he were distributing the prizes on speech day. Glatisant was still making a noise like thirty couple of hounds questing, outside the Tower door, and Galapas, with all the furniture piled against the door, was leaning out of the Tower window shouting for the fire brigade. The slaves giggled at him as they went out. Downstairs the occupant of cell No. 3 was busily collecting the Ascot Gold Cup and other trophies out of the giant's safe, while the publicity man was having a splendid time with a bonfire of truncheons, thumbscrews and anything else that looked as if it would melt the instruments of torture. Across the corridor of the now abandoned dungeons the inventor was carving a rude message with hammer and chisel, and this said, "Nuts to Galapas." The firelight and the cheering, with King Pellinore's encouraging remarks, such as "Britons never shall be slaves," or "I hope you will never forget the lessons you have learned while you were with us here," or "I shall always be glad to hear from any Old Slaves, how they get on in life," or "Try to make it a rule always to clean your teeth twice a day," combined to make the leave-taking a festive one, from which the two invisible visitors were sorry to depart. But time was precious, as Merlyn said, and they hurried off towards the Burbly Water.

Considering the things that had happened, there must have been something queer about Time, as well as its preciousness, for when the Wart opened his eyes in the solar, Kay was still clicking his chessmen and Sir Ector still staring into the flames.

"Well," said Sir Ector, "what about the giant?"

Merlyn looked up from his knitting, and the Wart opened a startled mouth to speak, but the question had been addressed to the vicar.

Reverend Sidebottom closed his book about Pallas, the son of Evander, rolled his eyeballs wildly, clutched his thin beard, gasped for breath, shut his eyes, and exclaimed hurriedly, "My beloved, the giant is Adam, who was formed free from all corruption. The wound from which he died is transgression of the divine command."

Then he blew out his cheeks, let go of his beard and glanced triumphantly at Merlyn.

"Very good," said Merlyn. "Especially that bit about remaining uncorrupted. But what about the candle and the needle?"

The vicar closed his eyes again, as if in pain, and all waited in silence for the explanation.

After they had waited for several minutes, Wart said, "If I were a knight in armor, and met a giant, I should smite off both his legs by the knees, saying, 'Now art thou better of a size to deal with than thou were,' and after that I should swish off his head."

"Hush," said Sir Ector. "Never mind about that."

"The candle," said the vicar wanly, "is eternal punishment, extinguished by means of a needle—that is by the passion of Christ."

"Very good indeed," said Merlyn, patting him on the back.

The fire burned merrily, as if it were a bonfire which some slaves were dancing round, and one of the gaze-hounds next to the Wart now went

"Hourouff, hourouff" in its sleep, so that it sounded like a pack of thirty couple of hounds questing in the distance, very far away beyond the night-lit woods.

Might Isn't Right

On the battlements of their castle at Camelot, during an interval of peace between the two Gaelic Wars, the young king of England was standing with his tutor, looking across the purple wastes of evening. A soft light flooded the land below them, and the slow river wound between venerable abbey and stately castle, while the flaming water of sunset reflected spires and turrets and pennoncells hanging motionless in the calm air.

The world was laid out before the two watchers like a toy, for they were on a high keep which dominated the town. At their feet they could see the grass of the outer bailey—it was horrible looking down on it—and a small foreshortened man, with two buckets on a yoke, making his way across to the menagerie. They could see, further off at the gatehouse, which was not so horrible to look at because it was not vertically below, the night guard taking over from the sergeant. They were clicking their heels and saluting and presenting pikes and exchanging passwords as merrily as a marriage bell— but it was done in silence for the two, because it was so far below. They looked like lead soldiers, the little gallow-glasses, and their footsteps could not sound upon the luscious sheep-nibbled green. Then, outside the curtain wall, there was the distant noise of old wives bargaining, and brats bawling, and corporals quaffing, and a few goats mixed with it, and two or three lepers in white hoods ringing bells as they walked, and the swishing robes of nuns who were kindly visiting the poor, two by two, and a fight going on between some gentlemen who were interested in horses. On the other side of the river, which ran directly beneath the castle wall, there was a man ploughing in the fields, with his plough tied to the horse's tail. The wooden plough squeaked. There was a silent person near him, fishing for salmon with worms—the rivers were not polluted in those days—and further off, there was a donkey giving his musical concert to the coming night. All these noises came up to the two on the tower smally, as though they were listening through the wrong end of a megaphone.

Arthur was a young man, just on the threshold of life. He had fair hair and a stupid face, or at any rate there was a lack of cunning in it. It was an open face, with kind eyes and a reliable or faithful expression, as though he were a good learner who enjoyed being alive and did not believe in original sin. He had never been unjustly treated, for one thing, so he was kind to other people.

The King was dressed in a robe of velvet which had belonged to Uther the Conqueror, his father, trimmed with the beards of fourteen kings who had been vanquished in the olden days. Unfortunately some of these kings had had red hair, some black, some pepper-and-salt, while their growth of beard had been uneven. The trimming looked like a feather boa. The moustaches were stuck on round the buttons.

Merlyn had a white beard which reached to his middle, horn-rimmed spectacles, and a conical hat. He wore it in compliment to the Saxon serfs of the country, whose national headgear was either a kind of diving-cap, or the Phrygian cap, or else this cone of straw.

The two of them were speaking sometimes, as the words came to them, between spells of listening to the evening.

"Well," said Arthur, "I must say it is nice to be a king. It was a splendid battle."

"Do you think so?"

"Of course it was splendid. Look at the way Lot of Orkney ran, after I had begun to use Excalibur."

"He got you down first."

"That was nothing. It was because I was not using Excalibur. As soon as I drew my trusty sword they ran like rabbits."

"They will come again," said the magician, "all six. The Kings of Orkney, Garloth, Gore, Scotland, The Tower, and the Hundred Knights have started already—in fact, the Gaelic Confederation. You must remember that your claim to the throne is hardly a conventional one."

"Let them come," replied the King. "I don't mind. I will beat them properly this time, and then we will see who is master."

The old man crammed his beard in his mouth and began to chew it, as he generally did when he was put about. He bit through one of the hairs, which stuck between two teeth. He tried to lick it off, then took it out with his fingers. Finally he began curling it into two points.

"I suppose you will learn some day," he said, "but God knows it is heartbreaking, uphill work."

"Oh?"

"Yes," cried Merlyn passionately. "Oh? oh? oh? That is all you can say. Oh? oh? oh? Like a schoolboy."

"I shall cut off your head if you are not careful."

"Cut if off. It would be a good thing if you did. I should not have to keep on tutoring, at any rate."

Arthur shifted his elbow on the battlement and looked at his ancient friend.

"What is the matter, Merlyn?" he asked. "Have I been doing something wrong? I am sorry if I have."

The magician uncurled his beard and blew his nose.

"It is not so much what you are doing," he said. "It is how you are thinking. If there is one thing I can't stand, it is stupidity. I always say that stupidity is the Sin against the Holy Ghost."

"I know you do."

"Now you are being sarcastic."

The King took him by the shoulder and turned him round. "Look," he said, "what is wrong? Are you in a bad temper? If I have done something stupid, tell me. Don't be in a bad temper."

It had the effect of making the aged nigromant angrier than before.

"Tell you!" he exclaimed. "And what is going to happen when there is nobody to tell you? Are you never going to think for yourself? What is going to happen when I am locked up in this wretched tumulus of mine, I should like to know?"

"I didn't know there was a tumulus in it."

"Oh, hang the tumulus! What tumulus? What am I supposed to be talking about?"

"Stupidity," said Arthur. "It was stupidity when we started."

"Exactly."

"Well, it's no good saying Exactly. You were going to say something about it."

"I don't know what I was going to say about it. You put one in such a passion with all your this and that, that I am sure nobody would know what they were talking about for two minutes together. How did it begin?"

"It began about the battle."

"Now I remember," said Merlyn. "That is exactly where it did begin."

"I said it was a good battle."

"So I recollect."

"Well, it was a good battle," he repeated defensively. "It was a jolly battle, and I won it myself, and it was fun."

The magician's eyes veiled themselves like a vulture's, as he vanished inside his mind. There was silence on the battlements for several minutes, while a pair of peregrines that were being hacked in a nearby field flew over their heads in a playful chase, crying out Kik-kik-kik, their bells ringing. Merlyn looked out of his eyes once more.

"It was clever of you," he said slowly, "to win the battle."

Arthur had been taught that he ought to be modest, and he was too simple to notice that the vulture was going to pounce.

"Oh, well. It was luck."

"Very clever," repeated Merlyn. "How many of your kerns were killed?"

"I don't remember."

"No."

"Kay said—"

The King stopped in the middle of the sentence, and looked at him.

"Well," he said. "It was not fun, then. I had not thought."

"The tally was more than seven hundred. They were all kerns, of course. None of the knights were injured, except the one who broke his leg falling off the horse."

When he saw that Arthur was not going to answer, the old fellow went on in a bitter voice.

"I was forgetting," he added, "that you had some really nasty bruises."

Arthur glared at his finger-nails.

"I hate you when you are a prig."

Merlyn was charmed.

"That's the spirit," he said, putting his arm through the King's and smiling cheerfully. "That's more like it. Stand up for yourself, that's the ticket. Asking advice is the fatal thing. Besides, I won't be here to advise you, fairly soon."

"What it this you keep talking about, about not being here, and the tumulus and so on?"

"It is nothing. I am due to fall in love with a girl called Nimue in a short time, and then she learns my spells and locks me up in a cave for several centuries. It is one of those things which are going to happen."

"But, Merlyn, how horrible! To be stuck in a cave for centuries like a toad in a hole! We must do something about it."

"Nonsense," said the magician. "What was I talking about?"

"About this maiden. . . ."

"I was talking about advice, and how you must never take it. Well, I am going to give you some now. I advise you to think about battles, and about your realm of Gramarye, and about the sort of things a king has to do. Will you do that?"

"I will. Of course I will. But about this girl who learns your spells. . . ."

"You see, it is a question of the people, as well as of the kings. When you said about the battle being a lovely one, you were thinking like your father. I want you to think like yourself, so that you will be a credit to all this education I have been giving you—afterwards, when I am only an old man locked up in a hole."

"Merlyn!"

"There, there! I was playing for sympathy. Never mind. I said it for effect. As a matter of fact, it will be charming to have a rest for a few hundred years, and, as for Nimue, I am looking backward to her a good deal. No, no, the important thing is this thinking-for-yourself business and the matter of battles. Have you ever thought seriously about the state of your country, for instance, or are you going to go on all your life being like Uther Pendragon? After all, you are the King of the place."

"I have not thought very much."

"No. Then let me do some thinking with you. Suppose we think about your Gaelic friend, Sir Bruce Sans Pitié."

"That fellow!"

"Exactly. And why do you say it like that?"

"He is a swine. He goes murdering maidens—and, as soon as a real knight turns up to rescue them, he gallops off for all he is worth. He breeds special fast horses so that nobody can catch him, and he stabs people in the back. He's a marauder. I would kill him at once if I could catch him."

"Well," said Merlyn, "I don't think he is very different from the others. What is all this chivalry, anyway? It simply means being rich enough to have a castle and a suit of armour, and then, when you have them, you make the Saxon people do what you like. The only risk you run is of getting a few bruises if you happen to come across another knight. Look at that tilt you saw between Pellinore and Grummore, when you were small. It is this armour that does it. All the barons can slice the poor people about as much as they want, and it is a day's work to hurt each other, and the result is that the country is devastated. Might is Right, that's the motto. Bruce Sans Pitié is only an example of the general situation. Look at Lot and Nentres and Uriens and all that Gaelic crew, fighting against you for the Kingdom. Pulling swords out of stones is not a legal proof of paternity, I admit, but the kings of the Old Ones are not fighting you about that. They have rebelled, although you are their feudal sovereign, simply because the throne is insecure. England's difficulty, we used to say, is Ireland's opportunity. This is their chance to pay off racial scores, and to have some blood-letting as sport, and to make a bit of money in ransoms. Their turbulence does not cost them anything themselves because they are dressed in armour—and you seem to enjoy it too. But look at the country. Look at the barns burnt, and dead men's legs sticking out of ponds, and horses with swelled bellies by the roadside, and mills falling down, and money buried, and nobody daring to walk abroad with gold or ornaments on their clothes. That is chivalry nowadays. That is the Uther Pendragon touch. And then you talk about a battle being fun!"

"I was thinking of myself."

"I know."

"I ought to have thought of the people who had no armour."

"Quite."

"Might isn't Right, is it, Merlyn?"

"Aha!" replied the magician, beaming. "Aha! You are a cunning lad, Arthur, but you won't catch your old tutor like that. You are trying to put me in a passion by making me do the thinking. But I am not to be caught. I am too old a fox for that. You will have to think the rest yourself. Is might right— and if not, why not, give reasons and draw a plan. Besides, what are you going to do about it?"

"What . . ." began the King, but he saw the gathering frown.

"Very well," he said. "I will think about it."

And he began thinking, stroking his upper lip, where the moustache was going to be.

There was a small incident before they left the keep. The man who had been carrying the two buckets to the menagerie came back with his buckets empty. He passed directly under them, looking small, on his way to the kitchen door. Arthur, who had been playing with a loose stone which he had dislodged from one of the machicolations, got tired of thinking and leaned over with the stone in his hand.

"How small Curselaine looks."

"He is tiny."

"I wonder what would happen if I dropped this stone on his head?"

Merlyn measured the distance.

"At thirty-two feet per second," he said, "I think it would kill him dead. Four hundred g is enough to shatter the skull."

"I have never killed anybody like that," said the boy, in an inquisitive tone.

Merlyn was watching.

"You are the King," he said.

Then he added, "Nobody can say anything to you if you try."

Arthur stayed motionless, leaning out with the stone in his hand. Then, without his body moving, his eyes slid sideways to meet his tutor's.

The stone knocked Merlyn's hat off as clean as a whistle, and the old gentleman chased him featly down the stairs, waving his wand of lignum vitae.

Merlyn Foresees His Fate

In Bedegraine it was the night before the battle. A number of bishops were blessing the armies on both sides, hearing confessions and saying Mass. Arthur's men were reverent about this, but King Lot's men were not—for such was the custom in all armies that were going to be defeated. The bishops assured both sides that they were certain to win, because God was with them, but King Arthur's men knew that they were outnumbered by three to one, so they thought it was best to get shriven. King Lot's men, who also knew the odds, spent the night dancing, drinking, dicing and telling each other dirty stories. This is what the chronicles say, at any rate.

In the King of England's tent, the last staff talk had been held, and Merlyn had stayed behind to have a chat. He was looking worried.

"What are you worried about, Merlyn? Are we going to lose this battle, after all?"

"No. You will win the battle all right. There is no harm in telling you so. You will do your best, and fight hard, and call in You-know-whom at the right moment. It will be in your nature to win the battle, so it doesn't matter telling you. No. It is something else which I ought to have told you that is worrying me just now."

"What was it about?"

"Gracious heavens! Why should I be worrying if I could remember what it was about?"

"Was it about the maiden called Nimue?"

"No. No. No. No. That's quite a different business. It was something— it was something I can't remember."

After a bit, Merlyn took his beard out of his mouth and began counting on his fingers.

"I have told you about Guenever, haven't I?"

"I don't believe it."

"No matter. And I have warned you about her and Lancelot."

"That warning," said the King, "would be a base one anyway, whether it was true or false."

"Then I have said the bit about Excalibur, and how you must be careful of the sheath?"

"Yes."

"I have told you about your father, so it can't be him, and I have given the hint about the person."

"What is confounding me," exclaimed the magician, pulling out his hair in tufts, "is that I can't remember whether it is in the future or in the past."

"Never mind about it," said Arthur. "I don't like knowing the future anyway. I had much rather you didn't worry about it, because it only worries me."

"But it is something I must say. It is vital."

"Stop thinking about it," suggested the King, "and then perhaps it will come back. You ought to take a holiday. You have been bothering your head too much lately, what with all these warnings and arranging about the battle."

"I *will* take a holiday," exclaimed Merlyn. "As soon as this battle is over, I will go on a walking tour into North Humberland. I have a Master called Bleise who lives in North Humberland, and perhaps he will be able to tell me what it is I am trying to remember. Then we could have some wild fowl watching. He is a great man for wild fowl."

"Good," said Arthur. "You take a long holiday. Then, when you come back, we can think of something to prevent Nimue."

The old man stopped fiddling with his fingers, and looked sharply at the King.

"You are an innocent fellow, Arthur," he said. "And a good thing too, really."

"Why?"

"Do you remember anything about the magic you had when you were small?"

"No. Did I have some magic? I can remember that I was interested in birds and beasts. Indeed, that is why I still keep my menagerie at the Tower. But I don't remember about magic."

"People don't remember," said Merlyn. "I suppose you wouldn't remember about the parables I used to tell you, when I was trying to explain things?"

"Of course I do. There was one about some Rabbi or other which you told me when I wanted to take Kay somewhere. I never could understand why the cow died."

"Well, I want to tell you another parable now."

"I shall love it."

"In the East, perhaps in the same place which that Rabbi Jachanan came from, there was a certain man who was walking in the market of Damascus when he came face to face with Death. He noticed an expression of surprise on the spectre's horrid countenance, but they passed one another without speaking. The fellow was frightened, and went to a wise man to ask what should be done. The wise man told him that Death had probably come to Damascus to fetch him away next morning. The poor man was terrified at this, and asked however he could escape. The only way they could think of between them was that the victim should ride all night to Aleppo, thus eluding the skull and bloody bones.

"So this man did ride to Aleppo—it was a terrible ride which had never been done in one night before—and when he was there he walked in the market place, congratulating himself on having eluded Death.

"Just then, Death came up to him and tapped him on the shoulder.

'Excuse me,' he said, 'but I have come for you.' 'Why,' exclaimed the terrified man, 'I thought I met you in Damascus yesterday!' 'Exactly,' said Death. 'That was why I looked surprised—for I had been told to meet you today, in Aleppo.'"

Arthur reflected on this gruesome chestnut for some time, then he said: "So it is no good trying to escape Nimue?"

"Even if I wanted to," said Merlyn, "it would be no good. There is a thing about Time and Space which the philosopher Einstein is going to find out. Some people call it Destiny."

"But what I can't get over is this toad-in-the-hole business."

"Ah, well," said Merlyn, "people will do a lot for love. And then the toad is not necessarily unhappy in its hole, not more than when you are asleep, for instance. I shall do some considering, until they let me out again."

"So they will let you out?'

"I will tell you something else, King, which may be a surprise for you. It will not happen for hundreds of years, but both of us are to come back. Do you know what is going to be written on your tombstone? *Hic jacet Arthurus Rex quondam Rexque futurus.* Do you remember your Latin? It means, the once and future king."

"I am to come back as well as you?"

"Some say from the vale of Avilion."

The King thought about it in silence. It was full night outside, and there was stillness in the bright pavilion. The sentries, moving on the grass, could not be heard.

"I wonder," he said at last, "whether they will remember about our Table?"

Merlyn did not answer. His head was bowed on the white beard and his hands clasped between his knees.

"What sort of people will they be, Merlyn?" cried the young man's voice, unhappily.

chapter 13

CLIVE STAPLES LEWIS:
THAT HIDEOUS STRENGTH

T H I S A N T H O L O G Y concludes with an apocalyptic answer to Arthur's question—one that is informed by a darkening vision of twentieth-century life, like the work of E. A. Robinson and T.H. White, but that also gives us a very different wizard and concludes by banishing supernatural evil from the earth. White's Merlin is a wise but predominantly comic figure who is anachronistic because he originates in modern times but lives backwards into the Middle Ages; Lewis's is archaic as well as anachronistic, a creature of the Dark Ages who has been preserved for a decisive battle between Good and Evil in modern England. Lewis's conception is made clear by a letter he wrote in 1950 to another Arthurian writer, Martyn Skinner, about Skinner's epic poem in progress *The Return of Arthur*. He urges "a style in which great or wise and almost numinous persons can speak. . . . Merlin must speak like one whose father was an aerial demon, and A[rthur] like one who has been in Avalon" (Glover, p. 220 n. 32).

That Hideous Strength: A Modern Fairy-Tale for Grown-Ups (1946) brings back to earth the "Space Trilogy" of which *Out of the Silent Planet* (1943) and *Perelandra* (1944) are the first two volumes. The trilogy presents our solar system as one in which physical nature is underpinned by a metaphysical order of divine beings. Following the example of Olaf Stapledon's *Star Maker* (1936), every planetary body is dominated by a master intelligence and associated lesser spirits. These "Oyeresu" and "eldils" are analogous to the angels of Christian theology, and earth is ruled by the "fallen" angels—which accounts for its tragic history. (After all, World War II looms in the immediate historical context of White's, Stapledon's, and Lewis's fiction.) Men, with their materialistic vision, are unaware of the spiritual presences; this ignorance enables the corrupt eldils of earth to manipulate them.

In the first novel of the trilogy a philologist named Elwin Ransom is kidnapped by a brilliant physicist named Weston and taken to Mars, where the men discover that an "unfallen" solar civilization exists outside earth. Because earth has been quarantined by this civilization, it is called Thulcandra, "the silent planet." In the second novel the creator spirit Maleldil transports Ransom to Venus, or Perelandra, to battle Weston again. The physicist's body has been taken over by Satan, earth's "Bent Eldil," who plans to corrupt prelapsarian Venus by tempting its Eve and her husband to sleep on a forbidden island. Ransom succeeds in destroying Weston, but suffers a permanent and painful wound in his heel.

That Hideous Strength augments the mythical and biblical elements of the first two novels with Arthurian legend. Ransom appears now as the "Director," or Mr. Fisher-King, his unhealing wound paralleling that of the Grail Castle's ruler. He has also inherited the mantle of the Pendragon, handed down secretly through the centuries, and so become Arthur's successor. Once again his opponents are the human agents of the Bent Eldil, who, thwarted in his designs beyond the silent planet, now seeks to encompass the utter enslavement of humanity. Ransom is prevented by his wound from directly intervening in this struggle; like Satan, he must work through human allies. Thus the action of the novel contrasts the opposing agencies and actors of Good and Evil.

Satan's agents are organized by the N.I.C.E.—a deliciously ironic acronym for the National Institute of Coordinated Experiments. The N.I.C.E. is not only secular and bureaucratic but fascist; its aim is to reorganize society along "scientific" lines and eventually to remold humanity itself by means like "sterilization of the unfit, liquidation of backward races. . . , selective breeding. Then real education, including pre-natal education" (p. 37). To gain popular support for its schemes, a "distinguished novelist and scientific popularizer" named Horace Jules has been appointed Director. However, the real power lies with a small coterie centered around John Wither, the Deputy Director, who like Weston serves as a human conduit for the evil eldils, and the dismembered head of a criminal scientist named Alcasan, which has been artificially preserved at N.I.C.E. headquarters in Belbury as the Bent Eldil's mouthpiece. Other members of the inner circle include Lord Feverstone (Weston's former assistant), Frost (like Wither a "full initiate" of the earthly eldils), "Fairy" Hardcastle (chief of the Institutional Police), Filostrato (a brilliant physiologist who has preserved Alcasan's head), and Straik (an unstable minister with millennial yearnings).

Ransom's circle is just as motley. It includes several people (Cecil and Margery Dimble, Ivy Maggs) who have been dispossessed of their homes by the Institute's takeover of Bracton College and the town of Edgestow, the skeptic John McPhee, the psychologist Grace Ironwood, a young couple named Arthur and Camilla Denniston, and a large black bear called Mr. Bultitude. Ivy Maggs' husband Tom, who is serving a brief term in prison, has been transferred into the custody of N.I.C.E. for its "experiments." The story focuses, however, on Jane and Mark Studdock, whose marriage is breaking apart because both are too concerned with their own independence to make a full emotional commitment to each other. Mark is recruited by N.I.C.E. and alternately enticed and bullied into the Belbury circle; Jane has a latent psychic talent, and her vivid dreams of a man lying on a stone bier underground and of Alcasan's head bring her to the attention of Ransom's group at St. Anne's. The Studdocks' deepening involvement in the conflict between the two groups is developed by contrasting scenes throughout the novel. It soon turns out that both groups are looking for Merlin, whom they suspect is buried under Merlin's Wood at Bracton College, and destined to awake soon.

Early on Cecil Dimble speculates about the mage's part in Arthurian legend: "He's the really interesting figure. Did the whole thing fail because he died so soon? Has it ever struck you what an odd creation Merlin is? He's not evil; yet he's a magician. He's obviously a druid; yet he knows all about the Grail. . . . I often wonder. . . whether Merlin doesn't represent the last trace of something the later tradition has quite forgotten about—something that became impossible when the only people in touch with the supernatural were either white or black, either priests or sorcerers" (p. 24). It is this half-human ambiguity as well as Merlin's magical power that makes him pivotal; N.I.C.E. intends to recruit him as the complement to their mastery of social and physical sciences and the linchpin for their conquest, while Ransom hopes to forestall them by appealing to the wizard's ancient allegiance. When he awakes, Merlin surprises them all.

Clive Staples Lewis (1898–1963), the writer of this remarkable work, which has one foot in Arthurian fantasy and one firmly in mid-twentieth-century England, was himself a remarkable individual. His early reading loves, much like his friend J.R.R. Tolkien's, included Celtic and Norse literature and the neomedieval romances of William Morris and George Macdonald. He won a scholarship to Oxford in 1916, but only went to the university after being wounded in World War I. In 1925 he became a Fellow of Magdalen College in Oxford, where he taught Anglo-Saxon, English literature, philosophy, and political science for thirty years before serving as Professor of English Medieval and Renaissance Literature at Cambridge for the last decade of his life. His scholarship produced *English Literature in the Sixteenth Century* (1954), which is Volume 3 in the Oxford History of English Literature, and *The Allegory of Love* (1936), a study of the courtly love tradition and literary technique that is still required reading for medievalists.

Lewis is better known to the general public, however, as a persuasive spokesperson for traditional Christian values in a singularly secular era. He himself moved from an agnostic to a Christian position, reversing the general tendency of his time; many of his eloquent books, like *The Screwtape Letters* (1942), a series of letters from an experienced devil to a young subordinate, argued for the genuine existence of the supernatural and urged a return to an orthodox and humane (if still patriarchal) morality. Yet his fantasies with strong moral themes, especially the Narnia books for children (1948–1956), remain the most popular and influential of all his writing.

Lewis's gift for espousing traditional religious values in urbane and imaginative forms gives him a special place in the Oxford triumvirate of J.R.R. Tolkien and Charles Williams, who along with Lewis and several others composed a famous group called the Inklings. They became familiar with each other's work through informal readings and discussion, and *That*

Hideous Strength shows the influence of both Tolkien and Williams. The clearest references are to "Numinor," the prototype of the sunken continent Atlantis in Tolkien's *Silmarillion*, and to the eldilic deities like those in Williams's novels and Tolkien's Valar/Maiar (including the spirits of Middle-earth corrupted by Melkor and Sauron). There is no sign that Lewis's Merlin is patterned upon Tolkien's Gandalf, although generally they possess similar roles and relationships to major characters.

Another important influence was Williams's complex Arthurian poems, which describe a conflict between the parallel realities of Logres and Britain. These poems so impressed Lewis that he added a lengthy commentary to Williams's unfinished prose discussion of the legend in *Arthurian Torso* (1948). Simply put, Logres embodies the ideal values sought by Arthur's chivalric Christian order and still potential in the legend of his return; while Britain represents the inhumanely materialistic and scientific bias that Lewis brings to a head in the N.I.C.E. The details of this conflict are best left to the selections that follow, but Lewis treats these elements in a unique fashion. In the end what he says of Williams proves true also for *That Hideous Strength*: "It is in one way a wholly modern work, but it has grown sponta-neously out of Malory and if the King and the Grail and the begetting of Galahad still serve, and serve perfectly, to carry the twentieth-century poet's meaning, that is because he has penetrated more deeply than the old writers themselves into what they also, half consciously, meant and found its significance unchangeable as long as there remains on earth any attempt to unite Christianity and civilization" (*Arthurian Torso*, pp. 199–200).

Bibliographic note: I have chosen to reprint selections from Chapters 9, 13, 15, and 16 of *That Hideous Strength*, which introduce the situation and include most of Merlin's appearances in the novel. By concentrating on the wizard, this arrangement inevitably departs somewhat from the alternation between scenes at St. Anne's and Belbury. Nevertheless, key contrasts have been retained, like that between the effects of the spirits' descent upon the company at St. Anne's and of Merlin's subsequent curse upon the dinner party at Belbury. The true character of the opposing forces in the novel is signaled by their respective uses (and abuses) of language, as well as by settings and actions.

The first edition was published in London and New York by Macmillan, 1946, and the novel has been reprinted many times in both cloth and paperback. Lewis's autobiography is *Surprised by Joy: The Shape of My Early Life* (New York: Harcourt Brace, 1956), and his relationship with the Inklings is chronicled in Humphrey Carpenter, *The Inklings: C.S. Lewis, J.R.R. Tolkien, Charles Williams, and Their Friends* (London: Allen & Unwin, 1979). Two good critical treatments of the novel that discuss Merlin are in Charles Moorman's *Arthurian Triptych: Mythic Materials in Charles Williams, C.S. Lewis, and T.S. Eliot* (Berkeley: University of California Press, 1960) and Donald Glover's *C.S. Lewis: The Art of Enchantment* (Athens: Ohio University Press, 1981).

That Hideous Strength

At the beginning the grand mystery for the Company had been why the enemy wanted Bragdon Wood. The land was unsuitable and could be made fit to bear a building on the scale they proposed only by the costliest preliminary work; and Edgestow itself was not an obviously convenient place. By intense study in collaboration with Dr. Dimble, and despite the continued scepticism of MacPhee, the Director had at last come to a certain conclusion. Dimble and he and the Dennistons shared between them a knowledge of Arthurian Britain which orthodox scholarship will probably not reach for some centuries. They knew that Edgestow lay in what had been the very heart of ancient Logres, that the village of Cure Hardy preserved the name of Ozana le Coeur Hardi, and that a historical Merlin had once worked in what was now Bragdon Wood.

What exactly he had done there they did not know; but they had all, by various routes, come too far either to consider his art mere legend and imposture, or to equate it exactly with what the Renaissance called Magic. Dimble even maintained that a good critic, by his sensibility alone, could detect the difference between the traces which the two things had left on literature. "What common measure is there," he would ask, "between ceremonial occultists like Faustus and Prospero and Archimago with their midnight studies, their forbidden books, their attendant fiends or elementals, and a figure like Merlin who seems to produce his results simply by being Merlin?" And Ransom agreed. He thought that Merlin's art was the last survival of something older and different—something brought to Western Europe after the fall of Numinor and going back to an era in which the general relations of mind and matter on this planet had been other than those we know. It had probably differed from Renaissance Magic profoundly. It had possibly (though this was doubtful) been less guilty: it had certainly been more effective. For Paracelsus and Agrippa and the rest had achieved little or nothing: Bacon himself—no enemy to magic except on this account—reported that the magicians "attained not to greatness and certainty of works." The whole Renaissance outburst of forbidden arts had, it seemed, been a method of losing one's soul on singularly unfavourable terms. But the older Art had been a different proposition.

But if the only possible attraction of Bragdon lay in its association with the last vestiges of Atlantean magic, this told the Company something else. It told them that the N.I.C.E., at its core, was not concerned solely with modern or materialistic forms of power. It told the director, in fact, that there was eldilic energy and eldilic knowledge behind it. It was, of course, another question whether its human members knew of the dark powers who were their real organisers. And in the long run this question was not perhaps important. As Ransom himself had said more than once, "Whether they know it or whether they don't, much the same sort of things are going to happen. It's not a question of how the Belbury people are going to act (the dark-eldils will see to that) but of how they will think about their actions. They'll go to Bragdon: it remains to be seen whether any of them will know the real reason why they're going there, or whether they'll all fudge up some theory of soils, or air, or etheric tensions, to explain it."

Up to a certain point the Director had supposed that the powers for which the enemy hankered were resident in the mere site at Bragdon—for there is an old and wide-spread belief that locality itself is of importance in such matters. But from Jane's dream of the cold sleeper he had learned better. It was something much more definite, something located under the soil of Bragdon Wood, something to be discovered by digging. It was, in fact the body of Merlin. What the eldils had told him about the possibility of such discovery he had received, while they were with him, almost without wonder. It was no wonder to them. In their eyes the normal Tellurian modes of being—engendering and birth and death and decay—which are to use the framework of thought, were no less wonderful than the countless other patterns of being which were continually present to their unsleeping minds. To those high creatures whose activity builds what we call Nature, nothing is "natural." From their station the essential arbitrariness (so to call it) of every actual creation is ceaselessly visible; for them there are no basic assumptions: all springs with the willful beauty of a jest or a tune from that miraculous moment of self-limitation wherein the Infinite, rejecting a myriad possibilities, throws out of Himself the positive and elected invention. That a body should lie uncorrupted for fifteen hundred years, did not seem strange to them; they knew worlds where there was no corruption at all. That its individual life should remain latent in it all that time, was to them no more strange: they had seen innumerable different modes in which soul and matter could be combined and separated, separated without loss of reciprocal influence, combined without true incarnation, fused so utterly as to be a third thing, or periodically brought together in a union as short, and as momentous, as the nuptial embrace. It was not as a marvel in natural philosophy, but as an information in time of war, that they brought the Director their tidings. Merlin had not died. His life had been hidden, sidetracked, moved out of our one-dimensioned time, for fifteen centuries. But under certain conditions it would return to his body.

They had not told him this till recently because they had not known it. One of Ransom's greatest difficulties in disputing with MacPhee (who consistently professed to disbelieve the very existence of the eldils) was that MacPhee made the common, but curious assumption that if there are creatures wiser and stronger than man they must be forthwith omniscient and omnipotent. In vain did Ransom endeavor to explain the truth. Doubtless, the great beings who now so often came to him had power sufficient to sweep Belbury from the face of England and England from the face of the globe; perhaps, to blot the globe itself out of existence. But no power of that kind would be used. Nor had they any direct vision into the minds of men. It was in a different place, and approaching their knowledge from the other side, that they had discovered the state of Merlin: not from inspection of the thing that slept under Bragdon Wood, but from observing a certain unique configuration in that place where those things remain that are taken off time's mainroad, behind the invisible hedges, into the unimaginable fields. Not all the times that are outside the present are therefore past or future.

It was this that kept the Director wakeful, with knitted brow, in the small cold hours of that morning when the others had left him. There was no doubt in his mind now that the enemy had bought Bragdon to find Merlin: and if they found him they would re-awake him. The old Druid would inevitably cast his lot with the new planners—what could prevent his doing so? A junction would be effected between two kinds of power which between them would determine the fate of our planet. Doubtless that had been the will of the dark-eldils for centuries. The physical sciences, good and innocent in themselves, had already, even in Ransom's own time, begun to be warped, had been subtly manoeuvred in a certain direction. Despair of objective truth had been increasingly insinuated into the scientists; indifference to it, and a concentration upon mere power, had been the result. Babble about the *élan vital* and flirtations with panpsychism were bidding fair to restore the *Anima Mundi* of the magicians. Dreams of the far future destiny of man were dragging up from its shallow and unquiet grave the old dream of Man as God. The very experiences of the dissecting room and the pathological laboratory were breeding a conviction that the stifling of all deep-set repugnances was the first essential for progress. And now, all this had reached the stage at which its dark contrivers thought they could safely begin to bend it back so that it would meet that other and earlier kind of power. Indeed they were choosing the first moment at which this could have been done. You could not have done it with Nineteenth-Century scientists. Their firm objective materialism would have excluded it from their minds; and even if they could have been made to believe, their inherited morality would have kept them from touching dirt. MacPhee was a suvivor from that tradition. It was different now. Perhaps few or none of the people at Belbury knew what was happening; but once it happened, they would be like straw in fire. What should they find incredible, since they believed no longer in a rational universe? What should they regard as too obscene, since they held that all morality was a mere subjective by-product of the physical and economic situations of men? The time was ripe. From the point of view which is accepted in Hell, the whole history of our Earth had led up to this moment. There was now at last a real chance for fallen Man to shake off that limitation of his powers which mercy had imposed upon him as a protection from the full results of his fall. If this succeeded, Hell would be at last incarnate. Bad men, while still in the body, still crawling on this little globe, would enter that state which, heretofore, they had entered only after death, would have the diuturnity and power of evil spirits. Nature, all over the globe of Tellus, would become their slave; and of that dominion no end, before the end of time itself, could be certainly foreseen. . . .

[*Both N.I.C.E. and the company of Logres send expeditions to find Merlin; meanwhile he awakes on his own and eludes them. N.I.C.E. brings back a tramp whom they have mistaken for Merlin, but Dimble, Denniston, and Jane Studdock glimpse him riding away on a horse. Then an apparition appears at St. Anne's.*]

"Stand! Stand where you are and tell me your name and business," said Ransom.

The ragged figure on the threshold tilted its head a little sideways like one who cannot quite hear. At the same moment the wind from the opened door had its way with the house. The inner door, between the scullery and the kitchen, clapped to with a loud bang, isolating the three men from the women, and a large tin basin fell clattering into the sink. The stranger took a pace further into the room.

"*Sta,*" said Ransom in a loud voice. "*In nomine Patris et Filii et Spiritus Sancti, dic mihi qui sis et quam ob causam veneris.*"[1]

The Stranger raised his hand and flung back the dripping hair from his forehead. The light fell full on his face, from which Ransom had the impression of an immense quietness. Every muscle of this man's body seemed as relaxed as if he were asleep, and he stood absolutely still. Each drop of rain from the khaki coat struck the tiled floor exactly where the drop before it had fallen.

His eyes rested on Ransom for a second or two with no particular interest. Then he turned his head to his left, to where the door was flung back almost against the wall. MacPhee was concealed behind it.

"Come out," said the Stranger in Latin. The words were spoken almost in a whisper, but so deep that even in that windshaken room they made a kind of vibration. But what surprised Ransom much more was the fact that MacPhee immediately obeyed. He did not look at Ransom but at the Stranger. Then, unexpectedly, he gave an enormous yawn. The Stranger looked him up and down and then turned to the Director.

"Fellow," he said in Latin, "tell the Lord of this House that I am come." As he spoke, the wind from behind him was whipping the coat about his legs and blowing his hair over his forehead; but his great mass stood as if it had been planted like a tree and he seemed in no hurry. And the voice, too, was such as one might imagine to be the voice of a tree, large and slow and patient, drawn up through roots and clay and gravel from the depths of the Earth.

"I am the Master here," said Ransom, in the same language.

"To be sure!" answered the Stranger. "And yonder whippersnapper *(mastigia)* is without doubt your Bishop." He did not exactly smile, but a look of disquieting amusement came into his keen eyes. Suddenly he poked his head forward so as to bring his face much nearer to the Director's.

"Tell your master that I am come," he repeated in the same voice as before.

Ransom looked at him without the flicker of an eyelid.

"Do you really wish," he said at last, "that I call upon my Masters?"

"A daw that lives in a hermit's cell has learned before now to chatter book-Latin," said the other. "Let us hear your calling, mannikin" *(homuncio)*.

"I must use another language for it," said Ransom.

"A daw could have Greek also in its bill."

---

[1] Stand. In the name of the Father and the Son and the Holy Ghost, tell me who you are and why you come.

"It is not Greek."

"Let us hear your Hebrew, then."

"It is not Hebrew."

"Nay," answered the other with something like a chuckle, a chuckle deep hidden in his enormous chest and betrayed only by a slight movement of his shoulders, "if you come to the gabble of barbarians, it will go hard but I shall out-chatter you. Here is excellent sport."

"It may happen to seem to you the speech of barbarians," said Ransom, "for it is long since it has been heard. Not even in Numinor was it heard in the streets."

The Stranger gave no start and his face remained as quiet as before, if it did not become quieter. But he spoke with a new interest.

"Your Masters let you play with dangerous toys," he said. "Tell me, slave, what is Numinor?"

"The true West," said Ransom.

"Well," said the other. Then, after a pause, he added, "You have little courtesy to guests in this house. It is a cold wind on my back, and I have been long in bed. You see, I have already crossed the threshold."

"I value that at a straw," said Ransom. "Shut the door, MacPhee," he added in English. But there was no response; and looking round for the first time, he saw that MacPhee had sat down in the one chair which the scullery contained and was fast asleep.

"What is the meaning of this foolery?" said Ransom looking sharply at the Stranger.

"If you are indeed the Master of this house, you have no need to be told. If not, why should I give account of myself to such as you? Do not fear; your horse-boy will be none the worse."

"This shall be seen to shortly," said Ransom. "In the meantime, I do not fear your entering the house. I have more cause to fear your escaping. Shut the door if you will, for you see my foot is hurt."

The Stranger without ever taking his eyes off Ransom swept back his left hand behind him, found the door handle, and slammed the door to. MacPhee never stirred. "Now," he said, "what of these Masters of yours?"

"My Masters are the Oyéresu."

"Where did you hear that name?" asked the Stranger. "Or, if you are truly of the College, why do they dress you like a slave?"

"Your own garments," said Ransom, "are not those of a druid."

"That stroke was well put by," answered the other. "Since you have knowledge, answer me three questions, if you dare."

"I will answer them, if I can. But as for daring, we shall see."

The Stranger mused for a few seconds; then, speaking in a slightly sing-song voice, as though he repeated an old lesson, he asked, in two Latin hexameters, the following question:

"Who is called Sulva? What road does she walk? Why is the womb barren on one side? Where are the cold marriages?"

Ransom replied, "Sulva is she whom mortals call the Moon. She walks in the lowest sphere. The rim of the world that was wasted goes through her.

Half of her orb is turned towards us and shares our curse. Her other half looks to Deep Heaven; happy would he be who could cross that frontier and see the fields on her further side. On this side, the womb is barren and the marriages cold. There dwell an accursed people, full of pride and lust. There when a young man takes a maiden in marriage, they do not lie together, but each lies with a cunningly fashioned image of the other, made to move and to be warm by devilish arts, for real flesh will not please them, they are so dainty *(delicati)* in their dreams of lust. Their real children they fabricate by vile arts in a secret place."

"You have answered well," said the Stranger. "I thought there were but three men in the world that knew this question. But my second may be harder. Where is the ring of Arthur the King? What Lord has such a treasure in his house?"

"The ring of the King," said Ransom, "is on Arthur's finger where he sits in the House of Kings in the cup-shaped land of Abhalljin, beyond the seas of Lur in Perelandra. For Arthur did not die; but Our Lord took him, to be in the body till the end of time and the shattering of Sulva, with Enoch and Elias and Moses and Melchisedec the King. Melchisedec is he in whose hall the steep-stoned ring sparkles on the forefinger of the Pendragon."

"Well answered," said the Stranger. "In my college it was thought that only two men in the world knew this. But as for my third question, no man knew the answer but myself. Who shall be Pendragon in the time when Saturn descends from his sphere? In what world did he learn war?"

"In the sphere of Venus I learned war," said Ransom. "In this age Lurga shall descend. I am the Pendragon."

When he had said this, he took a step backwards for the big man had begun to move and there was a new look in his eyes. Any who had seen them as they stood thus face to face would have thought that it might come to fighting at any moment. But the Stranger had not moved with hostile purpose. Slowly, ponderously, yet not awkwardly, as though a mountain sank like a wave, he sank on one knee; and still his face was almost on a level with the Director's. . . .

MacPhee, who had just been refuting both Ransom and Alcasan's head by a two-edged argument which seemed unanswerable in the dream but which he never afterwards remembered, found himself violently waked by someone shaking his shoulder. He suddenly perceived that he was cold and his left foot was numb. Then he saw Denniston's face looking into his own. The scullery seemed full of people—Denniston and Dimble and Jane. They appeared extremely bedraggled, torn and muddy and wet.

"Are you all right?" Denniston was saying. "I've been trying to wake you for several minutes."

"All right?" said MacPhee swallowing once or twice and licking his lips. "Aye. I'm all right." Then he sat upright. "There's been a—a man here," he said.

"What sort of a man?" asked Dimble.

"Well," said MacPhee. "As to that... it's not just so easy... I fell asleep talking to him, to tell you the truth. I can't just bring to mind what we were saying."

The others exchanged glances. Though MacPhee was fond of a little hot toddy on winter nights, he was a sober man: they had never seen him like this before. Next moment he jumped to his feet.

"Lord save us!" he exclaimed. "He had the Director here. Quick! We must search the house and the garden. It was some kind of impostor or spy. I know now what's wrong with me. I've been hypnotised. There was a horse too. I mind the horse."

This last detail had an immediate effect on his hearers. Denniston flung open the kitchen door and the whole party surged in after him. For a second they saw indistinct forms in the deep, red light of a large fire which had not been attended to for some hours; then, as Denniston found the switch and turned on the light, all drew a deep breath. The four women sat fast asleep. The jackdaw slept, perched on the back of an empty chair. Mr. Bultitude, stretched out on his side across the hearth, slept also; his tiny, child-like snore, so disproportionate to his bulk, was audible in the momentary silence. Mrs. Dimble, bunched in what seemed an uncomfortable position, was sleeping with her head on the table, a half-darned sock still clasped on her knees. Dimble looked at her with that uncurable pity which men feel for any sleeper, but specially for a wife. Camilla, who had been in the rocking chair, was curled up in an attitude which was full of grace, like that of an animal accustomed to sleep anywhere. Mrs. Maggs slept with her kind, common-place mouth wide open; and Grace Ironwood, bolt upright as if she were awake, but with her head sagging a little to one side, seemed to submit with austere patience to the humiliation of unconsciousness.

"They're all right," said MacPhee from behind. "It's just the same as he did to me. We've no time to wake them. Get on."

They passed from the kitchen into the flagged passage. To all of them except MacPhee the silence of the house seemed intense after their buffeting in the wind and rain. The lights as they switched them on successively revealed empty rooms and empty passages which wore the abandoned look of indoor midnight—fires dead in the grates, an evening paper on a sofa, a clock that had stopped. But no one had really expected to find much else on the ground floor. "Now for upstairs," said Dimble.

"The lights are on upstairs," said Jane as they all came to the foot of the staircase.

"We turned them on ourselves from the passage," said Dimble.

"I don't think we did," said Denniston.

"Excuse me," said Dimble to MacPhee, "I think perhaps I'd better go first."

Up to the first landing they were in darkness; on the second and last the light from the first floor fell. At each landing the stair made a right-angled turn, so that till you reached the second you could not see the lobby on the floor above. Jane and Denniston, who were last, saw MacPhee and Dimble stopped dead on the second landing; their faces in profile lit up, the backs of their heads in darkness. The Ulsterman's mouth was shut like a trap, his expression hostile and afraid. Dimble was open-mouthed. Then, forcing her tired limbs to run, Jane got up beside them and saw what they saw.

Looking down on them from the balustrade were two men, one clothed in sweepy garments of red and the other in blue. It was the Director who wore blue, and for one instant a thought that was pure nightmare crossed Jane's mind. The two robed figures looked to be two of the same sort ... and what, after all, did she know of this Director who had conjured her into his house and made her dream dreams and taught her the fear of Hell that very night? And there they were, the pair of them, talking their secrets and doing whatever such people would do, when they had emptied the house or laid its inhabitants to sleep. The man who had been dug up out of the earth and the man who had been in outer space ... and the one had told them that the other was an enemy, and now, the moment they met, here were the two of them, run together like two drops of quicksilver. All this time she had hardly looked at the Stranger. The Director seemed to have laid aside his crutch, and Jane had hardly seen him standing so straight and still before. The light so fell on his beard that it became a kind of halo; and on top of his head also she caught the glint of gold. Suddenly, while she thought of these things, she found that her eyes were looking straight into the eyes of the Stranger. Next moment she had noticed his size. The man was monstrous. And the two men were allies. And the Stranger was speaking and pointing at her as he spoke.

She did not understand the words; but Dimble did, and heard Merlin saying in what seemed to him a rather strange kind of Latin:

"Sir, you have in your house the falsest lady of any at this time alive."

And Dimble heard the Director answer him in the same language:

"Sir, you are mistaken. She is doubtless like all of us a sinner; but the woman is chaste."

"Sir," said Merlin, "know well that she has done in Logres a thing of which no less sorrow shall come than came of the stroke that Balinus struck. For, Sir, it was the purpose of God that she and her lord should between them have begotten a child by whom the enemies should have been put out of Logres for a thousand years."

"She is but lately married," said Ransom. "The child may yet be born."

"Sir," said Merlin, "be assured that the child will never be born, for the hour of its begetting is passed. Of their own will they are barren: I did not know till now that the usages of Sulva were so common among you. For a hundred generations in two lines the begetting of this child was prepared; and unless God should rip up the work of time, such seed, and such an hour, in such a land, shall never be again."

"Enough said," answered Ransom. "The woman perceives that we are speaking of her."

"It would be great charity," said Merlin, "if you gave order that her head should be cut from her shoulders; for it is a weariness to look at her."

Jane, though she had a smattering of Latin, had not understood their conversation. The accent was unfamiliar, and the old druid used a vocabulary that was far beyond her reading—the Latin of a man to whom Apuleius and

Martianus Capella were the primary classics and whose elegances resembled those of the *Hisperica Famina*. But Dimble had followed it. He thrust Jane behind him and called out,

"Ransom! What in Heaven's name is the meaning of this?"

Merlin spoke again in Latin and Ransom was just turning to answer him, when Dimble interrupted,

"Answer *us*," he said. "What has happened? Why are you dressed up like that? What are you doing with that bloodthirsty old man?"

MacPhee, who had followed the Latin even less than Jane, but who had been staring at Merlin as an angry terrier stares at a Newfoundland dog which has invaded its own garden, broke into the conversation:

"Dr. Ransom," he said. "I don't know who the big man is and I'm no Latinist. But I know well that you've kept me under your eyes all this night against my own expressed will, and allowed me to be drugged and hypnotised. It gives me little pleasure, I assure you, to see yourself dressed up like something out of a pantomime and standing there hand in glove with that yogi, or shaman, or priest, or whatever he is. And you can tell him he need not look at me the way he's doing. I'm not afraid of him. And as for my own life and limb—if you, Dr. Ransom, have changes sides after all that's come and gone, I don't know that I've much more use for either. But though I may be killed, I'm not going to be made a fool of. We're waiting for an explanation."

The Director looked down on them in silence for a few seconds.

"Has it really come to this?" he said. "Does not one of you trust me?"

"I do, Sir," said Jane suddenly.

"These appeals to the passions and emotions," said MacPhee, "are nothing to the purpose. I could cry as well as anyone this moment if I gave my mind to it."

"Well," said the Director after a pause, "there is some excuse for you all for we have all been mistaken. So has the enemy. This man is Merlinus Ambrosius. They thought that if he came back he would be on their side. I find he is on ours. You, Dimble, ought to realise that this was always a possibility."

"That is true," said Dimble. "I suppose it was—well, the look of the thing—you and he standing there together: like *that*. And his appalling bloodthirstiness."

"I have been startled by it myself," said Ransom. "But after all we had no right to expect that his penal code would be that of the Nineteenth Century. I find it difficult, too, to make him understand that I am not an absolute monarch."

"Is—is he a Christian?" asked Dimble.

"Yes," said Ransom. "As for my clothes, I have for once put on the dress of my office to do him honour, and because I was ashamed. He mistook MacPhee and me for scullions or stable-boys. In his days, you see, men did not, except for necessity, go about in shapeless sacks of cloth, and drab was not a favourite colour."

At this point Merlin spoke again. Dimble and the Director who alone could follow his speech heard him say, "Who are these people? If they are your slaves, why do they do you no reverence? If they are enemies, why do we not destroy them?"

"They are my friends," began Ransom in Latin, but MacPhee interrupted, "Do I understand, Dr. Ransom," he said, "that you are asking us to accept this person as a member of our organisation?"

"I am afraid," said the Director, "I cannot put it that way. He *is* a member of the organisation. And I must command you all to accept him."

"And secondly," continued MacPhee, "I must ask what enquiries have been made into his credentials."

"I am fully satisfied," answered the Director. "I am as sure of his good faith as of yours."

"But the grounds of your confidence?" persisted MacPhee. "Are we not to hear them?"

"It would be hard," said the Director, "to explain to you my reasons for trusting Merlinus Ambrosius; but no harder than to explain to him why, despite many appearances which might be misunderstood, I trust you." There was just the ghost of a smile about his mouth as he said this. Then Merlin spoke to him again in Latin and he replied. After that Merlin addressed Dimble.

"The Pendragon tells me," he said in his unmoved voice, "That you accuse me for a fierce and cruel man. It is a charge I never heard before. A third part of my substance I gave to widows and poor men. I never sought the death of any but felons and heathen Saxons. As for the woman, she may live for me. I am not Master in this house. But would it be such a great matter if her head were struck off? Do not queens and ladies who would disdain her as their tire-woman go to the fire for less? Even that gallows bird *(cruciarius)* beside you—I mean you, fellow, though you speak nothing but your own barbarous tongue; you with the face like sour milk and the voice like a saw in a hard log and the legs like a crane's—even that cutpurse *(sector zonarius)*, though I would have him to the gatehouse, yet the rope should be used on his back not his throat."

MacPhee who realised, though without understanding the words, that he was the subject of some unfavourable comment, stood listening with that expression of entirely suspended judgment which is commoner in Northern Ireland and the Scotch lowlands than in England.

"Mr. Director," he said when Merlin had finished, "I would be very greatly obliged if—"

"Come," said the Director suddenly, "we have none of us slept tonight. Arthur, will you come and light a fire for our guest in the big room at the North end of this passage? And would someone wake the women? Ask them to bring him up refreshments. A bottle of Burgundy and whatever you have cold. And then, all to bed. We need not stir early in the morning. All is going to be very well."

"We're going to have difficulties with that new colleague of ours," said Dimble. He was alone with his wife in their room at St. Anne's late on the following day.

"Yes," he repeated after a pause. "What you'd call a strong colleague."

"You look very tired, Cecil," said Mrs. Dimble.

"Well, it's been rather a gruelling conference," said he. "He's—he's a tiring man. Oh, I know we've all been fools. I mean, we've all been imagining that because he came back in the Twentieth Century he'd be a Twentieth Century man. Time is more important than we thought, that's all."

"I felt that at lunch, you know," said his wife. "It was so silly not to have realised that he wouldn't know about forks. But what surprised me even more (after the first shock) was how—well, how *elegant* he was without them. I mean you could see it wasn't a case of having no manners but of having different ones."

"Oh, the old boy's a gentleman in his own way—anyone can see that. But . . . well, I don't know. I suppose it's all right."

"What happened at the meeting?"

"Well, you see, everything had to be explained on both sides. We'd the dickens of a job to make him understand that Ransom isn't the king of this country or trying to become king. And then we had to break it to him that we weren't the British at all, but the English—what he'd call Saxons. It took him some time to get over that."

"I see."

"And then MacPhee had to choose that moment for embarking on an interminable explanation of the relations between Scotland and Ireland and England. All of which, of course, had to be translated. It was all nonsense too. Like a good many people, MacPhee imagines he's a Celt when, apart from his name, there's nothing Celtic about him any more than about Mr. Bultitude. By the way Merlinus Ambrosius made a prophesy about Mr. Bultitude."

"Oh? What was that?"

"He said that before Christmas this bear would do the best deed that any bear had done in Britain except some other bear that none of us had ever heard of. He keeps on saying things like that. They just pop out when we're talking about something else, and in a rather different voice. As if he couldn't help it. He doesn't seem to know any *more* than the bit he tells you at the moment, if you see what I mean. As if something like a camera shutter opened at the back of his mind and closed again immediately and just one little item came through. It has rather a disagreeable effect."

"He and MacPhee didn't quarrel again, I hope."

"Not exactly. I'm afraid Merlinus Ambrosius wasn't taking MacPhee very seriously. From the fact that MacPhee is always being obstructive and rather rude and yet never gets sat on, I think Merlinus had concluded that he is the Director's fool. He seems to have got over his dislike for him. But I don't think MacPhee is going to like Merlinus."

"Did you get down to actual business?" asked Mrs. Dimble.

"Well, in a way," said Dimble, wrinkling his forehead. "We were all at cross-purposes, you see. The business about Ivy's husband being in prison came up, and Merlinus wanted to know why we hadn't rescued him. He seemed to imagine us just riding off and taking the County Jail by storm. That's the sort of thing one was up against all the time."

"Cecil," said Mrs. Dimble suddenly. "Is he going to be any use?"

"He's going to be able to *do* things, if that's what you mean. In that sense there's more danger of his being too much use than too little."

"What sort of thing?" asked his wife.

"The universe is so very complicated," said Dr. Dimble.

"So you have said rather often before, dear," replied Mrs. Dimble.

"Have I?" he said with a smile. "How often, I wonder? As often as you've told the story of the pony and trap at Dawlish?"

"Cecil! I haven't told it for years."

"My dear, I heard you telling it to Camilla the night before last."

"Oh, *Camilla*. That was quite different. She'd never heard it before."

"I don't know that we can be certain even about that ... the universe being so complicated and all." For a few minutes there was silence between them.

"But about Merlin?" asked Mrs. Dimble presently.

"Have you ever noticed," said Dimble, "that the universe, and every little bit of the universe, is always hardening and narrowing and coming to a point?"

His wife waited as those wait who know by long experience the mental processes of the person who is talking to them.

"I mean this," said Dimble in answer to the question she had not asked. "If you dip into any college, or school, or parish, or family—anything you like—at a given point in its history, you always find that there was a time before that point when there was more elbow room and contrasts weren't quite so sharp; and that there's going to be a time after that point when there is even less room for indecision and choices are even more momentous. Good is always getting better and bad is always getting worse: the possibilities of even apparent neutrality are always diminishing. The whole thing is sorting itself out all the time, coming to a point, getting sharper and harder. Like in the poem about Heaven and Hell eating into merry Middle Earth from opposite sides ... how does it go? Something about 'eat every day' ... 'till all is *somethinged away.*' It can't be *eaten*, that wouldn't scan. My memory has failed dreadfully these last few years. Do you know the bit, Margery?"

"What you were saying reminded me more of the bit in the Bible about the winnowing fan. Separating the wheat and the chaff. Or like Browning's line: 'Life's business being just the terrible choice.'"

"Exactly! Perhaps the whole time-process means just that and nothing else. But it's not only in questions of moral choice. Everything is getting more itself and more different from everything else all the time. Evolution means species getting less and less like one another. Minds get more and more spiritual, matter more and more material. Even in literature, poetry and prose draw further and further apart."

Mrs. Dimble with the ease born of long practice averted the danger, ever present in her house, of a merely literary turn being given to the conversation.

"Yes," she said. "Spirit and matter, certainly. That explains why people like the Studdocks find it so difficult to be happily married."

"The Studdocks?" said Dimble, looking at her rather vaguely. The domestic problems of that young couple had occupied his mind a good deal less than they had occupied his wife's. "Oh, I see, Yes. I daresay that has something to do with it. But about Merlin. What it comes to, as far as I can make out, is this. There were still possibilities for a man of that age which there aren't for a man of ours. The Earth itself was more like an animal in those days. And mental processes were much more like physical actions. And there were—well, Neutrals, knocking about."

"Neutrals?"

"I don't mean, of course, that anything can be a *real* neutral. A conscious being is either obeying God or disobeying Him. But there might be things neutral in relation to us."

"You mean eldils—angels?"

"Well, the word *angel* rather begs the question. Even the Oyéresu aren't exactly angels in the same sense as our guardian angels are. Technically they are Intelligences. The point is that while it may be true at the end of the world to describe every eldil either as an angel or a devil, and may even be true now, it was much less true in Merlin's time. There used to be things on this Earth pursuing their own business, so to speak. They weren't ministering spirits sent to help fallen humanity; but neither were they enemies preying upon us. Even in St. Paul one gets glimpses of a population that won't exactly fit into our two columns of angels and devils. And if you go back further . . . all the gods, elves, dwarfs, water-people, *fate, longaevi*. You and I know too much to think they are just illusions."

"You think there are things like that?"

"I think there were. I think there was room for them then, but the universe has come more to a point. Not all rational things perhaps. Some would be mere wills inherent in matter, hardly conscious. More like animals. Others—but I don't really know. At any rate, that is the sort of situation in which one got a man like Merlin."

"It all sounds rather horrible to me."

"It was *rather* horrible. I mean even in Merlin's time (he came at the extreme tail end of it) though you could still use that sort of life in the universe innocently, you couldn't do it safely. The things weren't bad in themselves, but they were already bad for us. They sort of withered the man who dealt with them. Not on purpose. They couldn't help doing it. Merlinus is withered. He's quite pious and humble and all that, but something has been taken out of him. That quietness of his is just a little deadly, like the quiet of a gutted building. It's the result of having laid his mind open to something that broadens the environment just a bit too much. Like polygamy. It wasn't wrong for Abraham, but one can't help feeling that even he lost something by it."

"Cecil," said Mrs. Dimble. "Do you feel quite comfortable about the Director's using a man like this? I mean, doesn't it look a little bit like fighting Belbury with its own weapons?"

"No. I *had* thought of that. Merlin is the reverse of Belbury. He's at the opposite extreme. He is the last vestige of an old order in which matter and spirit were, from our modern point of view, confused. For him every operation on Nature is a kind of personal contact, like coaxing a child or stroking one's horse. After him came the modern man to whom Nature is something dead—a machine to be worked, and taken to bits if it won't work the way he pleases. Finally, come the Belbury people, who take over that view from the modern man unaltered and simply want to increase their power by tacking onto it the aid of spirits—extra-natural, anti-natural spirits. Of course they hoped to have it both ways. They thought the old *magia* of Merlin, which worked in with the spiritual qualities of Nature, loving and reverencing them and knowing them from within, could be combined with the new *goeteia*—the brutal surgery from without. No. In a sense Merlin represents what we've got to get back to in some different way. Do you know that he is forbidden by the rules of his order to use any edged tool on any growing thing?"

"Good gracious!" said Mrs. Dimble. "There's six o'clock. I'd promised Ivy to be in the kitchen at quarter to. There's no need for *you* to move, Cecil,"

"Do you know," said Dimble, "I think you are a wonderful woman."

"Why?"

"How many women who had had their own house for thirty years would be able to fit into this menageries as you do?"

"That's nothing," said Mrs. Dimble. "Ivy had her own house too, you know. And it's much worse for her. After all, I haven't got my husband in jail."

"You jolly soon will have," said Dimble, "if half the plans of Merlinus Ambrosius are put into action."

Merlin and the Director were meanwhile talking in the Blue Room. The Director had put aside his robe and circlet and lay on his sofa. The druid sat in a chair facing him, his legs uncrossed, his pale large hands motionless on his knees, looking to modern eyes like an old conventional carving of a king. He was still robed and beneath the robe, as Ransom knew, had surprisingly little clothing, for the warmth of the house was to him excessive and he found trousers uncomfortable. His loud demands for oil after his bath had involved some hurried shopping in the village which had finally produced, by Denniston's exertions, a tin of Brilliantine. Merlinus had used it freely so that his hair and beard glistened and the sweet sticky smell filled the room. That was why Mr. Bultitude had pawed so insistently at the door that he was finally admitted and now sat as near the magician as he could possibly get, his nostrils twitching. He had never smelled such an interesting man before.

"Sir," said Merlin in answer to the question which the Director had just asked him. "I give you great thanks. I cannot indeed understand the way you live and you house is strange to me. You give me a bath such as the Emperor himself might envy, but no one attends me to it; a bed softer than sleep itself, but when I rise from it I find I must put on my own clothes with my own hands as if I were a peasant. I lie in a room with windows of pure crystal so that you can see the sky as clearly when they are shut as when they are open, and there is not wind enough within the room to blow out an unguarded taper; but I lie in it alone with no more honour than a prisoner in a dungeon. You people eat dry and tasteless flesh but it is off plates as smooth as ivory and as round as the sun. In all the house there are warmth and softness and silence that might put a man in mind of paradise terrestrial; but no hangings, no beautified pavements, no musicians, no perfumes, no high seats, not a gleam of gold, not a hawk, not a hound. You seem to me to live neither like a rich man nor a poor one: neither like a lord nor a hermit. Sir, I tell you these things because you have asked me. They are of no importance. Now that none hears us save the last of the seven bears of Logres, it is time that we should open counsels to each other."

He glanced at the Director's face as he spoke and then, as if startled by what he saw there, leaned sharply forward.

"Does your wound pain you?" he asked.

Ransom shook his head. "No," he said, "it is not the wound. We have terrible things to talk of."

The big man stirred uneasily.

"Sir," said Merlinus in a deeper and softer voice, "I could take all the anguish from your heel as though I were wiping it out with a sponge. Give me but seven days to go in and out and up and down and to and fro, to renew old acquaintance. These fields and I, this wood and I, have much to say to one another."

As he said this, he was leaning forward so that his face and the bear's were almost side by side, and it almost looked as if those two might have been engaged in some kind of furry and grunted conversation. The druid's face had a strangely animal appearance: not sensual nor fierce but full of the patient, unarguing sagacity of a beast. Ransom's, meanwhile, was full of torment.

"You might find the country much changed," he said, forcing a smile.

"No," said Merlin. "I do not reckon to find it much changed." The distance between the two men was increasing every moment. Merlin was like something that ought not to be indoors. Bathed and anointed though he was, a sense of mould, gravel, wet leaves, weedy water, hung about him.

"Not *changed*," he repeated in an almost inaudible voice. And in that deepening inner silence of which his face bore witness, one might have believed that he listened continually to a murmur of evasive sounds: rustling of mice and stoats, thumping progression of frogs, the small shock of falling hazel nuts, creaking of branches, runnels trickling, the very growing of grass. The bear had closed its eyes. The whole room was growing heavy with a sort of floating anaesthesia.

"Through me," said Merlin, "you can suck up from the Earth oblivion of all pains."

"Silence," said the Director sharply. He had been sinking down into the cushions of his sofa with his head drooping a little towards his chest. Now he suddenly sat bolt upright. The magician started and straightened himself likewise. The air of the room was cleared. Even the bear opened its eyes again.

"No," said the Director. "God's glory, do you think you were dug out of the earth to give me a plaster for my heel? We have drugs that could cheat the pain as well as your earth-magic or better, if it were not my business to bear it to the end. I will hear no more of that. Do you understand?"

"I hear and obey," said the magician. "But I meant no harm. If not to heal your own wound, yet for the healing of Logres, you will need my commerce with field and water. It must be that I should go in and out, and to and fro, renewing old acquaintance. It will not be changed, you know. Not what you would call *changed*."

Again that sweet heaviness, like the smell of hawthorn, seemed to be flowing back over the Blue Room.

"No," said the Director in a still louder voice, "that cannot be done any longer. The soul has gone out of the wood and water. Oh, I daresay you could awake them; a little. But it would not be enough. A storm, or even a river-flood would be of little avail against our present enemy. Your weapon would break in your hands. For the Hideous Strength confronts us and it is as in the days when Nimrod built a tower to reach heaven."

"Hidden it may be," said Merlinus. "But not *changed*. Leave me to work, Lord. I will wake it. I will set a sword in every blade of grass to wound them and the very clods of earth shall be venom to their feet. I will—"

"No," said the Director. "I forbid you to speak of it. If it were possible, it would be unlawful. Whatever of spirit may still linger in the earth has withdrawn fifteen hundred years further away from us since your time. You shall not speak a word to it. You shall not lift your little finger to call it up. I command you. It is in this age utterly unlawful." Hitherto, he had been speaking sternly and coldly. Now he leaned forward and said in a different voice, "It never was *very* lawful, even in your day. Remember, when we first knew that you would be awaked, we thought you would be on the side of the enemy. And because Our Lord does all things for each, one of the purposes of your reawakening was that your own soul should be saved."

Merlin sank back into his chair like a man unstrung. The bear licked his hand where it hung, pale and relaxed, over the arm of the chair.

"Sir," said Merlin presently, "if I am not to work for you in that fashion, then you have taken into your house a silly bulk of flesh. For I am no longer much of a man of war. If it comes to point and edge I avail little."

"Not that way either," said Ransom, hesitating like a man who is reluctant to come to the point. "No power that is merely earthly," he continued at last, "will serve against the Hideous Strength."

"Then let us all to prayers," said Merlinus. "But there also . . . I was not reckoned of much account . . . they called me a devil's son, some of them. It was a lie. But I do not know why I have been brought back."

"Certainly, let us stick to our prayers," said Ransom. "Now and always. But that was not what I meant. There are celestial powers: created powers, not in this Earth, but in the Heavens."

Merlinus looked at him in silence.

"You know well what I am speaking of," said Ransom. "Did not I tell you when we first met that the Oyéresu were my Masters?"

"Of course," said Merlin. "And that was how I knew you were of the College. Is it not our pass-word all over the Earth?"

"A pass-word?" exclaimed Ransom with a look of surprise. "I did not know that?"

"But... but," said Merlinus, "if you knew not the password, how did you come to say it?"

"I said it because it was true."

The magician licked his lips which had become very pale.

"True as the plainest things are true," repeated Ransom. "True as it is true that you sit here with my bear beside you."

Merlin spread out his hands. "You are my father and mother," he said. His eyes, steadily fixed on Ransom, were large as those of an awe-struck child, but for the rest he looked a smaller man than Ransom had first taken him to be.

"Suffer me to speak," he said at last, "or slay me if you will, for I am in the hollow of your hand. I had heard of it in my own days—that some had spoken with the gods. Blaise my Master knew a few words of that speech. Yet these were, after all, powers of Earth. For —I need not teach you, you know more than I—it is not the very Oyéresu, the true powers of Heaven, whom the greatest of our craft meet, but only their earthly wraiths, their shadows. Only the earth-Venus, the earth-Mercurius; not Perelandra herself, not Viritrilbia himself. It is only . . ."

"I am not speaking of the wraiths," said Ransom. "I have stood before Mars himself in the sphere of Mars and before Venus herself in the sphere of Venus. It is their strength, and the strength of some greater than they, which will destroy our enemies."

"But, Lord," said Merlin, "how can this be? Is is not against the Seventh Law?"

"What law is that?" asked Ransom.

"Has not our Fair Lord made it a law for Himself that He will not send down the Powers to mend or mar in this Earth until the end of all things? Or is this the end that is even now coming to pass?"

"It may be the beginning of the end," said Ransom. "But I know nothing of that. Maleldil may have made it a law not to send down the Powers. But if men by enginry and natural philosophy learn to fly into the Heavens, and come, in the flesh, among the heavenly powers and trouble them, He has not forbidden the Powers to react. For all this is within the natural order. A wicked man did learn so to do. He came flying, by a subtle engine, to where Mars dwells in Heaven and to where Venus dwells, and took me with him as a captive. And there I spoke with the true Oyéresu face to face. You understand me?"

Merlin inclined his head.

"And so the wicked man had brought about, even as Judas brought about, the thing he least intended. For now there was one man in the world—even myself—who was known to the Oyéresu and spoke their tongue, neither by God's miracle nor by magic from Numinor, but naturally, as when two men meet in a road. Our enemies had taken away from themselves the protection of the Seventh Law. They had broken by natural philosophy the barrier which God of His own power would not break. Even so they sought you as a friend and raised up for themselves a scourge. And that is why Powers of Heaven have come down to this house, and in this chamber where we are now discoursing Malacandra and Perelandra have spoken to me."

Merlin's face became a little paler. The bear nosed at his hand, unnoticed.

"I have become a bridge," said Ransom.

"Sir," said Merlin, "what will come of this? If they put forth their power, they will unmake all Middle Earth."

"Their naked power, yes," said Ransom. "That is why they will work only through a man."

The magician drew one large hand across his forehead.

"Through a man whose mind is opened to be so invaded," said Ransom, "one who by his own will once opened it. I take Our Fair Lord to witness that if it were my task, I would not refuse it. But he will not suffer a mind that still has its virginity to be so violated. And through a black magician's mind their purity neither can nor will operate. One who has dabbled ... in the days when dabbling had not begun to be evil, or was only just beginning ... and also a Christian man and a penitent. A tool (I must speak plainly) good enough to be so used and not too good. In all these Western parts of the world there was only one man who had lived in those days and could still be recalled. You—"

He stopped, shocked at what was happening. The huge man had risen from his chair, and stood towering over him. From his horribly opened mouth there came a yell that seemed to Ransom utterly bestial, though it was in fact only the yell of primitive Celtic lamentation. It was horrifying to see that withered and bearded face all blubbered with undisguised tears like a child's. All the Roman surface in Merlinus had been scraped off. He had become a shameless, archaic monstrosity babbling out entreaties in a mixture of what sounded like Welsh and what sounded like Spanish.

"Silence," shouted Ransom. "Sit down. You put us both to shame."

As suddenly as it had begun the frenzy ended. Merlin resumed his chair. To a modern it seemed strange that, having recovered his self-control, he did not show the slightest embarrassment at his temporary loss of it. The whole character of the two-sided society in which this man must have lived became clearer to Ransom than pages of history could have made it.

"Do not think," said Ransom, "that for me either it is child's play to meet those who will come down for your empowering."

"Sir," faltered Merlin, "you have been in Heaven. I am but a man. I am not the son of one of the Airish Men. That was a lying story. How can I? ... You are not as I. You have looked upon their faces before."

"Not on all of them," said Ransom. "Greater spirits than Malacandra and Perelandra will descend this time. We are in God's hands. It may unmake us both. There is no promise that either you or I will save our lives or our reason. I do not know how we can dare to look upon their faces; but I know we cannot dare to look upon God's if we refuse this enterprise."

Suddenly the magician smote his hand upon his knee.

"*Mehercule!*" he cried. "Are we not going too fast? If you are the Pendragon,

I am the High Council of Logres and I will counsel you. If the powers must tear me in pieces to break our enemies, God's will be done. But is it yet come to that? This Saxon king of yours who sits at Windsor, now. Is there no help in him?"

"He has no power in this matter."

"Then is he not weak enough to be overthrown?"

"I have no wish to overthrow him. He is the king. He was crowned and anointed by the Archbishop. In the order of Logres I may be Pendragon, but in the order of Britain I am the King's man."

"Is it then his great men—the counts and legates and bishops—who do the evil and he does not know of it?"

"It is—though they are not exactly the sort of great men you have in mind."

"And are we not big enough to meet them in plain battle?"

"We are four men, some women, and a bear."

"I saw the time when Logres was only myself and one man and two boys, and one of those was a churl. Yet we conquered."

"It could not be done now. They have an engine called the Press whereby the people are deceived. We should die without even being heard of."

"But what of the true clerks? Is there no help in them? It cannot be that *all* your priests and bishops are corrupted."

"The Faith itself is torn in pieces since your day and speaks with a divided voice. Even if it were made whole, the Christians are but a tenth part of the people. There is no help there."

"Then let us seek help from over sea. Is there no Christian prince in Neustria or Ireland or Benwick who would come in and cleanse Britain if he were called?"

"There is no Christian prince left. These other countries are even as Britain, or else sunk deeper still in the disease."

"Then we must go higher. We must go to him whose office it is to put down tyrants and give life to dying kingdoms. We must call on the Emperor."

"There is no Emperor."

"No Emperor..." began Merlin, and then his voice died away. He sat still for some minutes wrestling with a world which he had never envisaged. Presently he said, "A thought comes into my mind and I do not know whether it is good or evil. But because I am the High Council of Logres I will not hide it from you. This is a cold age in which I have awaked. If all this West part of the world is apostate, might it not be lawful, in our great need, to look farther... beyond Christendom? Should we not find some even among the heathen who are not wholly corrupt? There were tales in my day of some such: men who knew not the articles of our most holy Faith, but who worshipped God as they could and acknowledged the Law of Nature. Sir, I believe it would be lawful to seek help even there. Beyond Byzantium. It was rumoured also that there was knowledge in those lands—an Eastern circle and wisdom that came West from Numinor. I know not where—Babylon, Arabia, or Cathay. You said your ships had sailed all round the earth, above and beneath."

Ransom shook his head. "You do not understand," he said. "The poison was brewed in these West lands but it has spat itself everywhere by now. However far you went you would find the machines, the crowded cities, the empty thrones, the false writings, the barren beds: men maddened with false promises and soured with true miseries, worshipping the iron works of their own hands, cut off from Earth their mother and from the Father in Heaven. You might go East so far that East became West and you returned to Britain across the great Ocean, but even so you would not have come out anywhere into the light. The shadow of one dark wing is over all Tellus."

"Is it then the end?" asked Merlin.

"And this," said Ransom, ignoring the question, "is why we have no way left at all save the one I told you. The Hideous Strength holds all this Earth in its fist to squeeze as it wishes. But for their one mistake, there would be no hope left. If of their own evil will they had not broken the frontier and let in the celestial Powers, this would be their moment of victory. Their own strength has betrayed them. They have gone to the gods who would not have come to them, and pulled down Deep Heaven on their heads. Therefore, they will die. For though you search every cranny to escape, now that you see all crannies closed, you will not disobey me."

And then, very slowly, there crept back into Merlin's white face, first closing his dismayed mouth and finally gleaming in his eyes, that almost animal expression, earthy and healthy and with a glint of half-humorous cunning.

"Well," he said, "if the Earths are stopped, the fox faces the hounds. But had I known who you were at our first meeting, I think I would have put the sleep on you as I did on your Fool."

"I am a very light sleeper since I have travelled in the Heavens," said Ransom. . . .

The whole house at St. Anne's was empty, but for two rooms. In the kitchen, drawn a little closer than usual about the fire and with the shutters closed, sat Dimble and MacPhee and Denniston and the women. Removed from them by many a long vacancy of stair and passage, the Pendragon and Merlin were together in the Blue Room.

If anyone had gone up the stairs and on to the lobby outside the Blue Room, he would have found something other than fear that barred his way—an almost physical resistance. If he had succeeded in forcing his way forward against it, he would have come into a region of tingling sounds that were clearly not voices though they had articulation; and if the passage were quite dark he would probably have seen a faint light, not like fire or moon, under the Director's door. I do not think he could have reached the door itself unbidden. Already the whole house would have seemed to him to be tilting and plunging like a ship in a Bay of Biscay gale. He would have been horribly compelled to feel this Earth not as the bottom of the universe but as a ball spinning, and rolling onwards, both at delirious speed, and not through emptiness but through some densely inhabited and intricately structured medium. He would have known sensuously, until his outraged senses forsook him, that the visitants in that room were in it, not because they were at rest but because they glanced and wheeled through the packed reality of Heaven (which men call empty space), to keep their beams upon this spot of the moving Earth's hide.

The druid and Ransom had begun to wait for these visitors soon after sundown. Ransom was on his sofa. Merlin sat beside him, his hands clasped, his body a little bent forward. Sometimes a drop of sweat trickled coldly down his grey cheek. He had at first addressed himself to kneel but Ransom forbade him. "See thou do it not!" he had said. "Have you forgotten that they are our fellow servants?" The windows were uncurtained and all the light that there was in the room came thence: frosty red when they began their waiting, but later lit with stars.

Long before anything happened in the Blue Room the party in the kitchen had made their ten o'clock tea. It was while they sat drinking it that the change occurred. Up till now they had instinctively been talking in subdued voices, as children talk in a room where their elders are busied about some august incomprehensible matter, a funeral, or the reading of a will. Now of a sudden they all began talking loudly at once, each, not contentiously but delightedly, interrupting the others. A stranger coming into the kitchen would have thought they were drunk, not soddenly but gaily drunk: would have seen heads bent close together, eyes dancing, an excited wealth of gesture. What they said, none of the party could ever afterwards remember. Dimble maintained that they had been chiefly engaged in making puns. MacPhee denied that he had ever, even that night, made a pun, but all agreed that they had been extraordinarily witty. If not plays upon words, yet certainly plays upon thoughts, paradoxes, fancies, anecdotes, theories laughingly advanced yet (on consideration) well worth taking seriously, had flowed from them and over them with dazzling prodigality. Even Ivy forgot her great sorrow. Mother Dimble always remembered Denniston and her husband as they had stood, one on each side of the fireplace, in a gay intellectual duel, each capping the other, each rising above the other, up and up, like birds or aeroplanes in combat. If only one could have remembered what they said! For never in her life had she heard such talk—such eloquence, such melody (song could have added nothing to it), such toppling structures of double meaning, such skyrockets of metaphor and allusion.

A moment after that and they were all silent. Calm fell, as suddenly as when one goes out of the wind behind a wall. They sat staring upon one another, tired and a little self-conscious.

Upstairs this first change had a different operation. There came an instant at which both men braced themselves. Ransom gripped the side of his sofa; Merlin grasped his own knees and set his teeth. A rod of coloured light, whose colour no man can name or picture, darted between them: no more to see than that, but seeing was the least part of their experience. Quick agitation seized them: a kind of boiling and bubbling in mind and heart which shook their bodies also. It went to a rhythm of such fierce speed that they feared their sanity must be shaken into a thousand fragments. And then it seemed that this had actually happened. But it did not matter: for all the fragments—needle-pointed desires, brisk merriments, lynx-eyed thoughts— went rolling to and fro like glittering drops and reunited themselves. It was well that both men had some knowledge of poetry. The doubling, splitting, and recombining of thoughts which now went on in them would have been unendurable for one whom that art had not already instructed in the counterpoint of the mind, the mastery of doubled and trebled vision. For Ransom, whose study had been for many years in the realm of words, it was heavenly pleasure. He found himself sitting within the very heart of language, in the white-hot furnace of essential speech. All fact was broken, splashed into cataracts, caught, turned inside out, kneaded, slain, and reborn as meaning. For the lord of Meaning himself, the herald, the messenger, the slayer of Argus, was with them: the angel that spins nearest the sun. Viritrilbia, whom men call Mercury and Thoth.

Down in the kitchen drowsiness stole over them after the orgy of speaking had come to an end. Jane, having nearly fallen asleep, was startled by her book falling from her hand, and looked about her. How warm it was . . . how comfortable and familiar. She had always liked wood fires but tonight the smell of the logs seemed more than ordinarily sweet. She began to think it was sweeter than it could possibly be, that a smell of burning cedar or of incense pervaded the room. It thickened. Fragrant names hovered in her mind—nard and cassia's balmy smells and all Arabia breathing from a box; even something more subtly sweet, perhaps maddening—why not forbid- den?—but she knew it was commanded. She was too drowsy to think deeply how this could be. The Dimbles were talking together but in so low a voice that others could not hear. Their faces appeared to her transfigured. She could no longer see that they were old—only mature, like ripe fields in August, serene and golden with the tranquility of fulfilled desire. On her other side, Arthur said something in Camilla's ear. There too . . . but as the warmth and sweetness of that rich air now fully mastered her brain, she could hardly bear to look on them: not through envy (that thought was far away), but because a sort of brightness flowed from them that dazzled her, as if the god and goddess in them burned through their bodies and through their clothes and shone before her in a young double-natured nakedness of rose- red spirit that overcame her. And all about them danced (as she half saw), not the gross and ridiculous dwarfs which she had seen that afternoon, but grave and ardent spirits, bright winged, their boyish shapes smooth and slender like ivory rods.

In the Blue Room also Ransom and Merlin felt about this time that the temperature had risen. The windows, they did not see how or when, had swung open; at their opening the temperature did not drop, for it was from without that the warmth came. Through the bare branches, across the ground which was once more stiffening with frost, a summer breeze was blowing into the room, but the breeze of such a summer as England never has. Laden like heavy barges that glide nearly gunwale under, laden so heavily you would have thought it could not move, laden with ponderous fragrance of night-scented flowers, sticky gums, groves that drop odours, and with cool savour of midnight fruit, it stirred the curtains, it lifted a letter that lay on the table, it lifted the hair which had a moment before been plastered on Merlin's forehead. The room was rocking. They were afloat. A soft tingling and shivering as of foam and breaking bubbles ran over their flesh. Tears ran down Ransom's cheeks. He alone knew from what seas and what islands that breeze blew. Merlin did not; but in him also the inconsolable wound with which man is born waked and ached at this touching. Low syllables of prehistoric Celtic self-pity murmured from his lips. These yearnings and fondlings were however only the fore-runners of the goddess. As the whole of her virtue seized, focussed, and held that spot of the rolling Earth in her long beam, something harder, shriller, more perilously ecstatic, came out of the centre of all the softness. Both the humans trembled— Merlin because he did not know what was coming, Ransom because he knew. And now it came. It was fiery, sharp, bright and ruthless, ready to kill, ready to die, outspeeding light: it was Charity, not as mortals imagine it, not even as it has been humanised for them since the Incarnation of the Word, but the translunary virtue, fallen upon them direct from the Third Heaven, unmitigated. They were blinded, scorched, deafened. They thought it would burn their bones. They could not bear that it should continue. They could not bear that it should cease. So Perelandra, triumphant among planets, whom men call Venus, came and was with them in the room.

Down in the kitchen MacPhee sharply drew back his chair so that it grated on the tiled floor like a pencil squeaking on a slate. "Man!" he exclaimed, "it's a shame for us to be sitting here looking at the fire. If the Director hadn't got a game leg himself, I'll bet you he'd have found some other way for us to go to work." Camilla's eyes flashed towards him. "Go on!" she said, "go on!" "What do you mean, MacPhee!" said Dimble. "He means fighting," said Camilla. "They'd be too many for us, I'm afraid," said Arthur Denniston. "Maybe that!" said MacPhee. "But maybe they'll be too many for us this way too. But it would be grand to have one go at them before the end. To tell you the truth I sometimes feel I don't greatly care what happens. But I wouldn't be easy in my grave if I knew they'd won and I'd never had my hands on them. I'd like to be able to say as an old sergeant said to me in the first war, about a bit of a raid we did near Monchy. Our fellows did it all with the butt end, you know. 'Sir,' says he, 'did ever you hear anything like the way their heads cracked.'" "I think that's disgusting," said Mother Dimble. "That part is, I suppose," said Camilla. "But ... oh if one could have a charge in the old style. I don't mind anything once I'm on a horse." "I don't understand it," said Dimble. "I'm not like you, MacPhee. I'm not brave. But I was just thinking as you spoke that I don't feel afraid of being killed and hurt as I used to do. Not tonight." "We may be, I suppose," said Jane. "As long as we're all together," said Mother Dimble. "It might be ... no, I don't mean anything heroic ... it might be a *nice* way to die." And suddenly all their faces and voices were changed. They were laughing again, but it was a different kind of laughter. Their love for one another became intense. Each, looking on all the rest, thought, "I'm lucky to be here. I could die with these." But MacPhee was humming to himself:

King William said, Be not dismayed, for the loss of one commander.

Upstairs it was, at first, much the same. Merlin saw in memory the wintry grass of Badon Hill, the long banner of the Virgin fluttering above the heavy British-Roman cataphracts, the yellow-haired barbarians. He heard the snap of the bows, the *click-click* of steel points in wooden shields, the cheers, the howling, and the ring of struck mail. He remembered also the evening, fires twinkling along the hill, frost making the gashes smart, starlight on a pool fouled with blood, eagles crowding together in the pale sky. And Ransom, it may be, remembered his long struggle in the caves of Perelandra. But all this passed. Something tonic and lusty and cheerily cold, like a sea breeze, was coming over them. There was no fear anywhere: the blood inside them flowed as if to a marching-song. They felt themselves taking their places in the ordered rhythm of the universe, side by side with punctual seasons and patterned atoms and the obeying Seraphim. Under the immense weight of their obedience their wills stood up straight and untiring like caryatids. Eased of all fickleness and all protestings they stood: gay, light, nimble, and alert. They had outlived all anxieties; care was a word without meaning. To live meant to share in this processional pomp. Ransom knew, as a man knows when he touches iron, the clear, taut splendour of that celestial spirit which now flashed between them: vigilant Malacandra, captain of a cold orb, whom men call Mars and Mavors, and Tyr who put his hand in the wolf-mouth. Ransom greeted his guests in the tongue of Heaven. But he warned Merlin that now the time was coming when he must play the man. The three gods who had already met in the Blue Room were less unlike humanity than the two whom they still awaited. In Viritrilbia and Venus and Malacandra were represented those two of the Seven Genders which bear a certain analogy to the biological sexes and can therefore be in some measure understood by men. It would not be so with those who were now preparing to descend. These also doubtless had their genders, but we have no clue to them. These would be mightier energies: ancient eldils, steersman of giant worlds which have never from the beginning been subdued to the sweet humiliations of organic life.

"Stir the fire, Denniston, for any sake. That's a cold night," said MacPhee. "It must be cold outside," said Dimble. All thought of that: of stiff grass, hen-roosts, dark places in the middle of woods, graves. Then of the sun's dying, the Earth gripped, suffocated, in airless cold, the black sky lit only with stars. And then, not even stars: the heat-death of the universe, utter and final blackness of nonentity from which Nature knows no return. Another life? "Possibly," thought MacPhee. "I believe," thought Denniston. But the old life gone, all its times, all its hours and days, gone. Can even Omnipotence *bring back?* Where do years go, and why? Man never would understand it. The misgiving deepened. Perhaps there was nothing to be understood.

Saturn, whose name in the heavens is Lurga, stood in the Blue Room. His spirit lay upon the house, or even on the whole Earth, with a cold pressure such as might flatten the very orb of Tellus to a wafer. Matched against the lead-like burden of his antiquity the other gods themselves perhaps felt young and ephemeral. It was a mountain of centuries sloping up from the highest antiquity we can conceive, up and up like a mountain whose summit never comes into sight, not to eternity where the thought can rest, but into more and still more time, into freezing wastes and silence of unnameable numbers. It was also strong like a mountain; its age was no mere morass of time where imagination can sink in reverie, but a living, self-remembering duration which repelled lighter intelligences from its structure as granite flings back waves, itself unwithered and undecayed but able to wither any who approach it unadvised. Ransom and Merlin suffered a sensation of unendurable cold; and all that was strength in Lurga became sorrow as it entered them. Yet Lurga in that room was overmatched. Suddenly a greater spirit came—one whose influence tempered and almost transformed to his own quality the skill of leaping Mercury, the clearness of Mars, the subtler vibration of Venus, and even the numbing weight of Saturn.

In the kitchen his coming was felt. No one afterwards knew how it happened but somehow the kettle was put on, the hot toddy was brewed. Arthur—the only musician among them—was bidden to get out his fiddle. The chairs were pushed back, the floor cleared. They danced. What they danced no one could remember. It was some round dance, no modern shuffling: it involved beating the floor, clapping of hands, leaping high. And no one while it lasted thought himself or his fellows ridiculous. It may, in fact, have been some village measure, not ill-suited to the tiled kitchen: the spirit in which they danced it was not so. It seemed to each that the room was filled with kings and queens, that the wildness of their dance expressed heroic energy and its quieter movements had seized the very spirit behind all noble ceremonies.

Upstairs his mighty beam turned the Blue Room into a blaze of lights. Before the other angels a man might sink: before this he might die, but if he lived at all, he would laugh. If you had caught one breath of the air that came from him, you would have felt yourself taller than before. Though you were a cripple, your walk would have became stately: though a beggar, you would have worn your rags magnanimously. Kingship and power and festal pomp and courtesy shot from him as sparks fly from an anvil. The pealing of bells, the blowing of trumpets, the spreading out of banners, are means used on earth to make a faint symbol of his quality. It was like a long sunlit wave, creamy-crested and arched with emerald, that comes on nine feet tall, with roaring and with terror and unquenchable laughter. It was like the first beginning of music in the halls of some King so high and at some festival so solemn that a tremor akin to fear runs through young hearts when they hear it. For this was great Glund-Oyarsa, King of Kings, through whom the joy of creation principally blows across these fields of Arbol, known to men in old times as Jove and under that name, by fatal but not inexplicable misprision, confused with his Maker—so little did they dream by how many degrees the stair even of created being rises above him.

At his coming there was holiday in the Blue Room. The two mortals, momentarily caught up into the *Gloria* which those five excellent Natures perpetually sing, forgot for a time the lower and more immediate purpose of their meeting. Then they proceeded to operation. Merlin received the power into him.

He looked different next day. Partly because his beard had been shaved; but also, because he was no longer his own man. No one doubted that his final severance from the body was near. Later in the day MacPhee drove him off and dropped him in the neighborhood of Belbury. . . .

Mark had fallen into a doze in the tramp's bedroom that day, when he was startled, and driven suddenly to collect himself, by the arrival of visitors. Frost came in first and held the door open. Two others followed. One was the Deputy Director; the other was a man whom Mark had not seen before.

This person was dressed in a rusty cassock and carried in his hand a wide-brimmed black hat such as priests wear in many parts of the continent. He was a very big man and the cassock perhaps made him look bigger. He was clean shaven, revealing a large face with heavy and complicated folds in it, and he walked with his head a little bowed. Mark decided that he was a simple soul, probably an obscure member of some religious order who happened to be an authority on some even more obscure language. And it was to Mark rather odious to see him standing between those two birds of prey—Wither, effusive and flattering on his right and Frost, on his left, stiff as a ramrod, waiting with scientific attention but also, as Mark could now see, with a certain cold dislike, for the result of the new experiment.

Wither talked to the stranger for some moments in a language which Mark could not follow but which he recognised as Latin. "A priest, obviously," thought Mark. "But I wonder where from? Wither knows most of the ordinary languages. Would the old chap be a Greek? Doesn't look like a Levantine. More probably a Russian." But at this point Mark's attention was diverted. The tramp, who had closed his eyes when he heard the door handle turning had suddenly opened them, seen the stranger, and then shut them tighter than before. After this his behaviour was peculiar. He began emitting a series of very exaggerated snores and turned his back to the company. The stranger took a step nearer to the bed and spoke two syllables in a low voice. For a second or two the tramp lay as he was but seemed to be afflicted with a shivering fit; then, slowly but with continuous movement, as when the bows of a ship come round in obedience to the rudder, he rolled round and lay staring up into the other's face. His mouth and his eyes were both opened very wide. From certain jerkings of his head and hands and from certain ghastly attempts to smile, Mark concluded that he was trying to say something, probably of a deprecatory and insinuating kind. What next followed took his breath away. The stranger spoke again; and then, with much facial contortion, mixed with coughs and stammers and spluttering and expectoration, there came out of the tramp's mouth, in a high unnatural voice, syllables, words, a whole sentence, in some language that was neither Latin nor English. All this time the stranger kept his eyes fixed on those of the tramp.

The stranger spoke again. This time the tramp replied at much greater length and seemed to manage the unknown language a little more easily, though his voice remained quite unlike that in which Mark had heard him talking for the last few days. At the end of his speech he sat up in bed and pointed to where Wither and Frost were standing. Then the stranger appeared to ask him a question. The tramp spoke for the third time.

At this reply the stranger started back, crossed himself several times, and exhibited every sign of terror. He turned and spoke rapidly in Latin to the other two. Something happened to their faces when he spoke. They looked like dogs who have just picked up a scent. Then, with a loud exclamation the stranger caught up his skirts and made a bolt for the door. But the scientists were too quick for him. For a few minutes all three were wrangling there, Frost's teeth bared like an animal's, and the loose mask of Wither's face wearing, for once, a quite unambiguous expression. The old priest was being threatened. Mark found that he himself had taken a step forward. But before he could make up his mind how to act, the stranger, shaking his head and holding out his hands, had come timidly back to the beside. It was an odd thing that the tramp who had relaxed during the struggle at the door should suddenly stiffen again and fix his eyes on this frightened old man as if he were awaiting orders.

More words in the unknown language followed. The tramp once more pointed at Wither and Frost. The stranger turned and spoke to them in Latin, apparently translating. Wither and Frost looked at one another as if each waited for his fellow to act. What followed was pure lunacy. With infinite caution, wheezing and creaking, down went the whole shaky senility of the Deputy Director, down onto its knees; and half a second later, with a jerky, metallic movement, Frost got down beside him. When he was down, he suddenly looked over his shoulder to where Mark was standing. The flash of pure hatred in his face, but hatred, as it were, crystallised so that it was no longer a passion and had no heat in it, was like touching metal in the Arctic where metal burns. "Kneel," he bleated, and instantly turned his head. Mark never could remember afterwards whether he simply forgot to obey this order or whether his real rebellion dated from that moment.

The tramp spoke again, always with his eyes fixed on those of the man in the cassock. And again the latter translated, and then stood aside. Wither and Frost began going forward on their knees till they reached the bedside. The tramp's hairy, dirty hand with its bitten nails was thrust out to them. They kissed it. Then it seemed that some further order was given them. They rose and Mark perceived that Wither was gently expostulating in Latin against this order. He kept on indicating Frost. The words *venia tua*[1] (each time emended to *venia vestra*) recurred so often that Mark could pick them out. But apparently the expostulation was unsuccessful: a few moments later Frost and Wither had both left the room.

As the door shut, the tramp collapsed like a deflated balloon. He rolled himself to and fro on the bed muttering, "Gor'blimey. Couldn't have believed it. It's a knock-out. A fair knock-out." But Mark had little leisure

---

[1] "With you kind permission," or "if you will pardon me."

to attend to this. He found that the stranger was addressing him and though he could not understand the words, he looked up. Instantly, he wished to look away again and found that he could not. He might have claimed with some reason that he was by now an expert in the endurance of alarming faces. But that did not alter the fact that when he looked on this he felt himself afraid. Almost before he had time to realise this he felt himself drowsy. A moment later he fell into his chair and slept. . . .

[*The figurehead director of N.I.C.E., Horace Jules, arrives at Belbury for a formal dinner that Merlin, still disguised as a Basque priest and silently manipulating the tramp, attends.*]

It was with great pleasure that Mark found himself once more dressing for dinner and what seemed likely to be an excellent dinner. He got a seat with Filostrato on his right and a rather inconspicuous newcomer on his left. Even Filostrato seemed human and friendly compared with the two initiates, and to the newcomer his heart positively warmed. He noticed with surprise that the tramp sat at the high table between Jules and Wither, but did not often look in that direction, for the tramp, catching his eye, had imprudently raised his glass and winked at him. The strange priest stood patiently behind the tramp's chair. For the rest, nothing of importance happened until the King's health had been drunk and Jules rose to make his speech.

For the first few minutes, anyone glancing down the long tables would have seen what we always see on such occasions. There were the placid faces of elderly *bons viveurs* whom food and wine had placed in a contentment which no amount of speeches could violate. There were the patient faces of responsible but serious diners, who had long since learned how to pursue their own thoughts, while attending to the speech just enough to respond wherever a laugh or a low rumble of serious assent was obligatory. There was the usual fidgety expression on the faces of young men unappreciative of port and hungry for tobacco. There was bright over-elaborate attention on the powdered faces of women who knew their duty to society. But if you had gone on looking down the tables you would presently have seen a change. You would have seen face after face look up and turn in the direction of the speaker. You would have seen first curiosity, then fixed attention, then incredulity. Finally you would have noticed that the room was utterly silent, without a cough or a creak, that every eye was fixed on Jules, and soon every mouth opened in something between fascination and horror.

To different members of the audience the change came differently. To Frost it began at the moment when he heard Jules end a sentence with the words, "as gross an anachronism as to trust to Calvary for salvation in modern war." *Cavalry*, thought Frost almost aloud. Why couldn't the fool mind what he was saying? The blunder irritated him extremely. Perhaps —but hullo! what was this? Had his hearing gone wrong? For Jules seemed to be saying that the future density of mankind depended on the implosion of the horses of Nature. "He's drunk," thought Frost. Then, crystal clear in articulation, beyond all possibility of mistake, came, "The madrigore of verjuice must be talthibianised."

Wither was slower to notice what was happening. He had never expected the speech to have any meaning as a whole and for a long time the familiar catch-words rolled on in a manner which did not disturb the expectation of his ear. He thought, indeed, that Jules was sailing very near the wind, that a very small false step would deprive both the speaker and the audience of the power even to pretend that he was saying anything in particular. But as long as that border was not crossed, he rather admired the speech; it was in his own line. Then he thought, "Come! That's going too far. Even they must see that you can't talk about accepting the challenge of the past by throwing down the gauntlet of the future." He looked cautiously down the room. All was well. But it wouldn't be if Jules didn't sit down pretty soon. In that last sentence there were surely words he didn't know. What the deuce did he mean by *aholibate?* He looked down the room again. They were attending too much, always a bad sign. Then came the sentence, "The surrogates esemplanted in a continual of porous variations."

Mark did not at first attend to the speech at all. He had plenty of other things to think of. The appearance of this spouting popinjay at the very crisis of his own history was a mere interruption. He was too endangered and yet also, in some precarious way, too happy to bother about Jules. Once or twice some phrase caught his ear and made him want to smile. What first awoke him to the real situation was the behaviour of those who sat near him. He was aware of their increasing stillness. He noticed that everyone except himself had begun to attend. He looked up and saw their faces. And then first he really listened. "We shall not," Jules was saying, "we shall not till we can secure the erebation of all prostundiary initems." Little as he cared for Jules, a sudden shock of alarm pierced him. He looked round again. Obviously it was not he who was mad—they had all heard the gibberish. Except possibly the tramp, who looked as solemn as a judge. He had never heard a speech from one of these real toffs before and would have been disappointed if he could understand it. Nor had he ever before drunk vintage port, and though he did not much like the taste he had been working away like a man.

Wither had not forgotten for a moment that there were reporters present. That in itself did not matter much. If anything unsuitable appeared in tomorrow's paper, it would be child's play for him to say that the reporters were drunk or mad and break them. On the other hand he might let the story pass. Jules was in many respects a nuisance, and this might be as good an opportunity as any other for ending his career. But this was not the immediate question. Wither was wondering whether he should wait till Jules sat down or whether he should rise and interrupt him with a few judicious words. He did not want a scene. It would be better if Jules sat down of his own accord. At the same time, there was by now an atmosphere in that crowded room which warned Wither not to delay too long. Glancing down at the second-hand of his watch he decided to wait two minutes more. Almost as he did so he knew that he had misjudged it. An intolerable falsetto laugh rang out from the bottom of the table and would not stop. Some fool of a woman had got hysterics. Immediately Wither touched Jules on the arm, signed to him with a nod, and rose.

"Eh? Blotcher bulldoo?" muttered Jules. But Wither, laying his hand on the little man's shoulder, quietly but with all his weight, forced him down into a sitting position. Then Wither cleared his throat. He knew how to do that so that every eye in the room turned immediately to look at him. The woman stopped screaming. People who had been sitting dead still in strained positions moved and relaxed. Wither looked down the room for a second or two in silence, feeling his grip on the audience. He saw that he already had them in hand. There would be no more hysterics. Then he began to speak.

They ought to have all looked more and more comfortable as he proceeded; and there ought soon to have been murmurs of grave regret for the tragedy which they had just witnessed. That was what Wither expected. What he actually saw bewildered him. The same too attentive silence which had prevailed during Jules' speech had returned. Bright unblinking eyes and open mouths greeted him in every direction. The woman began to laugh again—or no, this time it was two women. Cosser, after one frightened glance, jumped up, overturning his chair, and bolted from the room.

The Deputy Director could not understand this, for to him his own voice seemed to be uttering the speech he had resolved to make. But the audience heard him saying. "Tidies and fugleman—I sheel foor that we all—er—most steeply rebut the defensible, though, I trust, lavatory, Aspasia which gleams to have selected our redeemed inspector this deceiving. It would—ah—be shark, very shark, from anyone's debenture . . ."

The woman who had laughed rose hastily from her chair. The man seated next to her heard her murmur in his ear, "Vood wooloo." He took in the meaningless syllables and her unnatural expression at one moment. Both for some reason infuriated him. He rose to help her to move back her chair with one of those gestures of savage politeness which often, in modern society, serve instead of blows. He wrenched the chair, in fact, out of her hand. She screamed, tripped on a ruck in the carpet and fell. The man on the other side of her saw her fall and saw the first man's expression of fury. "Bot are you blammit?" he roared, leaning towards him with a threatening movement. Four or five people in that part of the room were now up. They were shouting. At the same time there was movement elsewhere. Several of the younger men were making for the door. "Bundlemen, bundlemen," said Wither sternly in a much louder voice. He had often before, merely by raising his voice and speaking one authoritative word reduced troublesome meetings to order.

But this time he was not even heard. At least twenty people present were at that very moment attempting to do the same thing. To each of them it seemed plain that things were just at that stage when a word or so of plain sense, spoken in a new voice, would restore the whole room to sanity. One thought of a sharp word, one of a joke, one of something very quiet and telling. As a result fresh gibberish in a great variety of tones rang out from several places at once. Frost was the only one of the leaders who attempted to say nothing. Instead, he had pencilled a few words on a slip of paper, beckoned to a servant, and made him understand by signs that it was to be given to Miss Hardcastle.

By the time the message was put into her hands the clamour was universal. To Mark it sounded like the noise of a crowded restaurant in a foreign country. Miss Hardcastle smoothed out the paper and stooped her head to read. The message ran *Blunt frippers intantly to pointed bdeluroid. Purgent. Cost.* She crumpled it up in her hand.

Miss Hardcastle had known before she got the message that she was three parts drunk. She had expected and intended to be so: she knew that later on in the evening she would go down to the cells and do things. There was a new prisoner there—a little fluffy girl of the kind the Fairy enjoyed—with whom she could pass an agreeable hour. The tumult of gibberish did not alarm her: she found it exciting. Apparently, Frost wanted her to take some action. She decided that she would. She rose and walked the whole length of the room to the door, locked it, put the key in her pocket, and then turned to survey the company. She noticed for the first time that neither the supposed Merlin nor the Basque priest were anywhere to be seen. Wither and Jules, both on their feet, were struggling with each other. She set out towards them.

So many people had now risen that it took her a long time to reach them. All semblance of a dinner party had disappeared: it was more like the scene at a London terminus on a bank holiday. Everyone was trying to restore order, but everyone was unintelligible, and everyone, in the effort to be understood, was talking louder and louder. She shouted several times herself. She even fought a good deal before she reached her goal.

There came an ear-splitting noise and after that, at last, a few seconds of dead silence. Mark noticed first that Jules had been killed: only secondly, that Miss Hardcastle had shot him. After that it was difficult to be sure what happened. The stampede and the shouting may have concealed a dozen reasonable plans for disarming the murderess, but it was impossible to concert them. Nothing came of them but kicking, struggling, leaping on tables and under tables, pressing on and pulling back, screams, breaking of glass. She fired again and again. It was the smell more than anything else which recalled the scene to Mark in later life: the smell of the shooting mixed with the sticky compound smell of blood and port and madeira.

Suddenly, the confusion of cries ran all together into one thin long-drawn noise of terror. Everyone had become *more* frightened. Something had darted very quickly across the floor between the two long tables and disappeared under one of them. Perhaps half the people present had not seen what it was—had only caught a gleam of black and tawny. Those who had seen it clearly could not tell the others: they could only point and scream meaningless syllables. But Mark had recognised it. It was a tiger.

For the first time that evening everybody realised how many hiding places the room contained. The tiger might be under any of the tables. It might be in any of the deep bay windows, behind the curtains. There was a screen across one corner of the room too.

It is not to be supposed that even now none of the company kept their heads. With loud appeals to the whole room or with urgent whispers to their immediate neighbours they tried to stem the panic, to arrange an orderly retreat from the room, to indicate how the brute could be lured or scared into the open and shot. But the doom of gibberish frustrated all their efforts. They could not arrest the two movements which were going on. The majority had not seen Miss Hardcastle lock the door: they were pressing towards it, to get out at all costs: they would fight, they would kill if they could, rather than not reach the door. A large minority, on the other hand, knew that the door was locked. There must be another door, the one used by the servants, the one whereby the tiger had got in. They were pressing to the opposite end of the room to find it. The whole centre of the room was occupied by the meeting of these two waves—a huge football scrum, at first noisy with frantic efforts at explanation, but soon, as the struggle thickened, almost silent except for the sound of labouring breath, kicking or trampling feet, and meaningless muttering.

Four of five of these combatants lurched heavily against a table, pulling off the cloth in their fall and with it all the fruit dishes, decanters, glasses, plates. Out of that confusion, with a howl of terror, broke the tiger. It happened so quickly that Mark hardly took it in. He saw the hideous head, the cat's snarl of the mouth, the flaming eyes. He heard a shot—the last. Then the tiger had disappeared again. Something fat and white and bloodied was down among the feet of the scrummers. Mark could not recognise it at first for the face, from where he stood, was upside down and the grimaces disguised it until it was quite dead. Then he recognized Miss Hardcastle.

Wither and Frost were no longer to be seen. There was a growling close at hand. Mark turned, thinking he had located the tiger. Then he caught out of the corner of his eye a glimpse of something smaller and greyer. He thought it was an Alsatian. If so, the dog was mad. It ran along the table, its tail between its legs, slavering. A woman, standing with her back to the table, turned, saw it, tried to scream, next moment went down as the creature leaped at her throat. It was a wolf. "Ai—ai!!" squealed Filostrato and jumped on the table. Something else had darted between his feet. Mark saw it streak across the floor and enter the scrum and wake that mass of interlocked terror into new and frantic convulsions. It was some kind of snake.

Above the chaos of sounds which now awoke—there seemed to be a new animal in the room every minute—there came at last one sound in which those still capable of understanding could take comfort. *Thud—thud—thud*; the door was being battered from the outside. It was a huge folding door, a door by which a small locomotive could almost enter, for the room was made in imitation of Versailles. Already one or two of the panels were splintering. The noise maddened those who had made that door their goal. It seemed also to madden the animals. They did not stop to eat what they killed, or not more than to take one lick of the blood. There were dead and dying bodies everywhere by now, for the scrum was by this time killing as many as the beasts. And always from all sides went up voices trying to shout to those beyond the door. "Quick. Quick. Hurry," but shouting only nonsense. Louder and louder grew the noise at the door. As if in imitation a great gorilla leaped on the table where Jules had sat and began drumming on its chest. Then, with a roar, it jumped down into the crowd.

At last the door gave. Both wings gave. The passage, framed in the doorway, was dark. Out of the darkness there came a grey snaky something. It swayed in the air; then began methodically to break off the splintered wood on each side and make the doorway clear. Then Mark saw distinctly how it swooped own, curled itself round a man—Steele, he thought, but everyone looked different now—and lifted him bodily high off the floor. After that, monstrous, improbable, the huge shape of the elephant thrust its way into the room: its eyes enigmatic, its ears standing stiffly out like the devil's wings on each side of its head. It stood for a second with Steele writhing in the curl of its trunk and then dashed him to the floor. It trampled him. After it raised head and trunk again and brayed horribly; then plunged straight forward into the room, trumpeting and trampling—continuously trampling like a girl treading grapes, heavily and soon wetly tramping in a pash of blood and bones, of flesh, wine, fruit, and sodden tablecloth. Something more than danger darted from the sight into Mark's brain. The pride and insolent glory of the beast, the carelessness of its killings, seemed to crush his spirit even as its flat feet were crushing women and men. Here surely came the King of the world . . . then everything went black and he knew no more.

When Mr. Bultitude had come to his senses he had found himself in a dark place full of unfamiliar smells. This did not very greatly surprise or trouble him. He was inured to mystery. To poke his head into any spare bedroom at St. Anne's, as he sometimes managed to do, was an adventure no less remarkable than that which had now befallen him. And the smells here were, on the whole, promising. He perceived that food was in the neighbourhood and—more exciting still—a female of his own species. There were a great many other animals about too, apparently, but that was rather irrelevant than alarming. He decided to go and find both the female bear and the food; it was then he discovered that walls met him in three directions and bars in the fourth. He could not get out. This, combined with an inarticulate want for the human companionship to which he was accustomed, gradually plunged him into depression. Sorrow such as only animals know—huge seas of disconsolate emotion with not one little raft of reason to float on—drowned him fathoms deep. In his own fashion he lifted up his voice and wept.

And yet, not very far away from him, another, and human, captive was almost equally engulfed. Mr. Maggs, seated in a little white cell, chewed steadily on his great sorrow as only a simple man can chew. An educated man in his circumstances would have found misery streaked with reflection; would have been thinking how this new idea of cure instead of punishment, so humane in seeming, had in fact deprived the criminal of all rights and by taking away the *name* Punishment made the *thing* infinite. But Mr. Maggs thought all the time simply of one thing: that this was the day he had counted on all through his sentence, that he had expected by this time to be having his tea at home with Ivy (she'd have got something tasty for him the first night) and that it hadn't happened. He sat quite still. About once in every two minutes a single large tear trickled down his cheek. He wouldn't have minded so much if they'd let him have a packet of fags.

It was Merlin who bought release to both. He had left the dining room as soon as the curse of Babel was well fixed upon the enemies. No one had seen him go. Wither had once heard his voice calling loud and intolerably glad above the riot of nonsense, *"Qui Verbum Dei contempserunt, eis auferetur etiam verbum hominis."*[1] After that he did not see him again, nor the tramp either. Merlin had gone and spoiled his house. He had liberated beasts and men. The animals that were already maimed he killed with an instantaneous motion of the powers that were in him, swift and painless as the mild shafts of Artemis. To Mr. Maggs he had handed a written message. It ran as follows: "Dearest Tom, I do hope your well and the Director here is one of the right sort and he says to come as quick as you can to the Manor at St. Anne's. And don't go through Edgestow Tom whatever you do, but come any way you can I should think someone had given you a Lift. Everything is all-right no more now. Lots of love ever your own Ivy." The other prisoners he let go where they pleased. The tramp, finding Merlin's back turned on him for a second, and having noticed that the house seemed to be empty, made his escape, first into the kitchen and thence, reinforced with all the edibles his pockets would hold, into the wide world. I have not been able to trace him further.

The beasts, except for one donkey who disappeared about the same time as the tramp, Merlin sent to the dining room, maddened with his voice and touch. But he retained Mr. Bultitude. The latter had recognized him at once as the same man whom he had sat beside in the Blue Room: less sweet and sticky than on that occasion, but recognisably the same. Even without the brilliantine there was that in Merlin which exactly suited the bear and at their meeting it "made him all the cheer that a beast can make a man." He laid his hand on its head and whispered in its ear and its dark mind was filled with excitement as though some long forbidden and forgotten pleasure were suddenly held out to it. Down the long, empty passages of Belbury it padded behind him. Saliva dripped from its mouth and it was beginning to growl. It was thinking of warm, salt tastes, of the pleasant resistances of bone, of things to crunch and lick and worry.

Mark felt himself shaken; then the cold shock of water dashed in his face. With difficulty he sat up. The room was empty except for the bodies of the distorted dead. The unmoved electric light glared down on hideous confusion—food and filth, spoiled luxury and mangled men, each more hideous by reason of the other. It was the supposed Basque priest who had roused him. *"Surge, miselle* (Get up, wretched boy)," he said, helping Mark to his feet. Mark rose; he had some cuts and bruises and his head ached but he was substantially uninjured. The man held out to him wine in one of the great silver cups, but Mark turned away from it with a shudder. He looked with bewilderment on the face of the stranger and found that a letter was being put into his hand. "Your wife awaits you," it ran, "at the Manor at St. Anne's on the Hill. Come quickly by road as best you can. Do not go near

---

[1]. They that have despised the word of God, from them shall the word of man also be taken away.

Edgestow—A. Denniston." He looked again at Merlin and thought his face terrible. But Merlin met his glance with a look of unsmiling authority, laid a hand on his shoulder, and impelled him over all the tinkling and slippery havoc to the door. His fingers sent a prickly sensation through Mark's skin. He was led down to the cloakroom, made to fling on a coat and hat (neither were his own) and thence out under the stars, bitter cold and two o'clock in the morning, Sirius bitter green, a few flakes of dry snow beginning to fall. He hesitated. The stranger stood back from him for a second, then, with his open hand, struck him on the back; Mark's bones ached at the memory as long as he lived. Next moment he found himself running as he had never run since boyhood; not in fear, but because his legs would not stop. When he became master of them again he was half a mile from Belbury and looking back he saw a light in the sky.